D1796165
9 78 9353605599

THE ROYAL
NATURAL HISTORY

LION AND LIONESS.

THE ROYAL NATURAL HISTORY

EDITED BY

RICHARD LYDEKKER, B.A., F.G.S., F.Z.S., Etc.

WITH PREFACE BY

P. L. SCLATER, M.A., Ph.D., F.R.S., Etc.
SECRETARY OF THE ZOOLOGICAL SOCIETY OF LONDON

ILLUSTRATED WITH

Seventy-two Coloured Plates and Sixteen Hundred Engravings

BY

W. KUHNERT, F. SPECHT, P. J. SMIT, G. MÜTZEL, A. T. ELWES, J. WOLF,
GAMBIER BOLTON, F.Z.S.; AND MANY OTHERS

VOL. I.

SECTION I.

LONDON
FREDERICK WARNE & CO.
AND NEW YORK
1894

MORRISON AND GIBB, PRINTERS, EDINBURGH

THE FIELD VOLE.

ERRATUM.

PAGE 37. The number of wrist bones should be eight and nine, as correctly stated on page 49.

PREFACE

THERE appears to be no limit to the demand for popular works on Natural History in these days, especially if they be accompanied by well-executed Illustrations. There can be little doubt, therefore, that *The Royal Natural History* will meet with a favourable reception, and, so far as I am acquainted with it, I have great confidence in commending it to my brother naturalists.

The text has been planned in such a way as to render it available not only for general information about the objects described in it, but also as a guide to their classification; and on such lines it will indeed be of priceless value to the travelling naturalist and to the resident in foreign countries. Applications for advice as to a good general book on Natural History are amongst those very frequently to be found in the foreign letter-box of the Secretary of the Zoological Society of London, and it will be a great satisfaction to him to be able to answer them in a definite way.

As regards the Illustrations to be employed in the present work, there need not be any apprehension as to their fitness for the purpose. They are mainly drawn from what is newest and most satisfactory in the current and largely augmented edition of Brehm's *Tierleben*, which is familiar to naturalists as one of the best illustrated works on popular Natural History ever issued. Specht and Mützel, for instance, to whose artistic pencils a large proportion of these pictures are due, are well known as being among the most charming portrayers of animal life of the present day, rivalling even Joseph Wolf and Keulemans in their sketches; and many of the other illustrators are of equally favourable reputation. Moreover, to this nucleus of acknowledged excellence there have been added many original drawings and engravings of a similar standard of pictorial merit, including not a few electrotypes from the *Proceedings of the Zoological Society* and other recognised sources of recent and trustworthy animal portraiture.

The public are much indebted to private enterprise for ventures of such magnitude as *The Royal Natural History*, in which, on an unusually wide scale, there is a genuine endeavour to give the results of modern investigation in a convenient and appropriate form, worthy in every respect of the subject, and under such arrangements as practically place the volumes within everybody's reach.

The study of Natural History has always been deservedly popular with young and old; its interest and its educational value as an incentive to thought and as a stimulant to observational power have ever held high place. The whole civilised world gains by any addition to the facilities of its pursuit, and by any enterprise that promotes inquiry into the structure and conditions of existence of the breathing myriads around us.

The Publishers have, I think, very wisely determined to devote a rather large proportion of the six volumes of *The Royal Natural History* to the Mammalian class. Mammals, as of all the animal kingdom approaching man most nearly in structure, are naturally of the greatest interest to him; they are, moreover, in most cases, the first objects likely to attract notice in a strange country, though on this point it must be admitted that in some parts of the world Birds run them hard. It can, however, be no matter of complaint on the part of the public in general if two volumes and a half of *The Royal Natural History* are devoted to Mammals.

Finally, I may remark that it is now more than ten years ago since the last general work of Natural History of this character was published in this country. Science moves fast nowadays, and during the past ten years numerous and remarkable discoveries have been made in every branch of zoology. These require to be annexed and incorporated in a new work. Knowing the energetic character of the Editor, how ably he is supported in his task, and how well acquainted he is with what is going on in every part of the zoological world, I have little doubt that *The Royal Natural History* will be quite up to the present level of information in every branch of this wide subject, and will form a Reference Work of the highest value.

P. L. SCLATER.

3 HANOVER SQUARE, LONDON, W.

NOTE

THE EDITOR desires to take this opportunity of stating that in such portions of the work as are not from his own pen, the Chapters will be signed by their respective authors. His thanks may, at the same time, be offered to the PUBLICATION COMMITTEE OF THE ZOOLOGICAL SOCIETY OF LONDON for the kind permission afforded to make use of numerous figures from the Society's publications; and they are likewise due to Messrs. MACMILLAN, Mr. JOHN MURRAY, Mr. T. SOUTHWELL, and Mr. ROWLAND WARD for similar permission.

FOX-TERRIER "SPOT," THE PROPERTY OF H.M. THE QUEEN.

CONTENTS

MAMMALS

Note.—This Section is the first half of the First Volume ; the Index to the complete Volume is in Section II.

LIST OF ILLUSTRATIONS

COLOURED PLATES

PAGE PLATES

TEXT ENGRAVINGS

THE ROYAL NATURAL HISTORY.

MAMMALS.

CHAPTER I.

General Characteristics,—Class **Mammalia**.

In describing any group of objects, whether they be artificial or whether they be natural, some method of classifying is absolutely essential to a right understanding of their relations to one another; and nowhere is this more important than in Natural History. To a certain extent such a classification is already made in our ordinary language, since we are accustomed to divide the higher animals into several distinct primary groups, under the names of Mammals or Quadrupeds, Birds, Reptiles, and Fishes; and these primary groups coincide in the main with those employed by zoologists. Such a popular classification depends almost entirely upon similarity or dissimilarity of outward appearance and form; and although this is a good and dependable guide in many cases, it is by no means always trustworthy, and may, indeed, frequently lead us into serious error. For instance, whales and dolphins are generally associated in the uninstructed mind with fishes, whereas, as a study of their internal structure at once reveals, they are really Mammals, which have been specially adapted for a purely aquatic life.

To arrive, therefore, at a correct idea of the mutual relations and affinities of animals, and thus to formulate a natural scheme of classification, it is absolutely essential to have a certain knowledge of their internal anatomy, as well as of their external appearance and their habits. Since, however, such intimate knowledge can only be attained after a protracted course of study quite impossible for the majority of persons to undertake, it is unavoidable that they must receive a good deal on trust from those who have devoted their time to such studies. And yet, with a certain amount of attention, every reader should be able to comprehend some of the main and leading characters in the structure of animals, by means of which they are classified and arranged in a series, which may either commence (as in this work) with the highest and descend to the lowest, or may take the opposite direction.

Species and Genera. In regard to classification, we commonly divide animals into what the zoologist terms species. Thus all the individuals of the animal we call a rat constitute a *species*, while all those to which we apply the name mouse form a second species. The rat and the mouse are, however, obviously closely allied species, and are accordingly grouped together by the zoologist as a *genus*, in this particular instance termed *Mus*. In the large majority of instances there is no great difficulty in deciding what is a species, but opinions may legitimately differ as to what amount of variation between particular species is necessary in order that they should be assigned to different genera.

Besides the rat and the mouse, there are, however, found in many parts of the world certain other animals, known as voles, which differ so markedly from rats and mice as clearly to form a distinct genus (in this case termed *Microtus*), although allied to them in so many points as to show that they are very near relations.

Families and Orders. Such nearly related groups of species or genera are accordingly grouped together in a *family*, which takes its name from one of the component genera. We, accordingly, have the genera *Mus* and *Microtus* constituting the family *Muridæ*; but the number of genera in a family may be much larger than this, while in a few instances a family is represented by one genus only.

All, however, who have ever observed with any ordinary attention such animals as rats, hares, beavers, and guinea-pigs, will have noticed that there is a general similarity in their outward appearance, and that all of them have a single pair of chisel-like teeth in both the upper and lower jaw, with which they are in the habit of gnawing their food, or any obstacles they may wish to remove. Animals thus obviously related to another, although differing in other respects too widely to be included in a single family, constitute an *order*, or assemblage of families; the animals to which we have alluded forming the order of Rodents, or *Rodentia*, which will thus include the families *Leporidæ* (hares and rabbits), *Muridæ* (rats and mice), *Castoridæ* (beavers), *Caviidæ* (guinea-pigs), and many others.

Classes. Our grouping by no means ends, however, with an *order*, for we find that groups of orders, from the possession of one or more common characters by all of them, may be brigaded together as classes. Thus the Rodents, the Hoofed Animals or Ungulates (pigs, deer, cattle, horses, etc.), and the Carnivores (cats, dogs, etc.), which form three distinct orders, all agree with one another in that their young are nourished by milk sucked from the mother. Consequently such animals, together with all others showing the same peculiarity, are grouped together to form the class of Mammals or Mammalia.

If, however, a mammal, a bird, a reptile, and a fish be compared together, it will be found that although the three latter differ from the former, in that the young are not suckled by the female parent, yet all agree in the possession of what we commonly call the *backbone;* this backbone consisting of a column running along the back of the animal, and composed of a number of jointed segments, which, although usually formed of bone, may be of cartilage. Such joints are technically known as *vertebræ,* and the whole column as the *vertebral column;* while all the classes possessing this vertebral column are grouped together under the name of Vertebrates, or Vertebrata, this largest group being known as a sub-kingdom.

We accordingly have a scheme of classification like the following :—

Subkingdom **VERTEBRATA,** or Vertebrates.

Class **Mammalia,** or Mammals.

Order RODENTIA, or Rodents.

Family *MURIDÆ*, or Rats and Voles.

Genus *Mus*, Rats and Mice.

Genus *Microtus*, Voles.

Structure of the Vertebrates. In saying that the Vertebrates, or highest of all animals, are characterised by the presence of a backbone or vertebral column, we have given only the primary feature of this great group ; and we must accordingly say a few words more on the subject of their structure. Now an essential feature in the structure of all Vertebrates is that on that side of the backbone lying nearest to the back there runs a tube or canal, formed by arches of bone or cartilage springing from the bodies of the vertebræ, within which tube is the so-called spinal marrow or cord, which is a rope-like structure formed of nerve-tissue, and running backwards from the brain to the hinder extremity of the body. On the opposite side of the backbone to that occupied by the spinal marrow there is a much larger cavity containing the viscera, such as the heart, lungs, stomach, etc. In a cross-section of the body of any vertebrate animal we therefore see two tubes—a small one containing the nervous system placed above the backbone, and a much larger one containing the viscera situated below the backbone.

Another noteworthy peculiarity of Vertebrates is that the limbs, which never exceed four in number, are always directed away from that part of the body which contains the nervous system, and towards that enclosing the viscera ; whereas in nearly all the lower animals, collectively known as the Invertebrates, the reverse is the case. Vertebrates are likewise distinguished by the circumstance that the two jaws work in a vertical plane, or, in other words, are upper and lower, instead of being right and left, as they are in insects.

Having said thus much as to the general characters of the Vertebrate sub-kingdom, we come to the consideration of those of its highest class, the Mammals.

With the exception of the word Beasts, we have no true English term for this group of animals. The term Quadrupeds was, indeed, long in popular use, but since it is inapplicable to whales, while it would also include most Reptiles, it is now largely superseded by the term Mammals, derived from the most obvious peculiarity of the class.

Characteristics of the Mammals. In addition to the presence in the females of mammary glands secreting the milk, by means of which the young are nourished, Mammals differ from the other higher Vertebrates by the mode in which the lower jaw is articulated to the skull. Thus in other Vertebrates this articulation is effected by the intervention of a separate squared bone, known as the quadrate, upon the lower end of which the articular hollow of the lower jaw plays, while its upper end is articulated to the skull proper. In Mammals, however, this intermediate bone is absent, and the lower jaw consequently articulates by means of a convex surface, or condyle, directly with the walls of the skull itself. Moreover, in all Mammals, each half of the lower jawbone consists of but a single bone, instead of several distinct bones joined together. Thus an isolated jawbone is always sufficient to prove whether its owner was a Mammal or some other Vertebrate. Another very important feature of Mammals is that they always have hair (although it may be only a few bristles on the mouth) on some portions of their bodies during a certain period of their existence. Again, that portion of the large cavity of the body which contains the heart and lungs is completely separated by a horizontal partition, known as the midriff or diaphragm, from the one containing the stomach and intestines. Moreover, at least in all living members of the class, the brain of Mammals is much more highly organised than that of other animals; one of its distinctive features being the presence of a transverse band on its lower surface, by means of which its two lateral halves are intimately connected together.

The above are a few of the chief features distinguishing Mammals from all other Vertebrates, but we may now briefly notice some in which they differ from certain of the lower classes, although agreeing with others. One of the most important of these differences is that the skull of Mammals is jointed to the first vertebra by means of a pair of transversely disposed bosses, or condyles, as they are technically called. In this respect Mammals are broadly distinguished from Birds and Reptiles, in which there is but a single condyle, placed in the middle line of the skull. Frogs and newts, constituting the class of Amphibians, agree, however, with Mammals in the mode by which the skull is jointed to the backbone; although they differ from them very widely in other parts of their organisation.

Circulation. On the other hand, Mammals differ from Fishes, Amphibians, and Reptiles, in having warm blood, which is propelled from a four-chambered heart through a double circulatory system; one part of this system causing the blood to pass through the lungs for the purpose of taking in a fresh supply of oxygen from the air, and the other being subservient to the supply of freshly oxygenated blood to the various organs and members of the body. This circulatory system also differs from that of Birds and Reptiles in that the blood for the nourishment of the body is propelled from the heart by a single vessel, known as the aorta, which passes over the left branch of the windpipe; whereas in the other two classes mentioned the aorta crosses either the right branch or both branches of the windpipe.

Respiration. All Mammals, whether they live on the land or in the water, breathe air by means of lungs suspended in the chest; and during no period of their life do they ever develop gills; neither do they ever undergo a metamorphosis analogous to that presented by the change of a tadpole into a frog. By these last two negative characters they are, therefore, sharply distinguished from the Amphibians, with which, as we have seen, they agree in the mode by which the skull is articulated to the first joint of the backbone.

Young. With the sole exception of the egg-laying Mammals, or Monotremes, of Australia and New Guinea, which are the lowest members of the class, the young of Mammals are invariably born in a living condition.

Vertebræ of Neck. A remarkable feature in Mammals is the circumstance that, with only three constant exceptions, the number of joints, or vertebræ, in the neck is seven; this number being equally constant in the enormously elongated neck of the giraffe, or in the extremely shortened one of the whale, where the vertebræ are reduced to thin plates of bone.

Structure. As a rule, Mammals have the two pairs of limbs characteristic of Vertebrates, but occasionally, as in the whales, the hinder pair may be wanting. In a large proportion of species the hind- and fore-limbs are of approximately equal length. In some cases, however, the hind-limbs may be enormously elongated at the expense of the fore-limbs, as we see in the kangaroos and jumping mice; and progression is then effected by means of leaps and bounds from these strong hind-limbs. The opposite extreme of limb-structure is shown among the bats, where, while the hinder pair retain their normal structure, the fore-limbs are enormously elongated to afford support to a leathery wing-like structure, by means of which these strangely modified creatures are enabled to fly in the air with the same ease and swiftness as Birds. In the whales and dolphins, which lead a purely aquatic life, we find the fore-limbs modified into paddles for swimming, while the hind ones are, as we have said, totally wanting. Similar conditions obtain in the dugongs and manatis; but in the true seals, which are less completely aquatic, the hind-limbs are still well developed, although directed backwards to form, in connection with the tail, a kind of rudder. The bats are the only Mammals which are wholly adapted for flight, but we meet with certain forms in other groups, such as the flying squirrels among the Rodents, and the flying phalangers among the Pouched Mammals, which are enabled to take long leap-like flights from tree to tree by means of a kind of a parachute formed of folds of skin running along the sides of the body from limb to limb. The limbs themselves are not, however, specially modified; and true flight, in the sense of propulsion caused by up-and-down strokes of the fore-limbs, is not performed by these Mammals. We shall have something more to add on the subject of limbs in the paragraphs devoted to the skeleton.

Almost as great variations are displayed in the modifications and uses of the tail of Mammals. In the majority of cases the tail is present and forms a tapering axis, often clothed with long hair, which may considerably exceed the total length of the body. The Mammal, in which the relative length of the tail is greatest, is a small one from Madagascar, belonging to the Insectivorous order, and named *Microgale,* in which the tail is nearly three times as long as the body. In some of the apes and monkeys the tail is absent; and it is very short in the bears among the Carnivores, and in many deer among the Hoofed Mammals, or Ungulates. In many Ungulates, however, such as cattle, it is of great length; and in that group it has its extremity furnished with a tuft of hair, and thus forms an effectual instrument for brushing away flies from the body. In the spider-monkeys of South America, as well as in the opossums and phalangers, in certain porcupines, and other forms, the tail is prehensile, and thus serves as an important aid in climbing, or to suspend its owner's head downwards. In the beaver the tail is expanded into a flattened oar-like form, which probably acts as a rudder in swimming. But the most remarkable modification of this useful organ occurs in the whales and dolphins, when it is expanded into a large forked structure, termed by whalers 'flukes,' and is the main organ in propelling the body through the water.

External Covering. In regard to the external covering, we have already said that hairs are always present on some portion of the body during some period of life. In the whales these hairs may, however, be reduced to a few bristles in the region of the mouth, which disappear when the animal attains maturity. Mammals never develop that modified kind of hair-structure known as feathers, which are peculiar to Birds. The body may, however, be covered with overlapping scales, like those so common in Reptiles, but this occurs only in the pangolins, or scaly ant-eaters of India and Africa. The tail of the common rat is an example of a part of the body covered with scales, having their edges in apposition; but in both these instances hairs are mingled with the scales. Still rarer than scales are bony plates, developed in the true skin. At the present day these structures are only met with among the well-known armadillos of South America, which are furnished with bucklers and transverse bands of these bony plates, and are in some cases able to roll themselves up into a ball, presenting on all sides an impenetrable coat of mail. In the Pleistocene, or latest geological period before the present, South America produced, however, a number of huge Mammals allied to the armadillos, and known as glyptodonts, which were covered with a continuous cuirass of bony plates, reaching in some cases more than an inch in thickness. That these huge and well-armoured forms, which one might regard as typical examples of animals fitted to withstand all enemies, have perished, while their smaller and less completely defended allies have lived on, show us that there are other causes at work than the attacks of foes in the destruction of animals. Between the plates of the armour of the armadillos hairs are always developed, and in one species these are so abundant as to completely hide the plates themselves, and render the general appearance that of an ordinary hairy mammal.

The use of hair is mainly to protect the body from cold, and thus to aid in the maintenance of a uniform high temperature; and when hairs are absent, we find this function performed by a more or less thick fatty layer beneath the skin, which, when it is excessively developed, as in the whales, is known as blubber. To compensate for the difference between the temperature of winter and summer, many Mammals which inhabit the colder regions of the globe develop a much thicker coat of hair in the former than in the latter season, of which we have an excellent example in the horse. In some Mammals, such as the hare and cat, the body is covered with only one kind of hair; but in other cases, as in the fur-seals, there is one kind of long and somewhat coarse hair, which appears at the surface, and another of a softer and finer nature, which forms the thick and warm under-fur. This under-fur is greatly developed in Mammals of all groups inhabiting Tibet, where it is locally known as 'pashm'; and it is this pashm of the goat of these regions which affords the materials for the celebrated Kashmir shawls. Curiously enough, too, animals which usually do not develop pashm almost immediately tend to its production when taken to the Tibetan region, as is notably the case with dogs. Less frequently the hair of the body takes the form of stiff bristles, as on the pig; and still more rarely this thickening is carried to such an extent as to produce spines, of which we have the best instances in the porcupine and hedgehog, belonging, it should be borne in mind, to distinct orders.

The solid horns of the rhinoceroses, and the hollow horny sheaths of cattle and antelopes are very similar in their nature to hairs, and may indeed be compared to masses of hair welded together into solid structures.

The Skeleton. Although a fair idea of Mammals as a whole may be gained without investigation into the nature of their soft internal parts, yet any one who desires to obtain any really accurate knowledge of them must make up his mind to acquire at least some slight idea of the general structure of the bony skeleton, and also of the form and nature of the teeth, since these parts are of the highest importance in classification.

We have already incidentally mentioned that the skull consists of two portions, —the skull proper, which contains the brain, and the lower jaw. It will suffice to mention, in addition, that the hinder part of the skull is

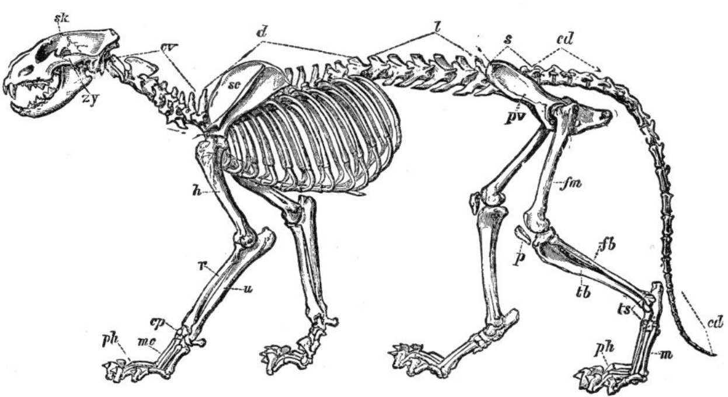

SKELETON OF THE LION.

sk. skull; *zy.* cheek-bone (zygomatic arch); *cv.* vertebræ of the neck; *d.* vertebræ of the back; *l.* vertebræ of the loins; *s.* sacrum; *cd.* vertebræ of the tail; *sc.* shoulder-blade (scapula); *h.* arm-bone (humerus); *r. u.* bones of fore-arm (radius and ulna); *cp.* wrist (carpus); *mc.* metacarpus; *ph.* toe-bones; *pv.* haunch-bone (pelvis); *fm.* thigh-bone (femur); *p.* knee-cap (patella); *tb. fb.* bones of lower leg (tibia and fibula); *ts.* ankle (tarsus); *m.* metatarsus.

known as the occiput, and that on the front surface the pair of bones roofing over the cavity of the nose are known as the nasals, while those behind them, forming the region of the forehead, are termed frontals. Further, in the upper jaw, the bones which carry the hinder or cheek-teeth are known as the maxillæ, while those in which the front cutting-teeth are implanted are termed the premaxillæ. All the other numerous bones of the skull have received distinct names; but the reader desirous of becoming acquainted with them must refer to other works. Our notice of the other parts of the skeleton must be equally brief. In the backbone or vertebral column, the first vertebra, or that which articulates with the skull is known as the atlas; following which is the axis vertebra, remarkable for having the body or basal portion of the atlas vertebra fixed to it, and known as the odontoid process. This separation of the body of the atlas vertebra from its proper segment is constant throughout the greater part of the vertebrate subkingdom. The remaining five of the cervical, or neck-vertebræ, are distinguished from the dorsal, or vertebræ of the region of the chest, by the absence of ribs. The ribs of most of the dorsal vertebræ articulate in the middle line of the inferior aspect of the body with the breast-bone, or sternum, which is itself composed of several segments. The dorsal vertebræ are succeeded posteriorly by a smaller number, forming the region of the loins, which have no ribs, and are termed lumbars. Behind the latter there are several coalesced vertebræ forming the so-called sacrum, to which the haunch-bones articulate; and these are again succeeded by the tail, or caudal, vertebræ, of which the number varies according to the length of the tail itself.

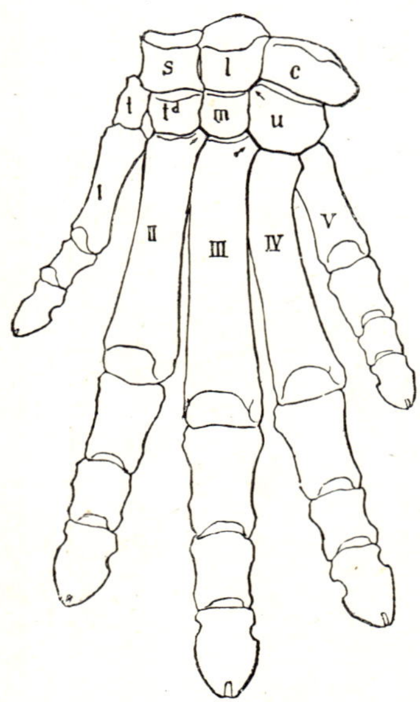

DIAGRAM OF THE BONES OF THE LEFT FORE-FOOT OF A FIVE-TOED MAM-MAL (*Phenacodus*). (½ nat. size.)

The bones marked *s, l, c, t, t^d, m,* and *u,* form the wrist; those numbered *I–V* are the metacarpals, and the remainder the finger or toe - bones.—After Osborn.

In the majority of Mammals the fore-limb is connected with the trunk simply by the blade-bone, or scapula, which lies on the back surface of the anterior ribs; and in front by the collar-bone, or clavicle, which connects the scapula with the sternum. The bones of the fore-limb are, firstly, the arm-bone or humerus, which has condyles at its lower end; and, secondly, the two parallel bones of the fore-arm, of which the outermost (when the palm of the hand is turned forwards) is the radius, and the other the ulna. The radius is always present, but in many Hoofed Mammals only the upper end of the ulna remains, which is fused with the radius. The radius articulates below with the upper of the two transverse rows of small solid bones forming the wrist or carpus; beyond these we have in man and monkeys, as well as in certain other groups, five elongated bones, termed metacarpals, the four outermost of which are succeeded by the three phalangeal bones of the fingers or digits. The thumb, or first digit, which lies on the same side as the radius, has, however, only two of these phalangeals.

The hind-limb differs from the fore-limb in that the innominate, or haunch - bones, which together form the pelvis, are connected by an immovable bony union with the sacral region of the vertebral column. The thigh-bone or femur, corresponding to the humerus of the arm, articulates with a cavity in the innominate, termed the acetabulum. The leg has two parallel bones articulating with the lower end of the thigh-bone or femur; of which the larger, or tibia, occupying the inner side of the limb, corresponds to the radius of the fore-arm, while the smaller outer bone, or fibula, represents the ulna. The ankle, or tarsus, corresponds to the carpus in the fore-limb, and likewise consists of two transverse rows of small bones. Two bones of the uppermost row, viz. the calcaneum or heel-bone, and the astragalus or ankle-bone, are specially modified. In the foot proper the bones correspond with those of the hand; those representing the metacarpals being, however, termed metatarsals. It will frequently be found convenient to speak of the extremity of the fore-limb, or hand, as the *manus;* while the hind foot may be termed the *pes.*

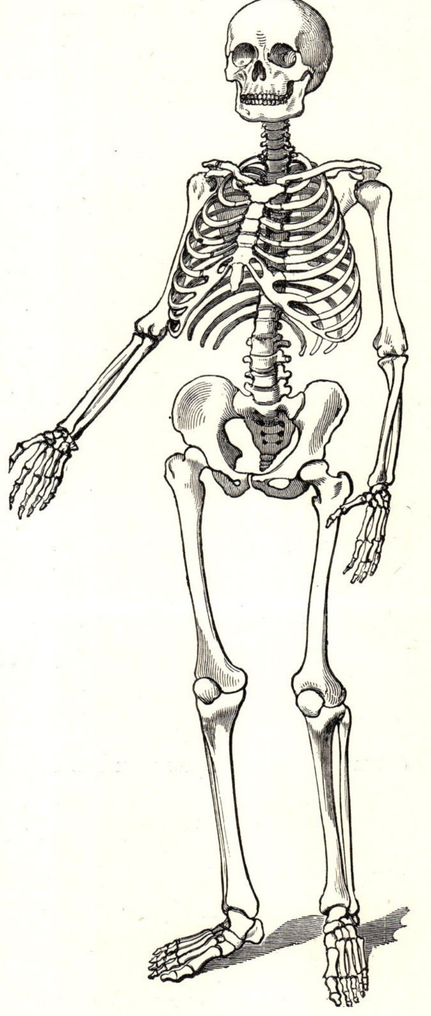

In the foregoing summary we have spoken of the hand and foot as consisting of five fingers and toes, or digits; and this is the case with most Monkeys, many Carnivores, Rodents, etc. In other cases, however, and especially among the Hoofed Mammals or Ungulates, there is a tendency to the reduction of the number of digits. Thus in the cattle and deer, commonly known as Ruminants, the number of functional digits is reduced to two, corresponding to the third and fourth of the typical series of five; while in the horse only a single digit remains, which in the fore-limb corresponds to the middle or third finger of the human hand, and in the hind-limb to the middle toe.

Arrangement of the Teeth. Almost all Mammals when adult have both jaws provided with a series of teeth, varying greatly in number and structure in the different groups. These teeth are almost invariably fixed in separate sockets; and while the front teeth have but a single root or fang, the side or cheek-teeth very generally have two or more such roots, each of which occupies a separate division of the socket. In all cases the teeth are fixed in their sockets merely by the aid of soft tissues connected with the gum, and are never welded to the jaws by a deposit of bone. Very generally there is a sharply-marked line of division, termed the neck, between the root, or portion of the tooth implanted in the jaw, and the crown or exposed portion.

In most of those Mammals, in which the teeth of different parts of the jaw differ in structure from one another, there are two distinct sets of teeth developed during life. The first of the two includes the milk- or baby-teeth, which are generally shed at a comparatively early age, are of small size and few in number, and are finally succeeded by the larger and more numerous permanent set, which remain during the rest of life, unless previously worn.

In those Mammals in which the permanent teeth differ from one another in form in different regions of the jaw, we are enabled from their position, and also from their relations to the temporary series of milk-teeth, to divide them into four distinct groups. Taking one side of the upper jaw, as that of the dog, of which the teeth are shown in the figure, we find the front bone, or premaxilla, carrying a small number (in this instance three) of simple cutting teeth, termed incisors. Behind these teeth, from which, as in the figure, it is generally separated by a longer or shorter gap, there is a tooth with a simple and often conical crown, which, like the incisors, is inserted in the jaw by a single root. This tooth, which is usually larger than the incisors, is termed the tusk, or canine tooth, and in the wild boar and most Carnivorous Mammals attains a very large size. It can always be distinguished from the incisors by the fact that it is implanted in the maxilla, or second bone of the jaw, or at least on the line of junction between that bone and the premaxilla. Behind the canine we have a series of teeth, which may be as many as seven, although only six in the figure, with more complicated crowns, and, except the first, inserted in the jaw by two or more roots. This series may be collectively known as the cheek-teeth; but they may be divided into two minor groups according as to whether they are preceded by milk-teeth or not. In the dog the four teeth immediately behind the canine, with the exception of the first, are the vertical successors of milk-teeth, and are known as premolars; while the two hindmost teeth, which have no such temporary predecessors, are known as true molars, or molars. In the lower jaw the tooth, usually larger

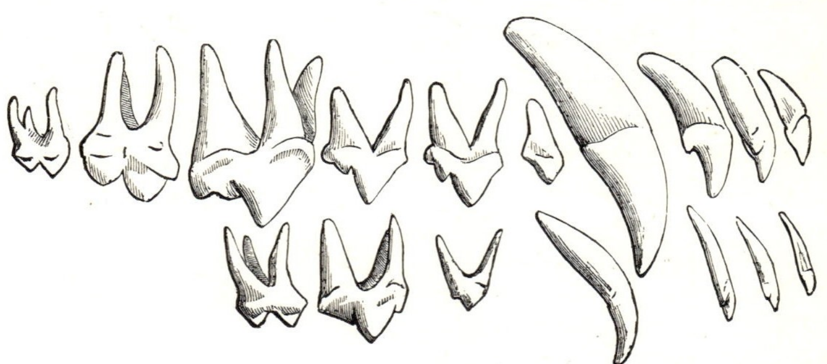

OUTER VIEW OF THE RIGHT MILK AND PERMANENT UPPER TEETH OF THE DOG.

The lower row are the milk-teeth, and the upper the permanent teeth.—After Sir W. H. Flower.

than the others, which bites in front of the upper canine is the lower canine. In advance of this tooth are the incisors, and behind it the premolars and molars, distinguished from one another in the same manner as are the corresponding teeth of the upper jaw.

With the exception of the Pouched Mammals, with which we shall not have to deal till we come to the middle of the third volume, there are, in practically all the Mammals with teeth of different kinds, never more than three incisors, one canine, four premolars, and three molars on either side of each jaw; so that the total number of teeth on both sides of the two jaws is not more than forty-four. In the figured upper jaw of the dog the number falls short of this full complement, owing to the circumstance that there are only two in place of three molars.

Dental Formulæ. As it would be exceedingly inconvenient always to have to describe the number of teeth in any given Mammal by writing them down at length, a graphic formula has been invented by which the number of teeth of each species can be shortly and clearly expressed. Thus, taking only one side of each jaw, and indicating the incisors by the letter i, the canines or tusks by c, the premolars by p, and the molars by m, and taking the numbers above the lines as representing the teeth of the upper, and those below the same the teeth of the lower jaw, we may express the number and kinds of the teeth of the dog by the formula: $i\frac{3}{3}, c\frac{1}{1}, p\frac{4}{4}, m\frac{2}{3}$. The total thus given is 21, and double this number will of course give the entire number of teeth on both sides of the two jaws, which in this case will be 42.

Structure of the Teeth. A few words must now be said regarding the internal structure of teeth, as without this it is quite impossible to understand the modifica-

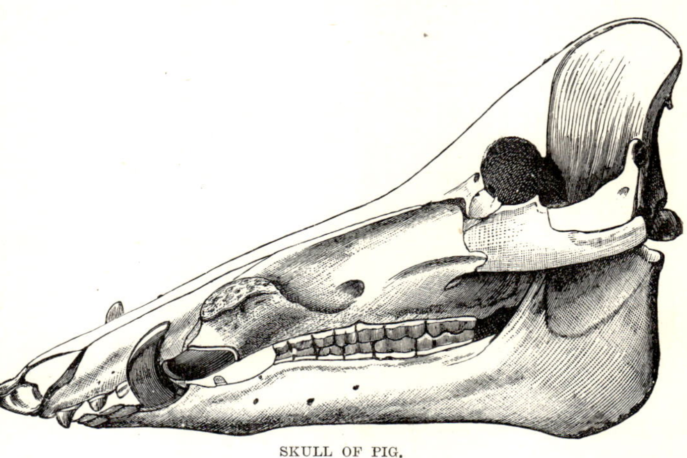

SKULL OF PIG.

To show distinction between incisors, tusks, and cheek-teeth.—After Nehring.

tions which they undergo in different groups of Mammals. Taking a simple more or less conical tooth like the tusk of a lion or tiger, or any tooth of a sperm whale, it may be observed that when such a tooth first appears above the gum it is open at the base, where it forms a hollow cone. And in teeth like the tusks of the elephant, which grow throughout the whole life of their owner, such a condition remains permanent. Usually, however, a tooth ceases to grow after a certain period, and the base of the root or roots then becomes completely closed, and assumes a pointed shape. A tooth of this simple conical type is composed internally of a substance known as the ivory or dentine, coated externally with a thin layer of a much harder nature and highly polished appearance, which is termed the enamel. Moreover, outside the base of the crown there may be patches of a coarser substance, called the cement. A model of such a tooth may be made by taking the finger of a kid glove, filling it with bees-wax, and putting some smears of sealing-wax at the base of the outer surface, when the bees-wax will represent the ivory, the kid the enamel, and the sealing-wax the cement. If we then cut off the summit of the finger we shall have a central disc of bees-wax (ivory) surrounded by a circle of kid (enamel), which will represent the condition of such a type of tooth when its summit has been worn away by use against the opposing tooth of the opposite jaw. If, however, before cutting off the end of our model, we indent the summit with several deep pits, and also mark the sides with one or more grooves, and fill up such pits and grooves with sealing-wax, it is obvious that we shall have a much more complex type of structure. This complex model will serve to explain the type of tooth structure found in many of the Hoofed or Ungulate Mammals; and it will be obvious that if we now cut off the summit of our model we shall find a series of irregular discs of bees-wax (ivory), each surrounded by a sinuous border of kid (enamel), in the folds of which will be masses of sealing-wax (cement). Such a model will enable us to understand the nature of the cheek-teeth of the Ungulate Mammals when we come to them.

Importance of Mammals to Man. From a utilitarian point of view Mammals are of extreme importance to man, since it is from them—and more especially from the Ungulate order—that by far the greater part of his animal food is procured, while their skins or fur furnish him largely with raiment; and it is from their ranks alone that all his beasts of burden and draught are recruited. Moreover, since these creatures are the highest representatives of the animal kingdom, among whom man himself must, from a zoological standpoint, be included, their study is one which commends itself most forcibly to all who are in any way interested in Natural History.

Mammals in the Past. Numerous as are the Mammals now living, it must never be forgotten that they form but a small moiety of those which flourished at earlier periods of the history of our earth. The Mammals of the present day may, indeed, be compared to the topmost branches and twigs of a giant forest tree, of which the larger limbs and trunk are concealed from our view. And it will accordingly be manifest that any one who confines his studies to the existing species will have but a very imperfect idea of the whole array of Mammalian life, and of the mutual connection of its various branches. The study of fossil Mammals is, however, a difficult one, and one requiring an extensive knowledge of comparative anatomy. All that can, therefore, be done in a work of the present nature is to call attention, as occasion arises, to some of these extinct Mammals which are of especial importance and interest as showing the manner in which groups now widely separated from one another were formerly more or less completely connected.

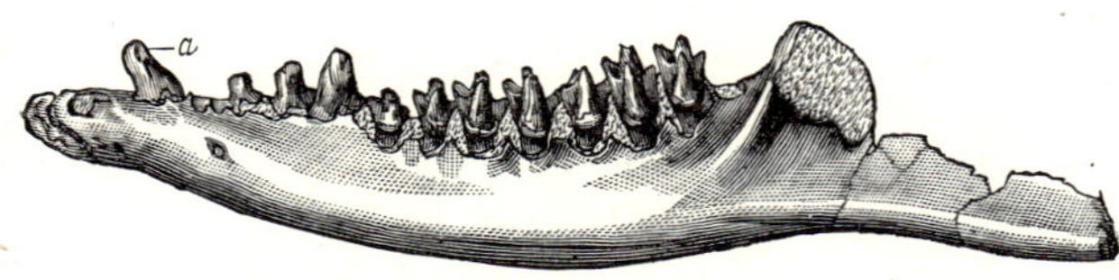

THE LEFT HALF OF THE LOWER JAW OF AN EXTINCT POUCHED MAMMAL.

From the Cretaceous Rocks of North America. The tusk is marked *a.*—After Marsh.

Although the number of extinct Mammals is very large, yet by far the greater proportion of these belong to the latest of the three great epochs into which the geological history of our globe has been divided. Whereas, during the long-past epoch known as the Secondary period, during which our chalk and oolites were deposited, the earth was tenanted by gigantic reptiles of strange form, it is not till we come to the rocks overlying the chalk, such as the London clay and overlying strata, that we find Mammals taking an important place among the inhabitants of the earth. It was, indeed, during this so-called Tertiary period that these animals attained the dominant position which they now occupy; and the present stage of the earth's history may be truly called the age of Mammals and Birds. We are not, however, to suppose from this that Mammals were unknown before the Tertiary period; a considerable number of species, mostly of small size, having been already discovered.

An additional importance attaches to the study of extinct Mammals, since it is by their means alone that we are able to explain several apparent anomalies in the geographical distribution of living groups. How, for instance, could we possibly explain the present existence of tapirs only in such widely remote areas as the Malay Peninsula and Islands and South America, unless we had learnt by geological explorations that these animals formerly roamed over large portions of Europe and Asia, from whence their descendants gradually migrated to the regions where they now remain?

The former occurrence of an epoch of great cold in the northern hemisphere known as the Glacial period, furnishes us with an explanation of how nearly related animals are now confined to isolated mountain chains; their ancestors having been enabled, during the prevalence of the cold, to spread over the plains of the temperate regions, from whence they retreated with the advent of warmer conditions to seek a congenial climate in the nearest mountain region.

Orders of Mammals. Mammals may be divided into eleven main groups or orders, which may be arranged as follows, and will be treated of in the same sequence, viz. :—

1. Apes, Monkeys, and Lemurs—PRIMATES.
2. Bats—CHIROPTERA.
3. Insectivores—INSECTIVORA.
4. Carnivores—CARNIVORA.
5. Hoofed Mammals—UNGULATA.
6. Manatis and Dugongs—SIRENIA.
7. Whales and Porpoises—CETACEA.
8. Rodents—RODENTIA.
9. Sloths, Anteaters, etc.—EDENTATA.
10. Pouched Mammals—MARSUPIALIA.
11. Egg-laying Mammals—MONOTREMATA.

It is not to be supposed that all these groups are separated from one another by differences of equal importance. For instance, No. 10 differs from the preceding groups by characters of far more importance than do any of those nine from one another; while the members of No. 11 differ fundamentally, not only from the first nine groups, but almost equally markedly from No. 10.

Having said thus much by way of introduction, we proceed to the consideration of the first order of Mammals.

CHAPTER II.

Apes, Monkeys, and Lemurs,—Order Primates.

The Man-like Apes.

Family *SIMIIDÆ*.

EVERYBODY knows what an ape or a monkey is, and the proverb "mischievous as a monkey" reveals the estimation in which the latter animals are commonly held. The more or less human-like form, the frequent tendency to assume an upright position, coupled with their hand-like feet, would be amply sufficient to distinguish the group to which these animals belong from all others, were it not for the circumstance that there are the less well-known creatures termed Lemurs, which, while evidently related to monkeys, yet differ from them in so many respects as to render it almost or quite impossible to give any characteristics which will absolutely distinguish the order to which they belong from all others. This is, however, a difficulty with which the zoologist has often to put up with, and to make the best of.

That the higher apes are closely related in their bodily structure to man is obvious to all, and it is a fact that the differences between some of these apes and man are, from a purely anatomical point of view, of far less importance than those by which the lower monkeys are separated from the higher apes. It has, indeed, been attempted to show that apes and monkeys are sharply distinguished from man by the circumstance that while man is two-handed, apes and monkeys are four-handed. The difference between the foot of one of the larger apes and that of man is, however, merely one of degree, and is much less than that between the apes and the lowest representatives of the order, as is well shown in the accompanying illustration, which illustrates the various forms assumed by the hand and foot of these animals.

Although the larger apes are those which come nearest to man in their general organisation, yet the strong ridges on the skulls of the adults, and the consequent overhanging and prominent eyebrows, give them an expression which, at the best, is but a gross caricature of the human countenance. It is, however, in the young of these animals, where the ridges on the skull are much less developed, and the tusks or canine teeth of the males have not attained the dimensions which they reach in the adult state, that we find a much more human-like cast of expression. Moreover, some of the smaller apes, in which the great ridges on the skull are never developed, approach much more nearly in the shape of their skulls to the human type. The larger apes are, indeed, repulsive animals in the adult condition; and it is usually only the smaller kinds of monkeys which are kept as pets.

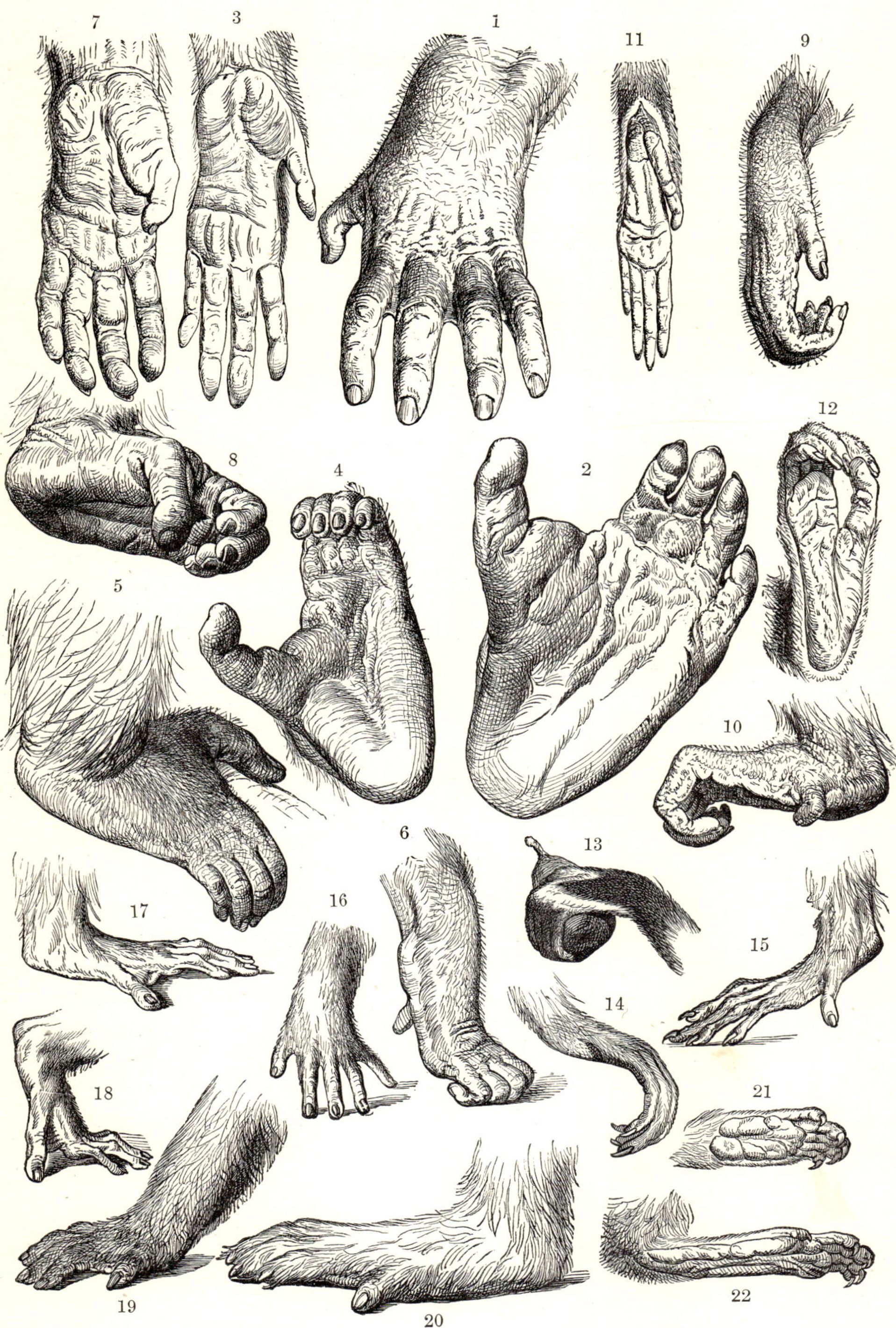

HANDS AND FEET OF APES AND MONKEYS.

1, 2, Gorilla ; 3–8, Chimpanzee ; 9, 10, Orang ; 11, 13, Gibbon ; 14, 15, Guereza ; 16–18, Macaque ;
19, 20, Baboon ; 21, 22, Marmoset.

Distribution. Most of the Primates are animals essentially adapted for living in warm climates, and are never found in regions which have not at least a hot summer. Some of them are, however, capable of withstanding a considerable amount of winter cold; and it is no uncommon sight in the outer ranges of the Himalaya to see troops of monkeys leaping from bough to bough of the snow-laden pines. Moreover, two species of monkeys inhabit the elevated regions of Eastern Tibet, where at least part of the winter must be intensely cold. With the exception of the apes found on the Rock of Gibraltar, which must either have reached their present habitation when Spain was united by land with Africa, or have been introduced by man at a later period, none of the Primates are found in Europe; they occur, however, throughout the warmer regions of the remainder of the globe, with the exception of the Australian region; but whereas all the apes and monkeys of the Old World belong to two well-marked families, those of the New World represent two other families closely allied to one another, but markedly different from both those of the Old World. The lemurs, as we shall see later on, are without exception Old World forms, and are especially characteristic of Madagascar, although also represented in India and on the continent of Africa, as well as in certain islands. In past times, however, lemurs were distributed over the greater part of the globe; and monkeys even roamed over the ancient forest-lands of Essex, as is proved by the discovery of a single tooth in the brick earth of Ilford in Essex; and they were also abundant over the more southern regions of Europe.

Nearly the whole of the Primates are adapted for a more or less completely arboreal life, most of them being inhabitants of forest regions. Aided by their hand-like feet, all of them are expert climbers, and many, like the oriental gibbons and the South American spider-monkeys, but rarely leave the trees, leaping from bough to bough, and thus from tree to tree, far above the heads of the travellers below, to whom their presence is made known only by their continual howling or chattering. The climbing powers of the South American monkeys are largely aided by their prehensile tails, which serve the purpose of a fifth limb. Owing to the warmth of the regions in which most of them dwell, no monkeys ever hibernate. Contrary, however, to what is often supposed to be the case, several of the smaller species are expert swimmers, and will fearlessly cross comparatively large rivers.

Characteristics. It is now time to take a glance at some of the more characteristic features which distinguish the order as a whole from other Mammals. In the first place, both the hand and the foot are, as a rule, provided with five digits, although in a few instances the thumb is wanting. Then, again, the hand is always adapted to act as a grasping organ, and, with the single exception of man, the same is the case with the foot, though it has recently been discovered that the foot of the newly-born human infant displays distinct traces of having been originally a grasping organ. In those cases where the hand attains its most perfect development, the thumb can be opposed to the fingers, but in some of the lower forms this action is only possible in a limited degree. The great toe is, in a similar manner, opposable to the other toes, although in man, as is well-shown in our figure of his skeleton, this action has been lost, and the bones of this toe lie parallel to those of the other toes. In this respect, as the figure shows, the foot of man is markedly different from that of the gorilla and the other apes. With the curious exception of the orang, in which the great toe is often entirely devoid of any trace of such appendage, all the fingers are furnished with nails. In the higher forms these nails are of a flattened shape in all the digits; and this flatness is always characteristic of the nail of the great toe, although the other digits of the lower forms have curved nails. In order to form an efficient support for these nails, the bones of the terminal joints of the digits, with the exception of the index finger of the lemurs, are transversely flattened out; and are thus very different from those of the Rodents and Carnivores. That the hand and foot should have perfect freedom of motion, it is of course necessary that the bones of the fore-arm and lower leg should remain completely separate from one another; and, as we see from the figured skeletons, the radius and ulna in the fore-arm, and the tibia and fibula in the leg, are both equally well developed and capable of motion upon one another. Another important point as regards the free use of the arms is the presence of complete collar-bones, which are always well developed in apes and monkeys, as they are in ourselves.

If we look once more at the figures of the skeletons of man and the gorilla we shall not fail to observe that in the skull the sockets, or orbits, of the eyes are completely surrounded by a ring of bone, and that the sockets themselves look almost directly forwards. This complete bony ring round the eye-sockets at once serves to distinguish the skulls of all the Primates from those of most of the Carnivores.

In correlation with the herbivorous habits of the majority of the species, the teeth of the Primates are adapted for grinding; the cheek-teeth having broad flattened crowns, which

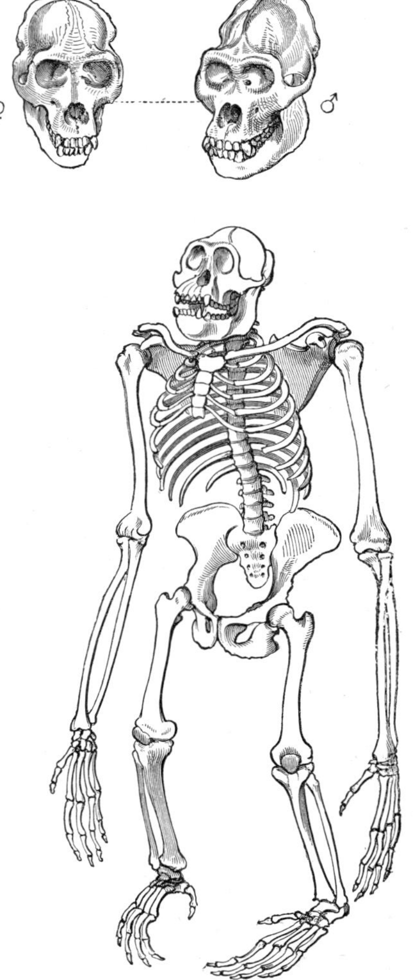

SKELETON OF THE GORILLA ;
and male (♂) and (♀) female skulls.

may either, as in ourselves, be surmounted by tubercles, or by transverse ridges. Except in one family of American monkeys, there are always three molar teeth in each side of either jaw, the last of which corresponds with our own "wisdom-tooth"; and these molar teeth are invariably larger and more complicated than the premolars. Very generally, as in ourselves, the number of the latter teeth is reduced to two on each side, and no living member of the order has more than three of these teeth. Very frequently again, and indeed invariably in the apes and monkeys, there are but two incisor teeth on each side of both the upper and the lower jaws.

With the single exception of the curious aye-aye of Madagascar, there are at least two mammæ situated on the breast of the females of all members of the order.

These, then, are the chief common characters possessed by apes and monkeys on the one hand and lemurs on the other; but, such as they are, they are considered of sufficient importance by a considerable number of zoologists to justify the inclusion of both groups in a single order. The two groups constitute, however, separate suborders, of which the first is termed the *Anthropoidea*, and the second the *Lemuroidea*. We shall point out how the latter group is distinguished from the former when we come to the consideration of the lemurs themselves; and we accordingly now proceed to consider the first family of the Apes and Monkeys.

The Man-like Apes. The Man-like Apes are but few in number, and are also those which come nearest, in point of structure, to man himself. Considered, indeed, from a purely zoological point of view, man represents merely a separate family—*Hominidæ*—of the Primates, which should occupy the place of honour at the head of all the other Mammals. Since, however, the special sciences, anthropology and ethnology, are devoted solely to the history of man, we shall here content ourselves by incidentally mentioning a few of the structural features by which he is distinguished from the Man-like Apes.

Apart, then, from man himself, the Man-like Apes include the largest representatives of the Primates. They are exclusively restricted to the Old World, where they are found only in the dense forests of the warmest and dampest regions. They are all characterised by their strikingly human-like form, although none of them habitually walk solely on their hind-limbs without obtaining additional support from their long arms.

Resemblance to Man. In all the larger species the resemblance to man is more marked in the young than in the adult; while in the adult the human characteristics are more pronounced in the female than the male. Dr. Robert Hartmann, of Berlin, who has devoted much attention to the Man-like Apes, observes that "in the gorilla, the chimpanzee, and the orang-utan, the external form is subject to essential modifications, according to the age and sex. The difference between the sexes is most strongly marked in the gorilla, and these differences are least apparent in the gibbons. When a young male gorilla is compared with an aged animal of the same species we are almost tempted to believe that we have to do with two entirely different creatures. While the young male still displays an evident approximation to the human structure, and develops in its bodily habits the same qualities which generally characterise the short-tailed apes of the Old World, with the exception of the baboon, the aged male is otherwise formed. In the latter case the points of resemblance to the human type are far fewer; the aged animal has become a gigantic ape, retaining indeed, in the structure of his hands and feet, the characteristics of the Primates, while the protruding head is something between the muzzle of the baboon, the bear, and the

A YOUNG CHIMPANZEE.

boar. Simultaneously with these remarkable alterations of the external structure there occurs a modification of the skeleton. The skull of an aged male gorilla becomes more projecting at the muzzle, and the canine teeth have almost attained the length of those of lions and tigers. On the upper part of the skull, which is rounded in youth, great bony crests are developed on the crown of the head and on the occiput. . . . The arches above the eye-sockets are covered with wrinkled skin, and the already savage and indeed revolting appearance of the old gorilla is thereby increased."

Teeth. In all the Man-like Apes the number of the teeth is the same as in man himself—that is to say, there are on each side of both the upper and lower jaws two incisors, one canine, two premolars, and three molars; the formula thus being: $i\frac{2}{2}$, $c\frac{1}{1}$, $p\frac{2}{2}$, $m\frac{3}{3}$, making a total of 32 teeth. Not only do the teeth agree in number with those of man, but, with the exception of the great size of the tusks, or canines, of the males, they likewise resemble them in structure. We are familiar with the form of our own molar teeth, which have wide crowns, with their angles rounded off and surmounted by four main tubercles set somewhat obliquely to one another; and the molars of the Man-like Apes are of the same general type of structure. In the apes, however, the whole series of teeth does not present the horse-shoe-like contour which is so characteristic of our own teeth; but, on the contrary, the cheek-teeth form nearly straight lines, having an angulated junction with the curved line of the front teeth.

Other Characteristics. None of these apes possess the peculiar pouches in the cheeks occurring in many of the monkeys, and none of them have any trace of a tail. Moreover, the naked patches so often found on the buttocks of the other Primates are either absent or, if present, are of very small size. All of these animals agree, however, with the monkeys, and thereby differ from man in the great length of the arms as compared with that of the legs; this difference being very clearly indicated in our figures of the skeleton of man and the gorilla. Another characteristic of the Man-like Apes shown in the figures last referred to is the great breadth and flatness of the breast-bone or sternum, this being a feature in which they agree with man, and differ from baboons and monkeys. Then, again, some of the Man-like Apes differ from the latter and resemble man in the absence of a small bone occupying a central position in the wrist, and hence known as the centrale of the carpus.

In addition to the points already mentioned, man is distinguished from the Man-like Apes by the greater relative size of his brain and the portion of the skull in which it is contained, as compared with the face and muzzle. His canine teeth are, moreover, but little longer than the other teeth, and are thus quite unlike the huge tusks of the male gorilla and orang. The great toe is also relatively longer, and is, at the most, only opposable in a very limited degree to the other toes. Moreover, the whole skeleton of man, as will be seen from our figure, is of a lighter and neater build, with certain peculiar curvatures of the lower part of the backbone, which permit of the assumption of the perfectly upright position without fatigue, and without need of any support from the arms, which do not reach below the middle of the thigh. Again, no ape has an ear modelled on the beautiful lines of that of the human species. The naked body of man is not, however, a character which a zoologist would consider of any importance as distinguishing him from the apes.

From their evident structural resemblance to man, the apes and monkeys are rightly placed at the head of the Mammalian class. This must not, however, by any means be taken to imply that all, or even any, of these animals are necessarily higher than the members of all the others. Although the intellect of the Man-like Apes may, and probably does, in some respects, exceed that of a dog; yet, for its own peculiar line of life, a dog is as fully and highly organised as an ape. Then, again, the lower monkeys and all the lemurs are far inferior in intelligence to the higher Carnivores, and indeed to the more highly-developed members of some of the other groups; but this is, of course, no bar to their being included in the order which heads the list.

With these remarks on the Man-like Apes in general, we proceed to the consideration of the various genera and species which comprise the family.

The Chimpanzee.

Genus *Anthropopithecus.*

Of all the large Man-like Apes, those which, on the whole, make the nearest approach in bodily structure to man are the chimpanzees of Western and Central Equatorial Africa, of which there appear to be two distinct species, one known as *A. niger* the other as *A. calvus.*

The chimpanzee has been long known in Europe. It has, indeed, been considered that the so-called "gorillas," met with by the Carthaginians of Hanno's voyage round the Cape in B.C. 470, on the rocky coasts of Sherboro Island, off Sierra Leone, were chimpanzees. According, however, to Mr. Winwood Reade, who travelled in Western Africa for the express purpose of obtaining authentic information about the chimpanzee and the gorilla, the creatures seen and captured by Hanno's party were neither gorillas nor chimpanzees, but dog-faced baboons. Be this as it may, that the chimpanzee was known in Europe as far back as 1598 is proved by an account brought back from the Congo by a Portuguese sailor, named Eduardo Lopez, and published at Frankfort by Pigafetta in his account of the Congo district. In 1613 there appeared, in Purchas's *Pilgrimages of the World,* the history of the wanderings of an English sailor, named Andrew Battel, in the lower part of Guinea, in 1590, who appears to have heard of or seen, not only the chimpanzee, which he designates the Enjocko (a corruption of N'djeko or N'Schego), but likewise the gorilla, which he calls the pongo.

Battel's account may be quoted at length, as follows. He states: "There are two kinds of monsters common to the woods of Angola; the largest of them is called Pongo in their language, and the other Enjocko. The pongo is in all its proportions like a man (except the legs, which have no calves), but he is of gigantic height. The face, hands, and ears of these animals are without hair; their bodies are covered, but not very thickly, with hair of a dunnish colour. When they walk on the ground, it is upright, with the hands on the nape of the neck. They sleep on trees, and make a covering over their heads to shelter them from the rain. They eat no flesh, but feed on nuts and other fruits; nor have they any understanding beyond instinct. When the people of the country travel through the woods they make fires in the night, and in the morning when they are gone the pongos will come and sit round it till it goes out, for they do not possess sagacity enough to lay on more wood. They go in bodies to kill many negroes who travel in the wood. When elephants happen to come and feed where they are, they will

HEAD OF CHIMPANZEE.

fall on them, and so beat them with their clubbed fists and sticks, that they are forced to run away roaring. The grown pongos are never taken alive, owing to their strength, which is so great that ten men cannot hold one of them. The young hang upon their mother's belly with their hands clasped about her. Many of them are taken by shooting the mothers with poisoned arrows."

From that date our knowledge of these animals has been gradually added to, although there is still room for fuller authentic accounts of their habits in a state of nature. Young chimpanzees have been frequently brought alive to Europe, and exhibited in the Zoological Gardens of this and other countries. They require, however, the greatest care and attention, and even with these they invariably die after a few years or months from the effects of our climate, which generally show themselves in various organic affections, although not, as has been supposed, in the form of tubercular disease of the lungs.

Structure. In all points of their structure the chimpanzees are very closely related to the gorilla, although the latter is now generally referred to a separate genus. Originally the chimpanzees were described under the name of *Troglodytes;* but since that name had been applied at an earlier date to the wrens, it has now been superseded by the somewhat cumbrous, although appropriate name of *Anthropopithecus.* This change is, however, not to be regretted on other grounds, since, as the name *Troglodytes* means a dweller in caves, while chimpanzees are purely forest animals, it is highly inappropriate to them.

In addition to certain distinctive features in the teeth, such as the relatively small size of the tusks or canines of the males, and the circumstance that the upper "wisdom-tooth" is smaller than either of the two molars in advance of it, chimpanzees may be readily distinguished from the gorilla by the circumstance that the males are but very slightly larger than the females. Moreover, the skull of the male chimpanzee is characterised by the absence of the enormous bony ridges which overhang the sockets of the eyes in that of the gorilla; while in the lower jaw the length of the bony union between the two lateral branches is much less than in the latter. In both these respects the chimpanzee is decidedly nearer to man than is the gorilla; and a further approximation to the human type is presented by the relatively shorter arms, which in the perfectly upright posture only reach a short distance below the knee. The hands and feet also are longer and more slender than those of the gorilla, as may be seen by comparing figs. 3–8 with 1 and 2 of the illustration on p. 15. Moreover, as in man, the middle finger is longer than either of the others; and although there is some degree of variation in the relative length of the thumb in different individuals, as a rule this digit reaches to the base of the first phalangeal joint of the index finger. The male chimpanzee does not appear to exceed five feet in height when full grown, and is thus considerably inferior in size to the male gorilla.

General Character. Dr. Hartmann remarks of the chimpanzees that, although the arched ridges above the eyes "are not so excessively prominent as in a gorilla of the same age, they are strongly developed, covered with wrinkled skin, and in this case also there is a species of eyebrow, stiff and bristly, with shorter hairs between. The large, wrinkled lids are furnished with thick eyelashes. A general physiognomical distinction between the gorilla and the chimpanzee consists in the fact that the bridge of the nose is shorter in the latter than in the former. In the chimpanzee this part of the organ is depressed, yet the depression is of a conical and convex form, and is covered with a network of wrinkles of varying depth. In the chimpanzee the interval between the inner angle of the eye and the upper lateral contour of the cartilaginous end of the nose is shorter than in the gorilla. There is also some difference in the form of the nose; it is on the whole flatter, the tip is less apparent, and the nostrils are not so widely opened, nor so thickly padded. The external ear of the chimpanzee has, on the whole, less resemblance to the human ear, and its contour is larger than that of the gorilla. But this organ varies so much in individuals that it is difficult to lay down any rule for its average size. The skin of the chimpanzee is frequently of a light, yet muddy flesh-colour, which sometimes verges upon brown. Spots, varying in size and depth of colour, sometimes isolated, sometimes in groups, and of a blackish-brown, sooty, or bluish-black tint, are found on different parts of the body of many individuals, especially on the face, neck, breast, belly, arms and hands, thighs and shanks, and more rarely on the back. The face, which, soon after birth, is of a flesh-colour, merging into yellowish-brown, assumes a darker shade with the gradual development of the body. The hairy coat is sleek, or only in rare cases slightly curled, and the coarser and bristly hair is generally stiff and elastic. The parting on the forehead is often so regular that it might have been arranged by the hairdresser's art. Close behind that part of the head at which the projecting ridges over the eyes of the gorilla generally meet there is in the chimpanzee (as is well shown in our figure of the head) an altogether bald place, or often only a few scattered hairs. Round the face the growth of hair streams downwards like a beard. On the neck it is of considerable length, and it falls in the same long locks over the shoulders, back, and hips. The hair on the limbs is not so long, and takes a downward direction on the upper arm, and an opposite direction on the fore-arm, while there is often a longitudinal parting on the centre of the inner surface of this part of the limb. On the back of the wrist the hair grows in a kind of whorl; the upper hairs turn upwards and backwards, the middle ones turn backwards, the lower ones backwards and downwards. The backs of the hands and the roots of the fingers are hairy. On the front of the thigh the hair takes a downward direction, while behind it grows backwards. On the shank it grows downwards in the region of the tibia, and turns back on the inside of the leg. The back of the foot and the roots of the toes are likewise hairy. There is a shorter growth of these hairs on the face, chin, and ears. In other cases the hair of the true chimpanzee is of a black colour. Short whitish hairs may be observed on the lower part of the face and chin, as well as round the posterior; and sometimes the colour of the hair is shot throughout with reddish- or brownish-black.

The foregoing description applies to the true chimpanzee, *Anthropopithecus niger*. Many varieties of this species seem to exist, some of which have been regarded as distinct species; but with the exception of the bald chimpanzee, to be mentioned immediately, it does not appear that any of these can be satisfactorily distinguished as true species. The natives of Africa have many names for chimpanzees in the various districts. In the Gabun region they are known as N'Schego, in Malimbu as Kulu, in Manyema as Soko, and in the Niam-Niam district as Ranja; while to the Arab traders they are known as the Bam or M'Bam.

The Bald Chimpanzee. In his *Equatorial Africa* Du Chaillu gave a description of a chimpanzee, which he said was known to the natives as the N'Schego M'Bouvé, and which he proposed to call *Troglodytes*, or as it should properly be, *Anthropopithecus calvus*. For a long period zoologists were in doubt whether this bald-headed chimpanzee was really a distinct species. In the autumn of 1883 a young chimpanzee was, however, purchased by the Zoological Society of London, which Mr. Bartlett, the superintendent of the Society's Gardens, recognised as being very different from the true or common chimpanzee, and which he regarded as in all probability identical with Du Chaillu's bald chimpanzee.

Writing of this animal, Mr. Bartlett remarks that, while "the colour of the face, hands, and feet in the chimpanzee are white or pale flesh-colour, the same parts of the animal under consideration are black or brownish-black. Another well-marked difference is to be found in the hair upon the head and face. In the true chimpanzee the hair on the top of the head, and that passing down from the centre (where it divides) to the sides of the face or cheeks, is tolerably long and full, forming what may be considered rather bushy whiskers; whereas the figure (given in the memoir), clearly shows the front, top, and sides of the head and face to be nearly naked, having only a few short hairs on the head, quite destitute of any signs of the parting so very conspicuous in the chimpanzee. Another striking difference may be noticed in the size and form of the head and ears. Out of the number of chimpanzees I have seen and examined, both old and young, none have possessed the large flat ears so conspicuous in this individual. The form of the head, the expression of the face, the expanded nostrils, the thicker lips, especially the lower lip, together with the more elevated skull, cannot fail to distinguish this animal from the chimpanzee. . . . Again, the habits of this animal differ entirely from those of the well-known or common chimpanzee. She has always shown a disposition to live upon animal food. Soon after her arrival I found she would kill and eat small birds; seizing them by the neck, she would bite off the head and eat the bird, skin, feathers, and all; for some months she killed and ate a small pigeon every night. After a time we supplied her with cooked mutton and beef-tea; upon this food she has done well. I have never found any ordinary chimpanzee that would eat any kind of flesh.

"Another singular habit was the producing pellets or 'quids,' resembling the castings thrown up by raptorial birds. They are composed of feathers and other indigestible substances, that had been taken with her food. Moreover, she is an expert rat-catcher, and has caught and killed many rats that had entered her cage during the night. Her intelligence is far above that of the ordinary chimpanzee. With but little trouble she can be taught to do many things that require the exercise of considerable thought and understanding; she recognises those who have made her acquaintance, and pays marked attention to men of colour, by uttering a loud cry of *bun, bun, bun.* She is never tired of romping and playing, and is generally in a good temper."

We shall have something to say in regard to the mental faculties of this chimpanzee later on, but we have now to consider, firstly, the geographical distribution of chimpanzees, and then their mode of life and habits.

Distribution. As already mentioned, chimpanzees inhabit Western and Central Equatorial Africa, where they range over a considerable area of country. On the west coast their range appears to be limited to the northward approximately by the river Gambia, while their southward range extends about to the river Coanza, which flows into the ocean at the boundary between Angola and Benguela. Their limits on either side of the Equator do not, therefore, exceed some twelve degrees, the northern range in latitude being greater than the southern.

With regard to the extent of their range across the continent to the eastward, chimpanzees are known to occur to the north-west of the great lakes in the Niam-Niam district, in 28° east longitude, and they are likewise recorded from Monbottu. Dr. Emin Pasha, writing to the secretary of the Zoological Society of London, considers, however, that they range to about the parallel of 32° east longitude. Dr. Emin's letter states, "It may be interesting for you to hear that an anthropoid ape exists in Uganda and Unyoro (the districts lying between the Victoria and the Albert Nyanza). I cannot say whether it is identical with the Monbottu chimpanzee or not. While staying in these countries the negroes told me much about this animal, and in a manuscript map which I forwarded to Dr. Petermann, I fixed its northern limit at 2° north latitude. Now I hear that this ape is frequent in the thick forests near Ugoma, and I hasten to beg my friend King Kabrega for some specimens." If this application to the king ever reached him it does not appear to have been successful. Later on, however, Dr. Emin forwarded to England the skull of a chimpanzee shot by himself near Lake Albert Nyanza, which does not appear to differ from that of the West African form.

Habits. Like all the other Man-like Apes the chimpanzees are forest-dwelling animals, although on the coast of the Loango district they are found in the mountains. Their food is usually the various wild fruits which grow abundantly in these dense forests, but, as we have seen, at least the bald-headed species will take kindly to an animal diet in captivity.

The following account of the habits of the chimpanzee is taken from Dr. Hartmann, who draws much of his information from the German traveller, Schweinfurth, as detailed in his work entitled *From the Heart of Africa.* Dr. Hartmann observes that the chimpanzee either lives in separate families or in small groups of families. "In many districts—as, for example, in the forest-regions of Central Africa—its habits are even more arboreal than are those of the gorilla. Elsewhere as, for instance, on the south-west coast, it seems to live more upon the ground. The Bam chimpanzee of Niam-Niam inhabits the galleries, as they were called by Piaggia and Schweinfurth—that is, the forest trees growing one above another in stages, of which the growth is so dense that it is difficult to get at them. The powerful stems, thickly overgrown with wild pepper, have branches from which hang long streamers of bearded moss, and also a parasitic growth of that remarkable fern to which Schweinfurth gave the name of elephant's ear. The large tun-shaped structures of the tree termites (white ants) are found on the loftier boughs. Other stems, rotten and decayed, serve as supports for the colossal streamers of *Mucuna urens* (a climbing leguminous plant with yellow or white flowers and large leathery seed-pods), and form bowers overhung with impenetrable festoons, as large as houses, in which perpetual darkness reigns.

" When the chimpanzee goes on all-fours, he generally supports himself on the backs of his closed fingers (compare Fig. 6 of the illustration on p. 15) rather than on the palm of the hand, and he goes sometimes on the soles of his feet, sometimes on his closed toes. His gait also is weak and vacillating, and he can stand upright on his feet for a still shorter time than the gorilla. At the same time he seeks support for his hands, or clasps them above his head, which is a little thrown back in order to maintain his balance."

Chimpanzees appear to be continually shifting their haunts in order to find fresh feeding-grounds, and will not unfrequently visit and pillage deserted native plantations. They utter loud cries, which may be heard resounding through the forests at all hours of both day and night. Dr. E. Pechuel-Loesche, who accompanied the expedition sent to Western Equatorial Africa during the years from 1873 to 1875, observes that chimpanzees "are really accomplished in the art of bringing forth these unpleasant sounds, which may be heard at a great distance, and are reproduced by the echoes. It is impossible to estimate the number of those who take part in the horrid noise, but we often seemed to hear more than a

THE CHIMPANZEE "MAFUKA."

hundred. They generally remain upon the ground among the dense underwood and thickets of *Amomum* (a member of the ginger family) and other scitamineous plants, and only climb trees for the sake of obtaining fruit. Their track may be plainly discerned on soft ground; they stop short wherever the *Amomum* grows, of which they are very fond, and the red husks of the fruit of which may be seen strewn around."

There seems to be no doubt but that chimpanzees build a kind of nest high up in the trees for their families; and it is stated that the male of the family takes up his position for the night beneath the shelter afforded by the nest. It is probable that this habit has given rise to the idea that these animals construct pent-houses for themselves; an elaborate illustration of such a structure being given in Du Chaillu's *Equatorial Africa*.

It is said that chimpanzees will generally take to flight at the sight of man, but that when driven to bay, or their retreat cut off, they will attack him fiercely, and are then very awkward customers to deal with. Dr. Livingstone, in his *Last Journals*, gave an account and sketch of a chimpanzee hunt by the Manyema tribe, describing these animals under their name of Soko, but apparently confusing them with the gorilla. The doctor's graphic sketch shows four chimpanzees surrounded by natives, one of the former having received its death-wound, a second with a spear in its back, and a fourth making a vigorous onslaught on one of the hunters, whose hand it has seized in its mouth. Dr. Livingstone states that the chimpanzee "kills the leopard occasionally, by seizing both paws and biting them, so as to disable them; he then goes up a tree, groans over his wounds, and sometimes recovers, while the leopard dies. The lion kills him at once, and sometimes tears his limbs off, but does not eat him. The soko eats no flesh; small bananas are his dainties, but not maize. His food consists of wild fruits, and of these one is large, a large sweet sop but indifferent in taste. The soko brings forth at times twins."

Intelligence in Captivity. In captivity chimpanzees, when in health, are gentle, intelligent, and affectionate, readily learning to feed themselves with a spoon, or to drink out of a glass or cup. Unfortunately, however, their span of life in this country is but brief. The longest period that a chimpanzee has hitherto lived in the Zoological Society's Gardens is eight years; "Sally," who died in 1891, having been kept there for that time.

One of the earliest accounts of the chimpanzee in captivity was given by the late Mr. Broderip, and is to be found quoted in most works on Natural History. It relates to a young male brought from the Gambia in the year 1835, which was deposited in the menagerie of the London Zoological Society. Dr. Hartmann has also published an interesting description of the habits of another male, which was exhibited in the Berlin Aquarium in 1876, and was remarkable for its unusually lively and cheerful disposition.

"Sally." More recent, and thus probably less widely known, is, however, the description by Dr. J. G. Romanes of the mental power of the bald chimpanzee, "Sally," already mentioned as having lived so long in London. This account was written in 1889, after the creature had been nearly six years in the Zoological Gardens. The intelligence of "Sally" is compared by Dr. Romanes to that of a child a few months before emerging from the period of infancy, and is thus far higher than that of any other Mammal (exclusive of man). In spite, however, of this relatively high degree of intelligence, the creature's power of making vocal replies to her keepers, or those with whom she was brought into contact, were of the most limited kind. Such replies were, indeed, restricted to three peculiar grunting noises. One of these indicated assent or affirmation; another, of very similar intonation, denoted refusal or distrust; while the third, and totally different intonation, was used to express thanks or recognition of favours. In disposition "Sally" was, like many of her sex, apt to be capricious and uncertain; although, on the whole, she was good-humoured and fond of her keepers, with whom she was never tired of a kind of bantering play, which was kept up at intervals

almost continually. By singing in a peculiar kind of monotone, in imitation of her
own utterance, her keepers were usually able to induce her to go through a series
of remarkable actions, the meaning of which is not very apparent. First she would
shoot out her lips into a tubular form, uttering at the same time a weird kind
of howling note, interrupted at regular intervals. The pauses would, however,

THE CHIMPANZEE "SALLY."

gradually become shorter and shorter, while the sing-song cry became louder and
louder, until it finally culminated in a series of yells and screams, not unfrequently
accompanied with a stamping of the feet, and a violent shaking of the netting
of her cage. After this climax the utterance of a few grunts terminated the
performance.

Some time previously to 1889, it occurred to Dr. Romanes (from whose account
we are paraphrasing) that "Sally" would be a good subject to test the powers of

the simiine intelligence by a series of special experiments.   It was found, however, that such experiments were seriously hampered by the effects on the creature of the visits of the numbers of people who were constantly passing in and out of the room in which she was kept; and there is consequently but little doubt that, under more favourable circumstances, the results obtained would have been more remarkable than they are.   Dr. Romanes, having secured the assistance of the keepers, caused them to ask "Sally" repeatedly for one, two, or three straws, which she was to pick up and hold out from among the litter strewing her cage.   The number of straws asked for was constantly varied, and never followed any regular order; and when the correct number was presented the animal was rewarded by a piece of fruit, while if the number was incorrect her offer was refused.   "In this way," observes Dr. Romanes,[1] "the ape was taught to associate these three numbers with their names.   Lastly, if two or three straws were demanded, she was taught to hold one or two in her mouth until she had picked up the remaining straw, and then to hand the two or three straws together.   This prevented any error arising from her interpretation of vocal tones.   As soon as the animal understood what was required, and had learnt to associate these three numbers with their names, she never failed to give the number of straws asked for.   Her education was then extended in a similar manner from three to four, and from four to five straws.   Here I allowed her education to terminate.   But more recently one of the keepers has endeavoured to advance her instruction as far as ten.   The result, however, is what might have been anticipated.   Although she very rarely makes any mistake in handing out one, two, three, four, or five straws, according to the number asked for, and although she is usually accurate in handing out as many as six or seven, when the numbers eight, nine, or ten are named, the result becomes more and more uncertain, so as to be suggestive of guess-work.   It is evident, however, that she understands the words seven, eight, nine, and ten to betoken numbers higher than those below them; and if she is asked for any of these numbers, she gives some number that is above six and not more than ten; but there is no such constant accuracy displayed in handing out the exact number named, as is the case below six.   On the whole, then, while there is no doubt that this animal can accurately compute any number of straws up to five, beyond five the accuracy of her computation becomes progressively diminished.   It is to be noticed that the ape exhibits some idea of multiplication; for she very frequently doubles over a long straw so as to make it appear as two straws.   Any of the rare errors which she makes in dealing with numbers below six are almost invariably due to her thus endeavouring to duplicate her straws.   In this connection it is to be remembered that, owing to the method above described, when any high number is demanded, a considerable tax is imposed upon her patience; and as her movements are deliberate, while her store of patience is small, it is evident that the doubling of the straws is intended to save trouble by getting the sum completed with greater rapidity.   Of course we do not recognise these doubled straws as equivalent to two straws, and therefore the persistency with which she endeavours to palm them off as such is the more noteworthy.   Moreover, I am disposed to think that the uncertainty which attends her dealing with the numbers six and seven is more due to her losing patience than to her losing count;

---

[1] We have somewhat abbreviated the extract.

although after seven I believe that her computation of the numbers becomes vague."

Before her death, as we have been informed by Dr. Romanes, "Sally" was able to count up to as many as ten straws; and if her life had been prolonged she might even have advanced beyond this. Dr. Romanes proceeds to state that it would be unreasonable to assume that this chimpanzee really employed any system of notation in delivering the correct tale of straws, and we may rather consider that she executed her task by a direct perception of the difference between a higher and

HEAD OF CHIMPANZEE "MAFUKA."

lower number, without any actual process of counting; this inference being confirmed by the power possessed by men of simultaneously estimating with accuracy the number of a low series of small objects set before them without any direct enumeration.

In addition to these attempts to determine "Sally's" capacity for numbers, Dr. Romanes instituted a series of experiments designed to test her powers of recognising and distinguishing between colours. "It appeared to me," says the experimenter, "that if I could once succeed in getting her to know the names of black, white, red, green, or blue, a possible basis might have been laid for further experiments wherein these five colours could have been used as signs of artificially associated ideas. The result, however, of attempting to teach her the names of colours has been so uniformly negative, that I am disposed to think the animal must be colour-blind. The method adopted in these experiments was to obtain a number of brightly and uniformly coloured pieces of straw—each piece being either white, black, red, green, or blue. Offered the straws two by two of different colours on each occasion, the ape was invited to select the straw of the colour named from the one whose colour was not named, and, of course, on choosing correctly was rewarded with a piece of fruit. In this way she quickly learned to distinguish between the white straws and the straws of any other colour; but she never could be taught to

SIDE VIEW OF HEAD OF CHIMPANZEE "MAFUKA."

go further. Now the distinction between the white straws and the straws of any other colour is a distinction which can be drawn by an eye that is colour-blind; and from the fact that the ape is always able to perceive this distinction, while she cannot be taught to distinguish any of the others, I conclude that her failure in this respect is not due to any want of intelligence, but to some deficiency in her powers of colour-perception."

Mafuka. We must conclude our notice of chimpanzees by the mention of a very remarkable ape which was brought from the Loango Coast in 1875, and exhibited in the Zoological Gardens at Dresden. This animal was a female, and from its peculiar physiognomy, as shown in our two figures of its head, has given rise to much discussion as to what species it really belonged. The creature was of a fierce disposition, and was generally known by the name of Mafuka. Although presenting many of the features of a chimpanzee, it had very projecting jaws, the ears were relatively small and placed rather high on the head, while the end of the nose was wide and expanded. The most remarkable feature about this animal was, however, the presence of a great bony ridge overhanging the eyes, very much as in the female gorilla. So like, indeed, was Mafuka to a gorilla in this respect, that Dr. Hartmann tells us when he first saw her he felt almost convinced that he had to do with a female gorilla which had not quite attained maturity. This opinion was, however, vigorously confuted by other zoologists; and it was subsequently suggested that the creature might be a half-breed between the chimpanzee and gorilla. Dr. Hartmann concludes by saying that "for me and many other naturalists Mafuka remains up to this time an enigma." Unless, which is very improbable, this animal indicates a third species of chimpanzee, we confess that the half-breed theory appears to us the most probable solution of the mystery.

Extinct Chimpanzee. A word in regard to a fossil-ape found in the north-west of India in rocks, belonging to the Pliocene or later division of the Tertiary period, and we have done with chimpanzees. It has always been a matter of surprise that no large Man-like Ape now inhabits the dense tropical forests of India or Burma, which would appear to be just as suitable for these creatures as are those of Borneo or Equatorial Africa. The discovery in India of a jaw of a large ape apparently belonging to the same genus as the chimpanzee shows us, however, that large Man-like Apes must have once roamed over the plains of India. Why chimpanzees, together with hippopotami and giraffes, which are likewise found fossil in India but are now confined to Africa, should have totally disappeared from the former country, is, however, one of those puzzling problems connected with the distribution of animals which we have but little hope of answering satisfactorily.

The fossil Indian chimpanzee was found in the arid districts of the Punjab, and since we know that the living Man-like Apes dwell in the deepest gloom and solitude of primeval forests, where vegetation grows luxuriously and offers a constant supply of fruits throughout the year, we may probably infer that the Indian chimpanzee inhabited a similar forest-clad country; and that, consequently, the present area of the Punjab was in parts at all events clothed with forests in which dwelt this ape, instead of being, as now, a sun-scorched and somewhat desolate region. Evidence of the former existence of these forests is afforded by the occurrence of numbers of fossil tree-stems in various parts of the same series of rocks from which the remains of the fossil chimpanzee were obtained.

THE GORILLA.

Genus *Gorilla.*

Under the heading of the Chimpanzee we have already seen how, as far back as 1590, the English sailor Battel heard of the existence of a gigantic ape living in the forests of Guinea, and known to the natives as the Pongo; this ape being

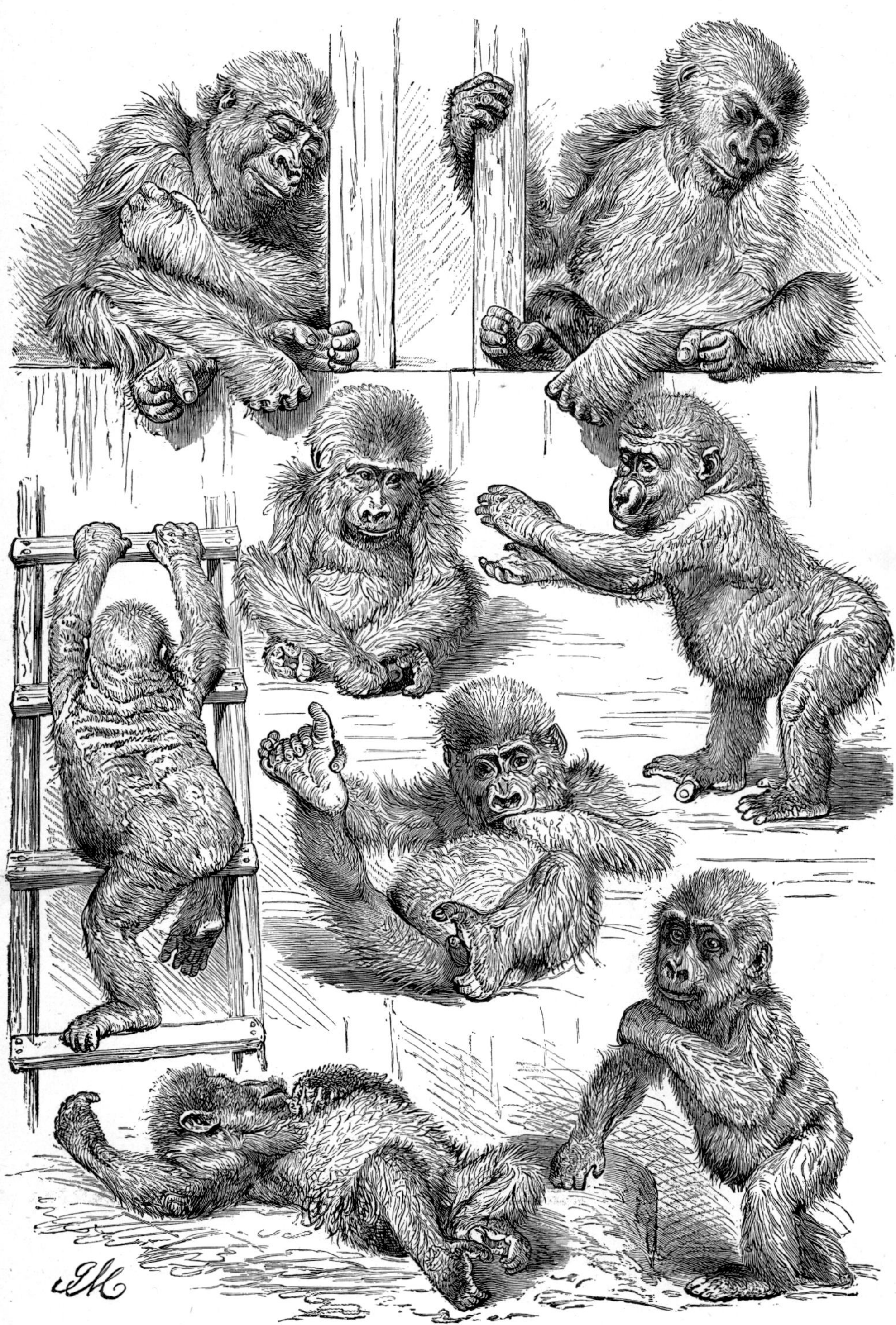

THE YOUNG GORILLA AT PLAY.

also known under the names of Jina, N'Jina, or Indjina, or N'Guyala, while by Europeans it is universally termed the Gorilla. The naturalist Buffon appears to have given credence to Battel's pongo (N'Pungu, or M'Pungu, as it is variously spelt); but his account was summarily rejected by the great Cuvier as a mere traveller's tale. Still, however, vague rumours of the existence on the West Coast of Africa of an ape of larger size and fiercer habits than the chimpanzee from time to time reached Europe; and in 1819 Bowdich, in his account of the " Mission from Cape Coast Castle to Ashanti," definitely stated that among the many curious apes found in the Gabun district the ingenu (or gorilla) was by far the largest and strongest. It was not, however, till the year 1847 that any precise evidence of the existence of this mysterious ape reached Europe. In that year, however, Dr. Savage, an English missionary stationed at the Gabun, wrote to the veteran comparative anatomist, Sir Richard Owen, enclosing drawings of the skull of an ape from that district, which was described as being much larger than the chimpanzee, and feared by the negroes more than they dread the lion, or any other wild beast of the forest. These sketches clearly showed the bold bony crests over the eye-sockets, which mark the skull of the gorilla as distinct from that of the chimpanzee. "At a later date in the same year," writes Sir Richard Owen, " were transmitted to me from Bristol two skulls of the same large species of chimpanzee as that notified in Dr. Savage's letter; they were obtained from the same locality in Africa, and brought clearly to light evidence of the existence in Africa of a second larger and more powerful ape." In the following year these specimens were described by the English anatomist under the name of *Troglodytes savagei*. It appears, however, that about the same time that Dr. Savage forwarded the sketches to Sir Richard Owen, he also sent a skull of the unknown ape, together with a description of the animal itself, by the hand of a fellow-missionary named Wilson, to Boston in the United States. And in an American scientific journal for the year 1847, the new ape was described, and named *Troglodytes gorilla*. Thus matters stood till the year 1851, when a Captain Harris presented to the Royal College of Surgeons the first skeleton of a gorilla that had ever been brought to England; while in the same year another skeleton was sent to Philadelphia by Mr. Ford. This at once made a great advance in our knowledge of the creature; and in 1852 a French naturalist came to the conclusion that the gorilla ought not to be included in the same genus as the chimpanzee; and he accordingly proposed for it the name of *Gorilla gena*. By the rules of nomenclature adopted among zoologists, he had, however, no right to supersede the specific name proposed by Sir Richard Owen; and the gorilla is accordingly now known scientifically as *Gorilla savagei*.

In 1856 the well-known African traveller, Du Chaillu, arrived at the Gabun, preparatory to his expedition into the interior; and two years later the British Museum received from the Gabun an entire gorilla preserved in spirits, the skin of which was soon afterwards mounted and exhibited to the public.

Such is the history of the gradual acquisition of our knowledge of the largest of the apes. On his return from the Gabun to America, Du Chaillu set to work to publish an account of his travels and adventures; and in 1861 the world was startled by the appearance of his *Explorations and Adventures in Equatorial*

Africa, which gave a full and illustrated narrative of numerous personal encounters with gorillas. Somewhat later, an Englishman, Mr. Winwood Reade, made an expedition to the Gabun for the purpose of verifying these accounts; the results of his journey being given in a work entitled *Savage Africa*, of which the first edition appeared in 1863. In this work it is asserted that neither Du Chaillu nor any other European had up to that date ever seen a wild, living gorilla in its native haunts, though he possibly did not refer to those driven to the shore in 1851; and his assertions are supported by the members of the German Loango Expedition of 1873–76. Be this as it may, Du Chaillu's accounts of gorilla-hunting have been so frequently quoted that we need hardly dwell on them here.

Characteristics. We now proceed to describe the gorilla, noticing especially the more important characters in which it differs from the chimpanzee. In the first place, it may, however, be observed that both these animals agree in the deep black colour of their skin, and the blackish hue of a large portion of the hair. One of the most obvious distinctive features of the gorilla, as distinguished from the chimpanzee, is that the males are very much larger than the females, while their skulls have the beetling, bony ridges overhanging the sockets of the eyes, which give to the living animals their peculiarly ferocious and forbidding aspect. Then, again, the arms are relatively longer than in the chimpanzee, reaching, in the upright position, some considerable distance below the knee, although never below the middle of the lower leg or shin. In regard to our figure of the skeleton of the gorilla, given on p. 17, it should, however, be observed that it is taken from one mounted in a somewhat slouching position, so that the hands reach lower down than would have been the case had it been set perfectly upright. Another point in which the gorilla differs from the chimpanzee, and thereby departs still further from the human type, is the greater length of the median bony union of the two branches of the lower jaw. Moreover, the "wisdom-tooth," or last molar, in the upper jaw, is larger than either of the two molars in front of it; this being another departure from the chimpanzee and man.

Such are some of the leading structural features by which the gorilla is distinguished from the chimpanzee, and they are those on which zoologists chiefly rely in referring these animals to different genera. We shall see, however, immediately that there are many other points of difference, but before noticing these we must mention certain characteristics by which the chimpanzee and gorilla are collectively distinguished from the lower Man-like Apes, and thereby agree with man. One of these is that the total number of joints in the backbone, or vertebræ, lying between the solid mass called the sacrum and the neck is seventeen, or the same as in man. It is true, indeed, that whereas in man only twelve of these vertebræ carry ribs, in the gorilla and chimpanzee thirteen are so provided; but this is a matter of minor import, which is entirely overbalanced by the numerical identity of the vertebræ. The other point is the absence of the central bone in the wrist; so that whereas in man, the chimpanzee, and the gorilla the total number of separate wrist-bones is but nine, in all the other Primates it is ten. This is a very important characteristic in connecting these two apes with man.

Relationship to Man. Here we may make a brief digression to explain what zoologists mean by the connection and relationship of these apes with man. A great deal of nonsense has been written about the impossibility of man being descended from the chimpanzee, a gorilla, or an orang. No one, however, who knows what he is talking about, can ever suppose for a single moment that such was the case. What zoologists do contend for is that, supposing some kind of evolution to be the true explanation of the origin of animals,—and all the available evidence indicates that it is so,—man is so intimately connected, so far as his bodily structure is concerned, with the higher apes that, in this respect at least, he cannot but be considered to have had a similar origin. And on this view both man and the Man-like Apes are regarded as diverging branches descended from a common ancestor,—" the missing link,"—long since extinct, and as much unlike any living ape, as such apes are unlike man himself. The gorilla and chimpanzee are presumed to be descended from apes which diverged from the common ancestral stock, subsequently to the assumption of the human attributes of seventeen vertebræ between the sacrum and the neck, and the loss of the central bone in the wrist.

With these few words on this deeply interesting and important subject, we proceed to a more detailed examination of the gorilla.

Structure. A full-grown male gorilla, if standing in a perfectly upright position, will generally measure rather more than six feet in height; and since his body is much more bulky, and his limbs are longer than those of a man, he is considerably the largest representative of the Primates. As in the chimpanzee, there are distinct eyebrows on the forehead and lashes to the lids of the eyes. The nose has a relatively long bridge, and its extremity is high, conical, and widely expanded; the whole length being divided by a distinct furrow running down the middle line, and becoming more marked as age advances. The upper lip is remarkable for its shortness; and the whole of the dark skin in the region of the nose, cheeks, and mouth is marked by a number of rugose folds. The massive jaws are extremely projecting, and with their huge tusks, or canine teeth, complete the repulsive aspect imparted to the expression by the overhanging eyebrows. The lower jaw has scarcely any indication of the prominent chin which is such a characteristic feature in the human countenance, but it slopes rapidly away from the middle line in front, so as to assume a somewhat triangular contour. The whole skin of the face is of deep black colour, of a glossy appearance, and sparsely sprinkled with coarse hairs. The ears are comparatively small, with their hinder border sharply angulated in the middle, and appear to be fastened above and behind to the sides of the face. Like the face and lips, the ears are of a deep black hue. The head is joined to the trunk by a very short and thick neck, which gives the appearance of its being set into the shoulders; and the term " bull-necked " is therefore strictly applicable to the creature. This great thickness and power of the neck is largely due to the backward projection of the occipital region of the skull, and the tall spines surmounting the vertebræ of the neck. In correlation with the great development of this region, we find the muscles of the shoulders and chest equally powerful, as is essential for the movements of the mighty arms. On the

GORILLAS AT HOME.

latter the arrangement of the hair is the same as in the chimpanzee; but we notice a great difference in the form of the hands, as may be seen from the illustration on p. 15. Thus, in marked contrast to that of the chimpanzee, the hand (1) is remarkable for its great width and stoutness, coupled with the shortness and generally clumsy make of the fingers, which are united together by a strong web, reaching nearly to the end of their first joints. The thumb is short in proportion to the fingers, reaching but slightly beyond the middle of the metacarpal bone of the index finger, and is nearly conical in shape at its extremity. The fingers, on the contrary, are somewhat flattened at their extremities. There is but little difference, as seen in our figure, between the lengths of the index, middle, and ring fingers; the former being some-times as long as, but at others shorter than the middle finger. In all cases, however, the "little" finger is true to its name in being shorter than either of the others. The skin on the back of the wrist is thrown into a number of deep folds, with an oblique direction; while a network of wrinkles covers the backs of the fingers, which have large callosities on the first and sometimes also on the second joints; these callosities being produced by the animal walking, when on all-fours, with its fingers doubled on the palms of the hands. On the deep black and naked skin of the palms of the hands, which are hard and horny, there are generally numerous wart-like growths.

With the exception of noticing its enormous bulk, especially in the lower part, we need not devote any particular attention to the body of the gorilla; and we accordingly direct our observation to the hind-limbs or legs. One of the most important features in these is that the calves are more developed than in any of the other Man-like Apes. The foot, as contrasted with that of the chimpanzee in the illustration on p. 15, is characterised by its great breadth and width, and also by the extreme shortness of the very thick toes. The great toe varies somewhat in length, as compared with that of the others, reaching in some individuals as far as the end of their first joints, and in others to the middle of the second. In con-trast to the thumb, the great toe is expanded at the end; and, in opposition to the other toes, forms a grasping organ of great power. None of the other toes are as thick as the great toe; the middle toe being slightly longer than either of the adjacent ones, while the little toe is considerably shorter. The sole of the foot is somewhat convex, but its upper surface is very flat, and there is no sort of re-semblance to the human instep in the whole foot. The upper surface of the foot, as far as the commencement of the toes, is thickly covered with hair, but on the latter the hairs become thinly scattered; while the sole is bare, and covered with a thick horny skin. Owing to the habit of its sometimes walking with the toes bent under the sole of the foot, the gorilla has callosities on the upper surface of the toes.

Colour. With regard to the colour of the hair, of which, as we have already said, the general hue is blackish, there is considerable individual variation, and likewise a change attendant upon age; very old gorillas becoming more or less completely grizzled. As a rule, we may notice a reddish-brown tint on the hair at the top of the head, although it may be dark brown, or even black; the hairs generally being differently coloured in different portions of their length. On the sides of the face the hair is greyish at the roots and dark at the tips; while on the neck and shoulders it tends to become lighter at the tips. A dark grey colour seems to characterise the tips of the hairs over the greater portion of the body and the upper parts of the limbs; but below the tips these hairs have a dark brown ring, beneath which they again become lighter. On the lower parts of the limbs and hands the hairs are darker at their tips, where they vary from brown to black; but in some individuals these portions of the limbs may be covered, like the trunk, with a mixture of grey and brown hairs.

External Covering. The hair consists of an outer coat of long stiff bristles, and of a shorter inner coat of fine short curly hairs, approximating to a woolly nature. The moderately long hair on the crown of the head is very stiff, and can be erected when the animal is enraged. Although the front and sides of the chin have but a short covering of hair, its under portion has a distinct beard or ruff. By far the longest hair on the upper part of the body is that growing on the shoulders, and hanging down thence on to the back and upper part of the arms. The length of this hair is, however, somewhat exceeded by that growing on the thighs. On the chest and the rest of the under parts the hair is much shorter; that on the chest generally taking an upward and outward direction. The woolly under-hair is not very thick, and has no tendency to mat together. The long hair of the shoulders, back, and thighs communicates a generally shaggy appearance to the gorilla, although this is much less marked than in the orang.

Female. The female gorilla, as we have already mentioned, is much smaller than the male, and does not generally exceed some four and a half feet in height. The whole build is, moreover, relatively weaker, the tusks are but slightly developed, and the skull is proportionately smaller and more rounded, without the huge bony arches over the eyes. It appears, moreover, that in the adult female the bridge of the nose is relatively shorter than in the male, while the cheeks are wider, and the upper lip longer than is usually the case in the latter. The general appearance of the female gorilla is, therefore, considerably less ferocious and repulsive than that of her lord and master.

Having now made our readers acquainted with the chief characters of the gorilla, we proceed firstly to notice the districts and nature of the country it inhabits, and then to say something as to its mode of life.

Geographical Distribution. The geographical range of the gorilla is very much more restricted than is that of the chimpanzee, being limited to that district of Western Equatorial Africa, lying between 2° north latitude and 5° south latitude, and apparently not extending further into the interior than 16° east longitude. This hot and miasmatous region includes the mouths of the rivers Ogavai, Gabun, and Muni, and also the range of mountains running for about a hundred miles in a northerly direction between the former and the Cameruns, known as the Sierra do Cristal. According to the medical missionary, Mr. H. A. Ford, already alluded to, gorillas are most common in the Sierra do Cristal, and have also been found a day's journey from the mouth of the Muni. During the years 1851 and 1852 numbers of gorillas, probably driven from the interior by want of food, were seen on the coast of the Gabun district, several of which were killed; the specimens sent by Captain Harris to London, and by Mr. Ford to Philadelphia being probably some of these. Subsequently to 1852 they appear never to have been seen on the coast. According to the report of the German Loango Expedition, already alluded to, gorillas are very rare in the Loango district near the coast, but are met with in or near the mountainous region further inland. Writing in 1859, Sir Richard Owen gave the following account of gorilla-land in the district between the Gabun and Muni (or Danger) river, which he appears to have derived from the narratives of correspondents residing in these regions. He observes, "The part where the gorilla has been most frequently met with presents a succession of hill and dale, the heights crowned with lofty trees, the valleys covered by coarse grass, with partial scrub or scattered shrubs. Fruit trees of various kinds abound both on the hills and in the valleys; some that are crude and uncared for by the negroes are sought out and eagerly eaten by the gorillas; and as different kinds come to maturity at different seasons, they afford the great denizens of the woods a successive and unfailing supply of these indigenous fruits." The professor then goes on to mention the various trees which have been identified among those which afford food to the gorillas. Among these the most important appears to be the oil-palm (*Elais*), of which the part eaten is the undeveloped spathe, known as the palm-cabbage; next we have the so-called grey plum-tree (*Parinarium excelsum*), bearing a grey, somewhat insipid fruit of the size of a large plum. Another is the papaw tree (*Larica*); two kinds of wild plantains (*Musa*); several sorts of *Amomum*, one of which produces the Malaquetta pepper—a tree bearing a walnut-like fruit, of which the gorilla is said to crack the shell with a stone, and which may be allied to the kind which produces the kola-nut. Lastly, we have a tree which, at the time when Sir R. Owen wrote, had not been identified, but which bears a fruit somewhat resembling a cherry. According to later accounts, gorillas will also visit the plantations of the natives, and do much damage to them.

Mode of Life. In regard to the actual mode of life of the gorilla there is a great dearth of authentic information. The old stories that these animals would seize with their foot natives passing beneath the trees on which they dwelt and drag them up, and likewise those to the effect that they gathered round the deserted camp-fires of the natives, as well as the legends that they drove off the elephant with clubs, were disposed of once for all by Du Chaillu. Unfortunately, however, we are equally unable to accept his own stories as to the male gorilla coming on to the attack in an upright position, and beating its chest with its fists, since, as we have already mentioned, Mr. Winwood Reade denies that Du Chaillu ever saw a living, wild gorilla. This is supported by the circumstance that all the skins of gorillas purchased by the British Museum from Du Chaillu show that their owners were killed by a wound in the back from the weighted spears which the natives are accustomed to suspend in the paths of these animals. The members of the German Loango Expedition frankly confess that they never saw a living, wild gorilla, although they brought home a young one which had been captured by some native hunters; neither did Winwood Reade himself ever come across these creatures in their native wilds. A later German traveller, Herr von Koppenfels, appears, however, to have been more fortunate, and states that he once observed a male and female with their two young quietly feeding.

From this account, and also from the natives, we know that gorillas habitually live in small families (as in our illustration), having young ones of various ages with them; and that they frequent the most gloomy recesses of the forest, where the light of day is reduced to a twilight so dim, that on cloudy days it might be supposed that the sun was eclipsed. The climate of these forests is hot and damp, suggestive of a Turkish bath or hothouse; and, as in most primeval forests, signs of animal life are extremely rare, although the stillness may be broken now and then by the voice of a bird. According to the account given by Herr von Koppenfels (although this does not appear to be supported by others) gorillas are in the habit of making a kind of nest in the trees by bending the boughs together and covering them with twigs and moss at a height of several yards above the ground. In this nest the female and young pass the night, while the male takes his station at the bottom of the tree, where he remains in a sitting posture during the night, ready to protect his family against the attacks of prowling leopards. This writer likewise assures us that gorillas do not frequent the same sleeping-place for more than three or four nights consecutively; and this is but natural when we reflect that these creatures must needs wander considerable distances in search of fresh supplies of suitable food.

Contrary to the custom of most wild animals, other than monkeys, gorillas appear to roam the forest in search of food solely during the daytime, and are totally stationary during the night. As a rule, they appear to walk on all fours; and while, in walking, the fingers of the hand are usually doubled on to the palm, the whole sole of the foot is applied to the ground. They can, however, walk with the fingers extended, and likewise with the toes bent down on the sole of the foot.

Although in appearance male gorillas are somewhat unwieldy creatures, yet, like all their kindred, they are most active and indefatigable climbers, and are said to ascend to the very tops of the forest trees, where they will pass from tree to tree almost as readily as the far lighter spider-monkeys of Brazil. They also appear capable of taking leaps from great heights to the ground without damage to themselves, since Herr von Koppenfels tells us he even saw an adult spring from a tree at a height of some thirty or forty feet, and on alighting rapidly disappear into the scrub.

Although when driven to close quarters the gorilla is doubtless one of the most terrible of foes, yet it appears certain that very exaggerated accounts have been given of the natural ferocity. Herr von Koppenfels, as quoted by Dr. Hartmann, informs us that so "long as the gorilla is unmolested he does not attack men; and, indeed, rather avoids the encounter." And when these creatures catch sight of men, they generally rush off precipitately in the opposite direction through the underwood, giving vent at the same time to peculiar guttural cries.

It appears that many gorillas are killed by the natives with the aid of a weighted spear suspended by a cunningly-devised system of cords in the creature's path. Others are, however, undoubtedly shot by the negroes, although it would seem that, at least in many instances, such animals have been accidentally met by the hunters as they travelled through the forest rather than deliberately sought out and tracked. As we have already seen, both the members of the German Loango Expedition and Mr. Winwood Reade express their belief that up to the dates of their respective explorations of the West Coast no European had ever shot a gorilla. According, however, to letters from Herr von Koppenfels, referred to by Dr. Hartmann, that traveller states that up to the early part of 1874 he had himself shot four gorillas.

In Captivity. With regard to gorillas in captivity, the accounts to hand are necessarily somewhat meagre; but, apart altogether from the climatal difficulties of keeping these creatures alive for any length of time in Europe, all authorities seem to be agreed that they are utterly untameable. Du Chaillu states that he had two young gorillas, the first of which was exceedingly ferocious and unmanageable, and both of which came to an untimely end. Herr Lenz, who published in 1878, at Berlin, under the title of *Sketches from West Africa,* the results of his African experiences, received from the natives of the Gabun a young male gorilla, of which he wrote an account in a letter addressed to and published by Dr. Hartmann. Nothing definite is, however, stated in this account as to the disposition of the animal, attention being mainly directed to the question how to accustom it to a diet such as could be obtained on board ship or in Europe. In spite of this training process, this gorilla died on the voyage to Germany.

We have already mentioned that the members of the German Loango Expedition received in 1875 a young male gorilla captured by native hunters. From the account of this animal, given in the report of the expedition by Herr Falkenstein, it appears that when first received at the station of Chinxoxo in Loango, the hardships which it had undergone in its transit down country had reduced the creature to a deplorable condition. By the aid, however, of a plentiful supply of wild and other fruits, and the milk of a goat, the young animal was gradually restored to something approaching its normal state of health; and preparations were then made for its transport to Berlin. Having been thus gradually accustomed to eat fruits and other food which could be procured on board ship, as well as to be in the company of Europeans, this young gorilla was finally shipped for Berlin. During the voyage it appears that it was never chained up, and it was soon allowed to wander freely about the ship, with but very slight supervision. This animal appears to have been of a gentle disposition, and although self-willed was never malicious. In taking its food it was remarkably well-behaved, helping itself from a plate with its thumb and two fingers; and even carrying small vessels of water to its mouth, and replacing them undamaged when empty. When larger vessels of liquid were put before it, it would lower its mouth to them and drink by suction. Its regard for personal cleanliness was also noteworthy; and when foreign substances adhered to it, it either brushed them off or held out its arms in a manner clearly indicating that it wished them removed.

When not able to obtain any article it desired, or when otherwise thwarted in its wishes, this young creature had recourse to various clever devices by which its object might be attained. For instance, it is related that "when he felt a desire for the sugar or fruit, which was kept in a cupboard in the eating-room, he would suddenly leave off playing, and go in an opposite direction to the room, only altering his course when he believed that he was no longer observed. He then went straight to the room and cupboard, opened it, and made a quick and dexterous snatch at the sugar-box or fruit-basket, sometimes closing the cupboard door behind him before beginning to enjoy his plunder, or, if discovered, he would escape with it; and his whole behaviour made it clear that he was conscious of transgressing into forbidden paths. He took a special, and what might be called a childish, pleasure in making a noise by beating on hollow articles, and seldom missed an opportunity of drumming on casks, dishes, or tin trays, whenever he passed by them." Strange noises, more especially thunder, alarmed him much.

This gorilla arrived safely at Berlin, where it was for a considerable period an inmate of the Aquarium. There it throve at first, and was docile, though inclined to be mischievous. Eventually, however, it succumbed to the malady which sooner or later carries off all the large Man-like Apes in our climate, dying of a rapid consumption in the autumn of 1877, after having lived for fifteen months in Berlin.

By the intervention of Messrs. Pechuel-Loesche and Falkenstein, a second living gorilla was obtained from the Loango district, and safely transported to Berlin, where it arrived in the early part of 1883. The journey during the winter appears, however, to have left its mark on the constitution of this animal, and after living for fourteen months in the Aquarium it died of the same disease as its predecessor in the spring of 1884. Dr. Hartmann states that there was a third live gorilla at Berlin in the autumn of 1881, which died soon after its arrival. There was also a young gorilla a few years ago in the London Zoological Gardens, which only lived a few months.

These appear to have been the only living gorillas which have been exhibited as such in Europe. Curiously enough, however, as far back as the year 1860, a travelling showman in England actually had a veritable living gorilla in his exhibition, which he considered to be a chimpanzee, no one suspecting till long after the creature's death the treasure he had possessed.

The Orang-Utan.

Genus *Simia.*

Partly from the reddish hue of its hair, and partly from the conformation of its face and skull, as well as from the much greater proportionate length of its arms, the great man-like ape of Borneo and Sumatra is a very different looking creature to either the chimpanzee or the gorilla. Owing, however, to the circumstance that our figures of these animals generally take the form of woodcuts, the marked contrast between the coloration of the orang (*Simia satyrus*), and that of its African cousins is unfortunately not presented to our view.

The name Orang-Utan (generally shortened in works on zoology to Orang) is a Malay word, signifying Man-of-the-Woods; and the ape so designated was known to Linnæus, at least as far back as the year 1766. It was not, however, till a considerably later date that it became fully known in Europe. It is true, indeed, that in 1780 Baron Wurmb, then the governor of the Dutch settlement of Batavia, transmitted to Holland the entire skeleton of an orang; but he did not recognise it as such, calling the animal to which it belonged the Pongo—a name which, as we have seen, belongs to the gorilla. In 1804 an orang was, however, living in the

ORANGS IN THEIR NATIVE WOODS.

menagerie that belonged to the Prince of Orange; and this example was in that year described and depicted by a naturalist named Vosmaer. Subsequently to this the identity of Wurmb's pongo with the orang was fully demonstrated; and from that period our knowledge of the structure and habits of this ape has gradually increased. Among those who have especially contributed to advance our knowledge of the orang in its living condition we may mention "Raja" Sir James Brooke, of Borneo, and Mr. A. R. Wallace, the latter of whom has given us such graphic accounts of the creature's habits, in his fascinating work, the *Malay Archipelago.*

In the uncongenial climate of Europe, orangs are as difficult to keep for any lengthened period in confinement as are the large Man-like Apes of Western Africa. The case is, however, very different in the moist subtropical climate of Calcutta, where adult orangs have thriven well in cages exposed to the open air, and have taught us many facts in relation to their habits.

Characteristics. The leading or, as zoologists say, generic characters distinguishing the orang from the chimpanzee and gorilla are to be found in the proportionately greater length of the arms—which in the upright position reach to the ankles—in the form of the skull—which is elevated almost into a point at the summit—as well as in a difference in the number of the joints in the backbone and of bones in the wrist. Thus there are sixteen (instead of seventeen) vertebræ in the backbone between the neck and the sacrum; twelve of these carrying ribs, as in man. In regard to the number of bones in the wrist, we find that the orang possesses the central bone which is wanting in man, the chimpanzee, and the gorilla; and thus has nine, in place of eight, bones in the wrist. In this respect the Bornean ape agrees with the lower members of its order; but in the absence of callosities on the buttocks it shows its kinship with the gorilla and chimpanzee.

All these characteristic features clearly indicate that the orang is decidedly lower in the scale than the two Man-like Apes of which we have already treated; but before going further we must examine more closely into its structure and appearance.

Structure. An adult male orang stands about 4 feet 4 inches in height when in an upright position, in which posture it can almost touch the ground with its fingers. The legs are extremely short and thick, and are twisted in such a remarkable manner that the knees are turned outwards, and the feet consequently set very obliquely to the line of the leg. From the peculiar structure of its legs and feet the orang walks entirely on the outer sides of its feet, of which the soles are turned inwards, so as to almost face one another. Although this arrangement is ill-adapted for walking rapidly on the ground, it is one admirably suited for climbing, in which these animals excel.

As shown in our illustration of the adult, the orang has a tall, elevated forehead, very different from the retreating one of the chimpanzee; and the whole aspect of the face is curiously flattened, with an oval contour. Not unfrequently there is a well-marked prominence in the middle of the forehead. Although there are slight ridges over the eyes, these are much less developed than in the chimpanzee, and have, therefore, no sort of resemblance to the enormous ones of the gorilla. The extraordinary height of the crown of the head is well exhibited in our figure of the head and shoulders of an immature individual, the whole of this part of the head being curiously shortened and compressed from back to front. In the immature animal, of which the head is figured, the jaws are not very prominent, but they become much more projecting in old males. The bridge of the nose is generally much depressed and flattened, but the whole nose is generally larger than in the chimpanzee and gorilla, and not so much expanded at its termination, the wings of the nose being arched and narrow, and the small oval nostrils separated from one another by a narrow partition. The mobile lips are usually comparatively smooth

HEAD OF ORANG.

and thin, the upper one being characterised by its great length and breadth. In the adult of the orang, as shown in our illustration, the neck is surrounded by a kind of collar formed of folds of skin containing an internal cavity communicating with the larynx or upper expansion of the windpipe. In some very old males these pouches attain enormous dimensions, and by no means add to the personal beauty of their owner. The ear is small and well formed, being much more human-like than that of the gorilla. Frequently the sides of the cheeks of the males have a warty protuberance, or callosity.

The body is by no means so powerfully built as that of the gorilla; and the sloping and stooping shoulders and extremely prominent abdomen make the whole shape of the animal ungainly in the extreme.

We have already alluded to the great length of the extremely powerful arms, which vastly augment the animal's climbing powers. The hand (shown in Fig. 9 of the illustration on p. 15) is even longer and more slender than that of the chimpanzee, and is characterised by the extreme shortness of the thumb, which scarcely reaches as far as the root of the first joint of the index finger. The fingers themselves are connected by a web, which extends for a third, or nearly half, the length of their first joints. With regard to the relative lengths of the fingers, there is some amount of individual variation; but the middle finger may exceed either of the others, while the ring finger is longer than the index, and the little finger relatively long. All the fingers are narrow and tapering, with well-formed arching nails.

The calves of the legs are less developed than in either the chimpanzee or gorilla, and the narrow flat heels are less projecting. The long and slender feet (shown in Fig. 10 of the illustration on p. 15) are likewise of a lower type of structure, as is particularly shown in the very small size of the great toe, which is peculiar among the Primates in frequently having no trace of a nail in the adult. Curiously enough old animals often lose the last joint of the great toe, apparently not through disease, but as a normal condition. Both the hands and feet on the backs, and the hands on their under surfaces, have wart-like callosities.

The general colour of the orang's skin is bluish-grey, although it may have a more or less decided tinge of brown. In marked contrast to the general slaty hue of the face, there often occur yellowish-brown rings round the eyes, nostrils, and upper lip. The full reddish-brown hair is long, shaggy, and bristly, with a small admixture of woolly under-hairs. The hair of the head may either have a natural parting in the middle, as in our figure of the head and shoulders, or may be tossed in wild confusion, in some individuals standing almost upright. Usually there is a well-developed beard on the cheeks and neck. On the whole of the under surface of the body the covering of hair is thin and scanty, and it is even less developed on the face, ears, and the backs of the hands and feet.

The tusks of the male are of enormous size. In the female they are, however, much smaller; and this sex is also characterised by the lesser development of the folds and pouches of skin around the neck.

Geographical Distribution. As we have said, orangs appear to be confined to the great islands of Borneo and Sumatra; and there has been considerable discussion as to whether there is more than one species. It was once thought that the large orang of Sumatra was specifically distinct from that of Borneo, and it accordingly received a separate scientific name. Later investigations indicate, however, that this is not the case, and that *S. satyrus* is common to both islands, although individuals vary considerably in their colour; and Dr. John Anderson is of opinion that a dark and a pale race may be distinguished, the latter being devoid of the warty callosities on the sides of the face of the males. The Dyaks of Borneo, by whom the orang is generally designated the Mias, appear to be fully acquainted with these two races, calling the one provided with cheek excrescences the *Mias pappan*, and the one without these appendages the *M. rambi*.

In addition to these two varieties of the true large orang, the Dyaks recognise a third kind, which they distinguish as the *M. kassir*. These animals are much smaller than the true orang, and never have the excrescences on the cheeks. A young individual of this orang was described many years ago by Sir Richard Owen as *Simia morio.* An orang which lived a short time in the London Zoological Society's Gardens was at first considered to be an adult of this form, and to prove its right to be regarded as a distinct species. The orang in question was presented to the Zoological Society, in whose Gardens it was received during the spring of 1891, by Commander E. Rason, R.N., who wrote to Mr. P. L. Sclater, stating that he obtained the animal at Kuching, near Sarawak, in Borneo, from some natives, who brought it to him slung on a pole. "At first it was extremely savage, and tried to bite, but soon became comparatively tame, and after a week would allow itself to be carried about and made a pet of. After three months' time, 'George,'" as Commander Rason calls his pet, "does not seem to have grown in height at all, and, judging by the look of his teeth, must be about ten years old; but, having had plenty to eat and but little exercise, has grown much fatter." On the death of this animal, it was found, however, that its age was much less than had been supposed, all the milk-teeth being still in place. Although the shape of its head was decidedly larger than in the ordinary orang, this specimen does not appear to indicate decisively that the lesser orang is a distinct species.

Mode of Life. Orangs are stated to be much more numerous in Borneo than in Sumatra; and, since dense, low-lying forests are essential to their existence, they are not found in the neighbourhood of Sarawak, where the ground is hilly. The unbroken, large areas of primeval forests, occurring in many parts of Borneo, are the true home of the orangs; such forests, according to Mr. Wallace, being like open ground to these apes, since they can travel in every direction from tree to tree, as easily as the North American Indian traverses his native prairie. In all their movements these apes are slow and deliberate; this being especially noticeable with the perfectly healthy adults which have been exhibited in the Zoological Gardens at Calcutta, where they enjoyed a climate not unlike their own. This deliberation in their movements is noticeable in Mr. Wallace's description of the manner in which orangs travel through the forest when undisturbed and at ease. We are told that they proceed with great circumspection along the larger branches of the trees in the half-upright position rendered necessary by the great length of their arms and the shortness of their legs. Almost invariably they select such trees as have their branches interlaced with the adjacent ones; and, when such boughs are within reach, they catch hold of them with their arms as if to try their strength, after which they deliberately venture upon them. Although the orang never leaps or jumps, and never seems to be in a hurry, yet he will make his way overhead in the forest as fast as a man can run on the ground below. In this progression the long powerful arms are of the greatest service; and it is by their aid that the orang plucks the choicest fruit from boughs too light to support his weight, and likewise gathers the leaves and young shoots to form his nest.

The orangs, like gorillas, go in small family parties, consisting of the parents accompanied frequently by from two to four young ones. Although they will devour leaves, buds, and young shoots,—more especially those of the bamboo,—the chief food of the orang consists of fruits of various kinds, the prime favourite being the luscious but ill-smelling durian or jack-fruit. Of this fruit they waste a vast quantity, throwing the rejected rinds on the ground below.

Mr. Wallace describes the nest, or sleeping-place, of the orang as being generally constructed in a comparatively small tree, at a height of from some 20 to 50 feet from the ground; a situation at this elevation being protected from wind by the taller surrounding trees. The Dyaks believe that the orang constructs a fresh nest every night; but, as Mr. Wallace remarks, if this were the case, the deserted nests would be much more common than they really are. These animals remain in their nests till the sun has risen sufficiently high to have dried the dew from the forest leaves. Their feeding-time is during the middle of the day; but it appears that they seldom return for more than two consecutive days to the same tree for this purpose. Mr. Wallace observes that the orang must have a task of considerable difficulty in getting at the interior of the durian, since this fruit is protected by a thick and tough skin, covered with strong conical prickles. Probably, however, the animal first bites off a few of these prickles or spines, and then makes a small hole into which it inserts its fingers, and thus manages to pull the fruit in pieces.

In Captivity. Many accounts have been given of the habits of orangs in captivity. Of these the earliest is the one by Vosmaer relating to the young female, which, as we have already mentioned, was living in the menagerie of the Prince of Orange in 1776. A later account of an orang brought to Java was given about the year 1830 by Dr. Clark Abel. On board ship this animal was allowed to roam freely about, and soon became on good terms with the sailors, whom it surpassed in the agility with which it ascended the rigging. It was, indeed, often pursued by the sailors from one part of the rigging to the other, when, finding itself unable to escape from them by direct speed, it would swing itself out of their reach by grasping a loose end of rope, and thus bring the chase to an end. On other occasions this animal would wait among the rigging, or at the mast-head, till the sailors were almost within touching distance, when it would suddenly lower itself to the deck by the nearest rope, or pass from one mast to another by means of the mainstay. Any attempts to dislodge the animal when aloft, by violently shaking or swaying the ropes by which it was suspended, were found to be quite ineffectual, although it often appeared to the spectator that the muscles of the orang would be unable to withstand the strain to which they were exposed. In its playful moods this orang is described as swinging itself suddenly within arm's length of one of its pursuers, and after having struck him a harmless blow with its outstretched hand, as suddenly swinging off in the opposite direction.

Dr. Abel states that while in Java this orang was lodged in a large tamarind tree growing near the house of his master. Here he was accustomed to form a kind of nest or bed for himself by plaiting the smaller boughs together, and strewing the platform thus made with leaves. In the daytime the animal was in the habit of lying in this couch with his head projecting over the edge, and thus watched with interest all the passers-by. When any of these happened to be carrying fruit, the ape would descend from his lair and endeavour to obtain a portion. At sunset, or even sooner, it would retire to its nest for the night; while at the first rays of dawn it would be again afoot, and endeavouring to obtain its usual food. When on board ship the mast-head formed its usual sleeping-place, where the creature would comfortably ensconce itself in the folds of a sail for the night. "In making his bed," writes Dr. Abel, "he used the greatest pains to remove everything out of his way that might render the surface on which he intended to lie uneven; and, having satisfied himself with this part of his arrangement, spread out the sail, and lying down upon it on his back, drew it over his body. Sometimes I preoccupied his bed, and teased him by refusing to give it up. On these occasions he would endeavour to pull the sail from under me or to force me from it, and would not rest until I had resigned it. If it was large enough for both he would quietly lie down by my side. If all the sails happened to be set, he would hunt about for some other covering, and either steal one of the sailor's jackets or shirts that happened to be drying, or empty a hammock of its blankets. His food in Java was chiefly fruit, especially mangosteens, of which he was extremely fond. He also sucked eggs with voracity, and often employed himself in seeking them. On board ship his diet was of no definite kind; he ate readily of all kinds of meat, and especially raw meat; and was very fond of bread, but always preferred fruits when he could obtain them. His beverage in Java was water; on ship-board it was as diversified as his food. He preferred coffee and tea, but would readily take wine, and exemplified his attachment to spirits by stealing the captain's brandy-bottle; since his arrival in London, he has preferred beer and milk to anything else, but drinks wine and other liquors. In his attempts to get food, he afforded us many opportunities of judging of his sagacity and disposition." The continuation of Dr. Abel's account is too long to be quoted at length, but he gives several other interesting particulars of the habits of the animal during the voyage from Java to England. Although habitually gentle, this orang could be excited into paroxysms of violent rage, which he expressed by opening his mouth, showing his teeth, and seizing and biting such persons as were in his vicinity. This animal survived its arrival in England for about fifteen months, when it fell a victim to the disease so fatal to its kindred in our climate.

The ferocious nature of the orang, when angered or driven to bay, is confirmed both by Sir James Brooke and Mr. Wallace. An instance of this is related by the latter writer in the following words :—" A few miles down the river there is a Dyak house, and the inhabitants saw a large orang feeding on the young shoots of a palm by the river-side. On being alarmed he retreated towards the jungle, which was close by, and a number of the men, armed with spears and choppers, ran out to intercept him. The man who was in front tried to run his spear through the animal's body, but the mias seized it in his hands, and in an instant got hold of the man's arm, which he seized in his mouth, making his teeth meet in the flesh above the elbow, which he tore and lacerated in a dreadful manner. Had not the others been close behind, the man would have been more seriously injured, if not killed, as he was quite powerless; but they soon destroyed the creature with their spears and choppers. The man remained ill for some time, and never fully recovered the use of his arm."

The same writer relates the history of a young orang which he received in Borneo when it was only a foot high. When first carried home this tiny creature took such a firm grasp of its new owner's beard, that it was with difficulty it could be made to loose its hold. At the time of its capture there were no signs of teeth

YOUNG ORANGS (1-5), AND GIBBONS (6-8).

in its mouth, but in the course of a few days two of the lower incisor teeth were cut. There was at the time unfortunately no means of attaining a supply of milk for the little ape; but Mr. Wallace overcame this difficulty by feeding it with rice-water sucked from a bottle with a quill through the cork. The animal soon managed to suck comfortably enough from this contrivance; and when sugar and cocoanut milk were added to the mixture it thrived well enough on the diet. If its owner introduced his finger into the creature's mouth, it first of all sucked away vigorously, but soon found out its mistake, and pushed the finger away with angry screams like those of a disappointed child. When caressed this ape was contented and happy, but when laid down soon began to scream; and for the first two nights of its captivity was very noisy and restless. It was kept in a kind of cradle, made of a box, with a soft mat at the bottom. The little orang seemed to appreciate a frequent bath; and, indeed, when it required one announced the fact by loud screams. The process of drying and rubbing after each bath seems to have been a source of great enjoyment; and this was likewise the case when its hair was combed and brushed. At first it clutched vigorously by all four limbs at any object in its neighbourhood, so that its owner had continually to be on his guard to save his beard. When it could find nothing better to do, it would nurse its own foot. Little by little the strength of the tiny creature's grip decreased, probably owing to the want of sufficient exercise. In order to remedy this, Mr. Wallace made a short ladder, from which the ape was suspended by its hands and feet for a quarter of an hour at a time. This exercise seemed at first to afford it pleasure, but afterwards it loosed its hold, first with one limb, and then with another, till it finally fell to the ground. These tumbles did not appear, however, to do it any material harm.

Mr. Wallace endeavoured to construct a kind of artificial mother out of buffalo hide, which the baby orang might fondle. For a time this appeared to afford satisfaction, but eventually was discarded, as the animal was nearly choked with the hair it had torn off the skin and swallowed. After a week's captivity, the young ape was fed from a spoon, containing a mixture of soaked biscuit, egg, and sugar, or, at other times, sweet potatoes. This food was swallowed readily, and with apparent satisfaction; the creature making droll grimaces to express either pleasure or the reverse. When it had swallowed anything which appeared grateful, it drew in its cheeks, and screwed up its eyes; while, when the food was distasteful from want of sufficient sugar or other cause, the creature, after turning it about in its mouth for a short time, finally ejected it. If this rejected food were again offered to it, the animal displayed marked displeasure by loudly screaming and throwing its arms about.

After three weeks a young macaque monkey was introduced to the orang, and the two, although very different in demeanour, soon became fast friends. Mr. Wallace particularly noticed the helplessness of the young orang when compared with the macaque; and it appears that this character distinguishes the young of all the Man-like Apes from those of the lower monkeys. Even after the young orang had been about a month in captivity, it was very unsteady when placed on its hands and feet, and would frequently overbalance itself and topple over. When it required attention, it would cry loudly for a time, but if this met with no reply, the young creature would remain quiet till a step was heard approaching, when its calls would be at once renewed. Although at the end of four weeks the two upper incisor teeth had been cut, the little creature, doubtless owing to improper food, had not increased perceptibly in weight; and soon after it sickened and died of a kind of intermittent fever, to the great regret of its owner.

The illustration on p. 55 shows some of the postures assumed by a young orang formerly living in the Aquarium at Berlin.

Fossil Apes. Under the head of the Chimpanzee we have already mentioned that a fossil species of ape apparently referable to the same genus has been found in the later Tertiary strata of Northern India. The same strata have also yielded the broken tusk, or canine tooth, of another large ape, which there is every reason to believe was a species of orang. If this be so, we shall be justified in considering that India was the original home of the ancestors of all the large Man-like Apes of the present day; and that from this centre their descendants have gradually dispersed to the eastward and south-westward. We thus have an easy explanation of the present peculiar geographical distribution of the various groups of large Man-like Apes now existing.

In addition to these fossil Indian apes we have, moreover, sure evidence that at an earlier part of the Tertiary Period, known as the Miocene Age, at least one species of large Man-like Ape inhabited Western Europe. This extinct creature has been named the *Dryopithecus*, and its remains have been found in France. It appears to have been about the same size as the chimpanzee; but differs from all the living Man-like Apes in the great length of the bony union between the two branches of the lower jaw. In this respect this ape, as we might have expected would be the case, approaches decidedly towards the lower monkeys.

The Gibbons.

Genus *Hylobates*.

With the gibbons we come to the last of the Man-like Apes, distinguished from those which we have hitherto considered, not only by their smaller size, lighter build, and longer arms, but also by the presence of small naked callosities on the buttocks, resembling those of the lower monkeys. They are, moreover, the only apes accustomed to walk in an upright position, in which, as shown in the illustration on p. 55, they are at times assisted by their long arms, although they can walk perfctly well with their hands clasped behind the neck.

Characteristics. The gibbons, or long-armed apes, comprise several species found in the warmer regions of South-Eastern Asia, and more especially in and around the Malay Peninsula. The largest of all the species only slightly exceeds 3 feet in height, while the others are not more than about 30 inches. Their arms are so long that they reach to the ankle, so that these animals can actually walk upright and at the same time touch the ground with their fingers. The head is well-shaped, without the upward prolongation of the crown that is so characteristic of the orang; and the lower jaw is remarkable for the great development of the chin, which is more human-like than that of any other ape. Moreover, from the absence of prominent ridges and crests, and the nearly

upright forehead, the whole skull strikes one as approaching the human type far
more nearly than do those of the other apes. This must not, however, be considered as an indication that the gibbons are of a higher type than the other
Man-like Apes, since the contrary is clearly demonstrated by their long arms and

THE WHITE-HANDED GIBBON.

the callosities on the buttocks. The resemblance of their skulls to the human
type is, indeed, merely a superficial one, due to the circumstance that small animals
must necessarily have proportionately larger brains than the larger members of
the same group; and also to the absence of the strong ridges which are necessary
for the powerful skulls of the larger forms, but would be quite useless in their
smaller cousins. The superficial human-like characters of the skulls of the gibbons
are, however, to a great extent destroyed by their long slender tusks, or canine

teeth, which project far beyond the level of the other teeth. The long and narrow hands and feet of these animals (shown in Figs. 11–13 of the illustration on p. 15) are characterised by the great extent to which the thumb and great toe are respectively separated from the other fingers and toes, as well as by the flatness of all the nails. In colour, the gibbons vary from black to yellowish-white; this variation occurring even in different individuals of the same species. The comparatively well-formed nose, as seen in our figure of the white-handed gibbon, imparts to their physiognomy an expression far less repulsive and forbidding than that which characterises the larger Man-like Apes.

Disposition. In disposition the gibbons are gentle and confiding; and when captured young they can be readily tamed. Their constitution is, however, even more delicate than that of the other Man-like Apes; and consumption soon terminates their existence in Europe, even when the greatest care and attention are bestowed upon them. In the Zoological Gardens at Calcutta, gibbons thrive excellently; and one, kept there some twelve years ago, was accustomed to make his presence known to people living more than a mile away by the loudness of his morning and evening cries.

Habits. All the gibbons are thoroughly arboreal in their habits; and in the rapidity of their movements among the trees they offer a marked contrast to the more deliberate and somewhat sluggish motions of the orang. So rapid and lightning-like are these movements that one species—the hoolock —has been observed, when in captivity at Calcutta, to catch birds on the wing that had flown into its cage; and there can be but little doubt that such habits are natural to these animals in their wild condition, when it is probable that birds thus captured constitute an appreciable portion of their food.

Although several of the species are found in the forests of the plains, the hoolock appears to be almost if not exclusively restricted to those of hilly districts. In marked contrast to the larger Man-like Apes, most of the gibbons go in large flocks or droves, which may comprise from fifty to a hundred, or even more individuals; although, as with most gregarious animals, solitary males are occasionally observed. The long arms are the chief agents in their active movements among the trees; and by their aid the distances they can swing from bough to bough, and thus from tree to tree, are of surprising length. When going down-hill they travel at an extremely rapid pace, by swinging themselves in a downward direction from one bough till they catch another on a lower level, and so from that to the next one.

Although walking rapidly when on the ground, gibbons, as Mr. W. T. Blanford tells us, can easily be overtaken by men. The same writer observes that, "when walking on the ground, the hoolock rests on its hind-feet alone, with the sole flat on the ground, and the great toe widely separated from the other digits. The arms are usually held upwards, sometimes horizontally, their great length (as shown in our illustration on p. 58) giving the animal a very peculiar aspect."

We have already mentioned the fondness of the hoolock .for small birds, and, in addition to this kind of diet, gibbons subsist mainly on various fruits and leaves, as well as young and tender shoots; they also feed on insects and spiders, and the eggs and callow nestlings of birds.

The habit which makes the gibbons known to (as well as cordially hated by) all who dwell in the districts which they frequent, is their custom of uttering at morn and even cries of a peculiarly loud and somewhat unearthly nature. These cries consist in the repetition of two syllables in quick succession; and the name hoolock is given to the Indian representative of the group in imitation of its cry.

The late Mr. Blyth observes that, "in all the genera of gibbon the thumbs of both the hands and feet are separated from the other digits to the base of the metacarpal and metatarsal bones," and then states that this character is also found elsewhere among the Primates only in two genera of lemurs (*Indris* and *Propithecus*). The same writer goes on to say that at the time of his writing it was "not generally understood that the long-armed apes are true bipeds when on the ground, applying the sole flatly, with the great toe widely separated from the other digits; the hands are held up to be out of the way, rather than for balancing, even when ascending a flight of steps, as I have seen repeatedly, but they are ever ready to seize hold of any object by which the animal can assist itself along, even as a human being commonly grasps a banister when ascending a staircase."

The Siamang (*Hylobates syndactylus*).

The siamang is the largest of all the gibbons, and since it also differs in certain structural peculiarities, it may be taken first. This fine species is apparently confined to Sumatra, and its habits were described many years ago by the French naturalist Duvaucel. The animal, when full-grown, stands a little over three feet in height when in the upright position. It is of a uniform glossy black colour, with the exception of a grey or whitish beard; the hair on the body and limbs being comparatively long. The hair on the fore-arm is directed upwards towards the elbow, as in the larger Man-like Apes, whereas the other members of the genus have it pointing towards the wrist. There are, moreover, two other features in which this species differs from the other gibbons. The first of these peculiarities, and the one from which the animal derives its scientific designation, is the circumstance that the second and third toes of the foot are joined together by a thin web of skin, reaching in the male as far as the last joint, but in the female only to the middle one. The second distinctive peculiarity of the siamang is the possession of a pouch formed by folds of skin round the neck and throat, resembling that which has already been mentioned as occurring in the orang. Moreover, the chin is better developed than in all the other gibbons.

Mode of Life. Duvaucel's is one of the earliest authentic accounts of the siamang that we possess. Writing from the neighbourhood of Benculen in Sumatra, he states that "this species is very common in our forests, and I have had frequent opportunities of observing it, as well in its wild state as in bondage. The siamangs generally assemble in numerous troops, conducted, it is said, by a chief, whom the Malays believe to be invulnerable, probably because he is more agile, powerful, and difficult to reach than the rest. Thus united, they salute the rising and setting sun with the most terrific cries, which may be heard at several miles' distance; and which, when near, deafen, when they do not frighten. This is the morning-call to the mountain Malays, but to the inhabitants of the towns it is a most insupportable annoyance. By way of compensation, they preserve a most profound silence during the daytime, unless when disturbed in their repose or sleep. These animals are slow and heavy in their gait; they want confidence when they climb, and agility when they leap, so that they may be easily caught, when they can be surprised. But nature, in depriving them of the means of readily escaping danger, has endowed them with a vigilance which rarely fails them; if they hear a noise which is strange to them, even though they be at a mile's distance, fright seizes them, and they immediately take flight. When surprised on the ground, however, they may be captured without resistance, being either overwhelmed with fear, or conscious of their weakness and the impossibility of escaping. At first, indeed, they endeavour to avoid their pursuers by flight, and it is then that their awkwardness in this exercise is most apparent. Their body, too tall and heavy for their short, slender thighs, inclines forwards, and availing themselves of their long arms, as crutches, they thus advance by jerks, which resemble the hobbling of a lame man whom fear compels to make an extraordinary effort."

Their want of agility when surprised on the ground is, however, amply made up for when in the trees, where they take long flying leaps. According to a German writer, Herr Rosenberg, siamangs inhabit forests in Sumatra at an elevation of some three thousand feet above the sea-level, rarely leaving the trees to descend to the ground. At any sudden fright they rush violently down the mountain sides, by leaping from bough to bough and from tree to tree in the manner already mentioned. According, however, to Mr. Wallace, in his *Malay Archipelago*, the siamang is decidedly slower in its movements than the other gibbons, not taking such tremendously long leaps, and keeping at a lower elevation in the trees. The extraordinary relative length of its arms is well indicated in the description of the same writer, who observes that in an individual about three feet in height, they measure five feet six inches from hand to hand, when stretched out at right angles to the body. A young siamang brought to Mr. Wallace, was at first somewhat savage, but soon became more amenable to discipline, feeding readily on rice and fruits. This individual, which Mr. Wallace had intended to transport to England, did not, however, long survive in captivity. And it appears that the Malays, who are stated to be adepts in keeping and taming wild animals, find it exceedingly difficult to keep siamangs for any length of time. Siamangs have been exhibited alive in the Zoological Gardens at Calcutta. In disposition they are regarded by the Malays as stupid and dull. Mr. Wallace considers that this species is found in the Malay Peninsula, but this is doubted by Mr. Blanford; and it appears, according to Mr. Wallace, to be but little known, even in Singapore, where the captive specimen, already mentioned, attracted a considerable amount of attention.

A white siamang is recorded by Sir Stamford Raffles as having been obtained by him in Sumatra.

The White-Handed Gibbon (*Hylobates lar*).

We may take as our first example of the more typical species of the group, all of which are very closely allied, the white-handed gibbon, represented in the figure on p. 58. This species, like all the other typical gibbons, is considerably smaller than the siamang, standing about thirty inches in height; and it is also of a lighter and more slender build. Although subject to great individual variation in colour, it may be always recognised by the pale colour of the hands and feet, of which the upper surfaces are usually either white or yellowish-white. Another distinctive characteristic is to be found in the usual presence round the black skin of the naked face of a complete ring of more or less nearly white hairs; which, as is well shown in our illustration, imparts a most peculiar physiognomy to the animal. Occasionally, however, this white ring is almost absent; different individuals showing a gradation in this respect from those in which it is but very slightly developed, to those in which it attains its full proportions. The general colour of the body and limbs of this gibbon varies from a full black, through various fulvous shades, to a yellowish-white. In opposition to what usually obtains in Mammals some individuals of this species have the back lighter than the under parts of the body; and it may occasionally be much variegated.

The white-handed gibbon is found throughout the Malay Peninsula, as far north as the province of Tenasserim, and may possibly reach into Lower Pegu. It inhabits the forests skirting the mountains, at elevations varying from about three thousand to three thousand five hundred feet above the sea-level.

Mode of Life. Colonel Tickell has given an excellent account of this gibbon, both in its wild state and in confinement. It appears from this description that the white-handed gibbon is somewhat more heavily built and less agile than the hoolock (to be noticed next); while it walks on the ground less steadily. It is also said to differ from the hoolock in its manner of drinking—scooping up water in its hands, and thus carrying it to its mouth, instead of applying its mouth directly to the surface of the water. The same observer also notices a great difference in the voice of the two species. The white-handed gibbons are also stated to go in smaller parties than the other species; the number in a drove, according to Colonel Tickell, being usually from six to twenty. They depend almost entirely on their hands in passing from bough to bough, and use their feet to carry food. He has seen a drove of these apes escape in this manner with the plunder stolen from a garden made by the Karen tribes near the forests which they frequent. Like other species of the group, the white-handed gibbon almost invariably has but a single young one at a time. The young are born at the commencement of the winter season; and cling to the body of the mother for nearly seven months, after which they shift for themselves.

THE HOOLOCK (*Hylobates hoolock*).

One of the best known of all the gibbons is the hoolock, or white-browed gibbon, which, as we have said, takes it name from its characteristic dissyllabic cry. This is the only species which occurs in India, where it is confined to the north-eastern districts, being found in the hill ranges south of the Assam valley, as well as in the provinces of Sylhet, Cachar, and Manipur. Thence it ranges to the east and southwards into the hill-forests of the Irawadi valley near Bhamo, in Upper Burma, and in the neighbourhood of Chittagong and Arakan. It may also occur near Martaban, in Upper Tenasserim; and the extent of its range on the

HOOLOCKS IN A BAMBOO JUNGLE.

east side of the Irawadi river is not yet definitely determined.

The hoolock may be readily distinguished from the white-handed gibbon by the presence of a white or grey band across the eyebrows, and also by the whole of the rest of the head, as well as the upper surfaces of the hands and feet, being of the same colour as the body. This general colour varies from black to a light yellowish-grey; the females being generally paler than the males. As we have seen, their build is rather lighter, while their habits are more active than those of the last-named species.

Mode of Life. All who have written of the hoolock agree as to its docile and engaging disposition, and the readiness with which, even when adult, it can be thoroughly tamed in a short space of time. Writing of a pet hoolock, formerly in his possession, Mr. R. A. Sterndale, in his *Mammalia of India* says, "Nothing contented him so much as being allowed to sit by my side with his arm linked through mine, and he would resist any attempt I made to go away. He was extremely clean in his habits, which cannot be said of all the monkey tribe. Soon after he came to me I gave him a piece of blanket to sleep on in his box, but the next morning I found he had rolled it up and made a sort of pillow for his head, so a second piece was given him. He was destined for the Queen's Gardens at Delhi, but, unfortunately, on his way up he got a chill, and contracted a disease akin to consumption. During his illness he was most carefully attended by my brother, who had a little bed made for him, and the doctor came daily to see the little patient, who gratefully acknowledged their attentions; but, to their disappointment, he died. The only objection to these monkeys as pets is the power they have of howling, or rather whooping, a piercing and somewhat hysterical ' whoop-poo! whoop-poo! whoop-poo!' for several minutes, till fairly exhausted."

Under the heading of gibbons in general we have already alluded to the wide distance over which the cries of a hoolock kept in the Zoological Gardens at Calcutta could be heard. Mr. Blanford, writing of the cries of these animals, observes that " at a distance the sound much resembles a human voice; it is a peculiar wailing note, audible from afar, and in the countries inhabited by these animals is one of the most familiar forest sounds. The calls commence at daybreak, and are continued until 9 or 10 A.M., several of the flock joining in the cry, like hounds giving tongue. After 9 or 10 o'clock in the morning the animals feed or rest, and remain silent throughout the middle of the day, but recommence calling towards evening, though to a less extent than in the earlier part of the day."

Like the white-handed gibbon, hoolocks have been exhibited, although less numerously, in the Gardens of the Zoological Society in Regent's Park.

The Hainan gibbon (*H. hainanus*), from the island of Hainan, China, is allied to the hoolock, but differs from that and all other species, except the siamang, by the absence of a white band on the forehead, and is thus black throughout.

THE AGILE GIBBON (*Hylobates agilis*).

According to Dr. John Anderson, the agile gibbon is subject to such an amount of individual variation that several so-called species, such as the Malay gibbon (*H. rafflesi*), of Sumatra, and the crowned gibbon (*H. pileatus*), of Siam, have been founded upon what appear to be nothing more than local races of one and the same species.

Inclusive of all these local varieties, the agile gibbon has a rather wide geographical distribution, ranging from Cochin-China to Siam; it is also found in Sumatra and Borneo, as well as in the small islands of the Sulu Archipelago lying between Borneo and the Philippines.

The activity of the agile gibbon is sufficiently attested by its name. It was this species which was first observed to have the power of catching birds while on the wing. According to Duvaucel, these animals are capable of taking clear leaps of forty feet when passing from bough to bough. They are stated to live generally in pairs rather than in droves; and are known to the natives of Sumatra as Ungka, or Ungka-puti.

In the typical form of the agile gibbon from Sumatra, the general colour is usually dark brown; the face being bluish-black or brown, and surrounded by whitish hair, through which the ears are only partially visible, and the hands and feet of the same general colour as the body. It may be distinguished by the prominent arches on the skull above the eyes, the comparatively flat nose, and the large nostrils. The colour of the back in the darker varieties is lighter than that of the under parts. The variety named after Sir Stamford Raffles, *H. rafflesi,* is of a nearly black colour, tending to brown on the sides and back. The Siamese variety, known as the crowned or tufted gibbon (*H. pileatus*), is likewise of a blackish colour, but differs in that the hands, feet, and a ring round the crown of the head are white. The white patch on the crown helps to distinguish this variety from the typical agile gibbon; although it must be confessed that all these Malay gibbons are singularly alike, and often difficult to distinguish even by the practised zoologist. This so-called variegated gibbon (*H. variegatus*) appears to be but another of the numerous varieties of *H. agilis.*

The Wou-Wou, or Silver Gibbon (*Hylobates leuciscus*).

The grey or silver gibbon, or wou-wou,—a name often incorrectly applied to the agile gibbon,—comes from the island of Java, and most zoologists agree in regarding it as a distinct species. It is characterised by its general ashy or bluish-grey colour; the presence of a large square black patch on the top of the head; and also by the white or grey fringe of hair surrounding the blackish face. The fur also appears to be longer, thicker, and of a more woolly nature than is the case in the other species; and the colour is stated to be usually lighter on the under parts than on the back. Specimens of both this and the preceding species have been exhibited in the London Zoological Society's Gardens.

Fossil Gibbons.

In the explorations which have been conducted in the caves of Borneo remains of gibbons, probably belonging to species still existing in the same regions, have been met with in a sub-fossil condition. This is only what we should naturally have expected to be the case. Very different, however, is the occurrence of fossil gibbons in fresh-water strata belonging to the middle portion of the Tertiary period in France and Switzerland; for it is quite certain that these animals could not have existed in a climate at all approaching that now characterising Europe. We shall, therefore, be safe in assuming that, at the period in question, portions of Southern Europe were clothed with dense forests, growing in a hot and moist climate closely resembling that of the Malay Archipelago of the present day. The evidence for the former prevalence of this tropical European climate does not, however, rest solely on the fossil gibbons, since many of the other animals found in the same strata are very similar to those now characteristic of the warmer regions of the East; while the presence of palms, resembling those of tropical regions, as well as other plants, supplements the evidence of the animals in a manner which must be convincing to all who pay any attention to the subject. After the middle or miocene division of the Tertiary period we have no evidence of the existence of gibbons in any part of Europe, although many kinds of monkeys were abundant until much later.

THE YELLOW BABOON.

CHAPTER III.

APES, MONKEYS, AND LEMURS,—continued.

THE OLD WORLD MONKEYS AND BABOONS.

Family CERCOPITHECIDÆ.

ALTHOUGH there is some degree of uncertainty as to the precise significance to be attached to the names Apes, Monkeys, and Baboons, we shall take leave to restrict the former term to the Man-like Apes described in the preceding chapter, and use the two latter for those other Old World Primates which do not belong to the group of Lemurs. The name Monkeys is, however, also applicable to one family of the Primates of the New World. Using, then, the terms Monkeys and Baboons in this sense, we may mention, in the first place, that zoologists include the whole of those inhabiting the Old World in a single family, for which they adopt the name *Cercopithecidæ*, taken from a genus of African monkeys. Our next point is to consider how all these numerous species are to be distinguished as a whole from the Man-like Apes on the one hand and from the American monkeys on the other.

66

Teeth. As regards the number of their teeth, all the Old World monkeys and baboons agree with the Man-like Apes; the total number of teeth being thirty-two, among which there are two premolars and three molars on both sides of each jaw. This character, as we shall subsequently see, will at once serve to distinguish any Old World monkey from an American monkey or marmoset. The Old World monkeys and baboons may, however, be distinguished from the Man-like Apes by the form of their cheek-teeth. We have, indeed, stated at the beginning of the preceding chapter that the premolar and molar teeth of the latter group closely resemble those of man; the crowns of the molars being relatively broad and surmounted by four low main tubercles situated at the four corners of each tooth, but arranged somewhat obliquely to its long axis. We may add that the last molar in the lower jaw is of the same general form as the two teeth immediately in front of it.

If, however, we take up the skull of any species of Old World monkey or baboon and carefully examine its molar teeth, we shall find that they will by no means accord with the foregoing description. We shall, indeed, recognise in these teeth the four tubercles at the corners; but instead of these tubercles being low, and set obliquely to one another, without any connection between those forming the front and hind pairs, we shall find that they are comparatively high, and are placed in pairs opposite one another, while each pair is connected together by a low imperfect transverse ridge. This two-ridged character of the molars, which is more distinct in the lower than in the upper teeth, is therefore a readily available method of distinguishing between an Old World monkey or baboon and a Man-like Ape. Moreover, with the single exception of one African genus of monkeys, and one Oriental species of another, the last lower tooth of all the monkeys and baboons of the Old World may be distinguished from that of the Man-like Apes by having a kind of projection or heel behind the second transverse ridge.

Nostrils. There are, however, other characters distinctive of the present group which must now be mentioned. In the first place, if we observe the nose of an Old World monkey we shall not fail to notice that the vertical partition dividing one nostril from the other is comparatively thin: this character affording a well-marked distinction from the monkeys and marmosets of the New World. **Tail.** We have already seen that no Man-like Ape has a tail; but there is great variation in this respect among the members of the present group, some of them having exceedingly long tails, others short tails, and a few no tails at all. In no instance, however, are the tails of this group endued with the power of prehension, as they are in the American monkeys. Here we may remark, in passing, that it has been very often considered that the term Monkey should be restricted to such species as have long tails, while those with short tails should be called Baboons, and those with no tails at all Apes. This application of terms will not, however, hold good when put in practice; since, if it were adopted, we should have to call certain of the different species of one single genus of monkeys by all the three names.

In all the monkeys and apes of the Old World, those peculiar patches of hard naked skin on the buttocks, known as callosities, which we have already mentioned as occurring in the gibbons, are invariably present. These callosities, which are not unfrequently bright-coloured, afford another character by which we can at once distinguish an Old World monkey from any and all of its American cousins. Their use is to afford a comfortable rest for the body in the upright sitting posture assumed by the monkeys and baboons of the Old World.

Cheek Pouches. Another feature absolutely peculiar to the monkeys and baboons of the Old World, although by no means common to the whole of them, is the presence of those pouches in the cheeks, with which all who have fed tame monkeys must be perfectly familiar. These cheek-pouches are formed by folds in the skin, and when empty lie flat on either side of the face. They can, however, be so distended as to contain a large quantity of food, and then stick out prominently on either side, so as to communicate a peculiarly bloated appearance to the face. The possession of these pouches must obviously be a great advantage to the monkeys in which they are found, since by their means a large quantity of food can be hurriedly gathered, stowed away, and afterwards eaten at leisure in some place of security. It might, indeed, be urged that the monkeys which do not possess these convenient receptacles appear to get on in life quite as well as their relations who are thus provided; and that, therefore, these pouches are of no real advantage. To this it may be replied that such Old World monkeys as have no cheek-pouches feed much more on leaves and shoots than on fruits; and that they are furnished with a peculiarly complex stomach in which this food can be rapidly stowed away previously to undergoing complete digestion.

Limbs. With regard to the limbs of the Old World monkeys and baboons, it may be observed that the arms never present that great excess in length over the legs which we have seen to be the case among the Man-like Apes; and the legs may, sometimes, be the longer of the two. The thumb of the Old World monkeys and baboons can in all cases be fully opposed to the fingers, except, of course, in the African species in which it is either absent or rudimentary, and therein have another marked point of difference from the American group.

Breast-bone. Finally, the skeletons of all members of the present group may be readily distinguished from those of the Man-like Apes by the breast-bone being narrow and flattened from side to side, instead of broad and flattened from back to front. Moreover, all of the species have a central bone in the wrist,—a characteristic they have in common with the gibbons and orangs among the Man-like-Apes.

Distribution. Such, then, are the leading features by which the monkeys and baboons of the Old World (forming a larger group than any other in the order) are distinguished from the groups immediately above and below them in the zoological scale; and the reader who has followed us carefully thus far ought to be able to tell at once whether any particular monkey that is set before him should or should not be included in the present group. When we speak of the members of this group occupying a position immediately below that of the Man-like Apes, we must guard ourselves from conveying the idea that the one can in any sense be regarded as the ancestor of the other. The difference in the structure of the molar teeth of the two groups is alone sufficient to prove that this cannot be the case; those of the Man-like Apes being of a more primitive type than are those of the monkeys and baboons.   The common ancestor of the two groups must indeed probably be sought in some long extinct type more nearly akin to the lemurs.

Although the majority of the Old World monkeys and baboons are inhabitants of the warmer regions of the eastern hemisphere, yet the group is by no means so strictly confined to tropical and sub-tropical regions as we have seen to be the case with the Man-like Apes.   Indeed, some of the Asiatic species are capable of withstanding a very considerable degree of cold, and may be found among the snows of the Himalaya and Tibet.

THE LANGURS.

Genus *Semnopithecus.*

With this group of long-tailed Asiatic monkeys, we come to the first of three nearly allied genera, all of which are characterised by their extremely slender and "lanky" build, by the excessive length of their tails, by the legs being longer than their arms, and by the absence of cheek-pouches.   All the above characteristics can be verified in the living animal, but there is one other for the examination of which we must turn to the dissecting-room of the anatomist.   This internal character relates to the stomach, which, instead of having the simple bladder-like form which it assumes in all other members of the order, is divided into a number of pouches or sacs.   When the peculiar pouched stomach was first described scarcely anything was known as to the habits and food of the monkeys in which it is found.   Sir Richard Owen, however, sagaciously suggested that from the analogy presented by this peculiar type of stomach to that which characterises the Ruminating Hoofed Mammals, as well as some other vegetable-feeding animals, it would be found that the food of these monkeys consisted in great part of leaves.   This suggestion has been fully confirmed by subsequent observations; and although the habits of the langurs are still but imperfectly known, yet it is stated by Mr. W. T. Blanford that they are more purely herbivorous than those monkeys which are provided with cheek-pouches, and that a very considerable portion of their food consists of leaves and the tender shoots and young twigs of trees.   The presence of this remarkable kind of stomach is, indeed, as we have already mentioned, a kind of compensation for the absence of cheek-pouches; it being more suited to the needs of these animals than the pouches would be.

The langurs are so-called from the name applied by the natives of Northern India to those species of the group which inhabit the outer ranges of the Himalaya. Langurs, which are known in Germany as *Schlankaffen,* or slender monkeys, are found over a large portion of South-Eastern Asia, being especially abundant in India and Burma, and represented by one species in the highlands of Tibet.

Structure.   As their German name implies, the bodies and limbs of these monkeys are exceedingly slender; while the tail is so long that very generally, and invariably in all the species from India, Ceylon, and Burma, it is actually longer than the whole length of the head and body together.   This is well shown in our figure of the true langur or hanumán monkey.   In all the species the thumb is well developed; this being a character of great importance, as the chief one by which these monkeys are distinguished from some closely allied African monkeys. The row of long stiff black hairs seen in our figure, projecting from above the eyebrows of the langurs, is another feature by which these monkeys may be easily recognised. Further, the skulls of all the langurs may be readily distinguished from those of all other monkeys, with the exception of the allied African group mentioned above, by the circumstance that the aperture for the

THE HANUMÁN MONKEY, OR TRUE LANGUR.

nostrils, which is exceedingly narrow, extends upwards between the sockets for the eyes, instead of stopping at about the level of their lower border.

Almost the earliest account that we have of the langurs relates to those of Ceylon, and was given in the year 1681 by one Robert Knox, an English seaman, who for nearly twenty years had been a prisoner in that island. Knox says that some of the Singalese monkeys "are as large as our English spaniel dogs, of a darkish-grey colour, and black faces, with great white beards round from ear to ear, which make them show just like old men. They do but little mischief, keeping in the woods, eating only leaves and buds of trees; but when they are catched they will eat anything. This sort they call in their language wanderows (wanderus)." This account has been thought to apply to the lion-tailed monkey (a macaque), which was formerly incorrectly called the Wanderu. That monkey is, however, black; and there is not the slightest doubt but that Knox described the langurs, which are the wanderus of the Singalese.

The Hanumán, or True Langur (*Semnopithecus entellus*).

Perhaps the best known of all the langurs, and the one which gives the scientific name to the genus, is the hanumán monkey, or true langur, of which we give a figure. This fine monkey is found throughout the northern part of Peninsular India, from South-Western Bengal and Orissa to Gujerat and Bombay, and is also found in Kattywar, and probably Katch, although unknown in Sind and the Punjab. Southwards it ranges into the Bombay Deccan; while its extreme northern limit extends to the outer ranges of the Himalaya, although there is still some doubt as to where the range of this species ends and that of the next begins.

The hanumán is one of four species of Indian langurs, characterised by having the hair covering the crown of the head radiating in all directions from a central point situated on the forehead. It is distinguished from its allies by the absence of any crest of hair on the head, of which the colour is scarcely, if at all, paler than that of the back; and by the full black colour of the upper surfaces of the hands and feet. The hair of the cheeks does not cover the relatively large ears. The general colour is greyish-brown, paler in some individuals than in others; but the face, ears, feet, and hands, are coal-black. In size a large male hanumán will measure some 30 inches in head and body; but average specimens will be about 25 inches, while their tail will measure as much as 38. As Mr. Sterndale has well observed, "the *tout ensemble* of the langur is so peculiar that no one who has once been told of a long, loose-limbed, slender monkey, with a prodigious tail, black face, and overhanging brows of long, stiff, black hair, projecting like a penthouse, would fail to recognise the animal."

Mode of Life. Langurs are exceedingly common throughout a large part of India, and in most districts are held sacred by the Hindus, by whom they are allowed to plunder the grain-shops at will. Mr. Sterndale considers, however, that the best times of the hanumán are over, and that it is not now allowed the free run of the bazaars so readily as it once was, while in some districts the aid of Europeans has even been invoked to rid the natives from the devastations of these monkeys, which take their name from the god Hanumán, to whom they are sacred.

As Mr. W. T. Blanford observes, the protection accorded to the hanumán by the Hindus of Northern India has caused these animals to be so tame, and so utterly disregardless of the presence of man, that there are but few mammals whose habits can be so well observed. The same writer states that "the hanumán is usually found in smaller or larger communities, composed of individuals of both sexes and of all ages, the youngest clinging to their mothers, and being carried by them, especially when alarmed. An old male is occasionally found solitary, as with so many other mammals. The story that males and females live in separate troops, though apparently believed by Blyth and quoted by Jerdon, I agree with Hutton in regarding as fictitious, though, as the latter observer justly remarks, females with very young offspring may keep together, and temporarily apart from the remainder of the troop to which they belong."

In regard to the cry of these langurs, Mr. Blanford observes that "their voice is loud, and is often heard, especially in the morning and evening. The two commonest sounds emitted by them are a loud, joyous, rather musical call, a kind of whoop, generally uttered when they are bounding from tree to tree, and a harsh guttural note, denoting alarm or anger. The latter is the cry familiar to the tiger-hunter, amongst whose best friends is the hanumán. Safely ensconced in a lofty tree, or jumping from one tree to another, as the tiger moves, the monkey by gesture and cry points out the position of his deadly enemy in the bushes or grass beneath, and swears at him heartily. It is marvellous to observe how these monkeys, even in the wildest forests where human beings are rarely seen, appear to recognise men as friends, or at least as allies against the tiger. It is a common but erroneous notion of sportsmen that this guttural cry is a sure indication of a tiger or leopard having been seen, whereas the monkeys quite as often utter it merely as an expression of surprise; I have heard it caused by the sight of deer running away, and I believe that it is frequently due to the monkeys catching sight of men."

The food of the hanumán consists largely of leaves and young shoots, and also grain of all kinds, especially in the towns. In disposition the hanumán is gentle, and appears never to attack human beings. Its constitution is delicate when in captivity,—probably from the want of suitable food,—but the species is generally well represented in the London Zoological Society's Gardens.

Their Battles. That troops of langurs sometimes engage in fierce contests is proved by an interesting account given by Mr. T. H. Hughes, from which the following extract is taken. Mr. Hughes says that "in April 1882, when encamped at the village of Singpur in the Sohagpur district of the Rewa State, my attention was attracted to a restless gathering of hanumáns in the grove adjoining the one in which my tent was pitched; and, wishing to form some idea as to its cause, I strolled to where the excitement was greatest, and found two opposing troops engaged in demonstrations of an unfriendly character. Two males of one troop, fair-sized brutes, and one of another, a splendid-looking fellow of stalwart proportions, were walking round and displaying their teeth. The solitary gladiator headed a much smaller following than that captained by the other two, and, strange to say, instead of the whole number of monkeys joining in a general *mêlée*, the fortune of the question that had to be decided appeared to have been intrusted to the representative champions. It was some time, at least a quarter of an hour, before actual hostilities took place, when, having got within striking distance, the two monkeys made a rush at their adversary. I saw their arms and teeth going viciously, and then the throat of one of the aggressors was ripped right open, and he lay dying. He had done some damage, however, before going under, having wounded his opponent in the shoulder; and matters then seemed pretty evenly balanced between the remaining strugglers. I confess that my sympathies were with the one champion who had gallantly withstood the charge of his enemies; and I fancy the tide of victory would have been in his favour had the odds against him not been reinforced by the advance of two females. I felt that the fight was not a fair one, but was deterred from interfering by a wish to see what the end of the affray would be, and the end, so far as the solitary hanumán was concerned, soon came. Each female flung herself upon him, and though he fought his enemies gallantly, one of the females succeeded in seizing him. Possibly he would have been killed outright had I not been present, but when I saw him so helpless, I interfered on the chance of being able to save him. He was, however, hopelessly mutilated, and before the morning he was dead. Not one of his own troop came to his aid. I presume they were either awed by the array of numbers on the other side, or they had full confidence in their leader. Had they assisted, they might in the end have been better off, for the result of the defeat of their champion was that the whole of the aggressors entered upon a guerilla warfare, and, isolating several of the members of the weaker troop, kept them prisoners under surveillance. Whenever the latter tried to break away, their guards stopped them, and then effectually watched them by occupying every piece of vantage-ground. One female with a young one was most viciously chased, and when, in her efforts to escape her enemies, she climbed to one of the highest limbs of a big tree, those in pursuit actually shook the branch on which she was, and jerked her to the ground. The fall was a nasty one, and she was so badly hurt that in the course of the night she went to swell the list of the fatally wounded. The defeated troops were thoroughly cowed, for one of the number actually allowed me to approach it quite closely without moving. I certainly do not ascribe the onslaught I saw to sexual excitement. It was plainly an incursion of a stronger troop into the domain of a weaker one ; and, under mistaken counsel, the weaker hesitated too long in yielding their feeding ground."

The Himalayan Langur (*Semnopithecus schistaceus*).

Very closely related to the hanumán is the Himalayan langur (*S. schistaceus*), so closely indeed that Dr. John Anderson considers it ought only to be reckoned as a variety of that species. In the opinion of Mr. Blanford—our most recent authority on Indian Mammals—it is, however, considered to be entitled to rank as a well-marked species ; and this observer gives the following characters by which it may be distinguished from the hanumán. The Himalayan species is characterised " by being somewhat larger,—although there is probably no great difference between large individuals of both species,—by the head being much paler in colour than the back, and by the feet being but little, if at all, darker than the limbs ; by the smaller ears, and by their being concealed by the long hair of the cheeks ; by the form of the skull."

This species is found throughout the greater part of the Himalaya proper, ranging from Bhutan in the south-east to the Kashmir valley and adjacent regions in the north-west. It appears not to be found below five thousand feet, and in the interior of Sikhim it ranges as high as twelve thousand feet. One of the first, if not actually the first record of the occurrence of the Himalayan langur in the interior of Sikhim will be found in Sir J. W. Hooker's *Himalayan Journals*. The author of that charming book of travel says, on arriving at a Tatar village, at an elevation of about nine thousand feet, " I saw a troop of large monkeys gamboling in a wood of *Abies brunoniana;* this surprised me, as I was not prepared to find so tropical an animal associated with a vegetation typical of a boreal climate." Other writers have observed these langurs in the outer ranges of the Himalaya in the neighbourhood of the hill stations of Simla or Mussuri, leaping from bough to bough of the snow-clad pines and deodars. And the present writer was himself once sufficiently fortunate to behold a similar sight when crossing a pass called the Rutten Pir, in the mountains to the south of the valley of Kashmir. On a sudden, when passing through a forest composed partly of pines and deodar cedars and partly of rhododendrons, a whole troop of these langurs dashed across the path, springing from tree to tree, and scattering in all directions the thick wreaths of snow with which the dark fir boughs were concealed; the season of the year being the middle of the spring.

In the autumn these langurs are to be found in large droves in the extensive forests of the higher valleys surrounding Kashmir. Here they are a decided nuisance to the hunter, as their cries will not unfrequently alarm the deer or bear which he may be pursuing. Desirous of securing a skull, the writer was once tempted to shoot a large male out of one of these droves; but the cries and expression of the poor wounded brute were so human-like that he never again could persuade himself to shoot a monkey of any kind.

The Madras Langur (*Semnopithecus priamus*).

In Madras and Ceylon the hanumán is represented by an allied species known as the Madras langur (*S. priamus*), distinguished by possessing a distinct crest of hair on the crown of the head, and by the upper surfaces of the feet and hands not being black. The following account of the habits of this species is taken from Sir J. Emerson Tennent's *Natural History of Ceylon,* where all the langurs are known as wanderus. The Madras langur "inhabits the northern and eastern districts and the wooded hills which occur in these portions of the island. In appearance it differs both in size and colour from the common wanderu (*S. cephalopterus*), being larger and more often greyish; and in habits it is much less reserved. At Jaffna, and in other parts of the island where the population is numerous, these monkeys become so familiarised with the presence of man as to exhibit the utmost daring and indifference. A flock of them will take possession of a palmyra palm; and so effectually can they crouch and conceal themselves among the leaves that, on the slightest alarm, the whole party becomes invisible in an instant. The presence of a dog excites, however, such an irrepressible curiosity that, in order to watch his movements, they never fail to betray themselves. They may frequently be seen congregated on the roof of a native hut; and, some years ago, the child of a European clergyman stationed near Jaffna, having been left on the ground by the nurse, was so teased and bitten by them as to cause its death."

The Malabar langur (*S. hypoleucus*), which is common not only in the forests, but likewise on the cultivated lands fringing the Malabar coast, is the last member of the group in which the hair of the crown of the head radiates from a single point on the forehead.

The Banded Leaf-Monkey (*Semnopithecus femoralis*).

A rare langur from Sumatra, Borneo, and the Malay Peninsula, extending as far north as Tenasserim, is the banded leaf - monkey, of whose habits little, unfortunately, is known. It differs from all those already mentioned in that the hair of the crown of the head radiates from two distinct points on the forehead. The hair on the hinder part of the head stands up so as to form a crest; while that over the temples bends forwards to overhang the eyes. In colour this monkey is much darker than any of the above species; it varies from blackish-brown to black over the greater part of the body, but is white over a larger portion of the under surface of the body and inner sides of the thighs; the white area always including the abdomen. The young are of a whitish hue throughout.

A closely allied, if not identical, kind of langur from the same regions has received the name of *S. chrysomelas,* and differs merely by some details of coloration.

It is a curious circumstance that the skulls of both these species or varieties of langurs can be distinguished from those of all others by the form of the last molar, or "wisdom-tooth," in the lower jaw. In all the other langurs this tooth has five tubercles, in the banded leaf-monkey it has but four, as in the under-mentioned group of guenons.

The Negro Monkey (*Semnopithecus maurus*).

Far better known than the last species is the negro monkey, or Budeng, as it is called by the inhabitants of Java, of which we give an illustration. This langur, which was originally obtained from Java, but, according to Dr. J. Anderson, is also found in Sumatra and the Malay Peninsula, takes its English name from the full black colour prevailing over all the body in the adult, except a portion of the under surface, and the root of the tail, where it is replaced by grey. It agrees with the last in the forward projection of the hairs on the front of the crown of the head, as is well shown in the figure. The length of the head and body of this monkey is about 24 inches; the tail being longer than the head and body, and frequently furnished with a small tuft at the extremity. The young are light-coloured, being of a yellowish or reddish tint; the dark colour of the adult appearing first on the hands, and then gradually spreading over the limbs and body. This light colour of the young shows that the dark tint of the adults is an acquired or specialised character.

Nearly allied to this species is another and much rarer monkey, found in Java, where it is called by the natives the lutong. It is known scientifically as *S. pyrrhus;* and it differs from the negro monkey in being of a ferruginous red colour at all ages, and is therefore evidently a less specialised form. So like, indeed, are the two that Dr. J. Anderson considered the lutong to be merely a light-coloured variety of the budeng. More recently, however, Dr. Jentiuk, of Leyden, has shown that the skulls of the two present considerable structural differences, and he has accordingly no doubt that the two forms indicate perfectly distinct species.

Although in Java these two monkeys have perfectly distinct names, the Malays call both by the name lutong, distinguishing the negro monkey as the *Lutong itam,* and the red species as the *Lutong mora;* the words *itam* and *mora* signifying respectively black and red.

NEGRO MONKEY.

The opinion that these two monkeys are distinct species is confirmed by a marked difference in their disposition, which was long ago pointed out by the late Dr. Horsfield, from whose work on the *Zoology of Java* we take the following account, with some slight verbal alterations. After observing that the black budeng is much more abundant than the red lutong, Dr. Horsfield observes that "the latter, both on account of its rarity and comparative beauty, is a favourite with the natives. Whenever an individual is obtained, care is taken to domesticate it, and it is treated with kindness and attention. The budeng, on the contrary, is neglected and despised. It requires much patience in any degree to improve the natural sullenness of its temper. In confinement, it remains during many months grave and morose; and, as it contributes nothing to the amusement of the natives, it is rarely found in their villages or about their dwellings.

The budeng is found in great abundance in the forests of Java; it forms its dwelling on trees, and associates in numerous societies. Troops, consisting of fifty individuals and upwards, are often found together. In meeting them in the forests, it is prudent to observe them at a distance. They emit loud screams on the approach of a man, and by the violent bustle and commotion excited by their movements, branches of decayed trees are not unfrequently detached, and thrown down on the spectators. They are often chased by the natives for the purpose of obtaining their fur. In these pursuits, which are generally ordered and attended by the chiefs, the animals are attacked with cudgels and stones, and cruelly destroyed in great numbers. The skins are prepared by a simple process, which the natives have acquired from the Europeans; and they conduct it at present with great skill. It affords a fur of a jet-black colour, covered with long silky hairs, which is usually employed, both by the natives and by the Europeans, in preparing riding equipages and military decorations."

THE CRESTED LUTONG (*Semnopithecus cristatus*).

The crested lutong of Sumatra and Borneo is closely allied to the negro monkey, from which it appears to be chiefly distinguished externally by the blackish fur being usually grizzled, or washed with greyish-white. A male obtained by Sir Stamford Raffles in Sumatra, and presented by him to the Indian Museum (now disestablished), is described by Dr. Anderson as of a brownish-black colour, with a fuliginous tinge on the flanks, fore-arms, and crest; the short crest on the vertex of the head being directed backwards, and the long black hair on the temples coming forwards. The same writer describes a female as black, with the tips of the hairs on the head and body of a lustrous grey tint; the hair of the limbs being yellowish-grey, except on the hands and feet, where they are black. On the under parts the hair is paler, with yellowish-grey tips; while the tail is black, tipped with grey above but yellowing underneath, more especially near the root. The face has a bluish-black hue.

The young of this monkey is yellow in colour; and Sir Stamford Raffles records the existence of a race in which the colour of the adult is either light grey or whitish.

THE NILGIRI LANGUR (*Semnopithecus johni*).

With the Nilgiri langur we come to the first of a large group of langurs, in which the hair of the crown, instead of radiating from one or more points on the forehead, is uniformly directed backwards without any trace of parting.

This species, which derives its Latin name from a former member of the Danish factory at Tranquebar in Madras, belongs to a subgroup characterised by the absence of a crest of hair on the crown of the head; the hair of the crown itself being not longer than that on the temples and the nape of the neck. The Nilgiri langur is a comparatively small species; the length of the head and body varying from about 21 to 23 inches, and that of the tail from 32 to 35; though larger individuals are occasionally met with. The hair of the body is long, fine, and glossy; and the general colour black to blackish-brown, with the exception of the head and rump, of which the former is brownish-yellow, and the latter ashy-grey. The young of this monkey are black throughout, and this appears to be the case in the next species. The character serves, therefore, to distinguish these langurs very markedly from those of the preceding group, in which, as we have seen, the young are light-coloured; and it may be taken as an indication that the present group is the most specialised of all the langurs, not only having acquired the black tint in the adult, but even in the earlier stages of their existence.

As its name implies, it is found in the Nilgiri Mountains (or Hills as they are commonly called by Anglo-Indians) of Southern India; and its range extends from the Wynaad southwards to Cape Comorin.

According to Mr. W. T. Blanford, this langur "is shy and wary, the result of human persecution. It inhabits the *sholas,* or dense but abruptly limited woods of the Nilgiris, and other high ranges of Southern India, and is also found in the forests on the slopes of the hills, usually in small troops of from five to ten individuals. It is very noisy, having a loud guttural alarm-cry, used also to express anger, and a long loud call. Jerdon relates that when the *sholas* of the Nilgiri range were beaten for game, these monkeys made their way rapidly and with loud cries to the lowest portion, and thence to a neighbouring wood at a lower level. In consequence of the beauty of their skins, and the circumstance that certain castes eat their flesh, these monkeys are more frequently shot than most of the Indian species, hence their shyness."

The Purple-faced Monkey (*Semnopithecus cephalopterus*).

The purple-faced monkey is the representative of this group in the island of Ceylon. It is known to be liable to considerable variations of colour, and at least, in a popular work like the present, we may follow Dr. Anderson in regarding the Singalese langurs known as the white monkey (*S. senex*), and the bear monkey (*S. ursinus*) as nothing more than well-marked varieties of this species.

There is a ready means of distinguishing the purple-faced monkey from the Nilgiri langur. In the latter the cheeks are of the same brown colour as the rest of the head, in the former they are always much paler than the crown. Typically this species is of small size, the length of the head and body being only 20 inches, and that of the tail $24\frac{1}{2}$ inches. The so-called bear monkey is, however, somewhat larger; the length of the head and body being 21, and that of the tail 26 inches. In colour the typical purple-faced monkey varies from dusky- to smoky-brown and black, more or less tinged with grey on the back and upper parts, this grey being always present on the haunches. In the head the long whiskers on the cheeks stand out in striking contrast to the brown hue of the rest of the head. Some varieties are more decidedly brown; and in the bear monkey dusky-brown is the prevalent hue, with complete absence of the grey on the haunches. The white monkey, which we are disposed to regard merely as a variety of this species, is a curious-looking animal, being of a general yellowish-white colour, with a faint brownish tinge on the head, and tending to a dusky hue on the shoulders and down the middle of the back. The face and ears retain the usual black colour, but the palms of the hands and the soles of the feet are flesh-coloured.

The typical form is found over the greater part of Ceylon at low or moderate elevations, and apparently not ascending above some thirteen thousand feet above the sea-level. The bear and white monkeys are, however, confined to the southern parts of Ceylon, and ascend to much greater elevations; the former variety being especially abundant in the high mountains in the neighbourhood of the town of Newera Ellia.

Mode of Life. Sir Emerson Tennent, writing of the typical purple-faced monkey, which he terms the wanderu of the low country, says that it is far the commonest of the Singalese langurs, and that " it is an active and intelligent creature, little larger than the common bonneted macaque, and far from being so mischievous as the other monkeys in the island. In captivity it is remarkable for the gravity of its demeanour, and for an air of melancholy in its expression and movements which are completely in character with its snowy beard and venerable aspect. In disposition it is gentle and confiding, sensible in the highest degree of kindness, and eager for endearing affection, uttering a low plaintive cry when its sympathies are excited. It is particularly cleanly in its habits when domesticated, and spends much of its time in trimming its fur, and carefully divesting its hair of particles of dust. Those which I kept at my house near Colombo were chiefly fed upon plantains and bananas, but for nothing did they exhibit a greater partiality than the rose-coloured flowers of the red hibiscus. These they devoured with unequivocal gusto; they likewise relished the leaves of many other trees, and even the bark of a few of the more succulent ones."

After referring to the white monkey, which he regards as merely a variety of the lowland wanderu, Sir Emerson Tennent proceeds with his account of the latter, and states that " when observed in their native wilds, a party of twenty or thirty of these creatures is generally busily engaged in the search for berries and buds. They are seldom to be seen on the ground, except when they may have descended to recover seeds or fruit which have fallen at the foot of their favourite trees. When disturbed, their leaps are prodigious; but, generally speaking, their progress is made not so much by leaping as by swinging from branch to branch, using their powerful arms alternately; and, when baffled by distance, flinging themselves obliquely so as to catch the lower boughs of an opposite tree, the momentum caused by their descent being sufficient to cause a rebound of the branch, that carries them upward again till they grasp a higher and more distant one, and thus continue their headlong flight. In these perilous achievements wonder is excited less by the surpassing agility of these little creatures (frequently encumbered as they are by their young, which cling to them in their career) than by the quickness of their eye and the unerring accuracy with which they seem almost to calculate the angle at which a descent will enable them to cover a given distance, and the recoil to attain a higher altitude."

The same writer then goes on to say that in the hills the typical black form of this monkey is replaced by the so-called bear monkey. "The natives, who designate the latter as the Maha, or Great Wanderu, to distinguish it from the Kala, or Black one (the typical purple-faced monkey), with which they are familiar, describe it as much wilder and more powerful than its congener of the lowland forests. It is rarely seen by Europeans, this portion of the country having till very recently been but partially opened; and even now it is difficult to observe its habits, as it seldom approaches the few roads which wind through these deep solitudes. At early morning, ere the day begins to dawn, its loud and peculiar howl, which consists of a quick repetition of the sounds *how, how!* may be frequently heard in the mountain jungles, and forms one of the characteristic noises of these lofty situations." There is a record of one of these monkeys having attacked a native laden with a bag of rice.

THE CAPPED LANGUR (*Semnopithecus pileatus*).

Of somewhat smaller dimensions than the hanumán is the capped langur of Assam and the neighbouring districts of North-Eastern India and Upper Burma. This species may be readily distinguished from the Nilgiri langur and the purple-faced monkey (with its varieties) by the hair of the crown of the head being longer than that on the occiput and temples, thus having somewhat the appearance of a cap, from which character the species derives its name.

In colour this monkey varies from a dusky-grey to a brownish ashy-grey on the upper parts; the upper part of the back, and sometimes also the crown of the head, being darker. The hands and feet are dark or black above, but occasionally some or all of the fingers may be yellowish. The tail is dark-brown, but may be black at the tip. The face is always black, but the sides and lower parts of the head, as well as the neck, vary from a golden brown or orange to a pale yellow or yellowish-white tint. The light colour of the sides of the face extends backwards to a line just above the ears, so that, with the light-coloured nape of the neck, the dark cap is well defined, and gives to this monkey a peculiar and distinctive appearance.

According to Mr. Blanford, nothing is known of its habits in a wild state, although they are probably very similar to those of most of the other species of the genus. In captivity it is said to be gentle if captured when quite young, but if not taken till adult it is morose and savage, this being especially the case with old males.

The so-called red-bellied langur (*S. chrysogaster*) is only known by an adult female and a young one preserved in the Museum at Berlin, and reputed to have been obtained from Tenasserim. In the adult the upper parts, the limbs, and the tail are jet black, with the lower portions of the individual hairs ruddy, and their extreme bases white; the band on the forehead, as well as the cheeks to behind the ears, and the sides and front of the neck, together with the chin and the upper part of the breast are pure white. The remainder of the under parts are of a deep bright ferruginous red, which also tinges the inner sides of the limbs, and gives the animal its distinctive appellation. The young are of a uniform reddish-white colour. The head of the adult appears to have a small crest, and by this it is distinguished from the typical capped langur.

From this description it would appear that this monkey is the most brilliantly coloured of all the langurs; and Mr. Blanford considers from this circumstance that if it really comes from Tenasserim other examples ought ere this to have been obtained. Dr. Anderson regards this monkey merely as a brilliantly coloured variety of the capped langur, but this view is not accepted by Mr. Blanford.

THE DUSKY LEAF-MONKEY (*Semnopithecus obscurus*).

The dusky leaf-monkey, which is found in Siam, the Malay Peninsula, and the Tenasserim provinces, while agreeing with the Nilgiri and the capped langur in the backward direction of the crown of the head, is distinguished by the possession of a distinct crest of longer hairs on the occiput, arranged in a pointed form.

The adult of this langur is of comparatively small size, the length of the head and body measuring 21 inches, and that of the tail 32. Usually the general colour of the head, body, and limbs is dark ashy-grey, but it may vary to blackish-brown. The under parts and tail are generally lighter, but the hands and feet are black. The crest on the back of the head is always distinctly lighter than that of the rest of the crown, and may be almost white. The young are of a bright golden ferruginous colour. According to Mr. Blanford this species is known to the Malays as *Lutong itam*, a title which appears properly to belong to the black variety of the negro monkey.

Closely allied to this species is Phayre's leaf-monkey (*S. phayrei*), distinguished by the crest of hair being placed on the crown of the head instead of on the occiput; and by this same crest being compressed and longitudinal, instead of pointed; while the colour of the body is dark grey above, and whitish underneath. Phayre's leaf-monkey inhabits Arakan, part of Pegu, and Northern Tenasserim.

Writing of this species, Mr. Blanford states that it "is found in dense, high forests, or amongst bamboos on the hill-sides and on the banks of streams, usually in flocks of twenty or thirty individuals. It is very shy and wary, and is consequently more often heard than seen; the whole flock when alarmed rushing through the forest, shaking the branches violently, and leaping from tree to tree. But occasionally, as Tickell observes, an old male stays behind in a safe post of vantage on the top of one of the highest trees, where he may be heard uttering his short, deep alarm-cry at frequent intervals. This cry is an angry bark, not unlike that of the hanumán. I was once well scolded from a tree by an old monkey, I believe of this species, on the edge of a half-deserted clearing in Southern Arakan, I had done nothing to offend his monkeyship, but he evidently considered me as something unusual and suspicious. Blyth observes that the young, besides making a whining noise to express their wants, emit a cry that might be mistaken for the mew of a cat."

Hose's Langur (*Semnopithecus hosei*).

This very handsome and peculiarly-coloured langur from Borneo belongs to the group in which the hair of the crown extends evenly backwards. It is about the same size as the dusky leaf-monkey. The crown has a longitudinal crest, starting about half an inch behind the centre of the forehead. The general colour of the body is a hoary grey, caused by the mixture of black and white hairs. The crest, as well as the centre of the crown of the head, the nape of the neck, and the eyebrows, are of a deep glossy black; and the hands and feet are of the same jetty hue. In marked contrast to these sombre tints is the brilliant white of the forehead, temples, sides of the head and neck, and chin. This white is continued down the throat and chest to the under surface of the body, and the inner sides of the upper parts of the limbs.

This exceedingly handsome species differs from all the langurs yet mentioned, in the marked contrast presented by its black crest to the brilliant white of the temples and cheeks. A specimen was obtained by Mr. John Whitehead on Kina Balu, the great mountain of Borneo, at an elevation of some four thousand feet above the level of the sea; and this explorer states that the species is fairly common in certain patches of forest on the mountain and in its neighbourhood.

The reader might well be excused for thinking that with this he had reached the end of the already long list of langurs; but there are several other species more or less closely related to those we have mentioned. As, however, even the enumeration of these might be wearisome, we pass on to the consideration of

THE DOUC (*Semnopithecus nemæus*).

The douc, or variegated langur, is an inhabitant of the forests of Cochin-China, where it is found near the coast, as well as in the interior, and is remarkable for its brilliant coloration. There seems to be great doubt as to the origin of the name Douc, which was applied to this monkey by Buffon, and it is stated to be unknown

THE DOUC.

in Cochin-China; it has, however, been so long in use that there would be no advantage gained by changing it.

The general form of the douc is so different from that of other langurs, that the late Dr. Gray proposed to make it the type of a distinct genus. Thus the general build is more robust, and the limbs are stouter, and of nearly equal lengths; whereas in the typical langurs the arms are considerably shorter than the legs.

The hair on the top of the head is directed backwards, without any crest; and the brilliant white whiskers have likewise the same direction, and are closely pressed to the face. The general colour of the head is brown, but there is a narrow band of bright chestnut passing backwards under the ears; and the naked face is of a brilliant yellow, which makes a bold contrast to the pure white whiskers. Owing to the hairs of the body having alternate dark and light rings of colour, the general tint of the body is a mottled, grizzled grey, darker on the upper than on the under parts. The upper parts of the arms and legs, as well as the hands and feet, are of a deep black; but the lower legs are of a full chestnut, and the fore-arms white. A large patch on the rump near the root of the tail, as well as the tail itself, are likewise white. All these colours are extremely brilliant, and sharply defined, without any tendency to blend with one another at their junctions, so that this monkey is one of the most gorgeously coloured Mammals known.

We have very little information as to the habits of the douc in a state of nature, and it does not appear that it has been exhibited alive (at least of late years) in this country. M. Rey, a French captain, who visited Cochin-China in the years 1819 and 1820, has given us an account of a number of doucs which he saw during an expedition into the interior of the country, in the course of which it is stated that a hundred individuals were slaughtered on a single occasion in the endeavour to capture some living specimens.

The Tibetan Langur,—*Semnopithecus roxellanæ.*

Perhaps the last place in which we should expect to find a living monkey would be the highlands of Eastern Tibet. Nevertheless, that one — and a very peculiar one—does exist in those elevated regions has been proved by the researches of the French missionary, Abbé David, who has done so much to increase our knowledge of the fauna of that inaccessible part of the world. The monkey in question, which may be known as the Tibetan langur, although a true *Semnopithecus*, may be recognised at a glance among all its congeners by its "tip-tilted" nose. Although short and small, the nose is so much turned up that its tip reaches to the level of the lower border of the eyes. Some writers, relying on this peculiar formation of the nose, have separated the species from the other langurs under the name of *Rhinopithecus*, but this multiplication of generic terms is confusing and unnecessary.

Although this remarkable monkey was first made known in Europe from specimens obtained in Eastern Tibet, subsequent researches have shown that it also ranges into North-West China, where it is found on the mountains of the province of Kansu. It appears, indeed, from the researches of the late Professor Moseley, that it has been known to the Chinese for an immensely long period. There is a Chinese work known as the *Shan Hoi King*, or mountain and ocean record, of very great antiquity,—so old, indeed, that one commentator even assigns to it as early a date as the year 2205 B.C.,—in which there is a woodcut representing a man of the Heu Yeung Kingdom, wherever that may be. Professor Moseley reproduces this figure in his *Notes of a Naturalist on the Challenger*, and says that it evidently represents a monkey closely allied to, and perhaps identical with, the species under consideration; the prominent nose turned up at the tip being clearly shown in the engraving. Professor Moseley adds that "the wide but unscientific distinction commonly drawn between men and the higher monkeys is an error of high civilisation, and comparatively recent. Less civilised races make no such distinction. To the Dyak the great ape of Borneo is simply the Man of the Woods —orang-utan." The Tibetan langur differs from the Indian langurs by its stouter build, and relatively shorter limbs. The upper surface of the body, the crown of the head, the outer sides of the limbs, and the whole of the tail, are an olive-brown colour, flecked with yellow; while the sides of the face, the lower part of the forehead, and all the under parts and the inner sides of the limbs, are of a brilliant yellow, tending to orange, the naked parts of the face being bluish-grey.

These langurs inhabit the forests of the mountain region between Moupin and Lake Khokonor, where snow is said to lie for a large portion of the year. They are stated to live in numerous troops, always ascending the loftiest trees, and feeding on fruits, but when pressed by hunger eating also the leaves and shoots of the bamboo.

FOSSIL LANGURS.

As we might naturally suppose would be the case, fossil remains of langurs have been found in their native land of India. Some of these have been obtained from caverns in the Madras Presidency, and do not date back much, if at all, beyond the human period. Other remains occur, however, in the much older Siwalik sandstones forming the ranges on the flanks of the Himalaya, and belonging to the upper part of that division of the Tertiary period known to geologists as the Pliocene. This does not, however, by any means limit the range of extinct langurs, since their remains have been found in the Pliocene deposits of the Val d'Arno in Tuscany, and also in strata of equivalent age in the south of France. We have, therefore, evidence that these monkeys, which are now confined to the Oriental region, were formerly widely spread over the eastern hemisphere.

THE PROBOSCIS MONKEY.

Genus *Nasalis.*

If the physiognomy of the Tibetan langur strikes us as ludicrous, it is hard to say what epithet we ought to apply to the far more grotesque-looking creature represented in the accompanying figure. The nose of the proboscis monkey is indeed so enormous in proportion to the face that it presents the appearance of an absolute deformity, and it is very hard to imagine of what possible advantage it can be to its owner.

The proboscis monkey (*N. larvatus*) is an inhabitant of Borneo, and its marked difference from other monkeys is one of the many proofs indicating the great antiquity of that island, and the long period during which it has been isolated from other lands. In general structure the proboscis monkey conforms so closely to the langurs that the peculiarity of its nasal organ would not alone justify its separation from that group as the representative of a distinct genus, although it was on this ground alone that the separation was originally made. Subsequent researches have, however, shown that the skull can be distinguished at a glance from that of any of the langurs, and also from those of the African genus *Colobus*, to be mentioned immediately, by the form of the aperture of the nasal cavity. Thus, whereas in the latter this aperture extends upwards between the sockets of the eyes, in the proboscis monkey the nose bones which roof over this aperture descend considerably below the lower margin of the eye-sockets. In this respect the species under consideration resembles the macaques and their allies.

The proboscis monkey was first made known to European science in 1781 by Baron Wurmb, sometime Dutch governor of Batavia. Wurmb described it under the name *Kahau*, a term apparently made up from a resemblance to its cry, but unknown to the native inhabitants of Borneo, by whom it is said to be called Bantajau. Specimens were subsequently sent to Europe by Sir Stamford Raffles, and it was considered by Messrs Vigors and Horsfield that these indicated two distinct species; but it was afterwards discovered that these supposed two species were founded upon the male and female of the one and only proboscis monkey, in which the two sexes differ considerably in point of size.

The proboscis monkey is a rather large animal, the combined length of the head and body of the male being about 30 inches, while the tail measures some 27 inches. The general colour is a kind of ochre-yellow, the head and upper parts of the body being chestnut. The under parts are lighter; a large patch on the rump above the root of the tail, as well as the tail itself, together with the

THE PROBOSCIS MONKEY ($\frac{1}{10}$ nat. size).

fore-arms and lower legs, being greyish-yellow. The forehead is very low, and the dark chestnut hair is directed backwards from a nearly straight line immediately over the eyes; while the hair of the temples is continued down the sides of the face as whiskers, which meet as a beard beneath the chin. The whole of the large naked face is, therefore, surrounded by a hairy frame. In stuffed or dried specimens the skin of the face fades to a dull leaden hue; but when the animal is alive the tint is of a reddish-brown flesh-colour.

The light-coloured area on the loins near the root of the tail usually takes the form of a number of large rectangular spots, producing a very peculiar and characteristic kind of coloration, which is, however, absent in the female.

The enormous nose, from which the proboscis monkey derives both its popular and scientific appellations, projects several inches in front of the mouth, with the nostrils placed on its under surface, although separated by a much narrower septum than in man. This excessive development of the nose is, however, only reached in the adult male; it being much less throughout life in the female, while in the young of both sexes it is comparatively small, and upturned as in the Tibetan langur.

No living examples of the proboscis monkey have, we believe, been exhibited in this country; and accounts of its habits in the wild condition are few. The following extracts are taken from a translation of the original account given by Baron Wurmb. After stating that these monkeys are found in large troops, the author says that "they assemble together morning and evening, at the rising and setting of the sun, and always on the banks of some stream or river; there they may be seen seated on the branches of some great tree, or leaping with astonishing force and rapidity from one tree or branch to another, at the distance of fifteen or twenty feet. It is a curious and interesting sight; but I have never remarked, as the accounts of the natives would have you believe, that they hold their long nose in the act of jumping; on the contrary, I have uniformly observed that on such occasions they extend the legs and arms to as great a distance as possible, apparently for the purpose of presenting as large a surface as they can to the atmosphere. The nature of their food is unknown, which renders it impossible to keep them alive in a state of confinement."

The Thumbless Monkeys.

Genus *Colobus*.

The langurs, which as we have seen are widely distributed over South-Eastern Asia, and more especially that portion forming the Oriental Region of zoologists, are replaced in Africa by a group of monkeys closely allied to them in all respects, but distinguished either by the total absence, or rudimentary condition, of the thumb. When present at all this digit merely takes the form of a small tubercle, which may or may not be provided with a minute nail. Such a point of difference from the langurs is rightly regarded as worthy of generic distinction, and these African monkeys have accordingly been described under the name of *Colobus*, in allusion to the feature in question. There is no popular name by which these monkeys are generally known, and we have accordingly entitled them the Thumbless Monkeys. Since, however, this term would be somewhat cumbersome when prefixed to another denoting the various species, it has been usual to anglicise the scientific name *Colobus*.

There are rather less than a dozen species of this group known to science. Our acquaintance with their habits is, however, extremely imperfect, and few of them have been brought alive to Europe, since, like their cousins the langurs, they are delicate, and do not thrive well in confinement. The sacculated stomach indicates that their food, like that of the langurs, is in all probability largely composed of leaves and twigs. If, however, their habits at all resemble those of the group last mentioned, it is not easy to see why they should have lost their thumbs,—unless, indeed, the small thumbs of their Indian cousins are practically useless.

In addition to being strictly African, all the thumbless monkeys, with one exception, appear to be confined to the west coast, where they must be very abundantly represented. Most of them are remarkable for the length and beauty of the silky hairs with which their bodies are clothed; their fur being largely imported into Europe for use as trimming for other furs and various kinds of apparel.

Our imperfect acquaintance with this group in their native haunts must be largely attributed to the neglect with which travellers and sportsmen treat monkeys and baboons. In every book of travel or sport we are sure to find chapter after chapter devoted to the hoofed mammals and the carnivores, but very seldom is there a word about monkeys. We have no desire to place any check on the continuous flow of information relating to any of the animals, but we venture to put in a plea that at least some attention may be devoted to these when opportunity offers.

Before noticing some of the species of this group it may be mentioned that the hair of all the thumbless monkeys is coloured uniformly, and by this character even a small piece of their fur may be distinguished from that of all other African monkeys, in which each individual hair is ringed with different hues.

The Guereza (*Colobus guereza*).

We commence our account of the thumbless monkeys with this strikingly handsome animal, which differs so much in external appearance from the other members of the group that it was referred by Dr. Gray to a distinct genus.

It is commonly reported to inhabit Abyssinia, but Mr. Blanford, who accompanied the Abyssinian Expedition under Lord Napier of Magdala, states that he never heard of the animal in the part of the country traversed by the army, and that the skins which are often offered for sale to travellers at Aden are really brought from the mountains in the interior of Somaliland. As, however, Somaliland and Abyssinia are continuous, it is highly probable that it may be found on the eastern borders of the former; and that it is found in Central Abyssinia in the neighbourhood of Samen, we have the evidence of several of the earlier travellers to prove. In Southern Abyssinia it appears to be of comparatively common occurrence in the district of Gojam, and thence it extends further to the southward into the Galla country. From the Galla country and Somaliland the guereza appears to range to the south-west into the Niam-Niam district, lying to the north-west of Lake Albert Nyanza, and to the southward as far as Kilima-Njaro on the east coast.

The head, body, and limbs of the guereza are covered with jet black hair of moderate length; but on either side of the back there arises a line of long hair, hanging down below the flanks, and forming a kind of mantle of a pure white colour. The dark face is also surrounded with a fringe of the same white hair, which forms long whiskers lying flat on the cheeks, and directed backwards. The long tail terminates in a white tuft. The contrast of the white of the mantle cheeks, and tail against the velvety black of the rest of the body is most striking and without exact parallel among other mammals, although the coloration of the skunk is somewhat suggestive of it.

Handsome as is the ordinary guereza in these respects, it is, however, exceeded by a variety occurring commonly at an elevation of about three thousand feet on the flanks of Kilima-Njaro, while the common race is believed to exist in the plains around. In the common guereza the first 12 or 16 inches of the tail are black and short-haired, the white tufted portion including only the last 8 or 10 inches; while the white mantle of hair depending from the back conceals only

THE GUEREZA MONKEY ($\frac{1}{10}$ nat. size).

about one-third of the black portion of the tail. In the Kilima-Njaro variety, or large-tailed guereza, only some 3 or 4 inches of the base of the tail are black and short-haired, while the remainder is covered with long white hair for a length of some 20 inches, each individual hair measuring from 8 to 9 inches. Moreover, the white hairs of the mantle entirely conceal the black of the root of the tail, so that the mantle and tail-brush practically become continuous. The tail of this variety reminds us of the larger tail of half-bred yaks used in India as fly flappers, under the name of *chowris;* and indeed the whole arrangement of the long hairs of the guereza, as well as its coloration, recalls a half-bred yak.

Habits.   The guereza has never been brought alive to this country. One of the earliest accounts of its habits is given by Pearce in his *Life and Adventures in Abyssinia,* in which it is stated that guerezas are common to the Galla country, and that while they are known in the Amharic dialect of Central Abyssinia under the name of Focha; in the Tigré tongue they are called Grazer (= Guereza). At this period, and even up to the date of Salt's second journey into Abyssinia in the first quarter of this century, these animals were supposed to be a species of lemur. Rüppell, however, definitely assigned the guereza to its proper zoological position, and has left us an account of its habits, from which the following particulars are taken.

The guereza is said to live in small companies, and usually inhabits the tallest trees it can find in the neighbourhood of running water. It is restless, and constantly on the move, but is said to be completely silent. The leaps which it takes from tree to tree are described as of tremendous length. It subsists mainly on various kinds of wild fruits, seeds, and insects; and it spends the whole day in collecting these, retiring to sleep high up in the trees. In Gojam, on the southern frontier of Abyssinia, it is common; and it is largely hunted for the sake of its fur, which is used for covering the shields of the Abyssinian soldiers.

There are good grounds for believing that this monkey is the true callithrix of the ancients, although this name is now applied in zoology to a totally different group of monkeys, as we shall see below.

The Black Colob (*Colobus satanas*).

In marked contrast to the pied coloration of the preceding species is the sable hue of the black colob, first described from specimens obtained at Fernando Po, on the West Coast of Africa, in 1838.

The uniform black colour of this monkey, of which a representation is given in the right-hand figure of the woodcut on p. 90, suffices indeed to distinguish it at once from all its congeners. In addition to this black coloration, the crown of the head has a crest of long hair projecting over the temples and eyes; and the whiskers are long and expanded. The whole of the body is covered with long and rather coarse hair; but the tail is short-haired throughout the greater part of its length, and has no trace of a tuft at the end. The whole of the hair has a dull and shaggy appearance, recalling, as an earlier writer has observed, that of the sloth bear of India. The length of the head and body is 32 inches, while that of the tail reaches 40 inches.

Although this species is mentioned by Du Chaillu as inhabiting Western Equatorial Africa, it is to be regretted that we have no record of its mode of life.

The King Monkey (*Colobus polycomus*).

The king monkey of Sierra Leone is one of the few colobs that have been exhibited alive in the Gardens of the London Zoological Society, a single specimen having been purchased in the spring of 1873. It has no crest on the head, but a long mane on the throat and chest; the hair of the sides of the body being likewise long. The general colour is black, but the mane, the forehead, and the sides of the face, as well as the whole of the tail, are of a dazzling white. The tail has a well-marked tuft at the end; and the entire coat of hair is very glossy.

The Ursine Colob (*Colobus ursinus*).

Closely allied to the last species is the so-called ursine colob from Fernando Po, in which the mane is greyish, and not longer than the hair on the sides of the body. Yet another nearly related West African monkey is the Angola colob

THE URSINE COLOB AND BLACK COLOB ($\frac{1}{8}$ nat. size).

(*Colobus angolensis*), which differs from the king monkey in that the chest and two-thirds of the lower portion of the tail are black.

The White-thighed Colob (*Colobus villerosus*).

More markedly distinct than the preceding from the king monkey, is the white-thighed colob of Western Africa. This species is distinguished by the absence of a mane on the head and throat, although it has a small fringe round the face. The general colour is glossy black; but that of the forehead, of the frill round the face, and on the chin, is white. The tail is also white; but the most distinctive characteristic of the species is the silvery-white of the thighs, from which it derives its name. The haunches are, moreover, generally grey. The white hair of the thighs is shorter than that on the body.

THE BAY COLOB (*Colobus ferrugineus*).

Very different in coloration from any of the species yet mentioned is the bay colob, definitely known from the Gambia and the Gold Coast, and of which a single specimen was brought alive to England in the autumn of 1890, but, unfortunately, did not long survive its arrival.

This handsome species has comparatively short hair, which, on the crown of the head and the back and upper part of the sides is blackish-grey, while the cheeks and throat, as well as the under parts and the limbs, are of a rich ferruginous bay. The upper part of the root of the tail is blackish, but the remainder of a reddish-brown. The ears and the greater part of the face are bluish, but the nose and lips are flesh-coloured. Altogether the bay colob is a striking species, which, once seen, will always be easily recognised.

THE CRESTED COLOB (*Colobus cristatus*).

The last of the thumbless monkeys we shall mention is the crested colob, which is likewise a West African species. It is readily distinguished by its short yellowish-brown fur, which becomes greyer on the front of the body; the shoulders and outer sides of the arms, the throat, chest, under parts, and inner sides of the limbs being greyish-white. It differs from all the other species in that the hair on the forehead radiates from two points on the temples, and that there is a low erect crest of longer hairs running along the middle line of the head.

CHAPTER IV.

Apes, Monkeys, and Lemurs,—*continued*.

The Old World Monkeys and Baboons,—*continued*.

In the preceding chapter we have considered such of the Old World monkeys as have no cheek-pouches, but possess sacculated stomachs, and in which the legs are longer than the arms. In systematic zoology these constitute the subfamily *Colobinæ,* of the family *Cercopithecidæ.* We have now to consider the remainder of the Old World monkeys, together with the baboons, which, although belonging to the same great family, constitute the separate large subfamily of the *Cercopithecinæ.* This group is characterised by the circumstance that all its members are furnished with cheek-pouches, but their stomachs are simple, and the arms and legs are of nearly the same length.

The Guenons.

Genus *Cercopithecus.*

Since we have no English name to distinguish this group of African monkeys from others of the same family, it will be found convenient to use the French name *Guenon,* meaning one who grimaces, which appears to have been especially applied to the monkeys of this group, as being those with which we are most familiar in menageries and shows.

As we have said, these monkeys are strictly confined to Africa, where they are represented by more than twenty species, of which the larger proportion are found on the western side of the continent. None of them are of large size, and they present the following features by which they are characterised as a genus.

Characteristics. In build they are comparatively slender, and their muzzle is either short, or at least not very long. Their tail is invariably long and slender, and the naked callosities on the buttocks are of comparatively small size. For another important point of distinction we must have recourse to the dried skulls, an examination of which will show that the last molar or wisdom-tooth on each side of the lower jaw consists of four tubercles only, and of these the front and hind pairs are connected by a pair of transverse ridges. In this respect the guenons differ, not only from the monkeys described in the last chapter, but likewise from all those to be subsequently noticed, in which the last lower molar has a fifth tubercle forming a kind of heel projecting from behind the second transverse ridge.

In general appearance, more especially as regards their slender build and long tails, the guenons are the members of the present subfamily which make the nearest approach to the langurs and their allies. All of them, like the other African monkeys to be subsequently mentioned, are characterised by each individual hair being marked by a series of different-coloured rings, which imparts to the fur the peculiar mottled appearance with which we are familiar.

In disposition these monkeys are docile and easily taught, and so well do they thrive in captivity that it is not uncommon for them to breed in menageries. In consequence of this docile disposition, and their comparatively hardy constitution, as well as from the facility with which they learn tricks, and to obey the word of command, they, or the representatives of the next genus, are generally chosen as companions by the peripatetic organ-grinders. Mischievous as a monkey, is truer of the guenons than of any other members of the order to which they belong; and it is largely to them that the monkey-house at the Zoological Society's Gardens owes it popularity.

Mode of Life. Like the langurs, the guenons are essentially arboreal; and they are found in their native wilds in large troops, which reveal their proximity by their incessant chattering. Not only, therefore, is the solitary monkey of the London organ-grinder to be commiserated for having exchanged the sunny atmosphere of his native African forests for the gloom of an English winter, but likewise for the loss of the merry companions with which he was wont to associate.

In saying that the guenons are docile, we should guard ourselves by adding, docile for a monkey, since in the strict sense of the word all monkeys are far less docile and less susceptible of education than many other Mammals. This, however, by no means implies that monkeys have not a very high degree of intelligence. In regard to this point we may quote a very suggestive paragraph from Mr. Blanford. "It is the commonest mistake," he writes, "amongst superficial observers, and even amongst naturalists, to confound docility and intelligence among animals, and to measure their intellectual powers by the facility with which they can be taught. Hence the very common, but, as it appears to me, very incorrect notion, that monkeys are of inferior intelligence to such animals as dogs and elephants. In reality they are less docile, less willing to learn, and less adapted to captivity; moreover, being of but little use to man, far less trouble has been taken in studying their habits. Thus while dog- and elephant - breaking engage all the time and mental resources of particular classes of men, the instruction of monkeys is left to the unaided efforts of amateurs and organ-grinders. The negro race amongst men appears to be far better adapted for slavery than most savage races, being more docile in a state of captivity; but it is scarcely proved to be more intelligent on that account. The same reasoning will doubtless apply to animals. I have often seen dogs and monkeys kept together, and in every instance it has appeared to me that the monkey ruled the dog, and that the dog, although the more powerful animal, feared the monkey; and I can only account for this by the superior intelligence of the monkey."

In their native condition the guenons go in separate families or droves, each under the leadership of an old male; and it appears that each drove has its own particular limits of territory beyond which it cannot go without intruding on the domains of another drove, an invasion which is treated as at once being a *casus belli.* Indeed, this principle of territorial rights appears to be so deeply implanted in the guenon nature that it persists even in captivity, when it is no uncommon sight to see two or more of these creatures religiously guarding one portion of the cage from all intruders.

In Ancient Egypt. As being the common monkeys of Africa the guenons would naturally be well known to the ancient Egyptians; and it is probable that most of the long-tailed monkeys we see on their old sculptures are either guenons, or mangabeys, as the members of the next group are called. The thumbless monkeys, as being almost exclusively West African, would be less likely to be intimately known to the inhabitants of Egypt. Not only were the guenons familiar to the Egyptians, but they appear to have been likewise imported into classic Greece and Rome; and it is believed that the Greek and Latin term *Cebus* was used to designate them, although the name is now applied to a South American genus.

The Talapoin Monkey (*Cercopithecus talapoin*).

The somewhat rare and tiny monkey from the Gabun and other regions of the West Coast of Africa is taken as our first example of the guenons, on account of the possession of a peculiarity which led Dr. Gray to separate it from all the others as the representative of a distinct genus (*Myopithecus*). This peculiarity is to be found in the circumstance that the last molar in the lower jaw has only three, in lieu of the ordinary four tubercles on its crown. Another distinctive feature, which can be observed in the living animal or in stuffed specimens, is the relative shortness of the hands as compared with those of the other guenons, and also the presence of a web uniting the bases of the fingers. The talapoin, which is scarcely larger than a squirrel, is the smallest of the guenons. In colour it is olive-green above and whitish beneath, with short whiskers of a pale golden yellow tint, forming a striking contrast to the face, which is black, with the exception of the upper lip and rings round the eyes, which are yellow or orange.

The Malbrouck Monkey (*Cercopithecus cynosurus*).

With the malbrouck monkey of Western Africa we come to the first of a group of guenons characterised by their oval heads and somewhat long muzzles, as well as by their stiff and backwardly-directed whiskers. The fur is invariably grizzled, each hair being marked with greenish or reddish rings.

The malbrouck is distinguished from the other members of this group by the large and broad face being flesh-coloured. The general hue of the fur is yellow, grizzled with black; a distinct band on the forehead, as well as the whiskers, throat, the under parts, and the inner surface of the limbs being whitish.

The first specimen of this monkey exhibited alive in England is described as having an unusually mild and gentle expression of countenance, and was calm, circumspect, and inactive in its general habits. It did not, however, appear anxious to become at all familiar either with its keepers or with strangers, and was always ready to resent any interference with its liberty.

WEST AFRICAN GREEN MONKEYS.

The Vervet Monkey (*Cercopithecus lalandi*).

Still better known than the malbrouck is the South African vervet monkey, or black-chinned vervet, as it has been called, in which, as in all the other members of this group of guenons, the rather small and narrow face is entirely black or blackish.

The fur of the vervet is of a greyish-green colour, finely speckled with black on the greater part of the body. The face, hands, and feet, and the terminal third of the tail, are of a deep black; while the cheek, throat, and under parts of the body are reddish-white, and the root of the tail and adjacent regions red. The band on the forehead is distinct, and yellowish. The red root and black tip of the tail and chin are absolutely distinctive of this species.

In size the vervet is somewhat smaller than the mona mentioned hereafter. With the exception of the samango monkey, it is the sole South African representative of the guenons. It is common in forest districts throughout the Cape Colony and adjacent regions, more particularly along the tract of coast extending from Cape Town to Algoa Bay, and thence through Kaffraria and Natal. It is said to feed chiefly on the gum from the acacias known to the Boers as camel-doorn and rhinaster-bosh; and its habits appear to be similar to those of the green monkey.

The Grivet Monkey (*Cercopithecus griseoviridis*).

As the vervet is one of two South African representatives of the guenons, so the grivet is one of two members of the group found in North-Eastern Africa. In colour the fur of this species is olive-green, speckled with yellow and black, while the chin, whiskers, and under-parts of the body are white, and the root of the tail and adjacent regions grey. The forehead has a broad whitish band, but faintly marked. The white chin and grey root to the tail serve to distinguish this monkey from the vervet, with which it agrees in size.

Writing of the grivets in Abyssinia, Mr. Blanford observes that they are but rarely seen, and then only in forest. "On the highlands," he states, "I only once saw a flock—this was near Dildi, south of Lake Ashangi. I met with large numbers on the Anseba, where they inhabited the high trees on the banks of the stream. The flocks seen were small, not exceeding twenty to thirty individuals. I had but few opportunities of observing their habits, but they appeared to differ but little from those of macaques, except that *Cercopithecus* is a quieter animal and less mischievous. In captivity they are well known as excessively docile and good-tempered, and fairly intelligent."

The Green Monkey (*Cercopithecus callitrichus*).[1]

One of the commonest of the guenons usually to be seen in menageries is the West African green monkey. The colour of the fur may be described as a mixture of black and yellow, giving a general dark green hue to the upper parts; the crown

---

[1] Frequently known as *Cercopithecus sabæus.*

of the head, the hands, feet, and the upper part of the root of the tail being blacker. There is generally no light band on the forehead, and if this be present it is very narrow. The whiskers, throat, and the under side and end of the tail are yellowish, sometimes tending to orange; and as in the last species, the base of the root of the tail is grey.

This monkey, of which we give a representation in the woodcut facing p. 97, is closely allied to the grivet, from which it may be distinguished by the more yellow-green hue of its upper parts, the yellowish whiskers, and the general absence of the white band on the forehead.

The green monkey is about the size of a large cat, the length of the head and body being 16 or 18 inches, and that of the tail rather more. It is one of the hardiest of the guenons, on which account it is so frequently seen in confinement, as it bears our climate well. Although gay and gentle during youth, it usually becomes morose and vicious when old, and is therefore not one of the species usually selected for exhibition by travelling organ-grinders. Like the other members of the group, it does not appear that the green monkey ever utters a sound when in captivity, and from an early account of the species it appears to be similarly silent in its wild condition.

The Mozambique Monkey (*Cercopithecus rufoviridis*).

The guenons are also represented in the Mozambique and Zambesi districts of the East Coast, although far less abundantly than on the West Coast. The Mozambique monkey agrees with the vervet in having the root of the tail and adjacent regions of a ferruginous red, but differs in the more yellowish-grey tint of the fur of the upper parts, which tends to a blacker hue on the crown of the head, the tail, and the outer sides of the limbs; while the under-parts and the inner sides of the limbs are pure white, instead of reddish-white.

The Patas Monkey (*Cercopithecus patas*).[1]

The West African patas, or red monkey, from Senegambia, differs from all the other members of this group of guenons yet noticed by the red colour of the fur of the greater part of the body; the nose, an arched band on the forehead, and the outer surfaces of the arms being blackish. The reader will, therefore, have no difficulty in recognising this species whenever he meets with it, and it is well represented in the accompanying figure. In addition to these leading features, we may notice that beneath the large and blackish ears there are thick bushy tufts of light grey hair, which extend forwards on to the cheeks and lower jaw, so as to cause the naked part of the face to be limited to a narrow space between the eyes and the upper lip. From these tufts the greyish-coloured hair is continued on the whole of the under surface of the body, as well as on the inner sides of the limbs. The hands are of a dusky brown colour, with very short fingers, and the thumb is reduced almost to the condition of a tubercle. The animal is about the same size as the green monkey. The black of the nose continuing upwards to the arched band of

---

[1] Frequently known as *Cercopithecus ruber*.

the same colour above the eyes communicates a very peculiar and characteristic physiognomy to the patas, which led Buffon to describe it as the monkey *à bandeau noir*.

One of the earliest accounts that we possess of the patas is given by an old French traveller, Brue, but it is not to be relied on in all particulars. A living example was first exhibited in the London Zoological Society's menagerie about the year 1834, since which date it has been abundantly represented. This original

THE PATAS MONKEY (⅛ nat. size).

example, which was very young, was described as being lively and active, but somewhat irascible if disturbed or handled.

The Nisnas Monkey (*Cercopithecus pyrrhonotus*).

On the opposite side of Africa, in Nubia and Somaliland, the place of the patas is taken by a closely allied monkey, known as the nisnas. So similar, indeed, are these two monkeys that Dr. Gray considered them merely as varieties of the same species; and it is quite probable that if we knew all the monkeys from the intermediate districts of North Central Africa we should find that the one passed into the other. However, as they are considered by the learned secretary of the Zoological Society to be distinct, we must, at least for the present, allow them to stand apart. According to Dr. Gray, the nisnas is distinguished from the patas merely by the red colour of the body being continued on to the shoulders and the outer sides of the arms, instead of those parts assuming a blackish tinge.

The nisnas is the species so frequently represented on the ancient Egyptian monuments; and it appears to be undoubtedly the *Cebus* of the ancients, which, on the authority of Pythagoras, was described by Ælian as inhabiting the Red Sea littoral, and was said to be of a bright flame-colour, with whitish whiskers and under-parts.

SYKES'S MONKEY (*Cercopithecus albogularis*).

With the nisnas we concluded our notice of the group of guenons in which the head is oval, the muzzle somewhat produced, the whiskers stiff, and the general colour greenish or red.

With the East African Sykes's monkey we come to the second and more typical group of these animals which are distinguished by the general form of the head being rounded, the muzzle very short, the whiskers short and rounded and not directed backwards, and the fur generally of a blackish hue, more or less tinged with yellow.

The present species appears to be the East African representative of the mona monkey, to be immediately mentioned, from which it is distinguished by the absence of the white spot on the haunches, and the pure white colour of the under-parts and chest, which extends on to the throat, and thus suggests the scientific name of the species. It is also of larger size than the mona, being the largest representative of the genus.

This monkey was originally brought to England by Colonel W. H. Sykes, by whom it was described in 1831. The original specimen was purchased at Bombay, and was said to have come from Madagascar (where, by the way, monkeys are unknown), but it was doubtless imported from Zanzibar.

In describing the original living specimen, Colonel Sykes observes that its manners "are grave and sedate. Its disposition is gentle, but not affectionate; free from that capricious petulance and mischievous irascibility which characterise so many of the African species, but yet resenting irritating treatment, and evincing its resentment by very sharp blows with its anterior hands. It never bit any person on board ship, but so seriously lacerated three other monkeys, its fellow-passengers, that two of them died of the wounds. It readily ate meat, and would choose to pick a bone, even when plentifully supplied with vegetables and dried fruits."

THE MONA MONKEY (*Cercopithecus mona*).

One of the most familiar of all the guenons is the mona monkey, represented in the upper figure of the accompanying woodcut. This beautiful little monkey may be always easily recognised by the presence of a large and distinct white spot of an oval shape, situated on each hip immediately in front of the root of the tail; the feature being quite peculiar to the species. In size it is rather smaller than the patas.

The mona is a West African monkey; and has no real right to its name, which is merely the Moorish word for monkeys in general. The general hue of the fur of this monkey is described by Dr. Gray as blackish-olive, finely grizzled with yellow; this gradually darkens towards the hinder parts of the body, so that the tail and the outer surfaces of the limbs are nearly black. The under surface of the

body is of a nearly pure white, these white parts being separated from the darker
regions by an abrupt division; and we have already alluded to the distinctive white
spot on each side near the root of the tail. The naked portions of the face are
purplish, with the exception of the lips and chin, which are flesh-coloured. The

THE MONA MONKEY AND DIANA MONKEY ($\frac{1}{8}$ nat. size).

bushy whiskers, which come forward so as to conceal a large part of the cheeks, are
straw-coloured, with a mixture of a few black hairs. A black transverse band,
surmounted by a thin streak of grey, extends from above the eyebrows to the base
of the ears; the latter, together with the hands and feet, being of a livid flesh-tint.

Writing of this species, which may be described as decidedly more docile and gentle than some of its allies, the French naturalist, Cuvier, observes that "if elegance of shape, gracefulness of movement, gentleness and simplicity of character, united with penetration and intelligence of expression, can inspire affection or make an animal sought after and admired, all these qualities are united in the small group of monkeys allied to the mona, itself distinguished not less by the variety of its colours than by its temper and disposition"—a somewhat flattering description applicable as a rule only to young individuals of both sexes, and to females of all ages, for the adult males are awkward and capricious creatures to manage.

The Diana Monkey (*Cercopithecus diana*).

Before noticing some of the beardless species more nearly allied to the mona, we must mention the well-known West African diana monkey, which derives its name from the distinct white crescent on the forehead above the eyebrows. Its most characteristic feature is, however, the long pointed white beard, so well shown in the lower figure of the woodcut on the preceding page; while the white streak on the haunches near the root of the tail is also distinctive.

The general colour of the fur is black, finely speckled with white, thus producing a greyish grizzle. In addition to the white beard and the crescent on the forehead, the cheeks, the chin, throat, chest, the front of the shoulders, as well as the inside of the thighs and the streak across the haunches, are likewise white. On the other hand, there is a broad streak down the back of a bay colour, and the same tint also prevails on the rump. The face, tail, and the outer sides of the wrists and legs are black, as well as the hands and feet.

All the colours of this animal are sharply defined from one another; and the long, narrow, black face, terminating below in the long and pointed beard, and surmounted by the crescent above the eyebrows, give it a peculiar and characteristic expression. The whole length of the head and body is about 18 inches, while the length of the tail reaches to some 24 inches.

The real name of the diana monkey in its native districts is said to be Roloway on the Gold Coast, although Exquima is given as its title on the Congo. In disposition it is one of the most gentle and easily tamable of the guenons; but, like the greater number of its tribe, its temper is milder in youth than in mature age. When young it appreciates caresses, and it nods and grins when pleased; but these expressions of feeling are generally abandoned at a later period.

The Bearded Monkey (*Cercopithecus pogonias*), Campbell's Monkey (*C. campbelli*), The Red-Bellied Monkey (*C. erythrogaster*), and Wolf's Monkey (*C. wolfi*).

We may notice under this collective heading four species of monkeys closely allied to the mona, but distinguished both from that species and the diana by the absence of any spot or streak of white on the haunches. While the first three species are West African, the fourth, which has only recently been described from a specimen living in the Zoological Gardens at Dresden, is from West Central Africa.

The bearded monkey, also known as Erxleben's monkey, has the fur of the upper parts either greyish or olive-brown, finely grizzled with grey or yellow. From above the eyes to the ears there is a black streak, while there is also a stripe down the back of the same hue; and the hands and feet, as well as the tail, are likewise black. The forehead, the whiskers, the small moustache, and the under parts of the body and the inner sides of the limbs are yellowish. This species has been obtained from Fernando Po and the Gabun.

Campbell's monkey, which inhabits Fernando Po and Sierra Leone, may be distinguished by the absence of the black streak running from above the eyes to the ears, and also by the whitish colour of the under-parts and inner sides of the limbs. The general colour is blackish-olive, washed with yellow.

The red-brown colour of the chest and under-parts, from which it takes its name, are amply sufficient to distinguish the red-bellied monkey; but as additional characters we may mention that the outsides of the thighs and legs are greyish-black, while the front of the thighs and the under surface of the tail are greyish-white.

Finally, Wolf's monkey, which has light under-parts, differs from the other species in the ferruginous colour of the legs, as well as by the light patches on the inner sides of the arms and thighs. This species is interesting as being the only representative of the mona group (if we exclude the larger Sykes's monkey) which is found eastward of Western Africa.

The Black-Bellied Monkey (*Cercopithecus pluto*).

The black-bellied or pluto monkey, from Angola, is another West African species, readily distinguishable by the dark colour of the under-parts of the body and the inner sides of the limbs, which are typically of a reddish-black.

Like the species of the mona group, there is no beard, but large bushy whiskers, well shown in the accompanying figure.

The general colour of the fur is black, finely grizzled with grey; the forehead has a white band, and the sides of the forehead, as well as the shoulders, chest, tail, and limbs, are entirely black, and there is no white on the haunches in the typical form.

Dr Anderson identifies, however, with this species the so-called diadem monkey (*C. leucocampyx*), which also has black under-parts, but is distinguished by a white streak across the haunches.

THE BLACK-BELLIED MONKEY.
(From Gray, *Proc. Zool. Soc.*)

The Moustache Monkey (*Cercopithecus cephus*).

In all the round-headed and short-muzzled guenons yet mentioned the nose and body are of the same colour. There is, however, another division of the guenons, in which the colour of the nose differs from that of the body. Out of the seven species of this subgroup recorded by Dr. Gray we shall select for notice the four which have been represented of late years in the Gardens of the London Zoological Society, premising that the whole seven are West African.

The leading characters of the moustache monkey are to be found in the presence of a triangular blue mark on the nose and in the yellow whiskers. Its general colour is olive-green, speckled with yellow; the throat and under-parts being grey, the face and temples black, and the feet and hands blackish.

The Hocheur Monkey (*Cercopithecus nictitans*).

The hocheur monkey is one of several species belonging to this subgroup of guenons, collectively known as white-nosed monkeys, from the circumstance that the nose in all of them is covered with white hairs. This particular species is distinguished by the blackness of the fur on both the upper and lower surfaces of the body, that of the back being finely speckled with yellow. The naked part of the face is of a bluish-black colour; the upper eyelids are flesh-coloured, and the hands and feet jet black.

This species, sometimes known as the larger white-nosed monkey, may be readily distinguished from the next, not only by its superior size, but also by its more prominent nose. It has been described as lively and good-natured, but not so gentle and familiar as the next species, and more resembling in its temper and general character the mona monkey. It has been obtained both from Fernando Po and Guinea.

The Lesser White-Nosed Monkey (*Cercopithecus petaurista*).

This elegant monkey, which comes from Guinea and Sierra Leone, is one of the smallest of the guenons. It was described in the works of the French naturalist Buffon under the well-chosen name of *Blanc-nez*; and is readily distinguished, as we have said, from the hocheur by its smaller size and the flatness of its nose, as well as by the lighter tint of the under-parts. In colour the fur of the back is olive-green, speckled with yellow; the face black; the white spot on the nose small and nearly triangular; and the cheeks, chin, under-parts of the body, the inner sides of the limbs, and the under side of the tail white.

The following account of the habits of this species in confinement is taken from an anonymous writer, who states that the manners of this monkey " are playful and engaging beyond any other species we have ever observed, and it has an amiability and innocence in its conduct and expression which, united to its lively and familiar disposition, never fail to make it a prime favourite with its visitors. An individual of this species, which formerly lived in the Gardens of the Zoological Society, was confined in the same cage with a young hanumán, whose gravity was sorely disturbed by the unwearied activity and playfulness of its mercurial companion. Whilst the white-nose was frolicking round the cage or playing with the spectators, the hanumán would sit upon the perch, the very picture of melancholy and apathy, with his long tail hanging down to the bottom; but his attention was roused and his security endangered every moment by the tricks of the restless little creature, which in its sports and gambols continually caught the hanumán's tail, either to swing itself out of the reach of the spectators, or, like a boy at his gymnastic exercises, to assist it in climbing up to the perch. All this, however, was done with great good-nature on both sides, and it was highly diverting to see the playful innocence of the one, and the gravity with which the other regarded it, like a fond parent enjoying the innocent follies of a favourite child."

The Ludio Monkey (*Cercopithecus ludio*).

The last of the guenons that we shall notice is the ludio monkey, which is another of the white-nosed group. Its fur is black, profusely grizzled with grey; the chin, chest, and the inner sides of the upper arms being white; while the temples, nape of the neck, shoulders, and the greater portions of the limbs, as well as the end of the tail, are pure black. The white spot on the nose has an oblong shape, and is higher than broad.

The species is said to range into Central Africa. The red-eared monkey (*C. erythrotis*), which is likewise West African, differs from the other members of the group in having red hairs on the nose and ears.

The Mangabeys, or White-Eyelid Monkeys.

Genus *Cercocebus*.

The mangabeys, or, as they are often called, white-eyelid monkeys, comprise a small group of four West African species, which, while agreeing in all external characters with the guenons, are distinguished by the presence of a projecting heel at the hinder end of the last molar tooth on each side of the lower jaw, so that the crown of this tooth carries five, in place of four tubercles. In this respect the mangabeys agree with the great group of macaques, which follow next in the series; and on this ground these monkeys have been separated from the guenons to form a distinct genus under the name of *Cercocebus*. There has been much discussion as to the advisability of thus separating the mangabeys, but it has at least the advantage of somewhat restricting the unwieldy group of the guenons.

The name Mangabey, it may be observed, is taken from the district Mangabe, or Manongabe, in Madagascar, and was applied by the French naturalist Buffon to these monkeys, from the mistaken idea that they came from that island, which in his time appears to have been a kind of refuge for the destitute, in regard to animals whose habitat was unknown. In spite, however, of this totally erroneous origin the name is a convenient one, and has been subsequently almost universally adopted for this group of monkeys.

All the mangabeys have an oval-shaped head, with a somewhat long muzzle; and they may be readily recognised in the living condition by their white eyelids. Moreover, their hairs differ from those of the guenons in not being ringed with different colours.

The Sooty Mangabey (*Cercocebus fuliginosus*).

We select as our first example of these monkeys, the sooty mangabey, represented in the accompanying woodcut. This monkey belongs to a group containing

THE SOOTY MANGABEY ($\frac{1}{6}$ nat. size).

three out of the four species, and characterised by the hair of the crown of the head being directed backwards, without any prolongation into a crest. As its name implies, the fur of the sooty mangabey is of a deep and dull black hue; the chin and under-parts being ashy. The face is livid, marked with dark brown blotches about the eyes, nose, muzzle, and cheeks; the ears, as well as the palms of the hands and the soles of the feet, being of a blacker brown.

At least, in captivity, this species is said to be characterised by the unusual habit of keeping its long tail turned forwards over the body. In confinement this mangabey is docile and good-tempered, and more amenable to instruction than is the case with the majority of the larger guenons. A specimen, which lived more than fifty years ago in the Zoological Society's Gardens, was said to be a most importunate beggar; "but instead of snatching the contributions of his visitors with violence or anger, like the generality of monkeys, he solicited them by tumbling, dancing, and a hundred other amusing tricks. He was very fond of being caressed, and would examine the hands of his friends with great gentleness and gravity, trying to pick out the little hairs, and all the while expressing his satisfaction by smacking his lips, and uttering a low surprised grunt."

The white-collared mangabey (*C. collaris*) may be easily distinguished from the sooty mangabey by its blackish-grey colour, the white round the neck, and the bay on the crown of the head; the white of the collar extending on to the cheeks, throat, and chest.

The third representative of this group is the white-crowned mangabey, which takes its name from a characteristic white spot on the crown, and is also distinguished by a white streak running down the middle of the back.

The Grey-Cheeked Mangabey (*Cercocebus albigena*).

The circumstance that the hair of the crown of the head is lengthened so as to form a distinct crest affords a ready means of distinguishing the grey-cheeked mangabey from its three congeners. The general colour of this monkey is blackish, but its name comes from the greyish hairs on the sides of the throat and cheeks, It was first made known to science in 1850 by the late Dr. Gray, from specimens sent home from the West Coast of Africa by Du Chaillu, previously to his great expedition of 1855.

The Macaques.

Genus *Macacus.*

After having devoted so much space to the monkeys of Africa, we turn to those Asiatic species known as Macaques, of which a group is represented in our coloured Plate.

We have already seen the curious origin of the term mangabey, applied to the group of African monkeys last mentioned, and it appears from what we have to say immediately that there is a kind of fatality in regard to the misapplication of names among monkeys. So far as can be learnt, the name *Macac* or *Macaque* seems to be a barbarous word which, in Margrave's *Natural History of Brazil*, published in the year 1648, is given as the native name of a monkey from the Congo and Guinea. Buffon, however, with a facility for misappropriation for which he was rather celebrated, transferred this name to the Indian group forming this part of our subject, and to them it has ever afterwards clung, having been Latinised into *Macacus*. In spite of its origin, the name is good enough, and so must remain.

Under the heading of the mangabeys we have seen how these monkeys differ from their cousins the guenons in having a heel, and thus five cusps, to their last lower molar teeth, and also in the uniform coloration of their individual hairs. As this is also the case in the macaques, it is obvious that in this respect the mangabeys form a transition to them from the guenons; and we may now consider how the macaques and mangabeys are to be distinguished from one another.

Characteristics. In the first place, macaques are always of stouter build than the mangabeys; and they are further distinguished by the considerably greater prolongation of the muzzle, and the larger size of the naked callosities on the buttocks. Some of the macaques have their tails as long as those of the guenons and mangabeys; in others these appendages are very short, while in a few they are actually wanting; thus showing that the presence or absence of a tail is of no import either as a generic character, or as indicative of a higher or lower degree of organisation. In common with all the monkeys we have hitherto considered, the nostrils of the macaques do not reach as far forwards as the extremity of the muzzle.

From these characters it will be apparent that while the macaques are sufficiently distinguished from the mangabeys to be entitled to rank as a separate genus, yet both groups are closely allied.

THE BURMESE PIG-TAILED MONKEY.
(From Sclater, *Proc. Zool. Soc.*, 1860.)

And, as we shall see that as in the opposite direction the macaques are intimately connected through one singular intermediate form with the baboons of Africa, we have evidence that an almost complete transition exists from the guenons through the mangabeys to the macaques, and thus to the baboons.

In speaking of the macaques as Asiatic monkeys, we must guard ourselves by mentioning that one solitary outlying species is found in the mountains of North-West Africa, and also on the opposite coast of Gibraltar. The greater majority of the species are, however, confined to India, Burma, the Malay Peninsula, and the islands of Borneo, Sumatra, etc. Some range as far east as China, while one is found even in Japan. To the northward, macaques extend into the outer ranges of the Himalaya, while a single species inhabits the secluded highlands of Eastern Tibet.

Habits. The whole of the large number of monkeys reckoned as macaques seem to have much the same general habits, being always found gathered together in troops, which may be of considerable numbers, and always comprise individuals of both sexes, and of all sizes and ages. They are forest-dwelling animals; and, while active and rapid in their movements, are less markedly so than their compatriots the langurs. As regards food, macaques have a varied appetite, most, if not all, of them eagerly eating insects as well as seeds and fruits. Moreover, they have occasionally been observed to devour lizards, and it is reported that frogs also form part of their food on rare occasions; while one species is known to subsist partly on crustaceans. Their cheek-pouches are of very large size, and it is the general habit of these monkeys to stuff these receptacles as full as they will hold on every available occasion.

According to Mr. Blanford, from whose works the above accounts of their habits is paraphrased, the voice and gestures of all the macaques are similar, and differ markedly from those of the langurs. In regard to these points, the same writer gives an interesting quotation from the manuscript notes of Colonel Tickell— an excellent observer of the habits of Indian animals—which we repeat. Colonel Tickell says, "Anger is generally silent, or, at most, expressed by a low hoarse '*heu*,' not so gular or guttural as a growl. Ennui and a desire for company by a whining '*hom*.' Invitation, deprecation, entreaty, by a smacking of the lips and a display of the incisors into a regular broad grin, accompanied with a subdued grunting chuckle, highly expressive, but not to be rendered on paper. Fear and alarm by a loud harsh shriek, '*kra*' or '*kraouk*,' which serves also as a warning to the others who may be heedless of danger. Unlike the langurs and gibbons, they have no voice if calling to one another."

In confinement most of the species are docile if caught young; but old males that have been captured when full grown are sometimes exceedingly spiteful; and the present writer has a vivid recollection of a pig-tailed macaque formerly in the Zoological Gardens at Calcutta that was very ferocious, and would fly at every visitor who approached his cage with open mouth and the most menacing gestures. In their wild state it also appears that these monkeys will occasionally show fight. Thus Mr. Sterndale tells us that on one occasion during the Indian Mutiny he came across a party of rhesus macaques, among whom were several females with young ones. He endeavoured, without success, to run them down, in order to capture the latter, when he was deliberately charged by the old males of the party, the leader of whom he had to despatch with a pistol-bullet. Several of the species will breed in captivity. As a rule, their manners when in the latter state are the reverse of pleasant.

Since the number of species of macaques is very large, we shall select for especial notice only some of the better-known types, commencing with those with the tails so long that their length exceeds three-quarters of the combined length of the head and body, and concluding with those in which the length of this appendage is less than three-quarters of that of the head and body.

The Bonnet Monkey (*Macacus sinicus*).

One of the best and longest known of the longer-tailed macaques is the South Indian bonnet monkey, which is one of two closely allied species characterised by

THE BONNET MONKEY.

the circumstance that the hair of the crown of the head is lengthened, and arranged in a radiating manner from the middle line. A representation of this monkey is given in the accompanying woodcut, and in Fig. 3 of the coloured Plate.

This species takes its name from the crest of hair on the crown, which instead of coming over the forehead, as a rule stops short of that part of the head, and thus assumes a toque-like form. On the forehead the short hair is usually parted down the middle line. The fur, which is of moderate length, and generally straight and smooth, is brown or greyish-brown above, and pale brown, or whitish on the under-parts. The face and ears are flesh-coloured, and in some examples the ends of the hairs are ringed. The tail is generally nearly or quite as long as the head and body; the length of the two latter being about 20 inches.

This macaque, which occurs all over Southern India and extends westward to Bombay, is the common monkey of those regions, being found not only in the forests, but likewise in the towns, where it pillages the shops of the *bhanias*, or native grain-sellers. It is exceedingly mischievous, and a ready mimic, although Mr. Blanford believes that the rhesus monkey is its equal in these respects.

In Ceylon this monkey is replaced by the closely allied toque monkey (*M. pileatus*), which appears only to differ in colour, although the long hair of the crest of the head seems to be more generally continued on to the forehead. It is shown in Fig. 5 of the coloured Plate.

Among the Singalese this monkey is known as the Rilawa. Sir Emerson Tennent speaks of it as being " the universal pet and favourite of both natives and Europeans. The Tamil conjurors teach it to dance, and in their wanderings carry it from village to village, clad in a grotesque dress, to exhibit its lively performances." After all, however, the mimicry and amusing tricks of a monkey in captivity are a mere shadow of what they are in its native condition, so that persons who have only seen these animals in confinement have but a faint idea of their true nature.

THE CRAB-EATING MACAQUE (*Macacus cynomolgus*).

This species derives its name from its peculiar habit of feeding largely on crabs from the brackish water of the lagoons and swamps on the coast. It is the true macaque of Buffon, and is known to the Malays, apparently from its cry, as the Kra. This monkey is shown in Fig. 6 of the coloured Plate.

It may be at once distinguished from the bonnet monkey by the circumstance that the hair on the crown of the head is neither longer than the rest nor distinctly radiated from the middle. In some individuals there is, however, a trace of a crest, with slight radiation of the hair from one or more points on the forehead. As a rule, the general colour of the fur of the upper parts varies from a dusky or greyish-brown to a rufous or golden-brown; the under-parts being either light greyish-brown or nearly white. The hairs of adult individuals vary in colour in different parts of their length, and are ringed at their tips. The naked parts of the face and the callosities on the buttocks are flesh-coloured or dusky. The eyelids are either white or bluish-white. The tail is nearly as long as the head and body, the combined length of the two latter reaching to 22 inches.

In the dark and smaller variety of this common monkey the fur is dusky; while in the lighter or golden-rufous variety, its hair is flesh-colour.

The range of the crab-eating macaque is a very wide one, extending from Siam in the east through the Malay Peninsula into Lower Burma and the Arakan coast. It is also found in the Nicobar Islands in the Bay of Bengal, although Mr. Blanford considers that it has probably been introduced there by human agency.

What induced the ancestors of this monkey to forsake the usual simian food and take to a diet of crabs and insects it is difficult to conceive; unless, indeed, they may have been driven to it during a season of scarcity, and found it so much to their liking that they have continued it ever since. Be this as it may, there is no doubt whatever as to the crustacean-devouring proclivities of this species. For instance, Sir Arthur Phayre mentions that "these monkeys frequent the banks of salt-water creeks and devour shell-fish. In the cheek-pouches of a female were found the claws and body of a crab. There is not much on record concerning the habits of this monkey in its wild state beyond what is stated concerning its partiality for crabs, which can also, I believe, be said of the rhesus in the Bengal sanderbans." According to Colonel Tickell, as quoted by Mr. Blanford, the crab-eating macaque is common on the tidal creeks and rivers of Burma and Tenasserim,

THE LION-TAILED MONKEY ($\frac{1}{10}$ nat. size).

especially in the delta of the Irawadi. They go usually in small family parties of from five to fifteen individuals, including an old male and four or five females with their offspring. Their home is among the roots and boughs of the mangrove trees, and they spend a large portion of their time in searching for insects and crabs. From the constant presence of human beings on the water-ways near which they dwell, these monkeys become very tame, and can be easily approached. They will even, Mr. Blanford tells us, pick up rice or fruit thrown down to them. Still more remarkable is the facility with which they can swim and dive. Colonel Tickell states that on one occasion a male of this species that had been wounded and placed for security in a boat, jumped overboard and dived several times over to a distance of some fifty yards, in order to prevent recapture. Like most macaques, this species is gentle if captured at a sufficiently early age, but the old males always become

MACAQUES.

fierce and morose. On account of the white eyelids of this monkey care must be taken not to confound it with the mangabeys noticed above.

The Lion-Tailed Monkey (*Macacus silenus*).

With the peculiar-looking lion-tailed monkey of Western India, well represented in the woodcut on the opposite page, and also in Fig. 2 of the coloured Plate, we come to the first of the macaques in which the length of the tail is less than three-quarters of that of the head and body taken together.

The lion-tailed monkey, often incorrectly called the wanderu (a term which as we have seen, should be restricted to the langurs of Ceylon), may be distinguished from all the other species by its general black colour, and the enormous grey beard and ruff, which surrounds the black face, with the exception of the middle of the forehead, where it stops short. The fur is long, and the slender tail is tufted at its extremity, and measuring from half to three-quarters the united length of the head and body. The thin and tufted tail, like that of a lion, is one of the characteristic features of this species, and that from which it derives its name. The enormous ruff, totally concealing the ears, is, however, that which especially attracts attention, and gives the owner somewhat the appearance of a black-faced old man with shaggy whiskers and beard.

These monkeys inhabit the Malabar, or Western, Coast of India, from Cape Comorin to about the fourteenth parallel of latitude, being especially abundant in the districts of Travancore and Cochin. They restrict themselves to the forest-lands on the range of trappean mountains known as the Western Ghats, and are always found at a considerable elevation above the level of the sea. Dr. Jerdon says that they associate in troops of from twelve to twenty or more in number. They are excessively shy and wary, and when caught are sulky and savage in captivity, so that it is only with great difficulty that they can be taught to perform any feats of agility or mimicry.

The Bengal Monkey (*Macacus rhesus*).

Perhaps the best known of all the macaques is the common Bengal or rhesus monkey, the bandar of the Hindus, which is found all over Northern India. It is shown in Fig. 1 of the coloured Plate.

This monkey presents but little resemblance to the last species, having no trace of a beard or a ruff, and its colour being brown, with a tinge of grey. As a species it is characterised by the straightness of its moderately long hair, and also by the buttocks being naked for some distance round the callosities. The tail is about one-half the length of the head and body, and tapers regularly from base to tip, without any trace of a terminal tuft. The face, as well as the callosities on the buttocks, are flesh-coloured, except in the adults, when they are bright red.

In India the Bengal monkey is found continuously northward from the valley of the Godaveri to the Himalaya, extending to the west coast at Bombay. It inhabits the valley of Kashmir and surrounding regions, at elevations of and above four thousand feet. In the neighbourhood of the hill sanitarium of Simla these monkeys are found at an elevation of between eight and nine thousand feet above the sea-level; and it is one of the regular expeditions from Simla to ride or walk to see the monkeys on their own hill, which rejoices in the appropriate name of Jako. Here they are regularly fed by a fakir, who has taken up his abode on the same mountain, and they come down in troops at his well-known call. Indeed, these monkeys are almost invariably found in large droves; usually in the forests or more cultivated lands, but occasionally near and in the towns. Although not regarded as sacred, it appears that the rhesus monkey is frequently protected by the Hindus, and in Kashmir the writer has seen them forming part and parcel of the appanages of the temples. In several parts of India the Hindus have, indeed, a strong objection to the slaughter of these monkeys.

The rhesus is an intelligent creature, and, if captured young, is docile and easily taught. It is the common monkey carried about by itinerant jugglers in Northern India, by whom it is taught many amusing tricks. Old animals, more especially ' males, become vicious and spiteful.

In their wild state these monkeys make a hideous noise with their incessant chattering, and they are always mischievous. In addition to the consumption of large quantities of fruit and seeds, they also subsist on insects

THE BENGAL MONKEY.

and spiders, and parties of them may frequently be seen carefully searching the ground for these delicacies. Mr. Blanford tells us that the rhesus, like the crab-eating macaque, swims well, and takes readily to the water.

Professor Ball relates a curious anecdote of these monkeys: "When at Malwa Tal [near the Himalayan Station of Naini Tal], which is one of the lakes where I spent a day, I was warned that, in passing under a landslip which slopes down to the lake, I should be liable to have stones thrown at me by monkeys. Regarding this as being possibly a traveller's tale, I made a particular point of going to the spot in order to see what could have given rise to it. As I approached the base of the landslip on the north side of the lake, I saw a number of brown monkeys (*M. rhesus*) rush to the sides and across the top of the slip, and presently pieces of loosened stone and shale came tumbling down near where I stood. I fully satisfied myself that this was not merely accidental; for I distinctly saw one monkey industriously, with both forepaws, and with obvious *malice prepense,* pushing the loose shingle off a shoulder of rock. I then tried the effect of throwing stones at them, and this made them quite angry, and the number of fragments which they then set rolling was speedily doubled. This, though it does not actually amount to throwing or projecting an object by monkeys as a means of offence, comes very near to the same thing, and makes me think that there may be truth in the stories of their throwing fruit at people from trees."

It is probable that the Bengal monkey ranges to the north-east into Assam and Upper Burma, and thence into the province of Yunnan, in Western China. In Szechuen, and eastwards into the interior, it is replaced by the closely allied Chinese rhesus (*M. lasiotis*).

Another nearly related species is the Himalayan macaque (*M. assamensis*), found at considerable elevations in the Eastern Himalaya, Assam, the Mishmi Hills, and parts of Upper Burma. According to Mr. Blanford it is distinguished from the Bengal monkey by the wavy nature of the hair, which in the Himalayan specimens assumes a decidedly woolly texture. Dr. Anderson tells us that it is larger than the last-named species, and more powerfully and compactly built, and thus approaches the under-mentioned pig-tailed monkey. Mr. Blanford further observes that, whether wild or tame, it is more sluggish in its movements than the Bengal monkey; and also that there is a slight difference between the voice of the two species.

THE PIG-TAILED MONKEY (*Macacus nemestrinus*).

The next species of macaque we select for notice is the one represented in the figure on the following page, and commonly known as the pig-tailed monkey. It is distinguished from those we have already mentioned by the shorter tail, which is thin and whip-like, and only about one-third the length of the head and body.

It is a comparatively stout and long-limbed monkey, easily recognised by the hair radiating from the centre of the head, the slender pig-like tail, and the very projecting muzzle, which approximates to that of the baboons. Dr. Anderson compares an adult full-grown male to a good-sized mastiff, both as regards size and strength. This monkey has been long known to science, and was described by Buffon as the maimon. It inhabits the province of Tenasserim, and thence extends southwards into the Malay Peninsula, and is also found in the islands of Borneo and Sumatra.

The voice and manners of this monkey are described as being very similar to those of the Bengal monkey. Its habits were long ago described by Sir Stamford Raffles from specimens observed by him in Sumatra; and this writer relates that the inhabitants of that island train these monkeys to ascend the cocoa-palms, and select and then throw down the ripest fruit. It seems probable that it must be only young or female individuals that are thus taught to serve their masters, since the old males are exceedingly fierce and vicious, and from their size and powerful build are formidable antagonists.

The Burmese Pig-Tailed Monkey (*Macacus leoninus*).

In Arakan and Upper Burma the place of the pig-tailed monkey is taken by the nearly allied species, known as the Burmese pig-tailed monkey, represented in the woodcut on p. 108.

This animal may be easily distinguished from its relations by its shorter limbs, shorter muzzle and longer hair, as well as by the black horseshoe-like crest on

THE PIG-TAILED MONKEY (⅓ nat. size).

the temples above the eyes, which stands out in marked contrast to the general brown colour of the rest of the fur. Moreover, the short tail, which is generally carried over the back, is more hairy, and more or less distinctly tufted at the end. The males are dark brown above, but the females somewhat lighter; the face in both sexes being of a dusky flesh-colour, while the combined length of the head and body is about 23 inches; the tail only measures some 8 inches, exclusive of the hair at its extremity, which adds another 2 inches to its length.

The late Mr. E. Blyth, who speaks of this species as the long-haired pig-tailed monkey, in contradistinction to the short-haired pig-tailed monkey (*M. nemestrinus*), says that it does not appear to be at all common, and that it chiefly inhabits the range of limestone mountains from the north of Arakan to an undetermined distance southwards. The Burmese pig-tailed monkey serves to connect the other species with the Bengal monkey.

The Brown Stump-Tailed Monkey (*Macacus arctoides*).

The brown stump-tailed monkey may be taken as an example of another group of macaques inhabiting Burma and the Malayan region, and thence ranging into China, Tibet, and Japan, and characterised by the reduction of their tails to a mere rudimentary stump.

The present species is characterised by the length of its dark brown or blackish-brown hair, which may measure more than 4 inches; and also by the bright red hue of the naked portions of the face and buttocks. As in the last-named species, the terminal portions of the hairs of old individuals are decorated with rings of different colours. The length of the head and body is probably about 24 inches, while that of the tail does not exceed 1 or 2 inches.

This monkey appears to range from the southern parts of Assam into Upper Burma, and is also found in Cochin China. We have not, however, full information on the subject of its geographical range, and absolutely none as to its habits, although it is said to be an inhabitant of hilly districts.

It has its tail sparsely clad with hair, or naked in old individuals. In the coldest and least accessible forest of Eastern Tibet the stump - tailed macaques are represented by a species (*M. tibetanus*) characterised by its larger size, and the thickly-haired tail. We have already seen how the same elevated regions are inhabited by a langur; and if Europeans ever obtain free access to Tibet, it will be an interesting subject of investigation to discover on what these monkeys subsist during the long and cold winters of that country.

The Moor macaque (*M. maurus*), which has received several distinct names— *M. ochreatus*, for instance—represents the stump-tailed monkeys in Borneo, Celebes, and probably some of the other Malayan islands, and is a dark and black-faced species.

In Japan the group is represented by the Japanese macaque (*M. fuscatus*), which is one of those in which the tail is thickly haired. We have, however, still much to learn as to the number of species of these stump-tailed macaques, and their exact geographical distribution; while information as to their mode of life is desirable.

The Magot, or Barbary Macaque (*Macacus inuus*).

In the preceding sections we have seen how a gradual shortening of the tail can be traced as we pass from the bonnet macaque, through the Bengal monkey and its allies, to the pig-tailed, and thence to the stump-tailed group. From the latter it is but a step to the total loss of the tail; and the magot, or Barbary macaque (the Barbary ape of many authors), presents us with the culminating member of the series. This total absence of a tail was long regarded as a reason for separating the magot as a distinct genus from the other macaques; but it is quite clear that there is no sort of justification for this view. The species is represented in Fig. 4 of the coloured Plate, as well as in the woodcut on the following page.

In addition to being the only tailless macaque, the magot is the sole existing species of the group which is not Asiatic. The magot inhabits, indeed, the north-west corner of Africa, in the districts of Morocco and Algeria, being especially common in the latter country in the neighbourhood of the city of Constantine. It is also found across the Straits in Gibraltar, and some of the neighbouring parts of Spain, but whether indigenous there, or introduced from the opposite

THE MAGOT ($\frac{1}{6}$ nat. size).

continent by human agency, does not appear to be clearly made out. The wide separation of this macaque from its Asiatic congeners suggests that it is the direct descendant from those extinct species which are found in the later geological deposits of various parts of Europe, at a date when we know that the genus was already in existence in India.

That the magot is the *Pithecus* of the ancients there is not a doubt, as the description given by Aristotle is enough to identify it. This species was indeed, in all probability, the only tailless member of the order with which the ancients were acquainted. It was, moreover, the animal from which the ancient Greeks obtained such knowledge as they possessed of human anatomy; and an account of its anatomy, given by Galen, has been handed down to our own times. The name Magot is of French origin, and was applied by Buffon.

This monkey is as large as a good-sized dog; and the upper parts of its body, and the outer sides of the limbs, are of a light yellowish-brown, becoming somewhat deeper on the head, and also along a line bordering the cheeks. The under-parts are of a dull yellowish-white, while the naked portions of the face, hands, and feet, as well as the callosities on the buttocks, are flesh-coloured. The rudiment of the tail consists merely of a little fold of skin, having no sort of connection with the end of the backbone.

One of the best early original accounts of the magot is given by the French naturalist, René-Luiche Desfontaines, who resided for some time in Algeria, during the closing decades of the last century. This writer observes that the magots "live in troops in the forests of the Atlas Mountains nearest to the seashore, and are so common at Stora that the surrounding trees are sometimes covered with them. They live upon the cones of the pine, sweet chestnuts, and the figs, melons, pistachio nuts, and vegetables which they steal from the gardens of the Arabs, in spite of all the pains taken to exclude these mischievous animals. Whilst in the act of committing these thefts, two or three detach themselves from the general body, and keep watch from the tops of the surrounding trees or rocks; and as soon as these sentinels perceive the approach of danger, they give warning to their companions, who presently scamper off with whatever they have been able to lay their hands on."

The Gibraltar "Apes of the Rock." A military officer, formerly stationed at Gibraltar, writing in 1880, has given the following excellent account in the *Field* newspaper of the magots at that place. After stating that Gibraltar is the only European locality where monkeys occur, the author observes, that young magots "may frequently be seen in summer in the Moors' part of the market-place, brought over from Barbary; and, doubtless, the ancestors of the existing colony were similarly imported. The census frequently taken by the sergeant in charge of the signalling department gives their present number as twenty-five. . . . These apes were formerly very numerous on the rock, and there were several gangs of them, but they were so predaceous in their habits, coming down to the gardens in the upper part of the town, and stealing fruit, especially figs, that they were killed by trap or poison, so as nearly to bring about their extinction. In November 1856, a garrison order was published for the guidance of the signalmaster," which forbade the destruction of the monkeys, and gave directions as to their being counted at regular intervals. "From that time," continues our author, "the register has been very regularly kept by the signalmaster. There were only four or five at this time, and but three in 1863, when General Sir W. Codrington, who was then governor, saved them from destruction by a fresh importation from Africa. The following note occurs in the Journal of the 26th May 1863, 'Turned out four apes, wild from Barbary, two males and two females, all young.' After some time the newcomers made friends with the apes of the old stock; and the band increased, but very slowly, however, owing to the great preponderance of females, until the present time, and it may be expected, as the signalmaster observes, now that there are two adult and rival males, that it will divide. Those who wish to see them will do well to remember that their haunts on the rock are determined by the direction of the wind. They prefer the ledges of the [to man] inaccessible, abrupt escarpment of the Mediterranean face; but cannot stand the cold damp Levanter wind which, as its name indicates, blows from the eastward, and compels them to resort to the western slopes on the town side of the rock. At the bottom of Charles V.'s wall, overhanging the Alameda Gardens, is a favourite spot. On the western side, the Monkeys' Alameda, a small bushy plateau half-way down the precipice, is another choice resort, as is also Monkeys' Cave, close to the sea. Of late years they have become sufficiently confident in their friend and protector, the signalmaster, frequently to enter the enclosure of the station, especially in the summer drought, when they come for water. In a letter to me, of the 3rd of May, Sergeant Brown [the signalmaster] says: 'The monkeys are sitting on the wall of the station as I write this—the first time this season that they have come up for water.'

"Their food consists of grass (the young blades of which I have seen them eating with avidity), and of a variety of roots and bulbs; those of the yellow Cape oxalis being much sought after. The fruits of the palmetto—*monkey-dates*, as the Gibraltar urchins, who also much appreciate the little brown viscous clusters, call them—are greedily devoured when ripe. The signalmaster has never observed them take any food left in their way at the station but a few grapes, of which they seemed very fond.

"In Sergeant Brown's letters I find several notes concerning these interesting animals, which may be here introduced. 'In the spring of 1872, two were shot by a young officer, who had been but a short time in the garrison, and probably did not know that the monkeys were so strictly preserved. He replaced them with either two or three of the same kind from Barbary, but the rock monkeys killed them. Some years ago, when first stationed at Gibraltar, I saw a very large male monkey in captivity at the signal station. He had been captured in one of the ammunition boxes in the enclosure, baited with fruit. It had taken the united efforts of three artillerymen, who rushed upon him with their cloaks, to secure him. After a while he got reconciled to his fate, but from his position, chained to the wall and overlooking the eastern precipice, he was always scanning the cliffs in great apparent anxiety and fear, which was quite unmistakable when his late comrades appeared in sight. If he had rejoined them he would probably have been torn in pieces. In June 1874,' says Sergeant Brown, 'a fire broke out on a Sunday afternoon, and a strong south-west wind carried it up the slope of the cliff. . . . The monkeys seemed in great distress while the fire was raging, and a full-grown one was missed afterwards, but several births kept up the total. In the spring of 1875 the troop consisted of six full-grown females and two large males, with several young ones. One of the males was very mangy, had a bowed back, and appeared very old; the other, a full-grown powerful monkey, I should judge to be nearly 3 feet long in the body, and standing nearly 5 feet high when stretched up. He was lord of the tribe, kept it in order by chasing or biting any refractory member, and took the lead when shifting from one side of the rock to the other, which they usually did a few hours before the wind changed. I missed the large male on August 7th, 1875, and in the beginning of September he was found dead.' The death of this monkey seems to have been a serious blow to the community, for writing again on the last day of 1877 Sergeant Brown says, 'There are now four very large adult females, four younger and rather smaller, four females, and one male of middle size, probably four years old, and five small ones just entering on their third year. I think there are four females and one male, but am not certain yet. There have been no births since 1875. They still travel together from place to place, but straggle more, and seem to squabble more among themselves since the old male died.'

"In a letter, May 3rd, 1880, the sergeant says, 'The monkeys are all doing well; the young male born in 1874 is now master of the troop. There were four young ones last spring, two of which had about an inch rudiment of tail. I expect seven or eight births this summer. One large female was found by a labourer on May 20th, 1879, looking very sick; he gave it some coffee, but it died; its breasts were full of milk, and it had probably just given birth to a young one, which was not found. Last July I saw two full-grown females, each with a young one; they sat down close to each other on the path, and were chattering and examining one another's young, when the male monkey came and sat down between them, and all three were chattering away together for several minutes. Through the summer the male was nearly always carrying one or other of the young ones.'

"Sometimes a fight occurs among the monkeys, when it is surprising to witness the rapidity with which they will follow an offender down the stupendous precipice of the eastern face; tumbling one after another, and catching at bits of bush or projecting ledges on their way, they descend hundreds of feet in a moment or two. Sometimes the sergeant dresses wounds on them, probably from this cause, but they soon heal up."

In captivity the magot, at least during youth, is lively, active, intelligent, and good-tempered; but with advancing years it becomes sullen and capricious, and finally spiteful and capricious. The French naturalist, Frederic Cuvier, observes that the natural instinct, which causes these monkeys when in a wild condition to associate together in troops, leads solitary individuals in confinement to make friends of such animals as they are thrown in contact with. Such animals, if sufficiently small, are carried about by the magots, who express their satisfaction by hugging and caressing their burdens, and become furious when any attempts are made to remove them.

The magot is perhaps brought oftener to Europe than any other monkey; its native climate being such as to permit of its existing with tolerable comfort in more northerly regions.

EXTINCT MACAQUES.

Under the heading of the magot, incidental reference has been made to the occurrence of fossil species of macaques, but as this is a subject of considerable interest in regard to the present geographical distribution of these monkeys, we must say a few words more. Asia being the headquarters of the group, it would only be naturally expected that we should find these monkeys represented in a fossil state on that continent. As a matter of fact, with the exception of India, we know comparatively little of the geology of Asia. In India, however, fossil remains of macaques are found in the caverns of Madras, and in certain deposits of comparatively late age in the Punjab which belong to that epoch of geological history known as the Pliocene.

In Europe fossil macaques occur in fresh-water deposits belonging to the same Pliocene period, both in the south of France, in Switzerland, and also in the north of Italy, in the valley of the Arno. The occurrence of these extinct monkeys need not imply any very great change of climate in those regions. The case is, however, very different with the single fragment of the jaw of a macaque which has been found fossil in our own country, near the village of Grays, in Essex, in strata which belong to the latest or Pleistocene epoch of geological history. This monkey must have lived in England during the time when man had already made his appearance; and there is no reasonable doubt that the climate must then have been considerably milder than it is at the present day, since it is impossible to imagine that monkeys could survive our English winters, even if they could find a living in our woods during the summer. We have already mentioned that these extinct European macaques may be those from which the magot has taken origin.

In addition to these extinct macaques, there occur in the Pliocene rocks of Attica and the south of France other monkeys which appear to indicate a transition from the macaques to the langurs. These monkeys, which are respectively known as the mesopitheque and the dolichopitheque, have indeed short and stout limbs like those of the macaques, but skulls resembling those of the langur. Unfortunately we shall never know the structure of their soft parts, so that their exact relationships cannot be determined.

The Black Ape.

Genus *Cynopithecus.*

The Island of Celebes is remarkable for possessing several altogether peculiar types of Mammals, among which is the so-called black ape (*Cynopithecus niger*), the sole representative of a genus in some respects connecting the preceding group of the macaques with the following one of the baboons. It was represented many years ago by one living example in the old menagerie at the Tower, and by another in that of Exeter Change. At that time, however, the true habitat of this animal was quite unknown, Cuvier suggesting that it came from the Philippines; but its home was subsequently found to be Celebes. This monkey, which is shown in the accompanying figure, is a decidedly handsome animal, the whole of the fur, as well as the naked parts of the face, hands, and feet, being of an intense black, the only exception to this coloration being the large callosities on the buttocks, which are flesh-coloured. The hair of the body is long and woolly, but that on the limbs shorter. The tail is represented by a mere tubercle, not more than an inch in length. The face is characterised by the marked protrusion of the muzzle, which is abruptly terminated; the nostrils opening obliquely, and placed some distance behind the extremity of the muzzle. It is this position of the nostrils which connects this monkey with the macaques, and distinguishes it from the true baboons, in which they are situated at the very end of the still more produced muzzle. The sides of the face have the peculiar longitudinal swellings characteristic of the latter, and the cheek-pouches are very capacious. On the top of the head the black ape has a broad tuft of long hairs, curling backwards, and forming a very characteristic crest.

The earlier specimens of this monkey brought to England are described as being rather violent in temper, and tyrannising over the other monkeys with which they were placed in company. Others, however, are stated to have been more

THE BLACK APE ($\frac{1}{6}$ nat. size).

gentle in disposition, and thus very different from the fierce baboons. But few specimens of this monkey have been exhibited of late years in the London Zoological Society's Gardens.

Dr. F. H. Guillemard, in his *Cruise of the Yacht Marchesa*, states that his party found the black ape very common in the forest near Wallace Bay, in Celebes; and describes these animals as swinging from bough to bough in small flocks. This monkey is also found in the small Island of Batchian, lying to the eastward of Celebes, and forming a part of the Molucca group. On account of the circumstance that none of the other Mammals of Celebes extend to Batchian, Mr. Wallace is inclined to consider that the black ape "has been accidentally introduced by the roaming Malays, who often carry about with them monkeys and other animals.

This is rendered more probable by the fact that the animal is not found in Gilolo, which is only separated from Batchian by a very narrow strait. The introduction may have been very recent, as in a fertile and unoccupied island such an animal would multiply rapidly." In its arboreal habits, and predilection for fruit, the black ape is essentially a macaque, and not a baboon.

The Gelada Baboon.

Genus *Theropithecus.*

The extraordinary-looking animal represented in the accompanying woodcut is our first example of the group of baboons, or dog-faced monkeys, so called from the

THE GELADA BABOON (⅛ nat. size).

great prolongation of their muzzles, which far exceeds that obtaining in the black ape, and gives to them an expression quite different from that of any other members of the order. We reserve our remarks for the other peculiarities of the baboons till we come to the more typical representations of the group mentioned under the next generic heading, and here content ourselves with indicating the chief characteristics of the species represented in the woodcut.

The gelada (*Theropithecus gelada*) is an inhabitant of the southern parts of Abyssinia, and is distinguished from the true baboons by the circumstance that the nostrils are placed some distance behind the extremity of the snout. In this respect, therefore, the gelada forms a connecting link between the black ape of Celebes and the true baboons.

This animal is of comparatively large size, and of a dark colour; the shoulders, back, rump, and fore-arms, as well as all the naked parts, being of a deep black, whereas the head, whiskers, neck, and sides are of a sooty grey, sometimes tinged with brown. The most peculiar feature about the creature, is, however, the great mantle of long black hair growing from the neck, and flowing over the shoulders. The chest is naked, while the moderately long tail is cylindrical, and furnished with a long black tuft at the end.

Taken altogether the aspect of the gelada forcibly suggests a large black poodle dog, with an unusually abundant mane. A good account of the habits of this baboon has been given by Dr. Rüppell, who travelled many years ago in Abyssinia. From this it appears that its mode of life is very similar to that of the true baboons. The geladas live in large troops, and are especially addicted to rocky regions, whence they descend to plunder the cultivated grounds of the natives, occasionally entering into conflict with troops of the Arabian baboon.

A few examples of the gelada have been exhibited from time to time in the Gardens of the London Zoological Society.

The True Baboons.

Genus *Cynocephalus*.

With the true baboons we come to the most hideous and repulsive-looking members of the order of Primates; their repulsive appearance being only equalled by the fierce and untamable disposition of several of the group. A party of these creatures is shown among their natural surroundings in our coloured Plate.

All the baboons are confined to Africa and the countries lying on the north of the Red Sea, so that they are totally absent from the Oriental region. They are found over the whole of Africa; but, as is so generally the case, are represented by a greater variety of species on the west coast than elsewhere, and it is also in that region that the most hideous representatives of the group are to be found. Next to the Man-like Apes, the baboons include the largest members of the Primates, some of the species being as large as a pointer dog.

While agreeing with the gelada baboon in the great length of their snouts, the true baboons are readily distinguished from that species by the nostrils being placed at the very extremity of their snout; indeed, in the Arabian baboon they actually project slightly beyond the upper lip, as is the case in most dogs. This canine form of countenance led the ancient Greeks and Romans to apply the name *Cynocephali* (dog-headed) to these animals; and it is this name which has been adopted in scientific phraseology as the distinctive appellation of the group. This great prolongation of the snout shows that the baboons are the lowest of the Old World monkeys, and they bear the most marked signs of relationship with the inferior orders of Mammals.

In addition to their long snouts, baboons are likewise distinguished by the large proportionate size of their skulls, this being most markedly the case with some of the West African forms. Moreover, the bones forming the upper jaws are greatly inflated, so as to give a swollen look to this part of the face in some of the species. They may also carry prominent oblique ridges, which form the support for the peculiar fleshy tumour-like structures occurring in certain West African examples.

In all the baboons the callosities on the buttocks are unusually large, and may be very brightly coloured. The tail is never very long, and may be short. The arms and legs, or, as they may be better termed, fore- and hind-legs, are nearly equal in length, and are thus far better adapted for progress on the ground than for climbing. Indeed, none of the baboons appear to be adepts at climbing, and many of them pass almost their whole time on the ground. As we shall have occasion to notice more fully later on, several species of this group show an especial predilection for rocky ground, and are accustomed to go in large troops—this association being probably necessary for defence against the attacks of leopards and other Carnivores, to which their terrestrial habits render them peculiarly liable.

Their defence does not, however, rest solely on the strength of numbers; for the male baboons, which are considerably superior in size and strength to their consorts, are armed with tusks of the most formidable dimensions. Indeed, a bite from one of these animals must be almost, if not quite, as severe and dangerous as a leopard's; and there are instances on record where leopards have been successfully attacked and mastered by a few old male baboons.

The great size of the head, coupled with their general bodily conformation, renders all the baboons much less capable of assuming and maintaining the erect posture than any of the other Old World monkeys. They are, indeed, accustomed to go almost invariably on all-fours; and when on tolerably flat ground can gallop at a pace that requires a horse to overtake them. When brought to bay, a baboon will, however, stand on its hind-quarters to defend itself more readily.

Habits. In the wild state scarcely any kind of food comes amiss to baboons; and although the bulk of their nutriment may take the form of seeds, fruits, roots, and the gum which exudes from the stems of many of the African acacias, they also search for and eat insects, lizards, and birds' eggs. In regions where cultivated lands exist much harm is done by the nocturnal excursions of baboons. During such raids most travellers agree in saying that a certain number of the troop are selected to act as sentinels and to give timely warning of the approach of an enemy. How much credence is to be given to the statements that on these occasions the marauders are accustomed to range themselves in long lines leading from the cultivated ground to their homes, and to pass the stolen plunder from hand to hand, it is not for us to decide.

In disposition all the baboons are the reverse of amiable, and they are accustomed to fly into paroxysms of fury at any object which enrages or excites them; but some of the species are capable of being more or less completely tamed, and even learning a certain number of tricks; and it appears that members of one species were habitually tamed by the ancient Egyptians.

We shall have occasion again to refer to the early period at which baboons must have been known to the Egyptians, and we have already mentioned that they take their scientific name from their ancient Greek title. To show that they were known in Europe at least two centuries ago, we extract an account which, though often quoted, is so interesting and so quaint that it will bear another repetition. This work is by one Ludolph, and relates to the ancient Ethiopia, the modern Abyssinia; the English translation being published in the year 1684. "Of apes," writes Ludolph, "there are infinite flocks up and down in the mountains, a thousand and more together; there they leave no stone unturned. If they meet with one that two or three cannot lift, they call for more aid, and all for the sake of the wormes that lye under; a sort of diet which they relish exceedingly. They are very greedy after emmets. So that having found an emmet-hill, they presently surround it, and, laying their fore-paws with the hollow downward upon the ant-heap, as fast as the emmets creep into their treacherous palms, they lick 'em off with great comfort to their stomachs; and there they will lie till there is not an emmet left. They are also pernicious to fruit and apples, and will destroy whole fields and gardens unless they be carefully look'd after. For they are very cunning, and will never venture in till the return of their spies, which they send always before; who giving information that all things are safe, in they rush with their whole body, and make a quick dispatch. Therefore they go very quiet and silent to their prey; and if their young chance to make a noise, they chastise them with their fists; but if they find the coast clear, then every one hath a different noise to express his joy. Nor could there be any to hinder them from further multiplying, but that they fall sometimes into the ruder hands of the wild beasts, which they have no way to avoid but by a timely flight, or by creeping into the clefts of the rocks. If they find no safety in flight, they make a virtue of necessity, stand their ground, and, filling their paws full of dust or sand, fling it into the eyes of their assailant, and then to their heels again."

Although Ludolph may have mixed up some other monkeys with them, there can be little doubt but that in the main this marvellous account refers to the Arabian baboon, which is still so common in Abyssinia. This identification is strongly supported by his mention of the large number of individuals in a troop, by the reference to rocks, by the search after insects, and also by the allusion to encounters with leopards. It must, however, be confessed that the figures of monkeys with which Ludolph's narrative is illustrated, bear but little resemblance to baboons, although this may well be explained by the degree of licence which the engravers of his epoch seem to have allowed themselves in such matters.

We now proceed to notice in detail the better known of the various species of baboons, commencing with the more typical ones with comparatively long tails, and concluding with the others, like the drill and mandrill, in which these appendages are reduced to their smallest dimensions. Our first example will be

The Arabian or Sacred Baboon (*Cynocephalus hamadryas*).

The Arabian, or sacred baboon, is the species so commonly represented on the ancient monuments of Egypt, and may be easily recognised by its generally ashy-

THE ARABIAN BABOON (⅛ nat. size).

grey colour, and the large mane with which the neck and shoulders of the males are covered, as is well shown in our illustration. The males of this species are about as large as a good-sized pointer dog. The tail is of considerable length, and terminates in a tuft of long hair. The face has long whiskers of a slaty colour, and is itself, like the ears, flesh-coloured. The hands are black, and the large naked callosities on the buttocks bright red. The shaggy mane on the neck and

BABOONS.

shoulders of the males extends backwards over a considerable portion of the body; and all the hairs are ringed with different colours, so as to produce that speckled appearance common to so many African monkeys. The females and young are quite devoid of this mane; the former being nearly as large as the males. The snout is very long, and has not the prominent tumour-like swellings characterising the short-tailed baboons. The nostrils project somewhat in front of the plane of the upper lip, like those of a dog, and are similarly divided by a vertical furrow. The eyes are surrounded by a light-coloured ring; and the whiskers are brushed back so as to cover the ears. If the gelada baboon be rightly compared to a black French poodle, the males of the present species might be still more appropriately likened to a grey one, did such a creature exist.

The Arabian baboon, as its name implies, inhabits Arabia, but it is more common on the African continent, in Abyssinia and the Sudan. It is not now found in Egypt, but it may have been in ancient times; although, on the other hand, it is quite probable that it may have been imported by the ancient Egyptians from the Sudan. It is just possible that the animal mentioned in the Scriptures under the name of satyr may be this species.

Early History. Among the ancient Egyptians the baboon occupied a prominent place in the long series of sacred animals, and was consecrated to the god Thoth. When sculptured by itself, it is the male that is represented, and it is always placed in a seated position, with the hands resting on the knees; the mane investing the body like a huge cloak. Hermopolis, the city of Thoth, was especially devoted to the cult of these animals; while in Thebes a special necropolis was arranged for the preservation of their mummified bodies. In spite, however, of its sacred character, the ancient Egyptians, if we may trust their sculptures, were not averse to making use of the sacred baboon in the ordinary affairs of life. For instance, there is a bas-relief extant representing a fruit-bearing sycamore, in the branches of which are three monkeys, which from their long snouts, well-developed tails, and thickly-haired shoulders and necks, may be at once recognised as Arabian baboons. On either side of the tree are two slaves, with baskets laden with sycamore-figs, others of which they are receiving from the hands of the baboons. It thus appears that the ancient Egyptians had succeeded in training these intractable animals to gather fruit and hand them to their masters, precisely after the fashion that the modern Malays are said to have trained a langur in Sumatra to perform a similar kind of service; the fruit in the one case being sycamore-figs, and in the other cocoa-nuts.

In addition to being represented on the monuments of Egypt, it appears highly probable that of two large monkeys sculptured on a bas-relief on one of the obelisks brought by Sir Henry Layard from Nimroud, the one depicted with a heavy mantle of fur on the shoulders is intended for the Arabian baboon.

Habits. Under the general heading of baboons we have already alluded to Ludolph's account of this species in the seventeenth century. There are many later descriptions of the habits of this species, but we shall content ourselves with some of the more recent of these. Mr. Blanford, in his account of the Natural History of Abyssinia, relates his first meeting with these baboons when on the march to Magdala in the following words:—" On rising the next morning I saw a singular spectacle. A large troop of baboons, at least two hundred in number, were hunting for any corn dropped upon the ground in the place where the horses had been picketed. They were the first I had seen, though the sight of these uncouth monkeys soon became familiar enough. The species (*C. hamadryas*) is the well-known dog-faced baboon of North-Eastern Africa and Arabia, the same which is frequently represented on Egyptian monuments. The male is a most formidable-looking animal, something between a lion and a French poodle in appearance, with long hair over his shoulders and fore-parts."

In another part of the same work the writer just quoted observes that in Abyssinia this baboon " was met with everywhere, from the plains around Annesley Bay to the top of the Dalanta plateau, although most abundant, perhaps, in the tropical and subtropical parts of the country. I saw a small herd close to Theodore's old camp at Baba, on the Dalanta plateau, at about nine thousand feet of elevation. In the passes leading from the table-land to the coast, immense numbers were constantly seen, and the animals evidently keep much to the sides of rocky ravines.

"The herds vary in number; some cannot include much less than from two hundred and fifty to three hundred monkeys of all ages. The old males usually take the lead when the troop is moving; some of them also bringing up the rear; others placing themselves on high rocks or bushes, and keeping a sharp look-out after enemies. A troop collected on a rocky crag presents a most singular appearance. I several times saw large numbers assembled around springs in the evening in the thirsty Shoho country between Komayle and Senafé. On such occasions every jutting rock, every little stone more prominent than the rest, was occupied by a patriarch of the herd, who sat, with the gravity and watchfulness befitting his grizzled hair, waiting patiently until the last of his human rivals had slaked his own thirst and that of his cattle. Around, the females were mainly occupied in taking care of the young; the smaller monkeys amusing themselves by gamboling about. Occasionally, if a young monkey became too noisy, or interfered with the repose of his seniors, he 'caught it' in most unmistakable style, and was dismissed with many cuffs, a wiser if not a better monkey."

The same writer mentions that the food of this baboon consists mainly of small fruits, berries, and seeds; although young shoots and buds of trees form a portion of its diet. Like the rest of its kind, it avoids forests and trees, and keeps mainly to the open country, preferring rocky spots. When it climbs, it does so in a heavy and ungainly manner, very unlike the active movements of the generality of monkeys. Its movements, when on the ground and in a hurry, partake more of the nature of a steady gallop than the bounding motion of other monkeys.

As Mr. Blanford observes, the association of these baboons in such large troops is doubtless for the purpose of mutual protection. The old males are, indeed, formidable antagonists, and there are many anecdotes of their attacking, or at least threatening, men. From the circumstance that none of the members of the Abyssinian expedition were attacked by these animals, Mr. Blanford is, however, of opinion that it is but seldom that such onslaughts take place. There is one well-authenticated instance of a troop combining to attack a leopard which had carried off one of their number.

Sir Samuel Baker's Observations.

We conclude our notice of the species with two accounts given by Sir Samuel Baker, when in the Sudan. "Troops of baboons," observes Sir Samuel, "are now exceedingly numerous, as, the country being entirely dried up, they are forced to the river for water, and the shady banks covered with berry-bearing shrubs induce them to remain. It is very amusing to watch these great male baboons stalking majestically along, followed by a large herd of all ages, the mothers carrying the little ones upon their backs, the latter with a regular jockey-seat riding most comfortably, while at other times they relieve the monotony of the position by sprawling at full length and holding on by their mothers' back hair. Suddenly a sharp-eyed young ape discovers a bush well covered with berries, and, his greedy munching being quickly observed, a general rush of youngsters takes place, and much squabbling for the best place ensues among the boys; this ends in great uproar, when down comes a great male, who cuffs one, pulls another by the hair, bites another on the hind-quarters just as he thinks he has escaped, drags back a would-be deserter by his tail and shakes him thoroughly; and thus he shortly restores order, preventing all further disputes by sitting under the bush and quietly enjoying the berries by himself. These baboons have a great variety of expressions, that may perhaps represent their vocabulary. A few of these I begin to understand, such as the notes of alarm and the cry to direct attention; thus, when I am sitting alone beneath the shade of a tree to watch their habits, they are at first not quite certain what kind of a creature I may be, and they utter a peculiar cry to induce me to move and show myself more distinctly."

On another occasion when a troop of about a hundred of these baboons were observed gathering gum from the mimosa trees, Sir Samuel Baker was asked by the natives whether Lady Baker would like to have a girrit, as these creatures are called by the Arabs of the Sudan. "Being answered in the affirmative, away dashed the three hunters in full gallop after the astonished apes, who, finding themselves pursued, went off at their best speed. The ground was rough, being full of broken hollows covered scantily with mimosas, and the stupid baboons, instead of turning to the right into the rugged and steep valley of Settite, where they would have been secure from the agageers [swordsmen], kept a straight course before the horses. It was a curious hunt. Some of the very young baboons were riding on their mothers' backs; these were now going at their best pace, holding on to their maternal steeds, and looking absurdly human; but in a few minutes, as we closely followed the Arabs, we were all in the midst of the herd, and with great dexterity two of the agageers, while at full speed, swooped like falcons from their saddles, and seized each a half-grown ape by the back of the neck, and hoisted them upon the necks of the horses. Instead of biting, as I had expected, the astonished captives sat astride of the horses, and clung tenaciously to the necks of their steeds, screaming with fear. The hunt was over, and we halted to secure the prisoners. Dismounting, to my surprise the Arabs immediately stripped from a mimosa several thongs of bark, and having tied the baboons by the neck, they gave them a merciless whipping with their powerful coorbatches of hippopotamus hide." This cruel treatment, which was eventually stopped by Sir Samuel Baker, was intended to make the unfortunate baboons docile, and prevent their biting.

The doguera baboon (*C. doguera*) is a closely allied species or variety, also found in Abyssinia. It is of a more olive colour than the sacred baboon. Dr. Anderson describes a male preserved in the Museum at Calcutta as being of a uniform yellowish-olive colour on the whiskers and all over the body, above and below, except on the hands and feet, which are nearly black. The coarse hair on the fore-part of the body is about 6 inches in length, and is ashy-grey in colour for the first 2 inches, while the remainder is banded with nine rings of orange and black.

The Chacma Baboon (*Cynocephalus porcarius*).

The species last noticed is an inhabitant of the countries bordering on the Red Sea littoral and the Upper Nile valley, but to reach the habitat of the chacma, or pig-tailed baboon, we have to travel to the southern extremity of the African continent. The name Chacma, it may be observed, is a somewhat euphonised rendering of the word T'chackamma, by which the Hottentots of South Africa designate this animal.

Like all the remaining representatives of the long-tailed baboons, the chacma differs from the Arabian baboon by the absence of the mane on the neck and shoulders of the males. We have, indeed, in this respect a gradual descending series from the gelada baboon, in which both sexes are maned, through the Arabian baboon, in which only the males are so ornamented, to the chacma, in which both males and females are maneless. In size the chacma is one of the largest of the group, and it has been compared in this respect, as well as in its bodily strength, with an English mastiff.

The general colour of this animal is greyish-black; but there is often a kind of greenish reflection in the fur when seen in certain lights. The head, as well as the hands and feet, are deep black; while the small whiskers on the sides of the face, which do not conceal the ears, are greyish. All the hair of the body is comparatively long and shaggy; while that on the nape of the neck, more especially in old males, forms a slender crest. The roots of the hairs are dun-coloured, but their extremities are ringed. The tail differs from that of the Arabian baboon by the absence of any distinct tuft at the end. The muzzle is perhaps even more prolonged than in the last-named species; but the nose is similarly extended beyond the upper lip. The naked callosities on the buttocks are smaller than is generally the case among the baboons. The naked part of the face is of a purplish hue, with the exception of a white ring round each eye, and the whole of the upper eyelids, which are likewise white. In the latter point, curiously enough, this species resembles the African mangabey monkeys already described. Like the other members of this group of baboons, the chacma carries its tail at first curved somewhat upwards, and then hanging straight down.

The chacma, like its cousin the Arabian baboon, is essentially a dweller in mountainous districts, and is found in all the mountain-ranges of the Cape district, such as the Snieuberg and the Drachenfels. How far it extends to the northward we have not been able to ascertain, since, as we have already had occasion to mention, travellers and sportsmen are, as a rule, very reticent on the subject of monkeys and their kindred.

Habits. The habits of this species appear to be very similar to those of its North African cousin, since we read that it goes in large troops, the members of which scramble up the rocks when their territories are invaded, and, having gained a safe refuge, seat themselves gravely down to gaze upon the strangers. In climbing up the rocky cliffs they are often much assisted by the tendrils of the creeping plants with which so many of the South African crags are clothed. Writing of the kind of scenery among which these animals dwell, the great African hunter, Gordon Cumming, says: "I continued my march through a glorious country of hill and dale, throughout which water was abundant. Beautifully wooded hills and mountains stretched away on every side; some of the mountains were particularly

THE CHACMA BABOON ($\frac{1}{8}$ nat. size).

grand and majestic, their summits being surrounded by steep precipices and abrupt parapets of rock, the abodes of whole colonies of black-faced baboons, which, astonished to behold such novel intruders upon their domains, leisurely descended the craggy mountain-sides for a nearer inspection of our caravan." It is said that there are instances where these animals have rolled down stones from the heights on a passing caravan, although there is no proof that such missiles were not merely fragments of rock accidentally detached.

The late Professor Moseley, who fell in with chacmas when at the Cape, during the *Challenger* expedition, states that they "live especially about the sea-cliffs and steep slopes leading down from there to the sea; but they are to be met with also on the open moorland above. They live in droves or clans of thirty, forty, or even up to seventy; and there were three such bodies of them in the country immediately about Simon's Bay, and in the tract stretching down to Cape Point. When on the feed, two or three keep watch, and one usually hears them before one sees them. The warning cry is like the German *hoch*, much prolonged. As soon as they see one, three or four of them mount on the scattered rocks so as to have a clear view over the bushes and heaths, and watch every movement of the enemy, so that it is extremely difficult to get within shot of them. If one stands still, or does not go any nearer, merely passing by, they employ themselves, as they sit unconcernedly, in scratching in the usual monkey fashion, but still never losing sight of their object of suspicion.

"Once I came across a troop on a sudden, on looking over a low cliff. They dashed off at a tremendous pace, galloping on all fours, till far out of shot, when they climbed up on to a rocky eminence, and calmly sat down to watch me. The baboons live on roots, which they dig up, and on fruits, and they turn over the stones to look for insects and such food underneath. It is striking thus to see monkeys roaming about on open moorland, where there are no trees.

"The track of the baboons on the sand is unmistakable. The foot makes a mark where the animal has been galloping, just like that of a child's foot; the fore-limb makes a mark not half so deeply indented, the hand being used merely to touch on, as it were, to prepare a fresh spring with the feet. I found the skeleton of one of the baboons in a cave at Cape Point. The animal had evidently crawled into the cave to die."

Mrs. A. Martin, in *Home Life on an Ostrich Farm*, also gives an excellent description of the habits of the chacma in the Cape district, from which the following extracts are taken: "On mountain excursions," writes this lady, "you frequently hear his surly bark, and sometimes see him looking out defiantly at you from behind a rock or bush, where possibly you have disturbed him in the midst of an exciting lizard-hunt, or careful investigation of loose stones in search of the centipedes, scorpions, and beetles hidden beneath. These creatures, uninviting though they appear to us, are among his favourite dainties, and he catches them with wonderful dexterity. In the silence of night his voice is so distinctly audible from the homestead that you would imagine him to be close by, though in reality he is far off in one of the *kloofs* of the mountains. One night, as we strolled up and down near the house, enjoying the bright moonlight, a loud chorus of distant baboons, to which we were listening, was suddenly interrupted, evidently by the spring of a hungry leopard, the moment's silence being followed by the agonised and prolonged yells of the victim. . . . No vegetable poison has the slightest effect on the baboon's iron constitution; and, indeed, if there exists any poison at all capable of killing him, it is quite certain that, with his superior intelligence, he would be far too artful to take it; and when the fiat for his destruction has gone forth, a well-organised attack has to be made on him with dogs and guns. He can show fight, too, and the dogs must be well trained and have the safety of numbers to enable them to face him; for in fighting he has the immense advantage of hands, with which he seizes a dog and holds him fast, while he inflicts a fatal bite through the loins. Indeed, for either dog or man, coming to close quarters with Adonis [as the chacma is ironically called by the Boers] is no trifling matter. One of our friends, travelling on horseback, came upon a number of baboons sitting in solemn parliament on some rocks. He cantered towards them, anticipating seeing the ungainly beasts take to their heels in grotesque panic; but was somewhat taken aback on finding that, far from being intimidated by his approach, they refused to move, and sat waiting for him, regarding him the while with ominous calmness. The canter subsided into a trot, and the trot into a sedate walk, and still they sat there; and so defiant was the expression on each ugly face that at last the intruder thought it wisest to turn back and ride ignominiously away."

The most general food of the chacma is afforded by the bulbous roots of an iris-like plant, known as *ixia*, of which there are several South African varieties, one of which is specially known as the baboon's ixia. These bulbs the chacmas dig up with their strong hands, and carefully peel before eating. Other kinds of bulbous and tuberous roots are also eaten by these animals; while buds and young twigs form a less important part of their food. In addition to this vegetable diet, the chacmas also search for and devour various kinds of insects and allied animals, such as locusts and scorpions; the latter being carefully deprived of their stings before being consumed. Lizards and frogs are dainties less commonly eaten; while birds' eggs, together with various worms and grubs practically complete the chacma's bill of fare.

These baboons are well represented in all menageries, where they thrive well. When young they are fairly tractable, but their temper steadily deteriorates with advancing age.

The Anubis Baboon (*Cynocephalus anubis*).

Although there existed for a long period much uncertainty as to their true habitat, it is now definitely known that the whole of the five species of baboons remaining for consideration are, with one exception, confined to the western side of Africa, and are therefore compatriots of the chimpanzee and the gorilla. It is probable, indeed, as we have already mentioned, that it was one of the short-tailed kinds that was met with in Hanno's voyage.

The anubis baboon, together with the two following species, may be readily distinguished from the chacma by the circumstance that the hairy parts of the hands and feet are of the same colour as the hair of the back, instead of being black. The general colour of the present species is olive-green, whence it is sometimes known as the olive baboon. There is a small crest on the nape of the neck; and the hairs are grey near the roots, and ringed with black and yellow at the tips.

Habits. The habits of these baboons appear to be much the same as those of the other species of the genus. They go in troops, and inhabit rocky mountainous regions, being especially common at a place some two hundred miles in the interior of Angola, known as the Black Rocks. Away from the river-valleys the country is arid in the extreme, and it is these thirsty districts which are the chosen abode of the baboons. Here they subsist largely on that very remarkable kind of West African plant known as the *welwitschia*. So remarkable is this plant, that we may venture to briefly describe it. The welwitschia is a plant which in its earlier stages of growth consists of the two ordinary seed-leaves. These appear to grow considerably, and extend horizontally outwards in opposite directions, raised but little above the surface of the sand; whilst the intervening stock thickens and hardens, assuming a somewhat conical shape, flattened at the top, and rapidly tapering below into the roots. In time the original pair of seed-leaves, having attained their full size, and acquired a hard and fibrous structure, instead of dying, gradually split up into shreds; at the same time the woody mass upon which they are borne, although rising but little in height, increases in width both above and below the insertion of the leaves, so as to clasp their bases in a deep slit on the margin. Every year several short flowering stalks are developed from the upper side of the base of the leaves. Each of these stalks forms an erect jointed stem, dividing in a fork-like manner, varying in height from 6 to 12 inches, and carrying at the end of each branch a cone, with the flowers and seeds beneath its scales. The result is that the country is studded with these tabular or anvil-like masses of wood, whose flat tops, pitted with the scars of old flower-stems, never rise to more than a foot above the ground, but vary, according to age, from a few inches to upwards of 5 or 6 feet in diameter. Even those which are not more than 18 inches in diameter are supposed to be fully a century old, although still retaining their original seed-leaves, which, albeit torn and tattered by the wear and tear of time, are, when entire, fully 6 feet in length. It is upon the stems and exposed portions of these extraordinary plants that the anubis baboons feed; tearing and ripping the woody tissue with their powerful tusks.

The Yellow Baboon (*Cynocephalus babuin*).

Our next example of this group is the yellow baboon, represented in the accompanying figure, and also on p. 66. This species may be distinguished from the preceding by the absence of a crest of hair on the nape of the neck, and likewise by its coloration. It takes its popular name from the pale brownish-yellow hue of the fur, which is rather darker on the sides of the back than elsewhere, while it tends to a whitish tint on the cheeks. The hair on the crown of the head is some-what elongated. As in the anubis baboon, the hairy parts of the hands and feet agree in colour with the body; but the naked parts of the face, hands, and feet are, as in the other members of the group, of a deep black.

It was long thought that the yellow baboon came from Nubia and the Sudan; it is now known to occur on the West Coast; but according to Mr. H. H. Johnston, there is a baboon found in the neighbourhood of Kilima-Njaro, on the East Coast, which he provisionally identifies with this species. He states that these baboons generally frequent the outlying parts of the plantations of the natives, subsisting largely on the maize and other products stolen therefrom. In certain localities they are extremely numerous, going about in troops composed of from about fourteen individuals of both sexes and of all ages. They have but little fear of man, and instead of running away will turn round and face an intruder, with threatening gestures, at a distance of only a few yards. The natives are in the habit of driving them away from the crops, when the baboons retreat in a leisurely manner, with their cheek-pouches crammed full, and often dragging off some of the plunder in their hands. In one instance it is related that a troop of these animals pursued a native lad for some time, until he had placed a river between himself and his pursuers. On another occasion Mr. Johnston relates how he killed a female out of a troop of baboons he encountered in these districts, who received him with snarlings and other expressions of hostility. After taking the carcase home, he proceeded to cook and eat a portion of it, and although he states that he found the flesh succulent and palatable, we venture to think that his

THE YELLOW BABOON ($\frac{1}{6}$ nat. size).

example will not be generally imitated by those who follow in his footsteps. As we shall see later on, the natives of Guiana are in the habit of eating roast monkey —or at least they were so in the time of Humboldt.

THE GUINEA BABOON (*Cynocephalus sphinx*).

There are few species of Mammals that have given rise to more confusion in Natural History literature than this one, of which examples have been described under at least two distinct names, and regarded as different species, though it is a well-ascertained fact that the common baboon, or papio, belongs to one and the same species as the sphinx, or Guinea baboon.

The Guinea baboon is characterised by the uniformly reddish-brown colour of its fur, which is washed with a yellowish tinge, more especially upon the head, shoulders, back, and limbs; the cheeks and throat being paler, and the whiskers fawn-coloured. As in the chacma, the upper eyelids are white. The nose projects rather beyond the upper lip, but is somewhat less elongated than in the chacma, and has small swellings corresponding with those so enormously developed in the next species.

As its name indicates, it is an inhabitant of Guinea; and although, judging from the number of specimens that are imported into Europe, it must be common, we have no record of its habits and mode of life in a state of nature. Of those in a state of confinement we have, however, numerous accounts, from the time of Buffon downwards; the species being frequently carried about by itinerant showmen.

The Mandrill (*Cynocephalus mormon*).

With the hideous creature represented in the accompanying woodcut we come to the first of two West African species of baboons, distinguished from all those we have hitherto considered by the reduction of the tail to a short stump, and also by the long tuberculous swellings on either side of the muzzle, which communicate the peculiarly hideous expression to the face. Moreover, the whole head is larger in proportion to the body than in the other baboons, and as the fore-quarters also appear to be relatively higher in proportion to the hinder parts, the general appearance is ungainly in the extreme. In fact, the whole appearance is far more suggestive of the forms imagined during a nightmare than is the case with any other living Mammals.

It has been suggested by several naturalists that these two species ought to be separated from all the other baboons in a genus by themselves; and the late Dr. Gray even went so far as to make each of them the type of a distinct genus. This separation is, however, uncalled for, since both are true baboons in all essential characters; the small size of the tail being merely analogous to the condition which we have seen in certain members of the macaque monkeys, while the huge swellings on the face are only exaggerated developments of the smaller ones found in the Guinea baboon.

The mandrill, as the species represented in the accompanying illustration is called, is the largest of all the baboons, and is, in truth, a brute of tremendous power and ferocity. Its leading characteristics as a species are to be found in the circumstance that its short and tuberculous tail has its under surface naked, and that the swellings on the face are ornamented with a brilliant coloration in the adult state, and are of enormous dimensions.

From the great development of these swellings on the sides of the muzzle, Pennant gave to the mandrill the name of rib-faced baboon, but this has generally been discarded by modern writers in favour of the former term. And here we may take the opportunity of mentioning that, according to the investigations of Professor Huxley, the name mandrill seems to signify a man-like baboon; the term drill being an old English word of which one meaning denotes a baboon or ape.

The limbs of the mandrill are characterised by their relative shortness and powerful build, and in correlation with these the form of the body is likewise powerful and robust. The ugly and massive head has scarcely any distinct forehead, the profile sloping almost uninterruptedly upwards from the muzzle to the occiput.

THE MANDRILL ($\frac{1}{10}$ nat. size).

The nose, instead of projecting in front of the upper lip, as in the sacred baboon, is somewhat truncated; while the projecting eyebrows and deeply sunk eyes communicate a forbidding expression to the whole countenance. The tubercular swellings on either side of the muzzle are supported on ridges arising from the swollen bones of this part of the skull, and are themselves almost the size of a man's fist. As a whole, they are somewhat sausage-shaped, and are marked with a series of prominent transversely-disposed ribs of light blue, with deep purple in the grooves, while the middle line and the tip of the nose are scarlet. The contrast between such brilliant colours and the general hue of the fur and the hazel eyes is most marked. The stump of a tail, which, as we have seen, is naked on the under side, is carried erect and bent over the back somewhat after the manner of that of a pug-dog. The general colour of the fur is a blackish-olive, darker on the crown of the head, the middle line of the back, the nape of the neck, and the flanks; and lighter on the cheeks. The summit of the head is crowned with a crest of dark hair directed backwards in a pointed and peaked form, while the chin is ornamented with a small pointed beard of an orange-yellow colour. To add to the strange effect of all these varied tints the large naked callosities on the buttocks are of a bright blood-red colour. The pointed crest on the crown gives to the whole head a somewhat triangular form; and in harmony with this peculiar contour we find the naked bluish-black ears angulated at their fore-and-aft borders, suggesting the appearance of having been cropped. The truncated muzzle is surrounded by a raised border like that of the swine; from which circumstance it has been considered by some writers that the mandrill is the problematical animal alluded to by Aristotle as *Chœropithecus* (hog-ape), but this identification is by no means certain.

Such are the colours of the adult male mandrill, but the brilliant scarlet of the middle and end of the muzzle is not assumed until the first, or milk-set of teeth have been replaced by the permanent series, while at a still younger age the whole of the face is black. Moreover, it is only in the adult of the male sex that the swellings on either side of the snout assume the enormous dimensions we have noticed. In both the young males and in the females of all ages, these swellings are but of moderate dimensions; and in the female they are coloured blue only. In correlation with the smaller size of the fleshy swellings, the skulls of females and young males are characterised by the much slighter development of the bony ridges underlying these structures, which form such prominent features in the skulls of old males.

Habits. In the wild state on the western coast of Africa mandrills appear to have habits very like those of other baboons, living in large troops; and on this account, as well as from their size and strength, being exceedingly formidable antagonists. The accounts given by the earlier travellers of their attacking men without being provoked require confirming; and we are in want of full information as to their habits in general.

In confinement the chief characteristic appears to be that the ferocity and moroseness common to the old males of all baboons is intensified. There is also a marked liking for spirituous liquors of all kinds, which is likewise a trait exhibited by other species of the genus. One of the earliest examples of an adult male mandrill exhibited in London was the famous " Jerry," immortalised by Mr. Broderip, which was kept first in the menagerie at Exeter Change, and then transferred to the Surrey Zoological Gardens. This animal had learnt to drink daily a pint of porter, which he seemed thoroughly to appreciate, and he had also been taught to smoke tobacco in a short clay pipe, although this accomplishment did not appear to be so much to his taste.

Of late years the mandrill has been represented by a comparatively small number of specimens in the London Zoological Society's Gardens. An extraordinary animal was born in the Society's menagerie in the autumn of 1878, being a female hybrid produced by a cross between a female mandrill and a male of the crab-eating macaque (*Macacus cynomolgus*)

The mandrill is strictly confined to the tropical parts of West Africa; the Gabun district being perhaps its headquarters.

THE DRILL (*Cynocephalus leucophœus*).

Although described by Frederic Cuvier as far back as the year 1807 as a distinct species, the West African baboon represented in the accompanying figure,

THE DRILL ($\frac{1}{16}$ nat. size).

and known as the drill, had for many years previously, in spite of a figure given by our countryman, Pennant, been considered to be merely the young of the mandrill, which had not acquired the characteristic coloration of the face. The acquisition of adult specimens of the drill by our museums and menageries proved, however, the correctness of the English and French naturalists' determination. It is exclusively West African, but its range in latitude appears to be somewhat more extensive than that of the mandrill.

It may be distinguished from its larger cousin the mandrill by the absence of any bright colours on the naked parts of the face, which are entirely black. The short tail is covered with hairs over the whole of its surface; while the general build, and especially that of the limbs, is of a much more slender type. Again, although the face has the long sausage-like swellings of the mandrill, these are considerably smaller and less inflated. The drill is ugly enough, but it is, to our eyes at least, one degree less repulsive than the male mandrill.

The general colour of the fur is brown, tending to a whitish tint on the forehead and the crown of the head, and darker on the shoulders and the limbs. The under-parts are also lighter, being either of a pale brown or a silvery grey tint. The hair of the upper parts is very long and fine, and is of a light brown colour at the root, but ringed with black and yellow at the tips. These rings of two colours give a greenish tinge to the fur when seen under certain lights. The whiskers are thin and directed backwards like those of the mandrill; and the drill also resembles that species in the presence of the peaked crest on the crown of the head, as well as in the small yellow beard beneath the chin. The apology for a tail terminates in a small tuft of hair. The naked jaw and ears are of an ivory-black appearance, and the swellings on the snout are not marked by the oblique transverse furrows and grooves which characterise those of the mandrill. The naked portions of the hands and feet are copper-coloured, while the bare callosities on the buttocks are bright red. The colour of such portions of the skin as are covered with hair is of a uniform dark blue. The female drill is distinguished from her lord and master by her smaller size, and also by the relatively shorter head and paler coloration, in which the young males resemble her.

We have already alluded to the unsatisfactory nature of our knowledge of the mandrill in its wild state, but in the case of the present species our information appears to be absolutely nil. In confinement, however, the drill seems to be very similar in its habits to the mandrill, and there can be no reasonable doubt but that there is the same similarity in the wild condition.

With the drill we conclude our notice of the living monkeys of the Old World; but before passing to those of the New World we must devote a short space to a few extinct baboons.

Extinct Baboons.

Our survey of the long series of Old World monkeys has shown us that as we pass from the Man-like Apes through the true monkeys to the baboons, we have been gradually receding further and further from a marked approximation to the human type, until we have reached forms that show a decided resemblance in their projecting muzzles and general contour to the lower orders of Mammals. These lowest forms being the baboons, it is but natural to assume that they are likewise old in the history of the animal kingdom, so that we should expect to find them in a fossil state. In Europe, however, no traces of fossil baboons have yet been discovered; while in Africa we only know of them as occurring in the superficial deposits of Algeria. The latter circumstance must not, however, be taken as an indication that other species of fossil baboons will never be found in Africa, since our knowledge of the geology of the greater part of that continent is of the most limited nature. We must, indeed, with our present knowledge, travel to the extreme north of India before we obtain evidence of fossil baboons belonging to a period antecedent to that during which man has existed on the globe. And it is in the sandstones forming the outer flanks of the mighty Himalaya to which we have previously alluded as containing the remains of the extinct Indian chimpanzee and orang, that those of the fossil baboons occur. These rocks, as we have elsewhere stated, belong to the lower part of that division of the Tertiary period which geologists designate the Pliocene. The remains of the Pliocene Indian baboons are, like those of all the Primates, extremely few, yet they are amply sufficient to prove the existence in that country of two distinct species. Both of these appear to have been closely allied to some of the longer-tailed African species; and we may therefore conclude that these Indian species were allied to the sacred baboon or the chacma. There is, moreover, evidence that baboons continued to exist in India to either the early human or Pleistocene period, since a single tooth has been obtained from deposits in a cavern in Madras which has likewise yielded remains of man.

We have, therefore, decisive proof that at a former epoch of the earth's history such an assembly of Primates was gathered together on the plains of India at a time when the Himalaya did not exist, as has been seen nowhere else beyond the walls of a menagerie. Side by side with langurs and macaques closely resembling those now found in that region, were chimpanzees and baboons as nearly related to those of modern Africa; while the extinct Indian orang recalls the existing species of Borneo and Sumatra. India, therefore, in the Pliocene period, seems to have been the central point whence the main groups of Old World Primates dispersed themselves to their far distant homes.

The generalised character, and the large size of the baboons, have suggested that it is to them we should look as the original ancestral stock from which the Man-like Apes took their rise. There is, however, found in the rocks of the Miocene period (the one immediately antedating the Pliocene) of Europe, a baboon-like ape known as the mountain ape (*Oreopithecus*), which combines to a certain extent the features now characteristic of the Man-like Apes and the baboons. It is this creature, therefore, which we should rather be justified in regarding as the ancestral stock of the Man-like Apes; the baboons being survivors from a still older stock, from which the mountain ape was itself derived.

Whether the relationship which must once have existed between the baboons and the inferior orders of Mammals will ever be revealed to us, is a question which time alone can decide.

CHAPTER V.

APES, MONKEYS, AND LEMURS,—*continued*.

THE AMERICAN MONKEYS.

Family *CEBIDÆ*.

THE monkeys of America differ so remarkably from those of the Old World, that they cannot be included in either of the families treated of in the two preceding chapters. The true monkeys of the New World form, indeed, a perfectly distinct family by themselves, known to zoologists as the *Cebidæ*. In addition to these, there is another group of American Primates known as the marmosets, which, although nearly related to the *Cebidæ*, constitute a second family, which will be treated of in the next chapter.

Not only is this distinction between the monkeys of the Eastern and Western Hemispheres a feature characteristic of the present state of the world's history, but, so far as we know, it was the case throughout geological history, for not a trace of a New World monkey has been found in any of the formations of the Old World, while those of the New World have yielded remains of species allied to those now inhabiting the same regions. We have thus decisive evidence that both these groups are of great antiquity; and it has even been suggested that they have taken their respective origins from animals probably allied to the lemurs quite independently of one another.

For a long period zoologists were accustomed to class the apes, monkeys, and baboons of the Old World in one group, to which they applied the name of narrow-nosed monkeys (*Catarhini*), from the circumstance that the partition between the nostrils is a thin one; while the American monkeys and marmosets, owing to the width of this partition, were grouped together as broad-nosed monkeys (*Platyrhini*). Although there is a certain amount of convenience in this arrangement, it has now, by common consent, been pretty generally abandoned; and the whole of the Primates, exclusive of the lemurs, are divided simply into four families, of which two belong to the Old World and two to the New. In the present chapter we shall take into consideration only the true monkeys (*Cebidæ*) of the New World,—the better known representatives of which are popularly designated howlers, spider-monkeys, sapajous, and titis—as it is to these alone that the term American monkeys should be restricted.

Characteristics. Proceeding to notice the characters by which these animals are distinguished from their distant cousins of the Old World, we have to mention, in the first place, that no New World monkey has naked callosities on the buttocks. This character will at once serve to distinguish any American monkey from all those of the Old World, except the larger Man-like Apes, with which there is not the slightest fear of its being confounded. Then, again, all the monkeys of the New World are characterised by the absence of cheek-pouches; so that whenever we see a monkey cramming nuts into his cheeks, we may be perfectly sure that he does not come from America. It is true, indeed, that this absence of cheek-pouches will not help us to distinguish an American monkey from an Indian langur or an African thumbless monkey, but then both the latter have naked callosities on the buttocks. Moreover, if we were to dissect

THE RED-FACED SPIDER-MONKEY ($\frac{1}{15}$ nat. size).

an American monkey, we should find that it had a simple stomach, quite different from the sacculated one which characterises the langurs and thumbless monkeys.

Another peculiarity of some, although unfortunately not all, of the American monkeys is that the tail is prehensile, and capable of being coiled round a bough so as to form a most efficient aid in climbing. These prehensile tails are characteristic only of the howlers and the spider-monkeys, and their kin; the tails of the titis and their allies being non-prehensile, like those of the Old World monkeys. The reader may note, however, that whenever he sees a monkey swinging suspended by its tail, he may at once put that animal down as an American.

Regarding this peculiar organ of the spider-monkey, Charles Waterton, who travelled so much in South America, writes as follows: "This prehensile tail is a most curious thing. It has been denominated, very appropriately, a fifth hand. It is of manifest advantage to the animal, either when sitting in repose on the branch of a tree, or when in its journey onwards in the gloomy recesses of the wilderness. You may see this monkey catching hold of the branches with its hands, and at the same moment twisting its tail round one of them, as if in want of additional support; and this prehensile tail is sufficiently strong to hold the animal in its place, even when all its four limbs are detached from the tree, so that it can swing to and fro, and amuse itself, solely through the instrumentality of its prehensile tail, which, by the way, would be of no manner of use to it did accident or misfortune force the monkey to take up a temporary abode on the ground. For several inches from the extremity, by nature and by constant use, this tail has assumed somewhat the appearance of the inside of a man's finger, being entirely denuded of hair or fur underneath, but not so on the upper part."

A more important feature of the American monkeys, as being common to the whole of them, is the great width of the vertical partition between the two nostrils, of which mention has already been made. This broad partition causes the end of the nose to be much expanded; and a comparison of any of our full-faced figures of the New World monkeys with those of the Old will show what a marked difference there is in this respect between the two groups.

TYPICAL SPIDER-MONKEYS.

Another character which we must not omit to notice is that in those of the American monkeys which are furnished with a thumb, this digit cannot be opposed to the other digits of the hand. The American monkeys agree, however, with their cousins of the Old World in having all their digits provided with well-developed nails.

We have left to the last the most important and perfectly constant distinction between the monkeys of the Old and New World, since it is one which can only be observed in the dried skulls. It will be remembered that in our description of the characters of the man-like apes, it was stated (p. 21) that in these and all the monkeys of the Old World, the total number of teeth was thirty-two. Of these, on each side of both upper and lower jaws, two were incisors, one was a canine, two were premolars, and three molars; the series being expressed by the formula $i\frac{2}{2}, c\frac{1}{1}, p\frac{2}{2}, m\frac{3}{3}$; total, 32.

If we now examine the skull of any American monkey (always excluding the marmosets) and count the teeth, we shall find that their total number is thirty-six, or four more than in the Old World monkeys. A closer examination will show that the additional tooth on each side belongs to the premolar series—the so-called bicuspids of human dentistry. Thus whereas all Old World monkeys have but two bicuspids on each side of both the upper and lower jaw, the American monkeys have three of these teeth; and the number of teeth in the latter may accordingly be expressed by the formula $i\frac{2}{2}, c\frac{1}{1}, p\frac{3}{3}, m\frac{3}{3}$; total, 36.

If we care to carry our examination a little further, we shall not fail to notice that the upper molar teeth of the American monkeys differ very decidedly in the form of their crowns from those of the monkeys of the Old World, so that a single detached specimen of one of these teeth is amply sufficient to decide to which of the two groups its owner belonged. Thus whereas in the Old World monkeys (exclusive of the man-like apes) the crowns of these teeth are tall and narrow, with the four tubercles arranged in pairs nearly at right angles to the long axis, and each tubercle nearly conical, in the monkeys of the New World the crowns of these teeth are much shorter and broader, with their pairs of tubercles arranged obliquely to the long axis; the outer tubercles being much flattened, and the inner crescent-shaped. Those acquainted with the details of anatomy will also find characters by which the skulls themselves of the Old and New World monkeys can be mutually distinguished.

Habits. Having now shown the leading characteristics by which the American monkeys, as a whole, are distinguished from those of the Old World, we may refer to a few other matters before proceeding to the description of the various species.

In the first place, none of the American monkeys make any approach in point of size to the large man-like apes, or even the baboons, of the Old World. Then, again, the whole of them are essentially adapted for a purely forest-life. Indeed, in the great primeval forests of the Amazon, where the ground is either swampy or entirely under water, the monkeys, together with several other animals, pass the whole of their lives in the tree-tops, travelling from tree to tree, and rarely, if ever, descending to the ground.

In this purely arboreal life it will be easily seen that the prehensile tail of those species which possess such an organ must be a great assistance to their owners in travelling from bough to bough, and thus from tree to tree. Considering, however, that the species, like the titis, in which the tail is not prehensile, are equally as arboreal in habits as those with prehensile tails, it is quite clear that the latter type of organ can only be regarded as a kind of luxury. Indeed, the whole question as to the reason why some monkeys have long tails, others short tails, and others, again, no tails at all, is involved in great obscurity.

The headquarters of the American monkeys are the great forest-regions of the Lower Amazon Valley, known as the Selvas; although they are also abundant in many other parts of Brazil, and likewise in the Orinoco Valley in Venezuela. All these animals are truly tropical and subtropical, although they extend to a longer distance on the south of the equator than they do on the north. To the northward, indeed, it appears that monkeys do not extend beyond the Tropic of Cancer in the southern half of Mexico; whereas in South America they are known to range as far as the Rio Grande do Sul, in latitude 30°.

In the vast forests of South America, monkeys make their presence known by their loud cries much more than in any other part of the world, unless, indeed, it be those parts of the Oriental region inhabited by the gibbons. The best description extant of the nocturnal noises of the American forests is that given by Humboldt. "After eleven o'clock," writes the great German traveller and philosopher, "such a noise began in the contiguous forest, that for the remainder of the night all sleep was impossible. The wild cries of the animals rang through the woods. Among the many voices that resounded together, the Indians could only recognise those which, after short pauses, were heard singly. There was the monotonous, plaintive cry of the aluates [howling monkeys], the whining, flute-like notes of the small sapajous, the grunting murmur of the striped night-monkey (*Nyctipithecus trivirgatus*), which I was the first to describe, the fitful roar of the great tiger [jaguar], the cuguar, or maneless American lion [puma], the peccary, the sloth, and a host of parrots, parraquas, and other pheasant-like birds. Whenever the tiger approached the edge of the forest, our dog, who before had barked incessantly, came howling to seek protection under the hammocks. Sometimes the cry of the tiger resounded from the branches of a tree, and was then always accompanied by the plaintive, piping tones of the monkeys, who were endeavouring to escape from the unwonted pursuit.

"If one asks the Indians why such a continuous noise is heard on certain nights, they answer, with a smile, that 'the animals are rejoicing in the beautiful moonlight, and celebrating the return of the full moon.' To me the scenes appeared rather to be owing to an accidental, long-continued, and gradually increasing conflict among the animals. Thus, for instance, the jaguar will pursue the peccaries and the tapirs, which, densely crowded together, burst through the barrier of tree-like shrubs which opposes their flight. Terrified at the confusion, the monkeys on the tops of the trees join their cries with those of the larger animals. This arouses the tribes of birds who build their nests in communities, and suddenly the whole animal world is in a state of commotion. Further experience taught us that it was by no means always the festival of moonlight that disturbed the stillness of the forest; for we observed that the voices were loudest during the violent storms of rain, or when the thunder echoed and the lightning flashed through the depths of the woods. The good-natured Franciscan monk, who accompanied us, used to say, when apprehensive of a storm at night, 'May Heaven grant a quiet night both to us and to the wild beasts of the forest!'"

In connection with this subject, we may mention that a subsequent traveller, the late Mr. Bates, when on the Tapajos River, writes: "I heard for the first and almost the only time the uproar of life at sunset which Humboldt describes as having witnessed towards the source of the Orinoco, but which is unknown on the banks of the larger rivers. The noises of animals began just as the sun sank beneath the trees after a sweltering afternoon, leaving the sky above of the intensest shade of blue. Two flocks of howling monkeys, one close to our canoe, the other about a furlong distant, filled the echoing forest with their dismal roaring."

We have already mentioned the circumstance that a European traveller on one occasion supped on roast baboon; and we may here call attention to the fact that in Humboldt's time monkey-flesh formed a by no means inconsiderable portion of the food of the natives of certain parts of South America, at least on particular occasions. Humboldt tells us that when his party was travelling in Ecuador, and had arrived at Esmeraldas, they found a native festival in progress. And in the room where the feast was held they observed numbers of large roasted monkeys (of what species we are not informed), blackened by smoke, and arranged round the walls. These monkeys were bent into a sitting posture, with the head generally resting on the long and skinny arms, and had been roasted by being placed on a grating of very hard wood over a clear fire. Humboldt observes that on seeing the natives devouring an arm or leg of one of these roasted monkeys, it was difficult not to believe that this habit of eating animals so closely resembling man in their physical organisation, had, to a certain degree, contributed to diminish among these people the horror of cannibalism.

The Sapajous, or Capuchin Monkeys.

Genus *Cebus*.

The long and prehensile-tailed monkeys so commonly seen in menageries, and known respectively as sapajous or capuchin monkeys, and spider-monkeys, may be regarded as the typical representatives of the family *Cebidæ*; and, together with two other genera, constitute a group which can be easily recognised, and as easily distinguished from all their cousins. With the exception of the howlers, of which more anon, this group of monkeys is indeed the only one furnished with prehensile tails; and, altogether apart from the question of voice, and the presence of certain structures connected therewith, all its members differ from the howlers by their rounded heads, and the nearly vertical plane of the face.

The sapajous may at once be distinguished from the three other genera included in this group by the circumstance that their tails, which are comparatively stout and of only moderate length, have no naked part on the lower surface of the extremity. In this respect they are not so perfectly adapted for the purpose of prehension as are those of the other genera. Another feature of these monkeys is that the hair does not partake of a woolly nature; while the general build of the body is rather stout; the arms and legs according in this respect with the body, not being excessively long nor excessively slender.

The native name of these monkeys on the Amazon is Caiarara, or "macaw-headed," the word Arāra meaning a macaw. It seems, however, that Caiarara is abbreviated frequently into Cai, and from the latter it appears that the name

Sajou or Sapajou has been evolved by a curious modification, originally due to the French naturalist, Buffon, using the word Sai (evidently the equivalent of Cai) for the weeper capuchin, and Sajou for another species of the genus. The term Capuchin doubtless takes its origin from the cowl-like appearance of the hair on the forehead.

The sapajous are represented by a large number of species, ranging from

THE WHITE-CHEEKED SAPAJOU (1), THE BROWN SAPAJOU (2), THE WHITE-THROATED SAPAJOU (3), THE SMOOTH-HEADED SAPAJOU (4)—($\frac{1}{6}$ nat. size).

Central America to the south of Brazil. Our knowledge as to the real number of species is, however, still very incomplete, as there is a great amount of individual and racial variation, and the whole group requires to be carefully revised before anything definite can be said in regard to this point. We shall therefore allude only to some of the better-known kinds.

Like most of the South American monkeys, the sapajous go in troops, and in Brazil ascend to the very summits of the lofty forest trees. The late Mr. Bates mentions one which he shot at a height of fully one hundred and fifty feet above the ground. Writing of one of the Chilian species, M. Germain states that "these monkeys usually have a permanent sleeping-place, whence they issue every morning to explore the neighbouring trees; the eggs and young of birds, insects, tender shoots, and, above all, fruits forming their chief food. I have never seen them," continues M. Germain, "on the ground, and I believe they never leave the tree-tops; while I have observed that they have particular routes in their journeys through the forest. The troops in which they live are not numerous, comprising from eight to a dozen individuals, under the leadership of an old and experienced male. When they arrive at the locality, where the fruits of which they are in search are to be found, each endeavours to seize as speedily as possible the best upon which it can lay its hands; but, both on its arrival and during its return, the band is far from being in disorder. In dangerous places, where a kind of gymnastic performance has to be undertaken, the troop passes in single file; each one not risking the jump till the one in advance has safely passed, and then seizing firmly the same boughs and jumping in just the same manner as the latter. I have sometimes seen them at a height of about one hundred and fifty feet from the ground suspend themselves by the tail from a branch, then balance themselves, with all four limbs stretched out, then, all of a sudden, let themselves go, and falling for a distance of some twenty or thirty feet, seize hold of another bough by the tail. In such falls the outstretched arms seem only ready in case of accident, for there is never any question of maladroitness."

Together with the spider-monkeys, the sapajous are the most docile and the most readily taught of all the American monkeys, and since they bear confinement and the European climate well, they are the most common of the monkeys carried about by the peripatetic organ-grinder.

THE WHITE-CHEEKED SAPAJOU (*Cebus lunatus*).

The white-cheeked sapajou, of which a representation is given in the middle upper figure of the woodcut on page 150, is an inhabitant of Brazil. According to Dr. Gray's description, this animal is characterised by the length of the hair on the head, which is directed backwards, while that round the jaw is longer, and curved so as to form a kind of crest on each eyebrow. On the cheeks the hair is short and flattened down. The fur of the body and head is long, soft, and silky, its general colour being blackish, but that on the cheeks and temples is yellowish-white. It is this light hair on the cheeks that gives its distinctive name to the species. The head is relatively large.

THE BROWN SAPAJOU (*Cebus fatuellus*).

In Guiana the sapajous are represented by a species commonly known as the brown sapajou, which presents a certain variation due either to differences of age, or to individual peculiarity, in regard to the form of the hair on the head, which has led to the supposition that there were two distinct species. In one of these forms, as represented in the upper right-hand figure of the woodcut on p. 150, the hair on the crown of the head is nearly flat, and directed backwards; this form having been described as *C. apella.* In the other variety, as shown in the left-hand figure of the accompanying engraving, the hair on the sides of the crown of the head is lengthened, so as to form a pair of more or less distinct longitudinal crests; this variety being hence known as the horned sapajou.

Although subject to great individual variation in this respect, the general colour of the thick and rather harsh fur is reddish-brown, becoming darker on the middle of the back, as well as on the legs and tail. The fore-arms, together with a

THE HORNED SAPAJOU AND THE WEEPER SAPAJOU (⅛ nat. size).

broad spot on the crown of the head and the whiskers, are nearly or quite black; while the front of the shoulders is yellowish. It is on either side of the dark spot on the crown of the head that the crests are situated in the "horned" variety. The face and other naked parts have a violet tinge.

This sapajou has been long known to science, a specimen having been exhibited in the King's Menagerie at Paris soon after the middle of the last century, and described by the French naturalist Brisson. Another example, described by Frederic Cuvier, was exhibited in the same collection in the year 1820. It is in winter, when the fur is longest, that the crests of the "horned" variety become most prominent; these never making their appearance until the animal has cut its permanent canine teeth. Like that of its congeners, the disposition of this species in captivity is mild and affectionate.

The Slender Sapajou (*Cebus pallidus*).

The slender or white sapajou appears to be a rare local species allied to the preceding, and inhabiting Bolivia in the neighbourhood of Santa Cruz. It is distinguished by the smaller size and lighter colour of the dark spot on the crown of the head, which is generally brown, and often has a small crest on each side. The general colour of the fur is fulvous, or greyish-fulvous, the limbs and tail being of a darker brown, and the beard a golden yellow. There is also a nearly white variety. Mr. Bates, who alludes to the slender sapajou as the Caiarara Branca, heard of its reported existence in the forests of the Tapajos River, which flows into the Amazon from the Cordillera Goral, on the Bolivian frontier of Brazil. His search was, however, in vain; and he was subsequently informed that the species only occurred across the watershed in Bolivia.

Another nearly related monkey, more widely spread in South America, is the tufted sapajou (*C. cirrifer*), in which the general colour of the short fur is black, but yellowish-white on the cheeks, chin, sides of the forehead, and a narrow band over the eyebrows. Two long, recurved tufts of hair, which often occur on the side of the head, give the distinctive name to this monkey.

A monkey known to the natives of the Lower Amazon valley as the Macaca Prego is provisionally identified with this species by Mr. Bates, who speaks of it as frequenting the cultivated lands; where it commits wholesale depredations with the most unblushing effrontery. The worst of these thefts is that, from the hasty and random manner in which the fruit is broken and plucked, the creature wastes far more than it can eat. When about to return to its native forest, it carries away as much plunder as it can hold in its hands and under its arms.

The Weeper Sapajou (*Cebus capucinus*).

One of the best-known and most common species of the genus is the weeper sapajou, or capuchin, of Brazil, represented in the right-hand figure on p. 152. It is characterised by the hairs on the crown of the head being short and directed evenly backwards, without any tendency to form crests on the sides. The colour of the fur is brown, with a golden tinge; the sides of the forehead, cheeks, throat, and chest, as well as the front of the shoulders, being pale yellow; while a black, or dark brown, line extends from the base of the nose to the back of the neck, gradually expanding as it goes backwards.

These sapajous have a wide range, extending right across Brazil, from Bahia in the east to Colombia in the north-west. With the exception of the occasions when they descend to drink, their whole life, according to Rengger, is spent in the trees of those regions of the forest where there is no underwood. They generally live in small parties, numbering from about six to ten or twelve individuals, of which the majority are females. From their shy and timid habits they are very difficult to observe. Their cry appears to be limited to a kind of low whistle, which serves to attract attention to them. On one occasion the traveller mentioned above observed a party of these sapajous despoiling an orange tree of its fruit. They were led on by an old male, the females carrying their young on their shoulders. When all had reached the tree, some commenced to eat the luscious fruit as soon as plucked, while others carried off their share to the stronger boughs of the neighbouring trees in order to secure a better resting-place in which to devour their plunder at leisure. These seated themselves on such boughs, with their tails firmly curled round the same, and, placing the oranges between their hind legs, tried to open the skin with their fingers. If they did not quickly succeed in this, they flung the fruit against another bough in order by this means to soften the rind, at the same time venting their displeasure at this unnecessary trouble by snarls and growls. Probably on account of its bitter taste, none of them attempted to tear off the rind with their teeth, but, as soon as an opening was made with their fingers, they proceeded to tear out the juicy pulp, licking up the juice as it flowed out, and then eating the pulp itself. When satisfied with their repast, the elder members of the family stretched themselves along the boughs to sleep; while the juniors gamboled around, swinging themselves by their tails from the branches, or going up them hand-over-hand, like sailors up a rope. The gambols of these young ones are, however, described as being awkward and ungainly, instead of light and graceful. The mothers exhibited great care towards their young, carefully tending them, and assiduously dressing and searching their fur.

On another occasion the same traveller had the good fortune to witness a troop of these sapajous descending from the forest to pillage a maize field. They were seen to climb cautiously down from the trees, and venture by twos and threes into the maize field; and, having hastily gathered a few cobs, returned with all speed to the forest to devour them at leisure. On the appearance of the spectator of their movements, the whole of the members of the troop in the field promptly scampered back to the trees, not forgetting, however, to carry with them their booty. Rengger then shot a female carrying off a young one, which, though badly wounded, clung for some time by her tail to a bough. At length, however, she fell lifeless to the ground, with the young one still tightly clinging to her body; and, indeed, it was not until the body had become cold that the hold was released. The young capuchin thus caught readily became tame, and would recognise its master even in the dark by the mere touch of his clothes. When wearied, it uttered a low whistling sound; and, when it had occasion to demand any particular object, it groaned. Its anger was expressed in rough tones resembling the syllables *"hu! hu!"* fear by shrieks, and pleasure by soft chuckles.

When captured young the capuchin is always easily tamed, but older animals refuse all food, become mopish, and do not live more than a few weeks. The younger ones soon take to their masters, and exhibit remarkable fidelity. They become, however, more readily attached to coloured than to white people; and they are generally very fond of other animals, so that in Paraguay it is a common custom to bring them up with a young dog, upon which they ride. To some persons they at once conceive a rooted dislike, which cannot be eradicated. Their intelligence is shown by the manner in which they learn to open an egg; most of the contents being lost at the first trial, but carefully secured at the second attempt.

Although they flourish in captivity if well attended to, great care must be taken to protect them from cold and damp. Their average term of life seems to be about fifteen years.

Like most other monkeys, captive capuchins are the very spirit of mischief, and are also prone to theft, more especially of eatables. When detected in the act of stealing, they will cry out before being touched; but, if not caught, they pretend perfect innocence, going about as if nothing had happened. When disturbed, small substances are hidden by these creatures in their mouths, and consumed subsequently at leisure. They are extremely covetous, and this covetousness is taken advantage of to capture them. The negroes are in the habit of removing the pulp of a gourd through a small aperture, and then putting sugar inside; such a prepared gourd is then placed near the haunts of the capuchins, who come down and endeavour to extract the sugar, and during the process they suffer themselves to be caught.

The White-Fronted Sapajou (*Cebus albifrons*).

The white-fronted sapajou is a common monkey in many parts of South America. It is allied to the last species, but is distinguished by its pale reddish-brown colour, which becomes redder on the back and the outer surfaces of the limbs. The most characteristic coloration is, however, the white which occupies the face, forehead, throat, shoulders, and chest.

Mr. Bates, who described this species as being of a light brown colour, states that it is pretty generally distributed over the forest-lands of the level parts of Brazil; and it was seen by this explorer in large flocks on the banks of the Upper Amazon. The members of such a flock are described as affording a wonderful sight when leaping from tree to tree; for, according to Mr. Bates, these monkeys (and we may presume their fellows of the same genus) are far-and-away the best performers in this gymnastic exercise. "The troops," observes Mr. Bates, "consist of thirty or more individuals, which travel in single file. When the fore-most of the flock reaches the outermost branch of an unusually tall tree, he springs forth into the air without a moment's hesitation, and alights on the dome of yielding foliage belonging to the neighbouring tree, maybe fifty feet beneath; all the rest following his example. They grasp, on falling, with hands and tail, right themselves in a moment, and then away they go along branch and bough to the next tree."

The same traveller, who had one of these monkeys as a pet, states that it kept the house in a perpetual uproar, screaming in a piteous manner when alarmed, excited, or hungry. It was always making a noise of some kind; frequently screwing up its mouth and uttering a succession of loud whistling notes, resembling those mentioned by Rengger in his account of the preceding species. Frequently this young sapajou, when following its master, would walk upon its hind-legs alone, although it had never been taught to do so. One day, however, in endeavouring to wrest some fruit from an owl-faced night monkey, it attacked the latter so fiercely that it cracked its skull with its teeth, upon which Mr. Bates considered that he had had enough of pet sapajous.

The White-Throated Sapajou (*Cebus hypoleucus*).

This species, represented in the lower figure of the illustration on p. 150, is an inhabitant of Central America. It belongs to the same group as the preceding one, from which it is distinguished by its coloration. Thus, while the general colour of the fur is black, the forehead and part of the crown of the head, as well as its sides, together with the throat and neck are white; while the naked portion of the face is of a pale flesh-colour.

The Smooth-Headed Sapajou (*Cebus monachus*).

The smooth-headed, monk, or yellow-headed sapajou, is a species from Rio Janeiro and other places in South-Eastern Brazil, which takes all its three names from the extremely close and short yellow hair with which the front of the head is covered. It is represented in the left-hand upper figure of the illustration on p. 150.

The fur of this species is very short and stiff. In colour the crown of the head, the whiskers and chin, together with the shoulders, haunches, limbs, and tail are pure black; the sides and back, more especially in the hinder half of the body, are yellow, more or less mixed with black; while the sides of the neck, the chest, and the front of the shoulders are yellow; the forehead and temples being whitish-yellow. Such is the striking coloration of the typical form of this species, but there are several variations therefrom, and the specimen represented in our illustration belongs to an olive-coloured variety, which has been described as a distinct species, under the name of *C. olivaceus.*

The Crested Sapajou (*Cebus robustus*).

The last member of this genus we shall notice is the crested sapajou of Brazil. This species is distinguished from all those previously mentioned by the long hair on the crown of the head forming a single central crest of a more or less conical shape. The general colour of the fur is bright red, with a black spot on the top of the crown, and the limbs and tail blackish.

The Woolly Monkeys.

Genus *Lagothrix.*

The woolly monkeys are best known by Humboldt's lagothrix (*Lagothrix humboldti*), first discovered by the traveller whose name it bears on the Orinoco, but also common in the upper part of the valley of the Amazon. This species, which is represented in our illustration, is the only one we shall describe, although three or four others are recognised by many zoologists.

The woolly monkeys take their name from the thick coat of woolly fur which is found beneath the longer hairs. This is one of the points by which they are distinguished from the sapajous. A more important point of difference is, however, to be found in the naked skin on the under part of the end of the tail—a character in which these monkeys resemble those of the next two genera. The woolly monkeys have, however, the same robust build as the sapajous, and thereby differ from the other members of this group of genera. They have well-developed

HUMBOLDT'S WOOLLY MONKEY ($\frac{1}{6}$ nat. size).

thumbs. The great length of the tail in the woolly monkeys, together with its naked tip, render it a prehensile organ of the most perfect type.

To the Portuguese colonists of Brazil these animals are known as Macaco Barrigudo, frequently abbreviated into Barrigudo; the full name signifying "big-bellied monkey," and being applied to them in allusion to their bulky build, as contrasted with the slender form of their cousins the spider-monkeys. The ordinary form of Humboldt's lagothrix has a general blackish-grey colour, with the head, chest, under-parts, and tail black. The individual hairs are dark grey, with very short black tips, on those parts of the body which are not black. Younger animals are more grey. Another form, which has been regarded as a distinct species by some zoologists, differs from the above variety in having grey fur on the head. Mr. Bates states that both these monkeys live together in the same places, and are probably only differently coloured individuals of one and the same species. In one of the largest examples obtained by that traveller, the length of the head and body was 27, and that of the tail 26 inches; these dimensions only being exceeded among the American monkeys by the black howler, whose head and body may measure 30 inches in length.

Mr. Bates observes that in Humboldt's lagothrix the skin of the face " is black and wrinkled, the forehead is low, with the eyebrows projecting; and, in short, the features altogether resemble, in a striking manner, those of an old negro. In the forests the barrigudo is not a very active animal; it lives exclusively on fruits, and is much persecuted by the Indians, on account of the excellence of its flesh as food. From information given me by a collector of birds and mammals, whom I employed, and who resided a long time among the Tucana Indians, near Tabatinga, I calculated that one horde of this tribe, two hundred in number, destroyed twelve hundred of these monkeys annually for food. The species is very numerous in the forests of the higher lands, but owing to long persecution, it is now seldom seen in the neighbourhood of the larger villages. It is not found at all on the Lower Amazon. Its manners in captivity are grave, and its temper mild and confiding, like that of the coaitas [spider-monkeys]. Owing to these traits the barrigudo is much sought after for pets; but it is not hardy like the coaitas, and seldom survives a passage down the river to Para."

From the account given by Mr. Bates as to the partiality displayed by the Indians of the Upper Amazon for this monkey as an article of food, it would seem that it is the one referred to in Humboldt's narrative of the roasted monkeys at Esmeraldas, quoted on p. 149.

The Woolly Spider-Monkeys.

Genus *Eriodes*.

The woolly spider-monkeys form a kind of connecting link between the woolly monkeys on the one hand, and the true spider-monkeys on the other; having the woolly under-fur of the former, but the slender build of the latter, while their thumbs are rudimentary. They differ, however, from both in that their nails are extremely compressed from side to side, and sharply pointed at the ends; while the partition between the nostrils is narrower.

Not much appears to be known of these monkeys, which have never been represented in the collection of the Zoological Society. They are confined to South-East Brazil; and have been divided into three species, mainly according to the degree of development of the thumb. The late Dr. Gray was, however, of opinion that these are merely varieties of a single species (*Eriodes arachnoides*), since some individuals have a rudiment of a thumb on one hand and not a trace of one on the other. In the typical variety, as represented in our illustration, the general colour is ashy brown, often tending to ferruginous at the base of the root of the tail, with the naked parts of the face flesh-coloured; the females being of a paler hue. The thumb is totally wanting. Another variety, with a distinct rudiment of a thumb, is of a dark brown colour, with white on the sides of the face.

THE WOOLLY SPIDER-MONKEY (⅙ nat. size).

THE SPIDER-MONKEYS.

Genus *Ateles*.

The spider-monkeys may be regarded as those members of the group most admirably adapted for a purely arboreal life, as is especially shown by their slight bodies, the long prehensile tail, naked below at the end, and the long spider-like limbs from which they derive their popular title. In the rudimentary condition, or total absence, of their thumbs, the spider-monkeys may be regarded as holding the same relationship to the sapajous as is presented by the thumbless monkeys (*Colobus*) of Africa, to the langurs (*Semnopithecus*) of India; and it is probable that in both instances the abortion of the thumb is due to the uselessness of this digit in a hand adapted to act merely as a kind of hook in swinging from branch to branch.

In general characters the true spider-monkeys agree with the woolly spider-monkeys, but are readily distinguished from them by the total absence of a woolly under-fur, the comparatively slight degree of compression in the nails, and the greater width of the partition between the nostrils; the thumb being generally absent. They are, moreover, of far more active habits; and in this respect are only equalled by the langurs and gibbons of the Old World, over which they have the advantage of the prehensile tail. To the description quoted from Waterton on p. 146, in which these monkeys are especially referred to, it may be added that they not unfrequently use this tail to convey fruit and other articles of food to their mouths. Those who have seen spider-monkeys swinging from rope to rope and leaping from side to side of their cages in menageries, can, when the cage is sufficiently large, gain some idea of their marvellous activity, although in such confined spaces their movements bear no comparison to what they are when in the boundless freedom of their native forests.

It is noteworthy that the stomachs of the spider-monkeys have a trace of the sacculated condition which distinguishes those of the long-limbed and long-tailed langurs and thumbless monkeys of the Old World. Their fur is generally smooth and stiff; and, as a rule, the hair on the crown of the head is directed forwards.

The number of species of spider-monkeys is very large, and we shall thus be compelled to limit our notice to some of the better-known types. The genus has a wide geographical range, extending from Uruguay in the south to Southern Mexico in the north.

The Red-Faced Spider-Monkey (*Ateles paniscus*).

The monkey represented in the figure on p. 145 is one of the best-known representatives of the genus, and is commonly termed the red-faced spider-monkey, although known to the natives of Brazil as the coaita. It is found over a large area of Brazil and Guiana; and, although exceeded in bulk by the woolly monkeys, is in absolute length of body the tallest of all the monkeys of these regions. It has been long known to science, its scientific name having been given by Linnæus, while its native designation, coaita, was in use in Europe as far back as the time of Buffon. The coarse fur is black in colour, and short on the crown of the head, although long and projecting on the forehead. The distinctive feature of the species is, however, the tawny flesh-coloured hue of the prominent naked portions of the face, from which it derives its name.

In Brazil this species is found all over the lowlands of the valley of the Amazon, but it does not range to the southward beyond the limits of the river-plains, where it is replaced by the white-whiskered spider-monkey. Like the other species, it lives in small parties; and is comparatively silent. Its flesh is much esteemed by the natives of Brazil, who capture it alive by shooting it with arrows tipped with weak urari poison, and restoring it, when fallen, with salt.

On one occasion when out hunting these animals on the Lower Amazon, Mr. Bates remarks that his attention was first called to one of them by hearing a rustling in the boughs above. "There was something human-like in its appearance," he says, "as the lean, dark, shaggy creature moved deliberately among the branches at a great height. I fired, but unfortunately only wounded it in the belly. It fell with a crash, headlong, about twenty or thirty feet, and then caught a bough with its tail, which grasped it instantaneously, so that the animal remained suspended in mid-air. Before I could reload, it recovered itself, and mounted nimbly to the topmost branches, out of the reach of a fowling-piece, where we could perceive the poor thing apparently probing its wound with its fingers.

THE CHAMECK, OR THUMBED VARIETY OF THE RED-FACED SPIDER-MONKEY ($\frac{1}{5}$ nat. size)

Coaitas are more frequently kept in a tame state than any other kind of monkey. The Indians are very fond of them as pets, and the women often suckle them when young at their breasts. They become attached to their masters, and will sometimes follow them on the ground to considerable distances. I once saw a most ridiculously tame coaita. It was an old female, which accompanied its owner, a trader on the river, in all his voyages. By way of giving me a specimen of its intelligence and feeling, its master set to and rated it smartly, calling it scamp, heathen, thief, and so forth, all through the copious Portuguese vocabulary of vituperation. The poor monkey, quietly seated on the ground, seemed to be in sore trouble at this display of anger. It began by looking earnestly at him, then it whined, and lastly rocked its body to and fro with emotion, crying piteously, and passing its long gaunt arms continually over its forehead; for this was its habit when excited, and the front of the head was worn quite bald in consequence. At length its master altered his tone. 'It's all a lie, my old woman; you're an angel, a flower, a good affectionate old creature,' and so forth. Immediately the poor monkey ceased its wailing, and soon after came over to where the old man sat." Mr. Bates adds that the disposition of these monkeys is mild in the extreme, having none of the painful, restless vivacity of their cousins the sapajous, and none of the surly and untamable temper of their more distant relatives, the howlers.

In the typical form of the red-faced spider-monkey, the thumb is absent. There is, however, a monkey similar to it in all respects, with the exception that it has a rudiment of the thumb on one or both hands. This monkey, which is known as the chameck, and is represented in the figure on the last page, has been regarded as a distinct species, under the name of *A. subpentadactylus*, but it seems preferable to consider it merely as a variety of the red-faced spider-monkey.

Other Species.

Black-Faced Spider-Monkey. In Eastern Peru the place of the red-faced spider-monkey is taken by a closely allied species (*A. ater*), in which the face is of the same black tinge as the fur. From this feature the species derives its distinctive title of the black-faced spider-monkey. According to Dr. Gray, it is further distinguished from the red-faced species by the shorter hair on the forehead.

Hooded Spider-Monkey. Passing by one or two species, such as the grizzled spider-monkey (*A. grisescens*), we come to a very well-marked form, known as the hooded, or black-capped spider-monkey (*A. cucullatus*), first described by Dr. Gray from a single example living in the London Zoological Society's Gardens, of which the exact habitat was unknown, although believed to be Colombia.

This species is distinguished by the length of the flaccid hair, which is of a mixture of black and silvery grey in colour; and on the crown of the head is elongated, so as to form a large hood, or penthouse over the eyebrows. The fur of the hands, the feet, the crown of the head, and the nape of the neck, is deep black; while the naked parts of the face are flesh-coloured.

White-Whiskered Spider-Monkey. The chuva, or white-whiskered spider-monkey (*A. marginatus*), has already been incidentally mentioned as found in the Lower Amazon valley, to the southward of the river-plains which are inhabited by the red-faced species.

It is of nearly the same size as the red-faced spider-monkey; but has moderately long hair, of a uniform black colour, with the exception of that on the forehead and the whiskers, which is white; the face being flesh-coloured. As in the last species, all trace of the thumbs has disappeared. It does not appear to be common, since Mr. Bates seems only to have come across one pair, both of which were shot, while specially searching for it in the valley of the Tapajos

River.   Being at the time unable to procure other animal food, this enterprising traveller was fain to try the flesh, and describes it as being the best-flavoured meat he had ever tasted, although it was with difficulty that he persuaded himself to make the attempt.

Brown Spider-Monkey.   This species (*A. hybridus*) is a native of Colombia, and is of an ashy-grey colour, sprinkled with black over the greater part of the body; the fur being very soft, with a tendency to curl, and mixed with a certain number of long and stiff blackish hairs.   Other parts, however, such as the crown of the head, the fore-arms, the thighs, and the greater part of the tail, are black; the face being blackish, with white hairs on the lip.   The inside of the thigh and upper arms are greyish.   This monkey is but little known in Europe.

Black-Handed Spider-Monkey.   In Central America, northwards of the Isthmus of Darien, this group of monkeys is represented by *A. geoffroyi*, noticeable as being found at very high elevations.   This species, which is also known as *A. melanochirus*, is the black-handed spider-monkey, readily recognised by the hands, feet, and the crown of the head being of a full black, while the fur of the body is generally some shade of pale or reddish-brown, although more rarely yellowish, or even yellowish-white, and indeed extremely variable in coloration.   It is commonly found on the volcanic mountain known as Orizaba, near Vera Cruz, in the south of Mexico, where it ranges up to an elevation of some two thousand feet, living in troops in the forests of the deep valleys.   In the neighbouring district of Oajaca it reaches, however, to a height of four thousand feet.

White-Bellied Spider-Monkey.   With the white-bellied spider-monkey (*A. belzebuth*) of Brazil we come to the first of a group of two or three species of spider-monkeys, distinguished from all those hitherto noticed by the under surface of the body and the inner sides of the lower legs and fore-arms being white or greyish-white. The present species is very variable in colour, shading from black to reddish, with the loins paler, and the under-parts and inside of the fore-arms, together with the front of the thighs, the inner surface of the legs, and the under side of the tail, whitish; the hair being rather long, and somewhat limp.

A Brazilian monkey, with rather longer hair and the under side of the tail black, has been described as a distinct species, under the name of the long-haired spider-monkey (*A. vellerosus*); but it may more probably be regarded as a well-marked variety of the species under consideration.   These monkeys have been long known, and were described by Cuvier under the name of *Coaita à ventre blanc*. Besides inhabiting Brazil, they were met with by Humboldt on the Orinoco.   They are stated to assemble in considerable troops.

THE VARIEGATED SPIDER-MONKEY (*Ateles variegatus*).

The last of the spider-monkeys we shall notice is the species represented in the figure on page 164.   It is remarkable for its brilliant coloration, and for its wide geographical distribution which extends from the upper reaches of the Amazon in Peru to the banks of the Rio Negro, flowing from Venezuela into the lower portion of the Amazon, and northwards into the Andes of Ecuador and Colombia.   It was originally described by the German naturalist Wagner, from specimens obtained on the Rio Negro. Later on, however, Dr. Gray described a monkey, brought by Mr. Bartlett from the River Tigri, which flows from the north into the Amazon soon after it takes its great easterly bend on leaving Peru, as a new species, under the name of Bartlett's spider-monkey (*A. bartletti*). It proved, however, to be identical with the variegated spider-monkey of the Rio Negro.

THE VARIEGATED SPIDER-MONKEY ($\frac{1}{6}$ nat. size).

The variegated spider-monkey is characterised by its thick, long, and soft hair. The general colour of the fur is black, but the cheeks are white. There is a band of bright reddish-yellow passing across the forehead a little distance above the eyes; while the under surface of the tail, the under parts of the body, and the inner surfaces of the limbs are yellow in the male and greyish-white in the female. With the above variations in colour it will readily be imagined that the male of this species is a striking animal. In addition to the more sombre tints of the female, the lines of separation between the colours are less marked.

On the River Tigri Mr. Bartlett describes these monkeys as living in small parties and travelling rapidly through the forests in the search of their favourite food, which is a berry resembling a gooseberry in size, but with a hard stone inside. Mr. Bartlett states that he had to ascend to the very summits of the ranges bordering the Tigri valley before his search was rewarded. " Here," he writes, " we came across a number of them—about eight or nine. I shot the male that is now in the British Museum, and my Indians brought down another with a poison dart. Having obtained two of them I was satisfied that I had found a new species. While, however, I was busily preparing the first specimen, my Indians had quietly placed the other on the fire, and, to my great horror and disgust, they had singed the hair off, and thus spoilt the specimen. Of course I was obliged to keep the peace, for they had not tasted meat for some days, and the monkey proved a very dainty dish."

The first example of this monkey brought alive to England came from the Upper Caura river in Venezuela, and arrived at the Gardens of the London Zoological Society on July 14th, 1870. Its stay there was, however, of the briefest, since it died on August 18th following.

The Douroucolis.

Genus *Nyctipithecus.*

The douroucolis, or nocturnal owl-faced monkeys, belong to a group of three genera, distinguished from all the American monkeys hitherto noticed by their long tails not being prehensile. All of them have well-developed thumbs, and their general form is massive. They agree with the members of the preceding group in the upright profile of the face, and also in the circumstance that the front or incisor teeth of the lower jaw are placed vertically.

The douroucolis, of which a party is represented in our illustration on p. 167, are distinguished from the other genera of the group by their rounded heads and the enormous size of their eyes. The latter are, indeed, so large that in the dried skull their sockets occupy almost its entire width, being separated from one another by a mere line of bone, considerably narrower than the opening of the nostrils. Another distinctive feature is the narrowness of the partition between the two nostrils, which is more like that of the monkeys of the Old World than of the other New World monkeys.

The ears are short, and the hair round the eyes is arranged in a radiating manner, after the fashion of the disc of feathers round the eyes of an owl. All the species are of relatively small size, and of purely nocturnal habits.

Apparently from the small size of their ears the traveller Humboldt gave them the name of earless monkeys (*Aotus*), but the name nocturnal monkey (*Nyctipithecus*) had been applied at an earlier date. We are unacquainted with the origin of the name douroucoli.

According to Mr. Bates, they are known to the inhabitants of Ega, on the Upper Amazon, by the name of *E-ia.*

Writing of them at Ega, he says : "I found two species, closely related to each other, but nevertheless quite distinct, as both inhabit the same forests, namely, those of the higher and drier lands, without mingling with each other or inter-crossing. They sleep all day long in hollow trees, and come forth to prey on insects, and eat fruits only in the night. They are of small size, the body being about a foot long and the tail 14 inches, and are thickly clothed with soft grey and brown fur, similar to that of a rabbit. Their physiognomy reminds one of the owl or tiger-cat. The face is round and encircled by a ruff of whitish hair; the muzzle is not at all prominent; the mouth and chin are small; the ears are very short, scarcely appearing above the hair of the head; and the eyes are large and yellowish in colour, imparting the staring expression of nocturnal animals of prey. The forehead is whitish, and decorated with three white stripes."

The Three-Banded Douroucoli (*Nyctipithecus trivirgatus*).

This species was first discovered by Humboldt on the banks of the River Cassiquiare, near the headwaters of the Rio Negro, in Venezuela; but it is likewise found in Guiana and Brazil. Its chief distinctive character is to be found in the circumstance that the three bands on the forehead continue distinct from one another on to the crown of the head. The fur is relatively short, and the tail cylindrical. The general colour is a greyish-brown, with a darker stripe down the middle of the back; the chest and under-parts being ferruginous, and the tail blackish-brown, except on the under part of its root, where it becomes yellowish.

The account given of this animal by Humboldt accords very closely with the descriptions of later naturalists. Humboldt refers to the difficulty of taming it, and states that one kept in his possession for nearly five months could not be reconciled to captivity. It slept during the day, concealing itself in the darkest corner it could find, and when awake could but seldom be induced to play with its master. Its agility in capturing flies was very remarkable. If irritated it hissed, and struck out with its paws after the manner of a cat, at the same time inflating its throat. Its voice, for so small an animal, was very powerful, and Humboldt compares its cry on some occasions to the roar of the jaguar, while at others it is described as a kind of mewing, accompanied by a deep guttural sound.

Mr. Bates describes how he kept an individual of this species for many months when on the Amazon. He observes that "these monkeys, although sleeping by day, are aroused by the least noise; so that when a person passes by a tree in which a number of them are concealed, he is startled by the apparition of a number of little striped faces crowding a hole in the trunk. It was in this way that my companion discovered the colony from which the one given to me was taken. I was obliged to keep my pet chained up; it never became thoroughly familiar." After referring to an individual of the next species, Mr. Bates states that his douroucoli " was kept in a box, in which was placed a broad-mouthed glass jar; into this it would dive head-foremost when anyone entered the room, turning round inside, and thrusting forth its inquisitive face an instant afterwards to stare at the intruder. It was very active at night, venting at frequent intervals a hoarse cry, like the suppressed barking of a dog, and scampering about the room, to the

GROUP OF DOUROUCOLIS.

length of its tether, after spiders and cockroaches. In climbing between the box and the wall, it straddled the space, resting its hands on the palms and tips of the outstretched fingers, with the knuckles bent at an acute angle, and thus mounted to the top with the greatest facility. Although seeming to prefer insects, it ate all kinds of fruit, but would not touch raw or cooked meat, and was very seldom thirsty. I was told by persons who had kept these monkeys loose about the house, that they cleared the chambers of bats as well as insect vermin. When approached gently, my Ei-a allowed itself to be caressed; but when handled roughly, it always took alarm, biting severely, striking out its little hands, and making a hissing noise like a cat." As is so frequently the case with small pets, this animal came to an untimely end, having been killed by the fierce attack of a sapajou monkey, as already related.

Other Species.

Feline Dourou-coli. The feline douroucoli (*N. vociferans*) takes its Latin name from the loud cry characteristic of all the monkeys of this genus. It is closely allied to the last species, from which it is distinguished by the circumstance that the three dark bands on the forehead meet on the top of the forehead itself, instead of continuing separately to the crown. It is an inhabitant of Brazil, dwelling in the same forests as the three-banded douroucoli, but always remaining separate.

Mr. Bates mentions that he once came across a perfectly tame individual of this douroucoli, belonging to the judge of Ega. It is described as being as lively and nimble as the sapajous, but far less mischievous, and more confiding in its disposition, delighting in being caressed by all visitors to the house of its owner, among whom it was a great favourite from the prettiness of its appearance, and its gentle ways. It was only, however, by a great attention and kindness, continued for many weeks, that the owner of this little monkey had been able to make it so perfectly tame.

Broad-Tailed Douroucoli. The broad-tailed, or lemurine douroucoli (*N. lemurinus*), derives its name from its broad and bushy tail, in which the hairs spread out on either side like those in the tail of a squirrel. It is further characterised by the greater length of the hair on the head and body, and also by the presence of a round pale-coloured spot over each eye, separated by a broad dark median line; the three frontal bands of the first two species being wanting. This douroucoli is an inhabitant of Colombia, but we have not met with an account of its habits, which are, however, doubtless, much the same as those of the other species.

The Squirrel-Monkeys.

Genus *Chrysothrix*.

The pretty little squirrel-monkeys comprise a small group of species closely allied to the under-mentioned titis (under which name those of the group are often included), but distinguished by several important features. In the first place, the eyes are very large, approaching in this respect those of the douroucolis, from which these monkeys are, however, distinguished by the wide partition between the nostrils, and the peculiar form of the head. The peculiarity in the shape of the head consists in its great elongation from front to back ; the aperture by which the spinal cord passes out from the brain to the backbone being situated far in advance of the hinder occipital region of the skull, which projects backwards behind the neck in a manner unknown in any other monkeys. Other characteristic points are to be found in the relatively large size of the tusks or canine teeth,

THE COMMON SQUIRREL-MONKEY ($\frac{1}{4}$ nat. size).

and also the comparatively short hair clothing the tail. The squirrel-monkeys, or saimaris, as they were called by Buffon, also differ from the douroucolis by their diurnal habits.

Common Squirrel-Monkey. The common squirrel-monkey (*C. sciurea*) is far the best-known representative of the genus ; it is an inhabitant of Brazil and the valley of the Orinoco. It is a small animal, not much larger than a squirrel, with the head grizzled grey, tending to blackish, and the hairs of the fur of the body also grey, with a black mottling, but more or less tinged with gold in the region of the back. The outer sides of the fore-arms are yellowish ; the paws whitish ; and the long and slender tail tipped at the end with black.

Writing of this species, the traveller Humboldt observes that no other monkey has so much the physiognomy of a child ; it exhibits a similar expression of innocence, a similar playful smile, and a similar sudden change from joy to sorrow, or *vice versâ*. When seized with fear its eyes are suddenly suffused with tears. The one in possession of Humboldt was extremely fond of spiders and insects; and when shown uncoloured figures of wasps, etc., in a work of Natural History, darted forward as if to seize the insect. It remained, however, perfectly indifferent to figures of heads and skeletons of Mammals.

When several of these monkeys confined in one cage were exposed to a shower of rain, they twined their tails round their necks, and huddled close together in order to impart to one another mutual warmth. The Indians of the Orinoco informed Humboldt that they often met with groups of ten or twelve of these monkeys thus cowering together, whilst others remained outside the group, uttering mournful cries at not being allowed to enter. By shooting poisoned arrows at such groups the natives are accustomed to obtain a number of young squirrel monkeys at a time; the young clinging to their dying mothers as they fall, and, unless wounded, not leaving them even when dead. All the movements of these little monkeys are rapid, light, and graceful. They have a habit of steadfastly watching the mouth of a person when speaking; and if allowed to sit on the shoulder of their master, they will frequently touch his lips, tongue, or teeth. Mr. Bates speaks of

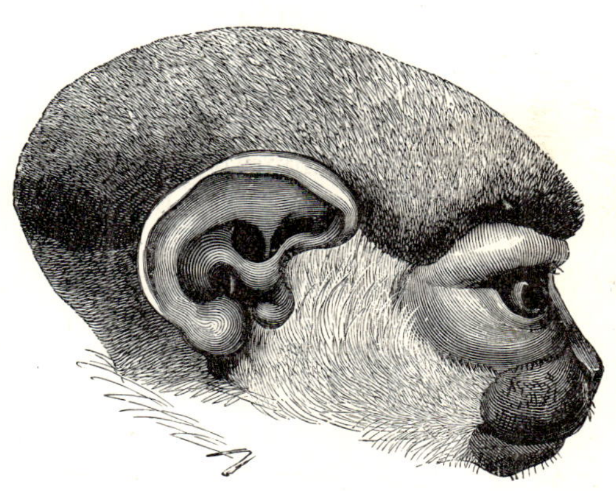

SIDE VIEW OF THE HEAD OF THE SHORT-TAILED SQUIRREL-MONKEY. (From Sclater, *Proc. Zool. Soc.* 1872.)

the squirrel-monkeys in Brazil as living in large flocks, and, when on the move, taking flying leaps from tree to tree.

Short-Tailed Squirrel-Monkey. This species (*C. usta*) is distinguished from the preceding one mainly by its shorter tail and naked ear. It inhabits the same regions as the last. In some specimens the outer side of the fore-arm is of the same colour as the body, but in others it is shot with gold, as in the typical squirrel-monkey. A side view of the head is given in the accompanying woodcut.

Black-Tailed Squirrel-Monkey. In Bolivia the squirrel-monkeys are represented by a well-marked species, (*C. entomophaga*), differing from both the above by its black head, and by the hairs of the body being yellow with long black tips. These parti-coloured hairs cause the general hue of the fur to be golden-brown. The upper part of the body is, however, of the same black hue as the head; and this colour likewise prevails on the tail, which is of moderate length. The face, throat, and the inner surfaces of the thighs are, on the contrary, of a yellowish-grey colour.

The Titi Monkeys.

Genus *Callithrix.*

The titis, which form the last members of the present group of American monkeys, are distinguished from the squirrel-monkeys by their round and well-formed heads, which are not elongated posteriorly; by their smaller eyes, less developed canine teeth, and the much longer hair clothing the tail.   They are chiefly inhabitants of Brazil and other parts of the Amazon valley, and are represented by some ten species; three of which have been exhibited alive in this country.   We shall notice only some of the species.

Red Titi. The red titi of Brazil, (*C. cuprea*), which belongs to a group in which the fur is soft but intermingled with a number of long, stiff hairs, takes it name from the reddish-bay colour of its hands, which forms a ready means of distinguishing it from the next species.   The colour of the upper parts is blackish mixed with grey, but the cheeks, throat, under-parts, feet, and legs are of the same reddish-bay hue as the hands; the tail being generally rather darker than the back, although instances are known in which it has a white tip.

Collared Titi. The second Brazilian species (*C. torquata*) is readily distinguished from the last by the white hair of the hands.   In general colour it is reddish-brown tending to black, the hairs being red at the root and black at the tips.   The face is surrounded by a narrow band of pure white hairs, and there is a narrow reddish-white collar round the neck, from which the species takes its name.   The forehead, feet, and tail are quite black.

The remarkable coloration of this animal has obtained for it among the creoles of Brazil the name of the Widow Monkey; the white rim round the face, the whitish collar, and the white hands being compared to the veil, handkerchief, and gloves worn by widows in its native country.

By the natives of Brazil this and other titis are known by the name of Whaipu-sai.   Although alluded to as the Moloch titi, it appears, judging by the reference to the long brown hair and the whitish hands, to be this species that was observed by Mr. Bates on the banks of the Tapajos River—the great southern tributary of the Lower Amazon.   Be the species what it may, his description is the best that we have in English of the habits of the titis.   He says that these animals have none of the restless vivacity of the sapajous and their allies, but are dull and listless; going in small parties of five or six individuals, and having the habit of running above the main branches of the forest trees   "One of the specimens which I obtained," he observes, "was caught on a low fruit tree at the back of our house, at sunrise one morning.   This was the only instance of a monkey being captured in such a position that I ever heard of.   As the tree was isolated, the animal must have descended to the ground from the neighbouring forest, and walked some distance to get at it.   The species is sometimes kept in a tame state by the natives; it does not make a very amusing pet, and survives captivity only a short time."

In Guiana this species is replaced by the closely allied white-chested titi (*C.*

amicta), which is distinguished by the presence of a pure white spot on the chest; the general colour being black tinged with red.

Moloch Titi. Another Brazilian species is the Moloch titi (*C. moloch*) which, while agreeing with those just noticed in the nature of the fur, differs in the colour of the hands and feet being of nearly the same grey hue as that of the back. The general colour of the upper parts is dark grey, with a grizzle of black and red; the cheeks, chest, and under-parts being reddish; and both the hands and feet dark grey.

The reed titi (*C. donacophila*) is a paler form, closely allied to the moloch. Mr. Bates states that while on the Lower Amazon, when going ashore early one morning, he found the forest resounding with the yelpings of a flock of whaiapu-sai monkeys, which he thought probably belonged to this species. Although unsuccessful in obtaining a specimen, he was enabled to see them for a moment, and describes them as of small size, and clothed with long fur of a uniform grey colour.

Black-Fronted Titi. The black-fronted titi (*C. nigrifrons*), differs from any of those yet noticed by its rigid and bristly fur, and also by both the hands and feet being black. Its general colour is grey, tinged with black; but it takes its name from the black forehead; the ears, a spot on each side of the neck, as well as the hands and feet, and the inner surfaces of the fore-arms and legs being of the same sombre tint. The fur of the tail has a reddish tinge; while the back of the crown of the head and the nape of the neck are of a whitish-grey.

The nearly related brown titi (*C. brunnea*), which is also known by the name of the masked titi, is subject to a great amount of individual variation in colour.

Black-Handed Titi. The last representative of these monkeys we shall notice is the black-handed titi (*C. melanochira*), which is one of two species which, while agreeing with the one last-mentioned in its black hands and feet, is readily distinguished from the whole of those yet mentioned by the fur being soft and woolly, without any intermixture of long stiff hairs. The general colour of this titi is reddish, but the crown of the head, the throat, and the inner surfaces of the limbs are a mixture of black and grey. There is a variety known in which the fur is bright red.

This species has been obtained from Bahia, on the eastern side of equatorial Brazil, but we have not come across any account of its habits, neither are we aware that it has ever been brought alive to Europe.

THE SAKI MONKEYS.

With the saki monkeys we come to a group containing only two genera, which, while resembling the douroucolis and their allies in the non-prehensile character of their tails, are distinguished from them (and likewise from all other American monkeys) by the circumstance that all the front or incisor teeth of the lower jaw, instead of being vertical, are inclined forwards. In this respect these monkeys resemble the lemurs. Like the titis, they approximate to the howling monkeys by having the sides of the hinder part of the lower jaw considerably expanded.

Most of the sakis are characterised by having long hair on the crown of the head, which may either be divided in the middle line, or may radiate from the centre; and they all have whiskers and a beard, the latter being either broad and single or separated by a division in the middle, and inclining back on either side. While in some species, like Humboldt's saki, the long hair covers the head, body, and tail; in others this long hair is confined to the head, where it may be present on the crown, cheeks, and chin, or only on the two latter.

THE WHITE-HEADED SAKI ($\frac{1}{4}$ nat. size).

The headquarters of the sakis appear to be Guiana and the Valley of the Amazon, although they are also found in other districts. Mr. Bates speaks of them as being delicate animals, difficult to keep in captivity. They are described as being gentle and inoffensive in disposition when in confinement; but we know very little of their habits in the wild state, although it appears that they are normally silent.

THE WHITE-HEADED SAKI (*Pithecia leucocephala*).

The white-headed saki, of which we give a figure, is an inhabitant of

Guiana, and may be regarded as the typical representative of the group. It is characterised by its white or yellowish forehead, marked by a central streak of black, the rest of the long fur being black, and the individual hairs of the same colour throughout. In common with the two following species, the hair on the crown of the head is arranged in a radiated manner, the beard is broad and single, and the tail clothed with long hair, which, like that on the body, is stiff and coarse.

HUMBOLDT'S SAKI (*Pithecia monachus*).

In the Amazon valley, as far west as Ecuador, the white-headed saki is replaced by a species distinguished by having no black streak down the middle of the white or yellowish forehead, and also by the greater length of the hair covering the head and body. This species is Humboldt's saki, also known as the hairy saki (*P. hirsuta*), and—by the inhabitants of the Upper Amazon—as the parauacu. The general colour is black with a grey grizzle, and the tip of each hair white. There is, however, a paler variety (*P. albicans*), in which the general colour is greyish-white, with only a large patch on the back and the tail black, the individual hairs being tipped with pure white, as in the ordinary variety.

When at Ega, far up on the Amazon, and at no very great distance from the frontier of Ecuador, Mr. Bates saw several specimens of this monkey. He describes it as being "a timid, inoffensive creature, with a long bear-like coat of speckled grey hair. The long fur hangs over the head, half concealing the pleasing, diminutive face, and clothes also the tail to the tip, which member is well-developed, being 18 inches in length, or longer than the body. The parauacu is found on the *terra firma* lands of the north shore of the Solimoens, from Tunantins to Peru. It exists also on the south side of the river, namely, on the banks of the Teffè, but there under a changed form, which differs a little from its type in colours." The variety here alluded to is the whitish one, which we have already mentioned, Mr. Bates goes on to say that this saki is "a very delicate species, rarely living many weeks in captivity; but any one who succeeds in keeping it alive for a month or two gains by it a most affectionate pet." Our author then proceeds to notice a specimen of the pale variety which belonged to a French inhabitant of Ega. This animal "became so tame in the course of a few weeks that it followed him about the streets like a dog. My friend was a tailor, and the little pet used to spend the greater part of the day seated on his shoulder, whilst he was at work on his board. It showed, nevertheless, a great dislike to strangers, and was not on good terms with any other member of my friend's household than himself. I saw no monkey that showed so strong a personal attachment as this gentle, timid, silent little creature. The eager and passionate cebi (sapajous) seem to take the lead of all the South American monkeys in intelligence and docility, and the coaita (spider-monkey) has perhaps the most gentle and impressible disposition; but the parauacu, although a dull, cheerless animal, excels all in this quality of capability of attachment to individuals of our own species. It is not wanting, however, in intelligence as well as moral goodness, proof of which was furnished one day by an act of our little pet. My neighbour had quitted his house one morning without taking the parauacu with him, and the little creature having missed its friend, and concluded, as it

seemed, that he would be sure to come to me, both being in the habit of paying me
a daily visit together, came straight to my dwelling, taking a short cut over gardens.
trees, and thickets, instead of going the roundabout way of the street.   It had never
done this before, and we knew the route it had taken only from a neighbour having
watched its movements.   On arriving at my house, and not finding its master, it
climbed to the top of my table, and sat with an air of quiet resignation waiting for

HUMBOLDT'S SAKI ($\frac{1}{3}$ nat. size).

him.   Shortly afterwards my friend entered, and the gladdened pet then jumped to
its usual perch on his shoulder."

It would appear that this interesting little creature did not long survive, as its
skin was brought home by Mr. Bates, and is now preserved in the British Museum,
If the life of these sakis is thus short, when in comparatively free captivity in their
native land, it must be doubly so when in our cold climate.   We find this confirmed
by the record of the two which have been exhibited of late years in the London
Zoological Gardens, one of which was received on the 15th of May 1866, and died on
the 26th of the following June.

Whiskered Saki.   The last representative of this group of sakis is the Brazilian
whiskered saki (*P. rufiventer*), which is distinguished, among other
features, by the hairs being marked by a yellowish ring near the end.   It is also
characterised in the adult state by the red colour of the under-parts, as well as by

the forehead being of the same greyish-black colour as the body. The moustache is yellow.

In the young of this species the moustache is white, while the under-parts of the body are grey.

The Red-Backed Saki (*Pithecia chiropotes*).

With the red-backed saki, which was first obtained by Humboldt on the banks of the Orinoco, and also occurs in Guiana, we come to the first of another group of the genus, distinguished in several points from all the species yet described.

THE BLACK SAKI (⅕ nat. size).

In the first place, the hair of the head, although radiating from a central point in the young, in the adult is divided by a median parting, and falls down on either side. Then the long beard is divided by a gap in the middle of the chin into two lateral moieties, while the fur on the body, instead of being long and harsh, is short and soft. The tail also has shorter hair than in the last group, and is thick and club-shaped. Finally, the hinder part of the lower jawbone is more expanded than in the typical group. The peculiar form of the neatly-divided and flattened hair of the head gives these animals the appearance of wearing a wig.

The general colour of the fur in this saki is blackish-brown, but there is a considerable area on the back and shoulders of a yellowish-red tint, from which the species derives its name. The tail is very thick and bushy, and the beard greatly developed.

Humboldt describes the red-backed saki as "a robust, active, fierce, and untamable animal; when irritated it raises itself on the hinder extremities, grinds its teeth, rubs the end of the beard violently, and darts upon the person who has excited its displeasure. In confinement it is habitually melancholy, and is never excited to gaiety, except at the moment of receiving its favourite food. It seldom drinks, but when it does so the operation is performed in a peculiar manner. Thus, instead of putting its lips, after the manner of other monkeys, to the water or the vessel containing it, this species conveys it to its mouth in the hollow of the hand, at the same time bending forward its head. It is not, however, easy to witness this singular trait of character, since the animal is unwilling to satisfy its thirst when watched or likely to be observed." In their wild state the same traveller relates that these animals live only in pairs. Their voice, which is but seldom heard, is described as a kind of disagreeable grunt.

Black Saki. Closely allied to the preceding species is the one represented in the figure on the previous page, (*P. satanas*), which is an inhabitant of Brazil. It is readily distinguished by the absence of the yellowish-red on the back and shoulders; the whole of the fur being of a uniform blackish-brown colour, generally tending to a more decided black in the males, and being browner in the female. In a male example in the Paris Museum the back is brown and the wig black, while in a female both the back and the wig are more fulvous. Unusually black individuals were described by Dr. Gray as a distinct species, under the name of *Chiropotes ater*.

The black saki, or cuxio, as this species is termed in Brazil, appears to be restricted to the lower parts of the Amazon valley. It was observed by Mr. Bates at Cameta, on the southern side of the Amazon delta, and is stated to dwell in the most retired parts of the forests, in regions where the ground is not subject to inundations. This naturalist was, however, unable to learn anything as to its habits in a wild state.

White-Nosed Saki. The last representative of these monkeys is the white-nosed saki (*P. albinasa*), which is likewise an inhabitant of the dense forests of the valley of the Amazon. It is of a deep black colour, with a paler tinge on the tips of the hair, except on the nose, which is pure white, and thus renders the animal easily recognisable.

THE UAKARI MONKEYS.

Genus *Uacaria*.

As we find among the monkeys of the Old World a great variation in regard to the relative length of the tail in closely allied forms, so in the New World there is a group of monkeys closely allied to the sakis, but distinguished by the extreme shortness of this appendage; and therein differing from all the other American monkeys. From their peculiar coloration two of the uakaris, as these monkeys are called, are among the most remarkable mammals in the world.

All the three species of uakari have long and silky hair, which is directed forwards on the forehead; but they have scarcely any distinct beard. The tail is very short, never being more than about a third the length of the body, and sometimes being reduced to a mere stump. From the shortness of their tails they received at first the very appropriate name *Brachyurus;* but since this term had been previously applied to another group of animals it had to be changed, and Dr. Gray proposed the uncouth name *Uacaria,* as a Latinised form of their native

THE BALD UAKARI ($\frac{1}{7}$ nat. size)

title. The shelving forwards of the lower incisor teeth, which we have already noticed as characteristic of the sakis, is still more marked in the uakaris.

THE BALD UAKARI (*Uacaria calva*).

The species represented in our figure is one of two closely allied monkeys found in the valley of the Upper Amazon, and readily distinguished by their brilliant scarlet faces, and the light colour of the long hair of their bodies. The length of the head and body of this species is about 18 inches; the whole of the body, from the neck to the tail, being clothed with long, straight, and shining hair of a whitish colour. The head is nearly bald, having only a very thin crop of short grey hairs. Beneath the chin and on the sides of the face there are bushy whiskers of a sandy colour; while the tint of the eyes is reddish-yellow. The contrast between these colours and the vivid scarlet of the naked part of the face must be very striking when the animal is alive; but, owing to the fugitive nature of the face-pigment, all this is lost in museum specimens.

This monkey has an extremely limited distribution, being found only on the left bank of the Amazon, in the neighbourhood of Ega; its small area being limited to the east by the River Japura, and to the west by the Putumayo, or Ica, as it is often called. Mr. Bates states that in this area the uakari "lives in small troops amongst the crowns of the lofty trees, subsisting on fruits of various kinds. Hunters say it is pretty nimble in its motions, but is not much given to leaping, preferring to run up and down the larger boughs in travelling from tree to tree. The mother, as in the other species of the monkey order, carries her young on her back. Individuals are obtained alive by shooting them with the blow-pipe and arrows tipped with diluted urari poison. They run a considerable distance after being pierced, and it requires an experienced hunter to track them. He is considered the most expert who can keep pace with a wounded one, and catch it in his arms when it falls exhausted. A pinch of salt, the antidote to the poison, is then put into its mouth, and the creature revives. The species is rare, even in the limited district which it inhabits.

"Adult uakaris, caught in the way described, very rarely become tame. They are peevish and sulky, resisting all attempts to coax them, and biting any one who ventures within reach. They have no particular cry, even when in their native woods; in captivity they are quite silent. In the course of a few days or weeks, if not carefully attended to, they fall into a listless condition, refuse food, and die. Many of them succumb to a disease which I suppose from the symptoms to be inflammation of the chest or lungs. The one which I kept as a pet died of this disorder, after I had had it about three weeks. It lost its appetite in a very few days, although kept in an airy verandah; its coat, which was orginally long, smooth, and glossy, became dingy and ragged, like that of the specimens seen in museums, and the bright scarlet colour of its face changed to a duller hue. This colour, in health, is spread over the features up to the roots of the hair on the forehead and temples, and down to the neck, including the flabby cheeks, which hang down below the jaws. The animal in this condition looks, at a short distance, as though some one had laid a thick coat of red paint on its countenance. The death of my pet was slow; during the last twenty-four hours it lay prostrate, breathing quickly, its chest slowly heaving; the colour of its face became gradually paler, but was still red when it expired. As the hue did not quite disappear until two or three hours after the animal was quite dead, I judged that it was not exclus- ively due to the blood, but partly to a pigment beneath the skin, which would probably retain its colour a short time after the circulation had ceased.

"After seeing much of the morose disposition of the uakari," continues Mr. Bates, "I was not a little surprised one day at a friend's house to find an extremely lively and familiar individual of this species. It ran from an inner chamber straight towards me, after I had sat down on a chair, climbed my legs, and nestled in my lap, turning round and looking up with the usual monkey's grin, after it had made itself comfortable. It was a young animal, which had been taken when its mother was shot with a poisoned arrow; its teeth were incomplete, and the face was pale and mottled, the glowing scarlet hue not supervening in these animals before mature age; it had also a few long black hairs on the eyebrows and lips. The frisky little fellow had been reared in the house amongst the children, and allowed to run about freely, and take its meals with the rest of the household.

"The uakari is one of the many species of animals which are classified by the Brazilians as *mortal*, or of delicate constitution, in contradistinction to those which are *duro*, or hardy. A large proportion of the specimens sent from Ega die before arriving at Para, and scarcely one in a dozen succeeds in reaching Rio Janeiro alive. The difficulty it has of accommodating itself to changed conditions probably has some connection with the very limited range, or confined sphere of life, of the species in its natural state, its native home being an area of swampy woods, not more than about sixty square miles in extent, although no permanent barrier exists to check its dispersal, except towards the south (where the Amazon flows), over a much wider space."

Mr. Bates then goes on to relate how he had a captive uakari on board his vessel, at the mouth of the Rio Negro, which escaped into the forest. On the day after its escape it, however, reappeared, and took up its accustomed position on the vessel, having evidently discovered that the forests of the Rio Negro were by no means so suited to its existence as those of the delta-lands of its native Japura River. Uakaris are never known to descend of their own accord to the ground, the forests inhabited by them being inundated during the greater part of the year. Hence the shortness of their tails is no indication of their habits being more terrestrial than those of the long-tailed sakis.

OTHER SPECIES.

Red-Faced Uakari. On the western side of the Putumayo River the bald uakari is replaced by a closely allied species, known as the red-faced uakari (*U. rubicunda*), which appears to have an equally confined distributional area, although the exact western limits of its range are unknown. This uakari differs from the preceding by the hair of the body and the limbs being of an almost uniform rich deep chestnut hue, only becoming rather paler on the neck. This is in marked contrast to the pale sandy white, tending slightly to rufous, on the under-parts and the inner surfaces of the limbs, characteristic of the bald-headed uakari. Both species agree, however, in their brilliant scarlet faces, and in having hair of a rich chestnut tint beneath the throat; and there can be no doubt but that they are extremely closely related, and have acquired their slight differences of coloration by being now completely separated from one another, although descended at no very distinct epoch from a common ancestor.

Black-Headed Uakari. The most northerly representative of these monkeys is the black-headed uakari (*U. melanocephala*), which is found in the forests to the north of the Rio Negro, especially on the Cassiquiare and the Rio Branco. It thus enters the basins of both the Amazon and the Orinoco, so that it has a considerably larger distributional area than either of the other species, from both of which it is widely different in coloration.

The general colour is blackish, but the back and sides of the body are yellowish, while the loins, the outer surface of the thighs, and the tip of the tail are reddish chestnut; the face, hands, and feet being completely black.

THE BLACK-HEADED UAKARI.

The Howling Monkeys.

Genus *Mycetes*.

The howling monkeys, or howlers, derive their name from their vociferous cries, which are sufficient in the living condition to distinguish them from all the other American monkeys. To produce this extraordinary noise—of which more anon—there is a peculiar hollow shell of bone joining on to the upper part of the windpipe, corresponding to the so-called hyoid bone of man, which is a very small and solid structure. The resonance of the voice within this cavity communicates to the cry its peculiar intensity. In order to provide space for this bony shell the sides of the lower jaw-bone are extremely deep, and by this character, as well as by the extreme flatness of the part containing the brain, the peculiar skull may always be recognised. A front view of the head of a howler is given in the wood-cut on the next page, to illustrate the form of the nostrils in the American monkeys.

The howlers differ from the two preceding groups, and agree with the spider-monkeys and their allies, in having prehensile tails, in which the under surface of the extremity is naked. In addition to the presence of the large bony swelling at the top of the windpipe, they may be at once distinguished from all other prehensile-tailed monkeys by the extreme obliquity of the plane of the face and

the projecting muzzle. This obliquity of the face is connected with the flattening
of the hinder part of the skull, already referred to; and is so marked that the
profile inclines backwards almost in a straight line from the muzzle to the crown.
Like all American monkeys, except the spider-monkeys and some of their allies, the
howlers have well-developed thumbs. Their face is naked, with the muzzle very projecting; the naked parts being surrounded by a fringe of long hair on the forehead,
cheeks, and chin. On the forehead this long hair may be directed either backwards
or forwards, but that of the whiskers and beard always hangs down. The hair of
the body, although shorter than that surrounding the face, is relatively long.

The howlers are especially abundant in Brazil, but they also range into Central
America. They are represented by a considerable number of species, but since
these are chiefly distinguished from one another by the colour of their hair, and
there is considerable individual and sexual
variation in this respect, it is in some cases
difficult to decide as to which variations we
ought to regard as indicating distinct species,
and which merely as local races. The food of
these monkeys is stated to consist entirely of
leaves.

Humboldt says that, when travelling in
the neighbourhood of the Orinoco, the rising of
the sun was always heralded by the cries of
the howlers. Frequently this traveller and his
companion, Bonpland, observed troops of them
moving slowly in procession from tree to tree.
A male was always followed by a number of
females, several of the latter bearing their
young on their shoulders. The uniformity
with which they perform their movements is
described as being very remarkable. According
to the observations of Humboldt, as detailed
by one of his biographers, whenever the
branches of neighbouring trees do not touch
one another, the male, who leads the party,
suspends himself by the naked prehensile part

HEAD OF THE VERA CRUZ HOWLING MONKEY.
(From Sclater, *Proc. Zool. Soc.*)

of his tail, and, letting fall the rest of his body, swings himself till in one of his
oscillations he reaches the neighbouring branch. The whole file performs the same
movements on the same spot. The Indians told the travellers that when these
monkeys filled the forests with their howling there was always one that chanted,
as leader of the chorus. During a long interval one solitary and strong voice
was generally distinguished, till its place was taken by another of a different pitch.

Writing in relation to a specimen of one of these monkeys, brought to him
when travelling on the Lower Amazon, Mr. Bates observes that "the howlers
are the only kind of monkeys which the natives have not succeeded in taming.
They are often caught, but they do not survive captivity many weeks. The one
of which I am speaking (apparently a female of the black howler), was not quite

full-grown. It measured 16 inches in length, exclusive of the tail; the whole body was covered with long and shining dingy-white hair, the whiskers and beard only being of a tawny hue. It was kept in a house, together with a coaita and a caiarara monkey (*Cebus albifrons*). Both these lively members of the monkey order seemed rather to court attention, but the howler slunk away when any one approached it. When it first arrived, it occasionally made a gruff subdued howling

THE BLACK HOWLER (⅛ nat. size).

noise early in the morning. The deep volume of sound in the voice of the howling monkeys, as is well known, is produced by a drum-shaped expansion of the larynx. It was curious to watch the animal while venting its hollow cavernous roar, and observe how small was the muscular exertion employed. When howlers are seen in the forest, there are generally three or four of them mounted on the topmost branches of a tree. It does not appear that their harrowing roar is emitted from sudden alarm; at least, it was not so in captive individuals. It is probable, however, that the noise serves to intimidate their enemies."

THE BLACK HOWLER (*Mycetes caraya*).

We select as our first example of that group of howlers in which the hair of the forehead is directed forwards so as to overhang the eyes, and the crown of the head is smooth, with radiating hairs, the black howler, either a young male or female of which is alluded to in the passage cited above.

It is a native of Brazil. The adult males have their fur mainly of a uniform black colour, interspersed with red hairs on the flanks and loins. The females and young males are of a dingy white, and were described as belonging to a distinct species, under the name of *M. stramineus*. At one time there were young males of the black howler in the Jardin des Plantes, at Paris, which actually changed from the white into the black state. Mr. Bates's example was obtained on the Madeira River, the largest southern tributary of the Amazon.

The yellow-handed howler (*M. belzebul*) is another Brazilian representative of this group, which has been known since the time of Linnæus. It appears to vary considerably in colour, so that one variety was described as a distinct species (*M. flavimanus*). According to the late Dr. Gray, the general colour of the fur may be either uniform black or reddish, with some brown hairs on the shoulders; but the hands and feet, as well as a line running down the middle of the upper surface of the tail, the tip of the same, together with a spot in front of each ear, and another on the knee, are invariably reddish-yellow. Mr. Bates states that the variety which is reddish coloured all over is the prevalent type of howler in Para, on the southern side of the delta of the Amazon; while in the island of Marajo, or Macajo, in the middle of the delta, this form is replaced by the darker one with yellowish hands and feet.

The red-and-yellow howler (*M. auratus*) is a third species from Brazil belonging to this group, in which the general colour is dark chestnut-brown, with the back and sides golden yellow, and the beard somewhat darker. Dr. Gray also applied distinct names to two other Brazilian howlers.

OTHER SPECIES.

Vera Cruz Howler. As the black howler is the most southerly representative of the genus, so *M. villosus*, the Vera Cruz howler (of which the head is figured on p. 183) is its most northerly example. This species differs from the black howler by its long soft hairs, which near their bases show a rufescent tinge, in the hair of the face being inclined forwards instead of reversed, and also in the colour of the female and young being black, like that of the male.

Red Howler. The red or golden howler (*M. seniculus*) is perhaps the best-known representative of the group in which the hair is bent back so as to form a ridge across the centre of the crown of the head. The general colour is a reddish-chestnut, but golden-yellow in the middle of the back. It appears that in young individuals the hairs are short and stiff, without any under-fur, and uniformly coloured throughout their length. In older individuals, however, they become long, soft, and silky, and are brown at the roots, and golden or chestnut - coloured at their tips; while at the same time a thick under - fur is developed. It was old individuals with this long silky kind of hair that Dr. Gray described as a distinct species, under the name of the silky howler (*M. laniger*).

This howler appears to be mainly a northern form, occurring in Colombia on the west, and in Guiana on the east side of South America; while, according to Mr. Bates, who describes its fur as being of a shining yellowish-red colour, it is the sole representative of the howlers in the Upper Amazon valley. It also occurs in Ecuador; and, according to Dr. Gray, is represented by a pale variety in Bolivia.

The red howler is one of the two species of this genus that have been exhibited in the Gardens of the London Zoological Society. It is, however, difficult to keep alive for any length of time, and of two specimens received from the Dekka River, near Cartagena, on August 28th, 1863, the one died on September 25th, and the other on October 7th of the same year. Writing of these howlers, which he states are known to the natives as ouarines, and on the Demerara in Guiana are commonly known as red monkeys, the traveller Charles Waterton states "that nothing can sound more dreadful than the nocturnal howlings of this red monkey. Whilst lying in your hammock amid these gloomy and immeasurable wilds, you hear him howling at intervals from eleven o'clock at night till daybreak. You would suppose that half the wild beasts of the forest were collecting for the work of carnage. Now it is the tremendous roar of the jaguar, as he springs upon his prey; now it changes to his terrible and deep-toned growlings, as he is pressed on all sides by superior force; and now you hear his last dying groan beneath a mortal wound. Some naturalists have supposed that these awful sounds, which you would fancy are those of enraged and dying wild beasts, proceed from a number of red monkeys howling in concert. One of them alone is capable of producing all these sounds; and the anatomists, on an inspection of his trachea (windpipe), will be fully satisfied that this is the case. When you look at him, as he is sitting on the branch of a tree, you will see a lump in his throat the size of a hen's egg. In dark and cloudy weather, and just before a shower of rain, this monkey will often howl in the day-time; and if you advance cautiously, and get under the high and tufted trees where he is sitting, you may have a capital opportunity of witnessing his wonderful powers of producing these dreadful and discordant sounds. Thus one single solitary monkey, in lieu of having others to sit down and listen to him, according to the report of travellers, has not even one attendant. Once I was fortunate enough to smuggle myself under the very tree, on the higher branches of which was perched a full-grown red monkey. I saw his huge mouth open; I saw the protuberance on his inflated throat; and I listened with extreme astonishment to sounds which might have had their origin in the infernal regions."

Brown Howler. The brown howler (*M. ursinus*) is a Brazilian species, apparently found only or chiefly south of the Amazon. Its usual colour is a blackish-brown, more or less washed with yellow; and some varieties are almost entirely yellow, this being most marked on the limbs and tail. The howler described as *M. fuscus*, of which specimens have been exhibited in the London Zoological Society's Gardens, is regarded by Dr. Gray merely as a variety of this species. It has been observed that the specimens of this monkey from the more northerly regions of Brazil are rufous or ferruginous in colour, while the females and those from the more southern regions are brown or blackish-brown. This species is very closely allied to the red howler.

Mantled Howler. In Costa Rica, and probably also in other districts of Central America, the howling monkeys are represented by a very well-marked species, known as the mantled howler (*M. palliatus*). This animal is characterised by the presence of a fringe of long brownish-yellow hair running along the lower part of the flanks, so as to form a kind of mantle on each side of the body. The general colour of the fur is blackish-brown, the hairs on the middle of the back, as well as on the upper parts of the sides, being yellowish-brown, with black tips.

FOSSIL AMERICAN MONKEYS.

In previous chapters we have seen how all the fossil monkeys of the Old World are more or less closely allied to the recent monkeys of that half of the globe, none of them showing any signs of closer affinity with their western cousins. The same holds good with regard to the extinct monkeys which have left their remains in the great caverns of Brazil, or in the fresh-water superficial deposits which cover such large areas of country in Argentina and other parts of South America; all these belonging either to existing genera, and in some cases even species, of American monkeys, or to extinct types of the same great family.

At the time when the huge ground-sloths known as megatheres and mylodons roamed over the pampas of South America, the forests of Brazil re-echoed as now with the cries of howling monkeys, apparently identical with the species still living; while titis and sapajous are known to have existed at the same

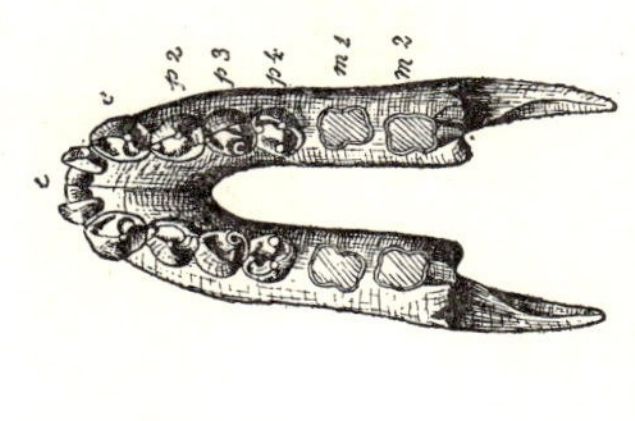
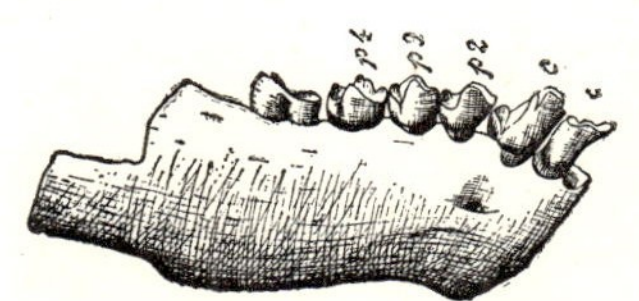

UPPER AND SIDE VIEWS OF LOWER JAW OF AMERICAN TERTIARY MONKEY (*Homunculus.*)—After Ameghino.

epoch, and remains of other living genera will doubtless also be found in the same deposits, which belong to what geologists term the Pleistocene period. At the same time, with these existing genera there also lived a totally extinct genus of monkeys, known by the name of *Protopithecus*. These monkeys appear to have been nearly related to the modern howlers, but were considerably larger than any living American monkey. In Argentina and Patagonia remains of monkeys, apparently belonging to this family, occur in much older strata, which have been correlated with the Eocene rocks of Europe. Marmosets are likewise represented in the superficial South American deposits.

CHAPTER VI.

Apes, Monkeys, and Lemurs,—*continued*.

The Marmosets.

Family *Hapalidæ*.

The last, and at the same time the smallest, of all the true Primates are the tiny and beautiful little creatures popularly known as marmosets and tamarins. These elegant little animals, many of which are much smaller than a squirrel, are confined to South and Central America, and, although agreeing in many points with the American monkeys (*Cebidæ*), yet differ in so many others as to render it necessary to refer them to a distinct family.

The most important point by which the marmosets are distinguished from the American monkeys relates to their teeth. It will be remembered that the American monkeys are distinguished from all their Old World cousins by having thirty-six in place of thirty-two teeth; the increase being due to the presence of an additional bicuspid or premolar on either side of each jaw. Now, if we take the skull of a marmoset and count its teeth, we shall find that their number is the same as in the Old World monkeys, viz. thirty-two. If, however, we carefully compare the cheek-teeth with those of an Old World monkey, we shall find that there is a very important point of difference. Thus, whereas in an Old World monkey there are on each side of both the upper and the lower jaw two bicuspids or premolars (teeth which are preceded by milk-teeth) and three molars, we shall find that in our marmoset there are three premolars and only two molars. That is to say, in place of there being two cheek-teeth with a pair of cusps on the crown, which are preceded by milk-teeth, and three teeth with four cusps which are not so preceded, there are three of the former type and only two of the latter. Although, then, a marmoset agrees with an Old World monkey in the total number of its teeth, yet in the much more important character of the number of premolars it resembles an American monkey, from which it differs by the comparatively unimportant feature of the loss of the last molar in each jaw. A marmoset may, indeed, be defined as a small American monkey which has lost its wisdom teeth; and the dentition of these animals may be expressed by the formula $i\frac{2}{2}, c\frac{1}{1}, p\frac{3}{3}, m\frac{2}{2}$; total 32.

The next most important feature in which the marmosets differ from the true American monkeys is that, with the exception of the great toe, all their fingers and toes are furnished with pointed claws, instead of more or less flattened nails; this character, like the presence of the additional premolar tooth in each jaw, clearly allying them to the lower types of Mammals. It is in this group, moreover, that we for the first time find the tail ringed with alternate dark and light bands; a feature occurring also in the lemurs, and in some of the lower Mammals.   As in the American monkeys, the thumb of the hand cannot be opposed to the fingers, neither are there naked callosities on the buttocks, nor are there pouches in the cheeks. None of the marmosets have prehensile tails.   Their hind-limbs are always considerably larger and more robust than the front ones, and the great toe is invari-

MARMOSETS—(1) COMMON MARMOSET, (2) BLACK-TAILED MARMOSET, (3) BLACK-EARED MARMOSET ($\frac{1}{4}$ nat. size).

ably of such small dimensions that, in a literal sense of the term, it has no sort of right to its name.

Many of the marmosets have the ears fringed with long pencils of hairs, which give them a very peculiar and unmistakable appearance.   Both in size and habits they are more like squirrels than monkeys, and they climb in the same way. They are, indeed, essentially arboreal animals, subsisting not only on fruits, but likewise to a large extent on insects.   As we shall see later on, marmosets usually live in small parties, and all of them appear to be gentle in disposition, although frequently requiring a considerable amount of trouble and patience before they can be tamed. Whereas other monkeys usually give birth to but a single young one at a time, marmosets normally have litters of two or three; and in this respect, therefore, show decided signs of their affinity with animals of inferior rank in the zoological scheme. They retain, however, the expressive and mobile faces characteristic of the higher monkeys.

There are a large number of kinds of marmosets, although there is still some uncertainty as to how many are entitled to rank as valid species. The whole of them are very similar in general appearance, but they may be conveniently divided into two genera, according as to whether the lower tusks or canine teeth are or not longer than the front teeth or incisors.

The Short-Tusked Marmosets.

Genus *Hapale.*

The marmosets of this group are characterised by the tusks not being longer than the incisors in the lower jaw, so that all the teeth present an even series. It is only in this genus that we meet with species in which the hair of the tail is marked by darker and lighter rings.

Common Marmoset. The common marmoset, or ouistiti (*H. jacchus*), is one of the best and longest known members of the family, having been first described by Linnæus. It is an inhabitant of Brazil, more especially the south-eastern regions of that country, and belongs to a group in which the ears are large and bald over the greater part of their expanse, but furnished with a pencil of long hairs, which forms an expanded tuft on the front edge of their aperture; the hair on the sides of the crown of the head being likewise elongated. The tail is alternately ringed with bands of black and white, and the back has likewise darker and lighter cross-bands.

The common marmoset, which is represented in the left figure of the woodcut on p. 189, is of a generally blackish colour, the back and outer surfaces of the thighs being marked with transverse bands of grey, and the head having a white spot on the upper part of the nose. The especial point of distinction is, however, that while the head is black and white, the tufts of hair on the ears are pure white.

The contrast between the black face and the white ear-tufts gives a very peculiar expression to this animal, reminding us somewhat of a white-haired negro. It is frequently brought to this country as a pet, and its behaviour in captivity has been many times described.

The following account of the habits of a favourite ouistiti is given by a writer in Loudon's *Magazine of Natural History* for the year 1829. This specimen was procured at Bahia, and at first it is described as being "exceedingly bold and fierce, screeching most vehemently when anyone dared to approach it. . . . It was long before it was so reconciled even to those who fed it as to allow the slightest liberty in the way of touching or patting its body; and it was almost impossible to do this by surprise, or by the most quiet and cautious approach, as the monkey was not steady a moment, but was constantly turning its head round from side to side, eyeing every person with the most suspicious and angry look. Its sense of hearing appeared to be excessively acute, so that the slightest whisper was sure to arouse it. The voice of this little animal was peculiarly sharp and disagreeable, consisting of a very quick succession of harsh and shrill sounds (imitated by the name ouistiti), so loud, that they might be heard from the remotest part of the ship.

"For a considerable time there was no evident change in its habits, as it continued to be nearly as wild as when I first got it, and showed none of the playfulness and vivacity which characterise most of the monkey tribe. As long as the fruit which we had on board lasted, it would eat nothing else; but, when these failed, we soon discovered a most agreeable substitute, which it appeared to relish above everything. By chance we observed it devouring a large cockroach which it had caught running along the deck of the vessel; and from this time till nearly the end of the voyage—a space of four or five weeks—it fed almost exclusively on these insects, and contributed most effectually to rid the vessel of them. It frequently ate a score of the largest kind, which are 2 or 2½ inches long, and a very great number of the smaller ones, two or three times in the course of the day. It was quite amusing to see it at its meal. When he had got hold of one of the large cockroaches, he held it in his fore-paws, and then invariably nipped the head off first; he then pulled out the viscera and cast them aside, and devoured the rest of the body, rejecting the dry elytra and wings, and also the legs of the insect, which are covered with short, stiff bristles. The small cockroaches he ate without such fastidious nicety. In addition to these, we gave him milk, sugar, raisins, and crumbs of bread. Hitherto the weather was warm, the thermometer never being below 65° or 60° Fahr.; but as we reached a more northern latitude, and approached England, the change of temperature affected the monkey very considerably, and now he would not even touch the cockroaches when given to him; the hair, especially that on the tail, fell off; and, at the end of the voyage, this organ was almost quite bare and naked. He kept constantly in the kennel, rolling himself up in a piece of flannel, which had been put in for warmth, except when he could reach a sunny part of the deck, where he might bask in the heat. There was a considerable continuance of cold north-easterly winds, the thermometer ranging as low as from 42° to 36°, and as the monkey ate little or nothing, and was quite inactive, I hardly expected to have kept it alive.

"When I got it on shore I kept it for some days in a warm room; it gradually recovered its nimbleness, running about the room, and dragging its kennel after it. Even then it would not eat any insects, and its food consisted of milk and crumbs of bread; it was particularly fond of any sweet preserve, as jelly, and of ripe fresh fruits."

Mr. Bates, who compares the ouistiti to a kitten, banded with black and grey all over the body and tail, and having a fringe of long white hairs around the ears, only observed this marmoset in the neighbourhood of Para. On a certain occasion he observed one of these animals comfortably seated on the shoulders of a mulatto girl, whom he met walking in Para; and, on inquiry, learnt that it had been captured in the island of Marajo, at the mouth of the Amazon.

Another closely allied form from Brazil has been named the white-necked marmoset (*H. albicollis*), and is distinguished from the common form merely by the circumstance that the hinder part of the head and the back of the neck are grey instead of black.

Black-Eared Marmoset. In South-Eastern Brazil there is yet a third nearly related form, known as the black-eared marmoset (*H. penicillata*), of which a representation is given in the right-hand figures of the illustration on page 189. The distinctive feature of this marmoset is to be found in the circumstance that not only the whole of the head and neck, but likewise the tufts of long hairs on the ears, are completely black.

There are other varieties or species, differing somewhat from either of the above in the coloration of the head and ears.

White-Eared Marmoset. The white-eared marmoset (*H. aurita*), which is likewise a Brazilian species, is the representative of a second group, in which the pencil of hairs on the ears is much more slender than in the common marmoset,

THE SILVER MARMOSET.

while the hair on the back is generally somewhat speckled, although faint traces of banding are occasionally observable. The tail is ringed like that of the common marmoset.

The general colour of this marmoset is blackish, minutely speckled with yellow or a reddish tint on the back; the sides of the head, the limbs, and the hinder part of the body being pure black; while the crown of the head is brown, and a spot on the forehead, as well as the tufts on the ears, are grey. In some instances, where the back is more decidedly red than usual, there are faint, paler cross-bands in this region, and more especially on the loins.

The white-shouldered marmoset (*H. humeralifer*) is a closely allied Brazilian form, distinguished by the face, shoulders, chest, and arms, as well as the tufts on the ears, being white; the thighs being a mixture of brown and white in colour.

Silver Marmoset. With the silver marmoset of Brazil (*H. chrysoleucus*) we come to the first of three species, distinguished from those yet noticed either by the absence of rings of colour on the tail, or by the arrangement or absence of the longer hairs on the ears. They are all tiny little creatures, not much larger than a rat, and have no bands of colour on the back.

The silver marmoset has large and nearly naked ears, covered on both sides near the margin with long hairs, forming a double fringe instead of a pencil. The fur of this elegant little creature is soft and silky, and either pure white or yellowish-white in colour. In the white variety the limbs and tail are, however, invariably yellowish; while in the variety in which the fur of the body is yellowish, that covering the limbs, tail, and under-parts may be chestnut-brown. These two varieties were regarded by Dr. Gray as distinct species, but this is not generally admitted by other writers.

Black-Tailed Marmoset. This species (*H. melanura*) is readily distinguished from the preceding by the absence of the fringe of hairs on the large and flesh-coloured ears, and likewise by the black tail. Usually the general colour of the fur is ashy-brown, paler on the front of the body, and whitish on the front of the thighs and loins; while the head and limbs are dark brown. There is, however, a variety which is entirely white, with the exception of the characteristic black tail. It is represented in the top figure of the illustration on p. 197.

Of this species, which he mentions under the name of *Midas argentatus*, Mr. Bates writes that it is one of the rarest of the American marmosets. "Indeed," says this writer, "I have not heard of its being found anywhere except near Cameta, where I once saw three individuals, looking like so many white kittens, running along a branch in a cacao grove; in their motions they precisely resembled the *M. ursulus*," of which a description is given later on. "I saw afterwards a pet animal of this species, and heard that there were many so kept, and that they were esteemed as great treasures. The one mentioned was full-grown, although it measured only 7 inches in length of body. It was covered with long, white, silky hairs; the tail being blackish and the face flesh-coloured. It was a most timid and sensitive little thing. The woman who owned it carried it constantly in her bosom, and no money would induce her to part with her pet. She called it Mico (the native name of these animals). It fed from her mouth, and allowed her to fondle it freely, but the nervous little creature would not permit strangers to touch it. If any one attempted to do so, it shrank back, the whole body trembling with fear, and its teeth chattered whilst it uttered its tremulous frightened tones. The expression of its features was like that of its more robust brother, *M. ursulus;* the eyes, which were black, were full of curiosity and mistrust, and were always kept fixed on the person who attempted to advance towards it."

Pigmy Marmoset. The third and last of the three diminutive species constituting this group is the pigmy marmoset, (*H. pygmæa*) which is likewise found in the primeval forest regions of Brazil. This species is distinguished by the smallness of its short ears, which, although slightly hairy on their outer surface, have no tuft or fringe of long hairs, and are entirely concealed beneath the backwardly-directed and elongated fur of the crown of the head. A further distinction is to be found in the presence of darker and lighter rings on the tail. The general colour of the body is a tawny or ferruginous brown, more or less varied with black and red on the back; the neck, under-parts, and inner surfaces of the limbs being yellowish, and the hands and feet yellowish-brown.

Three specimens of the pigmy marmoset were obtained by Mr. Bates on the upper Amazon, at San Paulo, near Ega. They are described as measuring only 7 inches in length, exclusive of the tail. The tiny little face is furnished with long brown whiskers, brushed back over the ears; the general colour of the body being brownish-tawny, but the tail elegantly ringed with black. Mr. Bates adds, that this marmoset ranges as far north as Mexico, and is the only Amazonian primate that wanders far from the great river plain. The silky marmoset has, however, also been recorded from Mexico.

THE PINCHÉ (⅛ nat. size).

THE LONG-TUSKED MARMOSETS, OR TAMARINS.

Genus *Midas.*

The marmosets of this group are at once distinguished from those of the preceding genus by the circumstance that the tusks, or canine teeth, of the lower jaw are considerably longer than the front, or incisor teeth; so that the whole series of lower teeth does not present the even and regular height characteristic of the short-tusked marmosets. Why Buffon applied the name tamarin to one member of this group, we are unaware; but it has been subsequently very generally adopted for two of the species, and is a short and convenient name by which to designate the entire genus. None of the tamarins have pencilled ears; neither, as we have already mentioned, have they ringed tails, although some of the species have the back marked with dark and light cross-bands.

THE NEGRO TAMARIN (*Midas ursulus*).

One of the best known of all the species is the common or negro tamarin, which is found in Guiana and the lower part of the Amazon valley. It belongs to a group in which both the forehead and face are hairy, and the hair of the head not longer than that of the body; the ears being large and naked. The colour is a nearly uniform black, especially on the nose, lips, and hands; but the hinder part of the body has the fur more or less mottled with greyish-white. Although not known as a distinct species at the time of Linnæus, this marmoset was described by the early French naturalists, and distinguished by Buffon as the *Tamarin nègre.*

Mr. Bates writes that the negro tamarin "is never seen in large flocks, three or four being the greatest number observed together. It seems to be less afraid of the neighbourhood of man than any other monkey. I sometimes saw it in the woods which border the suburban streets [of Para], and once I espied two individuals in a thicket behind the English consul's house at Nazareth. Its mode of progression along the main boughs of the lofty trees is like that of the squirrel; it does not ascend to the slender branches, or take the wonderful flying leaps which the *Cebidæ* do, whose prehensile tails and flexible hands fit them for such headlong travelling. It confines itself to the larger boughs and trunks of trees, the long nails being of great assistance to the creature, enabling it to cling securely to the bark; and it is often seen passing rapidly round the perpendicular cylindrical trunks. It is a quick, timid, restless little creature, and has a great share of curiosity, for when a person passes by under the trees along which a flock is running, they also stop for a few moments to have a stare at the intruder. In Para, *M. ursulus* is often seen in a tame state in the houses of the inhabitants. When full grown it is about 9 inches long, independently of the tail, which measures 15 inches. The fur is thick, and black in colour, with the exception of a reddish-brown streak down the middle of the back. When first taken, or when kept tied up, it is very timid and irritable. It will not allow itself to be approached, but keeps retreating backwards when any one attempts to coax it. It is always in a querulous humour, uttering a twittering, complaining noise; its dark, watchful eyes, expressive of distrust, observant of every movement which takes place near it. When treated kindly, however, as it generally is in the houses of the natives, it becomes very tame and familiar. I once saw one as playful as a kitten, running about the house after the negro children, who fondled it to their hearts' content. It acted somewhat differently towards strangers, and seemed not to see them seated in the hammock which was slung in the room, leaping up, trying to bite, and otherwise annoying them. It is generally fed on sweet fruits, such as the banana; but it is also fond of insects, especially soft-bodied spiders and grasshoppers, which it will snap up with eagerness when within reach. The expression of countenance in these small monkeys is intelligent and pleasing. This is partly due to the small facial angle, which is given as 60°; but the quick movements of the head, and the way they have of inclining it to one side when their curiosity is excited, contribute very much to give them a knowing expression."

Allied Species.

Red-Handed Tamarin. This species (*M. rufimanus*), which is the true tamarin of Buffon, is an inhabitant of Dutch Guiana, or Surinam, and differs from the preceding by its yellowish or orange-red hands; its habits being, doubtless, precisely similar. Like the negro tamarin, it has been exhibited alive in England.

Brown-Headed Tamarin. The brown-headed tamarin (*M. flavifrons*) is the Brazilian representative of several species or varieties distinguished from the two preceding forms by the face being brownish, with a few grey hairs, although the nose still remains black. The general colour is black, with a white mottling on the hinder part of the back; the head being pale brown, with some black markings. In the male the outer surface of the limbs generally has a bright rufous tinge, while the under-parts and the inner surfaces of the limbs are reddish-brown. The so-called black-and-red tamarin (*M. rufoniger*) would appear to be only a brighter coloured variety of this species, in which the back, loins, thighs, and legs are of a bright chestnut-red. It occurs in Brazil, and appears to have been met with by Mr. Bates on the upper Amazon in the neighbourhood of Ega. In referring to the marmoset, provisionally identified with this form, this traveller writes as follows:—"One day, whilst walking along a forest pathway, I saw one of these lively little fellows miss his grasp as he was passing from one tree to another along with his troop. He fell head-foremost from a height of at least fifty feet, but managed cleverly to alight on his feet in the pathway; quickly turning round, he gave me a good stare for a few moments, and then bounded off gaily to climb another tree." Mr. Bates adds that the habits of this animal are precisely the same as those of the negro tamarin.

Deville's tamarin (*M. devillei*), from Peru, is another nearly related species, with the head, neck, front of the back, fore-limbs, and tail black; the hinder part of the back marked with grey and black transverse bars; and the loins and legs bright chestnut-red.

Moustached Tamarin. This curious little creature (*M. mystax*) belongs to a well-marked group of two or three species readily recognised by having the tip of the nose and the lips covered with white hairs, giving a very peculiar look to the face. It is found in the upper Amazon valley, both in Brazil and Peru. It is black, with a brownish tinge on the back and thighs; the white hairs on the nose and lips being long, and forming a broad tuft. Mr. Bates, who met with this species on the upper Brazilian Amazon, near Tabatinga, says that, when seen from a short distance, it looks exactly as though it were holding a ball of snow-white cotton in its teeth.

The red-bellied tamarin (*M. labiatus*) is an allied upper Amazonian species, with a very smooth and glossy coat, of a deep blackish-brown colour on the back; while the under-parts are a mixture of rich black and reddish hues. The white hairs on the nose and lips are much shorter and less conspicuous than in the moustached tamarin; those on their lips merely forming a thin line on the margins, instead of a distinct tuft.

THE PINCHÉ (*Midas œdipus*).

In Colombia (New Granada) and Panama the tusked marmosets are represented by two closely allied species differing in certain points from all the species found in the more southerly or easterly regions. Both have the face and sides of the head but sparsely haired, while there is a distinctly marked patch of hair different from the rest on the crown of the head, and the hair on the neck is elongated.

The present species is restricted to Colombia, and has been long known in Europe; it received its name of Pinché—on what grounds we know not—from the French naturalist Buffon. It is represented in our illustration on p. 194, and is of a greyish-brown colour on the back; the outer surface of the limbs and the root of the tail being tinged with red, while the long tuft of hair which forms a crest on

SILKY MARMOSETS ($\frac{1}{4}$ nat. size).

the top of the head, as well as the throat, under-parts, arms, and the front of the legs, are white; the tip of the tail being black.

Geoffroy's marmoset (*M. geoffroyi*), which is the representative of the Pinché in Panama, is distinguished from that species by the hair on the crown of the head not being elongated into a crest, but being short, and forming a narrow patch of an oblong shape. Its coloration is very nearly the same as that of the Pinché, with the exception that the hair on the nape of the neck is chestnut-coloured.

The Silky Marmoset (*Midas rosalia*).

The last group of the marmosets is represented by the well-known silky marmoset, shown in the figure on the preceding page, and the golden-headed marmoset; both of which inhabit the forests of South-Eastern Brazil, and are commonly exhibited in the menageries of Europe. They are distinguished by having the head and part of the neck covered with long hair, forming a kind of mane; the hair round the face being directed backwards. The face itself is but sparsely haired; and the naked ears are partly concealed by the mane. The colour is a bright golden yellow, more or less tinged with red; but there is a variety in which the head, hands, and feet, as well as the end of the tail, are blackish.

The silky marmoset was known to Buffon under the name of the Marikina; and has also been described as the lion marmoset (*M. leoninus*). Mr. Bates, who alludes to it under the latter name, which is due to the long mane of brown hair hanging from the neck giving it very much the appearance of a miniature lion, states that he once saw a tame individual of this species when on the upper Amazon. After commenting on its playful and intelligent disposition, he observes that it was familiar with every person in the house where it was kept; and seemed to take particular pleasure in climbing about the bodies of the various visitors who entered. "The first time I went in," writes Mr. Bates, "it ran across the room straightway to the chair on which I had sat down, and climbed up to my shoulder; arrived there, it turned round and looked in my face, showing its little teeth, and chattering, as though it would say, 'Well, and how do you do?' It showed more affection towards its master than towards strangers, and would climb up to his head a dozen times in the course of an hour." These marmosets are described as keeping to the very top of their cages—a habit probably retained from the native one of living in the tree-tops. When descending they always come down backwards, with the tail pendent. Mr. Swainson, who observed these animals in their native Brazilian forests, states that their ways are very similar to those of the common marmoset. He mentions, however, their habit of bounding from tree to tree with incredible rapidity, which is scarcely consonant with the account given by Mr. Bates of the movements of marmosets in general. They are stated to utter sharp but weak cries of alarm when frightened.

The total length of this marmoset is rather less than two feet, of which one is occupied by the long tail.

The golden-headed marmoset (*M. chrysomelas*) may be regarded as a black representative of the preceding species; its general colour being black, with the face, fore-arms, hands, feet, and the base of the tail tawny.

CHAPTER VII.

Apes, Monkeys, and Lemurs —*continued*.

The Lemurs.

Family *LEMURIDÆ*.

THE whole of the animals treated of in the four preceding chapters, as possessing many characters in common, to which we have alluded in the course of our description, are regarded by zoologists as collectively constituting one great group of the order Primates. And since this group is also taken in zoological classification to include man himself, it is spoken of as the Anthropoid or Human-like group; the individual members thereof being referred to as Anthropoids.

We now come to another and lower group of animals, which, while sufficiently nearly allied to the above to be included in the order Primates, are so different as to be entitled to stand as a group of equivalent rank. These animals are primarily represented by the lemurs. The group also includes two other creatures which cannot be classed in the same family as the lemurs, and of which we shall treat in the succeeding chapter. As it is desirable to have a common name for all the members of this group, and as it would be incorrect to allude to the whole of them as lemurs, the term Lemur-like creatures, or, shortly, Lemuroids, has been proposed, and will be found convenient.

Although these Lemuroids may always be distinguished at a glance from the apes and monkeys by their foxy, expressionless faces, it is difficult to point out the important structural features by which they differ from the former without entering into anatomical details unsuited to a popular work like the present. The reader must, therefore, take it on trust that there are such important differences between the Anthropoids and the Lemuroids. In spite, however, of these differences, there are such resemblances between the two groups as to suggest that the lemurs and their allies are not far removed from the group from which we may presume (if the doctrine of evolution be the true key to the book of nature) the apes and monkeys to have originated.

Characteristics. That the lemurs are much lower in the zoological scale than the apes and monkeys is shown by the simpler structure of their brains, which have far fewer foldings on their surface than is the case with those of the latter; the amount of such foldings, as giving a larger extent of superficial surface, being indicative of the mental powers of the owners of the brains.

A peculiar feature of all the lemurs and their allies is to be found in the circumstance that the second toe of the foot (corresponding to the index finger of the hand) is always furnished with a sharp claw. All lemurs have a well-developed thumb and great toe; but, curiously enough, in some of them the index finger of the hand is rudimentary. They may or may not have tails, but these are never prehensile, although, as in some of the marmosets, they may be marked by alternate dark and light rings.

A point of resemblance to the monkeys and apes is shown by the number of incisor, or front teeth, being very frequently two on each side of both jaws, in place of the three which are so commonly present in other Mammals. In the apes and monkeys, however, the central pair of incisors in the upper jaw are in

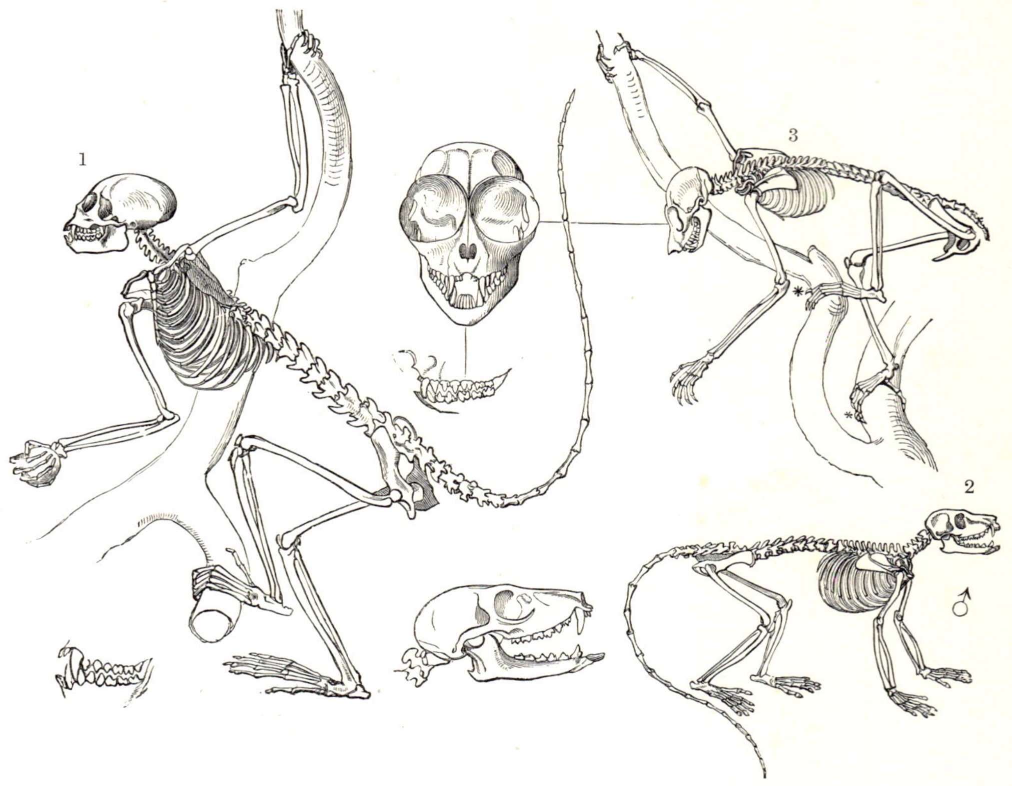

SKELETON OF SQUIRREL-MONKEY (1), OF MONGOOSE LEMUR (2), AND OF SLENDER LORIS (3).

contact with one another, while in the lemurs they are almost invariably separated by a gap in the middle line. This affords a ready means of distinguishing the skull of a lemur at a single glance from the skulls of almost all other Mammals except bats and some of the Insectivores. The lower front, or incisor, teeth of the lemurs shelve forwards, after the manner we have already mentioned as characteristic of one group of the American monkeys (p. 173).

Many lemurs are purely nocturnal animals, and it was probably from this circumstance, coupled with their silent habits and stealthy movements, that Linnæus was induced to give them the name by which they are now universally known. It is, perhaps, almost superfluous to mention that the name lemur is taken from the Latin term *lemures*, which, together with that of *larvæ*, was applied by the ancient Romans to such shades of the dead as were supposed to be of malignant propensities. It is somewhat curious that both these terms should have been introduced into zoological nomenclature; the former to denote the animals of the present group, while the latter is applied to the grub stage of insects.

Distribution. Altogether, there are somewhere about fifty species of lemur-like animals, of which the distribution presents some very remarkable features. In the first place, they are all restricted not only to the Old World, but also to the southern regions of the great land masses of that hemisphere, none of them being found to the northward of the tropic of Cancer, while the tropic of Capricorn very nearly limits their southward range. Within this area a few species are found respectively throughout the warmer regions of Africa, and in Southern India and Ceylon, while their eastern limits are marked by the island of Celebes and the Philippines. In all these regions the number of species is comparatively few, and they form but an unimportant element in the general fauna of the country. The case is, however, very different in the great island of Madagascar, which is the headquarters of the whole group. Here we find them constituting no less than one-half the entire Mammalian fauna of the island, being represented by six genera, which include more than thirty species; most of the other Mammals being comparatively small forms, unknown either on the continent of Africa or in Asia. The true lemurs occur only in Madagascar, and it is very remarkable that all the species of the group found in that island scarcely show any closer relationship to those of the African mainland than they exhibit to those of Asia. So abundant, indeed, are lemurs in Madagascar, that, according to Monsieur Grandidier, who has done so much to increase our knowledge of this group, at least one individual is almost sure to be found in every little copse throughout the island.

It will be evident that such a numerous population of helpless animals like lemurs could not exist in a land overrun with large carnivorous animals; and in the whole of Madagascar we find only a few civets and an allied creature known as the foussa. Now to account for these peculiar features—the absence of all large Carnivores, except civets, and the abundance of lemurs—we have to call in the aid of the geologist. He will tell us that lemur-like animals, accompanied by civet-like Carnivores, existed in England, France, and other parts of Europe during the early part of the Tertiary period. And we are accordingly led to conclude that the lemurs and civets of Madagascar obtained an entrance into that island, doubtless by way of Africa, at a time when that continent was still free from the presence of the large Carnivores and the host of hoofed mammals which now form such a dominant feature in its animal population. After the lemurs and civets had obtained an entrance into Madagascar that country became separated from the adjacent mainland, and it has remained as an island ever since. There, secure from molestation, the lemurs have attained a development unequalled at any time in any part of the globe, and afford us an admirable instance of the importance a group of animals may attain when living under favourable conditions.

Habits. We have already said that many lemurs are essentially nocturnal creatures. To this we may add that they are all of essentially arboreal habits. Indeed, except when compelled to descend to the ground to obtain water, or for the purpose of crossing from one plantation or coppice to another, they but rarely leave the trees. Their diet is extremely mixed, scarcely anything coming amiss to them, as will be inferred when we mention that leaves, fruits, insects, reptiles, birds' eggs, and birds themselves are eagerly consumed by most of these animals.

By the natives of Madagascar the lemurs are looked upon with suspicious

FEMALE BLACK LEMUR WITH YOUNG. (From Sclater, *Proc. Zool. Soc.*, 1885.)

awe, and are consequently but seldom molested. This is doubtless due to their nocturnal habits and ghost-like movements; while the large eyes essential to these and all other nocturnal creatures have perhaps contributed to this feeling. In Ceylon and India, as we shall subsequently see, the large glaring eyes of one of the prettiest of the lemurs used to lead to the unfortunate creatures being put to a cruel death. None of the lemurs attain any very large size, and all of them, when unmolested, are perfectly harmless and inoffensive animals, except to the birds, reptiles, and insects upon which they prey. The nostrils of a lemur, which are always situated at the extremity of the muzzle, differ markedly in form from those of a monkey. In all the latter, whether they be thin-nosed like the Old World kinds, or broad-nosed like those of America, the nostrils are always more or less rounded in form, and thus approach to the human type. In lemurs, on the other hand, the nostrils are always in the form of a curved slit, widest above, and with the convexity directed outwardly, as is well shown in the figure on p. 206. The nostrils of a lemur are in fact almost precisely similar to those of a dog or a cat, and we have in this another proof of a relatively low zoological position.

In the lemurs proper, the first point to be noticed is that the upper front, or incisor teeth are always two in number on either side of the jaw, and that the middle pair are separated from one another by a distinct gap. The upper premolar teeth may be either two, as in the Old World monkeys, or three, as in their cousins, of the New World; the molars being invariably three in number. The front teeth in the lower jaw, together with the one corresponding to the tusk, or canine, always shelve forwards, and are of small size. This small size and shelving direction of the lower tusk renders it necessary that some other tooth should be enlarged so as to bite against the upper tusk. And we accordingly find that the first premolar in the lower jaw takes on the form and size of a tusk, and bites against the true tusk, or canine tooth of the upper jaw. It has been mentioned in the introductory chapter that whereas true tusks, or canines, have usually but a single root, premolar teeth nearly always have two roots, except when there are four of these teeth, in which case the first generally has but one root. Now the tusk-like lower premolar of the lemurs has the usual two roots, and hence we have a ready means of distinguishing a lemur's skull from that of most other Mammals; that is to say, by the lower tusk having two distinct roots.

The last feature we shall mention as being distinctive of the lemurs proper, is that, with the exception of the second toe of the foot, all the fingers and all the toes have well-formed flattened nails like those of the majority of monkeys.

The Indri Lemur.

Genus *Indris*.

The peculiar-looking animal represented in the illustration on the next page is one of the numerous lemurs from Madagascar, and occupies the proud position of being the largest member of the entire group. It is likewise the sole representative of its genus; and in scientific parlance is designated *Indris brevicaudata*, its second title referring to its apology for a tail. The name indri, or indris, is a corruption from the native name Endrina, used in certain districts by the inhabitants of Madagascar for this animal. In other districts it is, however, designated Babakoto, or " little old man."

The indri is the first of a group of three genera, restricted to Madagascar, which present certain characteristics in common not found in other lemurs. Among these characters the most obvious is the large proportionate size of the legs as compared with the arms. Another is, that with the exception of the great toe (which is capable of being fully opposed to the others), the toes of the foot are joined together by a web as far as the end of their first joints. For those who desire to enter more fully into the structure of these lemurs, it may be mentioned that the total number of teeth in the adult condition is limited to 30; the series being represented by the formula $i\frac{2}{1}, c\frac{1}{1}, p\frac{2}{2}, m\frac{3}{3}$. All the members of this group differ from the other lemur-like animals in that they do not give birth to more than a single young one at a time. From this circumstance, together with certain features in their structure, these indris are regarded as the most highly organised of all

THE INDRI LEMUR ($\frac{1}{8}$ nat. size).

the lemurs, and are accordingly placed at the head of the list. They subsist exclusively on a vegetable diet.

The indri is sufficiently distinguished from the other two genera included in the group by its mere stump of a tail; although there are also certain other features which support its right to stand as the representative of a distinct genus.

We have already mentioned that the indri is the largest of all the lemurs; and in a fully adult animal the length of the head and body is about two feet. Although there is great individual variation in this respect, the indri is very strikingly coloured. Very frequently the forehead is blackish, but, like the cheeks and throat, it may be grey. The head, shoulders, back, and arms are of a full velvety black; and the black ears are large and prominent, and covered with longer hairs than those on the head.

From the loins to the tail there is a large triangular patch of either pure white or of a yellowish tinge; this patch terminates in front in a sharp point, and is bordered on all sides with black. The flanks are also light-coloured; and the dark bands which usually separate the light area of the loins from that of the flanks are continued down the front of the legs; but the sides of the legs are in general whitish, and their hinder surface grey; the heel being reddish. The hands and feet are black, and, unlike the specimen we figure, they are, as a rule, almost denuded of hair.

Such are the common colours in the larger number of specimens of the indri. In almost every flock, however, individuals are found in which the light-coloured areas intrude more or less extensively upon those which are usually black; and from these intermediate forms a complete transition can be traced to others in which the whole of the fur is white. The intermediately coloured individuals very generally retain the broad black streak down the front of the leg, and the black ears.

Instead of being distributed over the whole of Madagascar, the indris are confined to the forests on the east coast of the island; this restricted distribution being due to the great range of mountains running longitudinally through Madagascar, which cuts off these animals from the plains on the western side.

Habits. In contradistinction to most of the lemurs, the indris are purely diurnal in their habits; they are commonly found in small parties of four or five, although during the day single individuals, more or less widely separated from their companions, may frequently be seen. Their general habits appear to be similar to those of the propitheques, to which we shall refer later on. Unless injured so badly as to be unable to make its escape, the indri does not give utterance to the least sound when wounded; if, however, it is so severely hit as to fall to the ground, which it will only do when its extraordinary powers of holding on to the branches of the trees are exhausted, it gives vent to piercing shrieks.

It is related by Grandidier that some of the inhabitants of Madagascar have an extraordinary superstitious veneration for the indri, and will on no consideration harm it. Different families assign different reasons for this special veneration; and while it may be of the most marked description in one village, in a neighbouring one it may be totally wanting. The author referred to considers that it may be largely due to the plaintive and mournful cries with which these animals frequently make the forests resound,—cries which can be heard at great distances, and have a more or less marked resemblance to agonised human wailings.

The Propitheques, or Sifakas.

Genus *Propithecus.*

The sifakas, as they are called by the native inhabitants of Madagascar, constitute the only genus of this group of lemurs which is represented by more than a single species. Although closely allied to the indri, they are at once distinguished by their long tails; the muzzle is also rather shorter, and the ears are considerably smaller, and are partly concealed by the fur, as is shown in our figure of the head of one of the species. Their skin is of a deep black; but the general colour of the fur is usually white, more or less tinged with yellow, and, in some individuals, passing into red or even black. The fur on the breast is always much thinner than that of other parts of the body.

Three species of the genus are recognised, which are restricted to different parts of the island; but of these species there are several more or less distinct races, which are likewise confined to particular localities. It has been observed that while those individuals of the several species which tend to assume a black coloration are found in the damper parts of the island, those which are most completely white frequent the drier regions at the northern extremity of Madagascar. The sifakas, as Grandidier observes, live in bands of from six to eight individuals. They are completely diurnal in their habits, and may be observed at morning and evening, when the heat is not too great, leaping in the forests from tree to tree in search of food. At sunrise they may often be seen sitting on the horizontal bough of a tree, close to where it branches off from the main stem, with their long legs bent, so as to touch their chin, and their hands resting on their knees. At other times they will be seen sitting in the same position, but with their arms extended, so as to receive the genial warmth from the rising sun on their bodies. During the heat of the day they conceal themselves in the depths of the foliage. When sleeping, they incline the head forwards on the chest, and cover it with their arms; at the same time the tail is either curled up spirally between the legs, or allowed to hang straight down.

HEAD OF VERREAUX'S SIFAKA.—After Grandidier.

Their shelving lower front teeth are admirably adapted for removing part of the rind of the fruits on which they so largely subsist, and thus making an aperture through which the pulp is removed piecemeal. The skins of the fruits are always rejected; and it is stated that sifakas exhibit a marked preference for green rather than ripe fruit.

In all ways they are admirably adapted for a purely arboreal life. So strong indeed are their hind limbs that they can readily take leaps of from ten to eleven yards in passing from bough to bough; and so rapid are their motions that Grandidier speaks of them as appearing to fly rather than leap. On the rare occasions when they descend from their favourite trees, they advance by means of long leaps, as owing to the shortness of their arms it is not easy for them to walk on the ground on all-fours like the majority of monkeys. To see them, observes Grandidier (from whom the whole of this account is taken), resting on their hind feet, and at each leap throwing up their arms in the air, the spectator might be led to think for a moment that he was looking at children at play. Indeed, a troop of these creatures advancing across the plains in the manner described, is said to be a truly ludicrous sight. Not only are the hands of the sifakas of no use to their owners in walking, but they are almost equally useless as organs of prehension; and when a sifaka has occasion to pick up a fruit from the ground, he will usually stoop down and seize it in his mouth. When conveyed to the hand, such an object is grasped between the bent fingers and the palm, and not between the fingers and thumb. As purely grasping organs, adapted to afford a firm hold to the branches of trees, both the hands and feet of these lemurs are, however, perfect.

In disposition the sifakas are described as being gentle, and they but seldom attempt to bite, while if they do so the wound they inflict is not serious. At certain seasons, however, the males are wont to engage in contests among themselves, the results of which are frequently visible in their torn and tattered ears. Unlike many other lemurs, they are, as a rule, silent; but when frightened or angry they give vent to a low cry somewhat resembling the clucking of a fowl. In a word, so far as character goes, these animals may be described as being but little active, but little restless, and but little intelligent.

Diademed Sifaka. The diademed sifaka (*P. diadema*), known to the natives of Madagascar as the simpona, is the largest of the three species, and at the same time the one which was first brought to the notice of science, having been described by E. T. Bennett in the year 1832. It takes its name from the band of white hairs running across the forehead, which, with the grey fringe of hair on the cheeks and chin, surrounds the black face, and thus gives to the animal a peculiar and striking physiognomy. The crown and back of the head, together with the outer surface of the ears and the nape of the neck, are a dark brown colour, and the same tint extends over the shoulders, so as to give somewhat the appearance of a mantle, and ends in a point on the back; this point in some individuals being only just below the neck, while in others it reaches as far back as the loins. Occasionally this dark mantle-like area, instead of being dark brown, is of a grey tint. The loins and flanks are generally grey, varying considerably in different individuals; the grey passing gradually into the brown of the back and the orange round the tail, and extending on to the upper parts of the arms, or even enveloping the whole of the upper arm. The fore-arms, together with the region round the tail and the legs, are generally of a bright orange yellow, although occasionally yellowish-white with some intermixed black hairs. The hands are mainly black, but the feet have a good deal of yellow in them; the basal half of the tail is yellowish, while the rest of it is grey.

Such are the colours of the typical form of this species. In the moist regions of the south of Madagascar there is, however, a nearly or quite white race of this lemur, while in the dry regions of the north there is a black race; in each case intermediate forms occurring which connect these varieties with the ordinary type.

The diademed sifaka inhabits the narrow strip of forest-land extending along the whole length of the eastern coast of Madagascar, and bordering the chain of granite and slaty mountains which dips down towards the sea on the east, and is the cause of almost daily rain. It is where this chain almost dies out at the northern end of the island that the black race occurs.

Verreaux's Sifaka.　　This and the next species, which are smaller than the last, and are those which are known to the natives as the sifakas, are restricted to the western and southern coasts of Madagascar.　Here they are only found in the thick forests which here and there occur among the desolate solitudes of the western and southern sides of the island,—regions of sandy plains where fertilising rains but seldom occur.

The fur of *P. verreauxi* (of which the head is figured on p. 206) is woolly and soft to the touch; its colour being typically white with a faint tinge of yellow. The summit and hinder part of the head are, however, often of a marone colour, and more rarely reddish, while some individuals show more or less marked grey tints in various regions of the body.　In no case, however, does the brown of the head ever extend on to the neck and back, as it does in the diademed species. There are two well-marked varieties of this species, one being pure white, with the exception of patches of bright red on the arms and thighs.

A writer relates how he once had for some time two females and their young of this species in a cage.　"Nothing was more touching than to see these poor mothers holding their young lying in their arms.　At the least movement, the young sifaka left its mother's breast and leapt upon her back, where, with its hands resting on her shoulders, and its feet buried in her fur, it took so firm a grasp that it was impossible to make it leave go; and one could thus readily understand how that, whatever leaps the mother might take, the offspring would never be unseated."

Crowned Sifaka.　　The last species of the propitheques (*P. coronatus*) agrees in size with the preceding, to which it is closely allied.　It has, indeed, a crest of long blackish hairs on the forehead, from which it derives its name; but since a similar crest is found in some individuals of Verreaux's sifaka, this cannot be taken as the ground for specific distinction.　Neither can its coloration, peculiar though it be, form the distinction, since the difference in this respect from the typical form of the latter species is scarcely if at all greater than that occurring between the various races included under that heading.

It is, indeed, mainly from the characters of the skull that the crowned sifaka is ranked as a distinct species.　Thus the skull is altogether larger than that of the preceding species, in addition to which it has a proportionately larger muzzle; while there are other distinctive features, into the consideration of which it would be beyond the scope of the present work to enter.

In colour, the forehead, the crown of the head, and the cheeks are blackish-brown; in bold contrast to which stands out the white fur with which the ears are covered.　The neck and upper parts of the body, as well as the limbs, are of the same white colour, having a more or less distinct rosy tinge on the limbs and at the root of the tail; this rosy tint being most distinct in the more southern race of this species, in which it may extend on to the back.　There is a patch of grey or brown, varying in size, on the nape of the neck.　The tail and hands are invariably pure white.

This species is restricted to a small area on the north-west coast of Madagascar, situated to the north-eastward of Cape St. André, and bounded to the east by the River Betsiboka, and by the Manzaray River to the west.

In concluding their notice of these animals, Messrs. Milne-Edwards and Grandidier remark how curious it is to find the various races and species so sharply separated from one another that it is sufficient to cross a river—it may be of no great width—in order to find that, while on one bank all the sifakas belong to one race, on the opposite bank they will be of another race, if not of a distinct species. No satisfactory explanation of these peculiar features in topographical distribution has, however, suggested itself to the authors quoted.

The Avahi Lemur.

Genus *Avahis*.

The third and last genus of the present group of lemurs is represented only by the avahi or woolly lemur (*Avahis laniger*); a species discovered at the same time as the indri in the year 1870 by the French traveller Sonnerat. The avahi, although furnished with a long tail like the sifakas, is readily distinguished by the still shorter muzzle, and also by the ears being completely concealed by the fur, which is of a woolly instead of a silky nature. Although these differences are amply sufficient to distinguish the avahi from the sifakas when they are seen together, it is not on these alone that the zoologist relies when referring them to distinct genera. There are, indeed, well-marked differences in their teeth; but it will be sufficient for our present purpose to merely record the existence of these points of distinction. The avahi differs, moreover, from all the other members of the group to which it belongs in being of nocturnal instead of diurnal habits.

The avahi is the smallest member of all this group of lemurs, its dimensions being rather less than two-thirds of those of the diademed sifaka. In colour, the long hairs on the forehead immediately above the eyes are grey at the base and pinkish at the tips; while there is in some individuals a small white or yellowish band, more or less irregular, across the crown of the head. The rest of the head, the neck, the back, and the arms are covered with woolly fur, of which the individual hairs are grey at the roots, reddish in the middle, and black at the tips; an arrangement which communicates a peculiar appearance to the whole fur. The concealed ears are reddish, and the cheeks grey. The loins and flanks are of a much lighter colour than the back, especially in the region of the tail, where there is a large triangular patch of pinkish-white running forwards into the dark area of the body. The hind-limbs are still lighter in colour, and as the hairs here tend to grow into bunches or tufts, they reveal their grey bases and pinkish tips, thus giving to the pelage a mottled appearance. The bushy tail is of a decidedly pink tint, more especially for the first third of its length. The hands and feet are reddish.

There are, however, great variations of colour among different individuals of the avahi, inhabiting even the same district; some having the pelage almost uniformly reddish, while in others all the parts above the thighs are nearly pure white.

According to Messrs. Milne-Edwards and Grandidier, the avahis, instead of living in small troops like the indris and sifakas, are found either solitary or in pairs. They are completely nocturnal, sleeping during the day curled up in the fork of a branch, and issuing forth in search of food with the falling shades of evening. Like their allies, they are sluggish in their movements, and but seldom descend to the ground, and, when they do so, they walk in the same peculiar manner as the sifakas.

The avahis are found in two parallel bands of forest on the east side of Madagascar, and also in the woods of a small area on the north-west. They are, however, totally unknown on the west and south coasts, where the vegetation and climate are totally different. The members of the colony on the north-west coast are of smaller size and somewhat different coloration from those on the east side of the island. From their smaller size and nocturnal habits the avahis are less noticed by the natives of Madagascar than are the other members of this group, and do not figure conspicuously either in their legends or in their superstitions. The name avahi is the one by which they are known to the Antanala tribe. By other tribes they are, however, termed Ampongi, Fotsi-fe, or Fotsi-afaka; the two latter terms respectively meaning "white legs" or "white fork," in allusion to the peculiar coloration of the hinder parts of these animals.

The True Lemurs.

Genus *Lemur*.

With the true lemurs, which are likewise confined to the island of Madagascar, we come to the first of a group differing in several respects from those already noticed. The first and most easily recognised feature by which the true lemurs and their allies may be distinguished from the group containing the indri and the avahi, is that the toes of the foot are not connected together at their bases by a web. In none of those animals are the legs so long in proportion to the arms as we have seen to be the case in the

HEADS OF COMMON (A) AND SMOOTH-EARED (B) BLACK LEMUR.
(From Sclater, *List of Animals in Zool. Gardens.*)

members of the preceding group; while the whole of them have long tails. Then, again, it may be mentioned that the members of this group are distinguished by the presence of an additional front tooth on either side of the lower jaw, and likewise by having one more premolar tooth on each side of both jaws; thus bringing up the total number of teeth from thirty to thirty-six. The formula is $i\frac{2}{2}, c\frac{1}{1}, p\frac{3}{3}, m\frac{3}{3}$; which may be compared with that given on p. 204, as distinctive of the indri group.

The true lemurs are confined to Madagascar and the Comoro islands, which are situated half-way between it and Zanzibar. Although some of them are nocturnal, and others diurnal in their habits, all these lemurs differ from the indri group in subsisting on a mixed diet; insects, small reptiles, birds' eggs, and the callow young of birds forming at least as important a part of their food as fruits. It is probably owing to this mixed diet that they are of a much hardier disposition than are those of the indri group, so that they flourish in confinement in this country so well as not unfrequently to breed; the number of young produced at a birth being either one or two.

In consequence of their arms being longer in proportion to their legs than in the indri group, the true lemurs and their allies, when on the ground, are in the habit of going on all-fours, although capable of taking leaps of great length. The true lemurs may be distinguished from the other members of the group to

THE RING-TAILED LEMUR ($\frac{1}{4}$ nat. size).

which they belong by the length of their snouts, and the large size of their tufted ears, as well as by their diurnal habits.

RING-TAILED LEMUR (*Lemur catta*).

One of the best known, and at the same time the most easily recognised of all the true lemurs, is the ring-tailed lemur, represented in the accompanying woodcut. This animal, which may be compared in appearance to a very small fox, is of an ashy grey colour, darker on the back, and white on the under-parts, as well as on the sides of the face, ears, and the middle of the forehead. Its most distinctive feature is, however, to be found in the alternate rings of black and white on the tail, from which it derives its name. It has no fringe round the face.

The ring-tailed lemur is found in the central parts of Madagascar, ranging on the west coast to Mouroundava, and on the east coast to Andrahoumbe. Like the other members of the group, this lemur lives in small parties, and is most active at early morning and evening; sleeping during the night with its bushy tail curled round its body, and likewise taking a siesta during the heat of the day. Unlike the members of the indri group, it is a noisy creature; and the whereabouts of a troop in the morning or evening is discoverable by the loud cries which they are continually uttering.

In captivity this species thrives well, and it is generally numerously represented in the menagerie of the London Zoological Society, although it does not appear that it has ever bred there.

Mr. G. A. Shaw, writing of the ring-tailed lemur, states that they are found only in the south and south-western borders of the Betsileo province of Madagascar. This province is about one hundred and fifty miles in length, by fifty or sixty in width, and is situated on the central table-land, about one hundred to two hundred and fifty miles south of Antananarivo, the capital of Madagascar. A forest extends along the whole eastern side of this province, fringing the table-land, and covering all the slopes down into the lowland bordering the sea; but nowhere in these forests have the ring-tailed lemurs been found. Their habitat in the south and south-west is among the rocks; over which they can easily travel where it is impossible for the people, although bare-footed, to follow. An examination of their hands will show that they are pre-eminently adapted for this kind of locomotion. The palms are long, smooth, level, and leather-like, and enable the animal to find a firm footing on the slippery wet rocks, very much on the same principle as that which assists the fly to walk up a pane of glass. The thumbs on the hinder hands are very much smaller in proportion than in the lemurs inhabiting the forests, which depend upon their grasping power for their means of progression. These spring from tree to tree, and rarely, if ever, touch the ground, except in search of water. Hence the ring-tailed lemurs are an exception to the general habits of the *Lemuridæ*, in that they are not arboreal. There are very few trees near their district; and those which do grow there are very stunted and bushy.

OTHER SPECIES.

Red-fronted Lemur. The whole of the other species of true lemurs are readily distinguished from the preceding by their uniformly coloured tails. The number of nominal species is, however, too large to permit of reference to all of them, and the one which we select as the next representative of the genus is the red-fronted lemur (*L. rufifrons.*)

This lemur may be easily recognised by the two small white stripes running across each side of the rump. The general colour of the fur is grey; the throat and under-parts being reddish; the nose and the middle of the forehead black; while the sides of the nose, the cheeks, and a large spot on either side of the forehead are white. The tail is blackish, with a reddish tinge at the root.

Mungoose Lemur. The species represented in the accompanying figure (*L. mungoz*), was described as far back as the time of Linnæus. It inhabits the western coast of Madagascar; and may always be known by its black nose and the iron-grey spot on each side of the forehead. The fur, which is of a somewhat woolly nature, is reddish-grey in general colour; but the face, chin, the middle line of the forehead, and a streak across the crown of the head are black; while the cheeks and the sides of the forehead are grey. There is considerable individual variation in the width of the black band across the head.

White-fronted Lemur. The white-fronted lemur (*L. albifrons*) appears to be restricted to the north-east coast of Madagascar. It is mainly distinguished from the allied species by its colour; its most distinctive feature being a broad band of white woolly hairs extending across the forehead, and including the base of the ears, the cheeks, and part of the throat and neck. The prevailing colour of the back and flanks is a grizzled brown, tinged with red; the long muzzle and face, together with the hands and feet, and the end of the tail being black. The under-parts and inner surfaces of the limbs are whitish-grey. This pretty lemur

THE MUNGOOSE LEMUR (½ nat. size).

was first described by the French naturalist Geoffroy St. Hilaire; and was exhibited in the London Zoological Gardens as far back as 1830.

Black-fronted Lemur. This (*L. nigrifrons*) is another closely allied lemur, also first made known to science by the naturalist last mentioned. In comparing it with the preceding species, E. T. Bennett, who had the opportunity of seeing living examples of both, observes that "their size, it is true, is nearly equal, and there is little if any difference in their form; but their colours, invariable as we have hitherto found them, furnish sufficient ground for regarding them as distinct. The present animal has the elongated muzzle of the last, but the black colour embraces in it the forehead and sides of the face, as well as the base of the muzzle; and the hair on the former parts, instead of being long and woolly, is short, smooth, and even. While the black is thus extended backwards over the head, it is bounded on the fore part of the muzzle, which instead of being uniform in colour, as in the preceding species, becomes grizzled towards its extremity, and at last almost white. The general colour of the upper parts of the body is a dark ashy grey, most of the hairs terminating in a tawny tip, which is so strongly marked on the back as to give a decided tinge. The tail is light grey at the base, and darker towards the tip; the outside of the limbs is of a light ashy grey; the chin, chest, and throat are pure white; and the under-parts, together with the inner side of

THE BLACK LEMUR ($\frac{1}{6}$ nat. size).

the hind-limbs, pale rufous. The hands, which are blackish, have the same tendency to become grizzled as the fore part of the muzzle."

In captivity this and the preceding species are described as being perfectly tame and good-natured, without any tendency to the petulant and mischievous habits of the smaller monkeys. In a wild state the habits of these allied species are doubtless similar.

BLACK LEMUR (*Lemur macaco*).

With the black lemur, which is represented in the accompanying figure, we come to the first of a group of three very well-marked species, differing considerably from those already noticed; this difference being chiefly shown by the presence of a more or less well-marked ruff fringing the cheeks and chin, and frequently also by a fringe of hairs on the margins of the ears. Moreover, all these lemurs are subject to great variation in colour, which in one case appears to be merely individual, while in another it is distinctive of the two sexes. So great, indeed, is this variation, that the two species of which we shall treat have been described under at least four distinct scientific names; thereby showing how great is the need of caution in such matters.

The black lemur comes from the north-west coast of Madagascar; and the male, upon the evidence of which the species was originally described, is of a uniform black colour, with a well-developed ruff round the cheeks and neck, and a long fringe to the ears. Very different, however, is the female, which was at first described under the name of the white-whiskered lemur (*L. leucomystax*). In this sex the general colour of the fur is brown, with a patch on the lower part of the back, and the ruff round the face and the fringe on the ears are white.

A female of this species in the Gardens of the London Zoological Society twice gave birth to a young one, and thus afforded an opportunity of seeing the curious manner in which the true lemurs carry their offspring. This is shown in the woodcut on p. 202. The young one born on the 24th of March 1884 proved to be a female, and was of the same brown colour as its mother. On the 3rd of April in the following year the second young one was born, which was a male, and at the time of birth it was of the black hue of its father. Each of these young ones was carried lying nearly across the abdomen of its mother, with its tail passed round her, and thus on to its neck, so as to afford a firm attachment; and it is believed that, at least in the wild state, the young are at a later period carried on their mother's back.

A nearly allied lemur, of which the male was described by Dr. Sclater, may be called the smooth-eared black lemur (*L. rufipes*), and is distinguished by the smaller size of the ruff round the throat, and the absence of a fringe on the ears of the male; the difference in the heads of the two forms being shown in the figure on page 210. The female of this lemur was described by Dr. Gray, and has reddish feet.

The Ruffed Lemur (*Lemur varius*).

The last, and at the same time the largest, of the true lemurs is the ruffed lemur, which inhabits the north-east coast of Madagascar. As its name implies, it is remarkable for the extraordinary individual variation in the colour of the fur; such variations being apparently independent of sex. Frequently the colour is a mixture of black and white, disposed in patches on different parts of the body, but occasionally white individuals are met with. Other individuals are, however, of a nearly uniform reddish-brown colour; this variety having been regarded as a distinct species, under the name of the red lemur (*L. ruber*).

A specimen of the red variety in the Menagerie of the London Zoological Society had the upper surface of the body of a bright rufous brown, while the under-parts were of a deep black. The reddish area included the sides of the face, ears, back, and flanks, and the outer surfaces of the limbs; while the black embraced the forehead and face, the throat, chest, and abdomen, the inner surfaces of the limbs, and the hands and feet, with the exception of a narrow stripe of white across their

THE RUFFED LEMUR (¼ nat. size).

upper surface. On the back of the neck there was a large white patch. The length of the head and body of this animal was two feet, and that of the tail somewhat more.

THE GENTLE LEMUR.

Genus *Hapalemur.*

The gentle lemur (*Hapalemur griseus*), like all the members of the group under consideration, is an inhabitant of Madagascar, but differs so decidedly from the true lemurs that it has been made the type of a distinct genus, of which it is the only well-defined species.

It may be readily distinguished from the true lemurs by its rounded head and extremely short muzzle, the ears being likewise very short. A peculiar feature is the presence of a small bare patch on the front surface of the fore-arm, a little above the palm of the hand, which is covered with small spines. The colour is a dark iron-grey, with a tinge of yellow, becoming somewhat paler on the under-parts and the inner sides of the limbs. The individual hairs are black, with a reddish band near their tips.

The species differs from the true lemurs in being purely nocturnal in its habits. It is chiefly found in bamboo-jungles, and subsists mainly on the young tender shoots of these plants, as well as on their leaves. In such jungles its capture is difficult, and hence living examples are rare in our menageries. One living in the Zoological Society's Gardens in the year 1870 was regarded by the late Dr. Gray as a new species, and described as the broad-nosed lemur (*H. simus*), but it does

THE GENTLE LEMUR (¼ nat. size).

not appear to be more than a variety. According to a French traveller, the gentle, or grey lemur is known to the natives of Madagascar as the Bokombouli.

THE WEASEL-LEMUR.

Genus *Lepidolemur*.

The slender, or weasel-lemur, is the last representative of the present group, and belongs to a genus containing two species, which differ from all other lemur-like animals in having, when adult, either no upper front (incisor) teeth at all, or merely a single pair of minute rudimentary ones. This character will at once suffice to distinguish these animals from the gentle lemur, which they resemble, however, in being of purely nocturnal habits.   A further distinction is afforded by the greater length of the muzzle; and also by the ears being bald and somewhat larger.   The tail is long, and covered with close-set short hair.

The weasel-lemur (*Lepidolemur mustelinus*) is chiefly found in the north-west of Madagascar, and is characterised by having no upper front teeth at all

THE FORKED MOUSE-LEMUR ($\frac{1}{4}$ nat. size).

when quite full grown.   Its head and body together measure about 10 inches in length, while the length of the tail is 14 inches.   This is one of the lemurs which are subject to great individual variation of colour, in consequence of which it has received several distinct scientific names.   In one variety the general colour of the upper parts is dark grey tinged with yellow, the back having a darker stripe, while the under-parts, as well as the throat, are whitish-grey.   The dark stripe on the back may, however, be wanting; and some specimens are redder above and yellower beneath; indeed, scarcely any two individuals are alike in these respects.

The weasel-lemur, during its nocturnal rambles, is marvellously active, and is capable of taking tremendous leaps among the trees in which it dwells; its slender build and long limbs being admirably adapted for such a mode of progression. Like the gentle lemur, it subsists solely on leaves; and it is much sought after as an article of food by the natives of Madagascar, to whom it is known by the name of Fitili-ki. It is killed by being knocked on the head with a stick while curled up during the day in its nest of leaves, to which it has been tracked down at the end of its nocturnal excursions.

The hoary-headed lemur (*L. caniceps*) is a closely allied species, chiefly distinguished by having a minute rudimentary pair of front or incisor teeth in the upper jaw, but further characterised by the hoary grey of the hair on the crown of the head.

The Mouse-Lemurs.

Genus *Chirogaleus.*

With the tiny creatures known as the mouse-lemurs, we come to the first of a group of two genera which differ from all the members of the lemur tribe in that the bones of the upper part of the ankle are enormously elongated, thus causing the whole foot to be much longer than in the preceding groups.

The mouse-lemurs themselves are confined to Madagascar; and include the smallest of the lemurs, some of them being even inferior in size to a rat. They have long tails, and rather large ears, which are hairy at their base, and cannot be folded upon themselves.

The most remarkable feature connected with the mouse-lemurs, and one for a knowledge of which we are indebted to the observations of Grandidier, is that they are in the habit of what is generally called hibernating, or remaining dormant for a portion of the year. But as their quiescent season is during the hottest and driest time, the term æstivation would be more appropriate. By no means all the mouse-lemurs thus hibernate; and we may fairly presume that the species in which this habit occurs are those dwelling in the more arid regions. To prepare for this protracted period of dormant energies, during which they maintain the heat of their bodies by the consumption of their own substance, the mouse-lemurs feed so vigorously that when the hot season arrives they are in an extremely fat and sleek condition. Curiously enough the great accumulation of fat which then takes place is mainly restricted to the region of the base of the tail; and when they retire at the close of the rainy season, during which food is extremely abundant, their tails are swollen to a prodigious size. The wasting process which goes on during hibernation leaves them, however, with their tails shrunk to a very small diameter. In order to make themselves comfortable during their long sleep, they follow the example of our own dormice, and prepare snug little nests of twigs and other substances; some of their habitations being described as marvels of neat construction. Their food is mainly of a vegetable nature; although this diet is largely supplemented by insects, and even small birds are said not to come amiss. Having large round eyes, by which they are enabled to see small objects in the darkest nights, they are in the habit of stalking nocturnal moths and beetles when settled on the boughs of trees, and then rushing upon and seizing them with a final spring.

Forked Mouse-Lemur. The largest, and at the same time one of the longest-known of the mouse-lemurs is the species (*C. furcifer*) represented on p. 218, which takes its name from the black streak running down the middle of the back, and dividing on the top of the head so as to form a distinct fork-like mark between the eyes. The colour of the remainder of the body is grey, with a black tip to the tail.

This species is found in the forests on both the east and west coasts of Madagascar, though more abundant in the latter region. It is known to the natives as the Walouvi; and is not one of those species that hibernate.

Murine Mouse-Lemur. This species (*C. murinus*) differs from the preceding by the absence of the dark stripe down the back. The general colour is a pale reddish-grey, with a broad whitish streak up the middle of the face; the cheeks and under-parts being also light-coloured, but the slender tail more brown. The mouse-lemur represented in the figure on the opposite page, which is often described as the myoxine mouse-lemur (*C. myoxinus*), appears to be very closely allied to this species.

Coquerel's Mouse-Lemur. This mouse-lemur (*C. coquereli*) is characterised by the soft and woolly nature of the fur, of which the prevailing colour is greyish-brown, tinged with gold. It makes well-formed nests, composed of twigs, dead leaves, and grass, and having a diameter of some 18 inches. In this nest it sleeps during the day, to prowl forth at night in search of food.

Brown Mouse-Lemur. Another mouse-lemur (*C. milii*), which is one of the hibernating species, takes its name from M. Milius, a governor of Reunion, in the first quarter of the present century, by whom two of these creatures were sent to Paris. They were described by Frederic Cuvier in the year 1821 as the *maki nain*, or small lemur. The species is some 9 inches in length, exclusive of the long tail; and it is of a greyish-brown colour, with black whiskers, and white throat and under-parts; the fur being silky. The specimens sent to Paris throve for some time, and became so tame that they were allowed to leave their cages. They would, however, only play about if the apartment was kept perfectly dark and still; and when this was done they could be heard frolicking in high glee. During the day they rolled themselves up into a ball and slept.

Dwarf Mouse-Lemur. The smallest of all is the dwarf mouse-lemur (*C. pusillus*), not unfrequently referred to as the Madagascar rat, on account of its having been described by Buffon under the name of *le rat de Madagascar*. The head and body of this diminutive representative do not exceed 4 inches in length, while the tail measures 6 inches. The prevailing colour is a pale grey; the chin and under-parts being pale yellow, and the outer surface of the ears light brown, while a white streak runs up the nose and between the eyes. The eyes themselves are surrounded by black rims, giving to the face the appearance of wearing a pair of spectacles.

The dwarf mouse-lemur builds beautifully constructed nests of twigs, lined with hair, in the tops of the lofty trees where it delights to dwell. These nests somewhat resemble those of a rook both in form and size, and are used not only as diurnal resting-places but as cradles for the young. The species is remarkable for the extreme beauty of its brilliant eyes.

Mr. G. A. Shaw writes that the dwarf lemurs "inhabit a belt of forest-land stretching from the eastern forest into the heart of Betsileo, a few miles north of Fianarantsoa, where they are tolerably abundant. They live on the tops of the highest trees, choosing invariably the smallest branches, where they collect a

THE MURINE MOUSE-LEMUR (½ nat. size).

quantity of dried leaves, and make what looks from below like a bird's-nest. So close is the resemblance, that it requires good eyes to distinguish the one from the other. Their food consists of fruit and insects, and most probably honey. I have frequently seen them catching the flies that have entered their cage for the honey; and I have supplied them with moths and butterflies, which they have devoured with avidity. They are extremely shy and wild. Although I have had between thirty and forty caged at different times, I have never succeeded in taming one. They are also very quarrelsome, and fight very fiercely, uttering a most piercing, penetrating sound, somewhat resembling a very shrill whistle."

The Galagos, or African Lemurs.

Genus *Galago.*

The galagos are the only long-tailed lemurs found throughout the length and breadth of Africa. The name is said to be that by which one of the species is known to the natives of Senegal. They resemble the mouse-lemurs in having the bones of the upper half of the ankle greatly elongated, and thus have the same lengthy foot. Although some are much bigger, there are others quite as small as the smaller mouse-lemurs. There is, however, a readily recognised external

THE GREAT GALAGO (⅙ nat. size).

character by which a galago can be at once distinguished from a mouse-lemur. This consists in the large size of the ears, which are quite bare, and have the unique peculiarity that they can be partially folded upon themselves at such times as their owners please, so as to lie nearly flat upon the sides of the head. This may be for the purpose of protecting these delicate organs when passing through thick foliage, especially if wet.

This distinctive peculiarity of the ears is, of course, sufficient to enable us at once to separate a galago from a mouse-lemur; and, indeed, from every other kind of lemur. Zoologists are, however, by no means satisfied with distinguishing animals merely by external characters; and they have succeeded in finding a feature in the teeth by which a galago differs markedly from a mouse-lemur, although, unfortunately, this point of distinction can only be seen in a dried skull. If, however, we take the skull of a mouse-lemur we shall find that while the last three upper teeth, or molars, have broad crowns and are alike, the tooth in advance of these, which is the last premolar, has a smaller and simpler crown, of a triangular shape. In a galago's skull, on the contrary, this last upper premolar, although slightly smaller than the molars, has a similarly shaped crown, broad on the inner side, and nearly quadrangular in shape.

The galagos are widely distributed over the " dark continent," one kind being found as far south as Natal, while there are several on the western side and two on the eastern. Like the mouse-lemurs, they are essentially nocturnal; and are, of course, confined to those regions where thick forest prevails. When not enjoying their diurnal repose, they are lively and interesting. They subsist on a mixed diet, including fruits, insects, and small birds and their eggs. Some of the smaller species will readily devour locusts, and the peculiar leaf-like mantides, or praying insects. When on the ground the galagos recall the lemurs of the indri group, in that they generally sit in the upright position, and progress by a series of leaps or hops. They usually have two or three young at a birth; and are stated to have bred in captivity in Africa, although we are not aware whether they have done so in Europe. Many of them, however, thrive well in our menageries; where some have been represented by a considerable number of individuals. It is stated that the galagos resemble the mouse-lemurs in building nests, which are situated in the forked branches of trees; but it is probable that this is only true of the smaller species. They appear, however, to be peculiar in that several individuals will inhabit the same nest, out of which they all rush when suddenly disturbed. The total number of teeth, both in the galagos and the mouse-lemurs, is the same as in the true lemurs.

THE GREAT GALAGO (*Galago crassicaudata*).

With the exception of a closely-allied kind from the West Coast, the great, or thick-tailed galago, of Mozambique and the Lower Zambesi Valley, is the largest of all the species. This animal of which a figure is given on p. 222, is in point of size about equal to a cat of average dimensions; and, indeed, the peculiar manner in which it carries its thick bushy tail high above its back is highly suggestive of a pampered Persian cat. This bushy tail is about one-fourth longer than the head and body. The great galago belongs to a group of three or four species, in which the ears are unusually long, and the muzzle is considerably elongated, while the feet are comparatively broad and short, and the fingers and toes have broad disc-like expansions at their extremities. The colour of the fur is a uniform dark brown.

Writing of this species, Sir J. Kirk observes that " it is confined to the maritime region, so far as I know never penetrating beyond the band of wood generally known as the mangrove forests. By the Portuguese it is named 'rat of the cocoa-nut palm,' that being its favourite haunt by day, nestling among the fronds; but if it be disturbed, performing feats of agility, and darting from one palm to another. It will spring with great rapidity, adhering to any object as if it were a lump of wet clay. It has one failing, otherwise its capture would be no easy task. Should a pot of palm-wine be left on the tree, the creature drinks to excess, comes down, and rushes about intoxicated. In captivity they are mild; during the day remaining either rolled up in a ball, or perched half asleep, with ears stowed away like a beetle's wing under its hard and ornamented case. I had half a dozen squirrels with one in the same cage; these were good friends, the latter creeping under the golgo's" (Sir J. Kirk's way of spelling galago) "soft fur and falling asleep. On introducing a few specimens of (elephant) shrew, the golgo seized one and bit off its tail, which, however, it did not eat. The food it took was biscuit, rice, orange, banana, guava, and a little cooked meat. Stupid during the day, it became active at night, or just after darkness set in. The rapidity and length of its leaps, which were absolutely noiseless, must give great facilities to its capturing live prey. I never knew it give a loud call, but it would often make a low, chattering noise. It has been observed at the Luabo mouth of the Zambesi, at Quillimane, and at Mozambique. When I had my live specimen at Zanzibar, the natives did not seem to recognise it; nevertheless, it may be abundant on the mainland."

On the West Coast of Africa, in Angola, the great galago is represented by the closely allied Monteiro's galago (*G. monteiri*), which is of slightly larger size than the East Coast form; the length of the head and body being 12, and that of the tail 16 inches. Although these two galagos differ mainly or entirely by their coloration, yet, according to Sir. J. Kirk, the eastern form is confined to the coast region, and it is probable that there is a wide area separating the habitats of the two, which suggests the advisability of regarding them as distinct species. As a rule, Monteiro's galago is of a uniform pale grey colour, with the sides of the nose somewhat darker, and the throat and tail nearly or quite white. The fur is soft, with the component hairs slate-coloured at their roots, and white at the tips.

Garnett's Galago (*Galago garnetti*).

Garnett's, or, as it is sometimes rather inappropriately called, the black galago, is a species belonging to the same group as the preceding forms, from which it differs by its inferior size. It is an inhabitant of Eastern Africa, and is of a dark brown colour, tending to yellowish on the under-parts, with black ears, and a white streak on each side of the loins.

One of these animals, formerly in the London Zoological Society's menagerie, when let loose one night in the apartments of the superintendent, exhibited to perfection the leaping habits and extreme agility characteristic of its tribe. It leaped, after the manner of the kangaroo, clearing several feet at a single spring, and hopping on to the table and other articles of furniture which were in the room. Strange to say, it exhibited no signs of fear of the dogs and cats with which it was confronted.

The pale-coloured galago (*G. pallida*), of Western Equatorial Africa, is a species connecting in some respects the three above-mentioned species with those of the group now to be described. It was met with by Du Chaillu, who believed that he had discovered a new species. The general colour is pale grey, and the tail unusually long.

ALLEN'S GALAGO (*Galago alleni*).

With the West African species we come to the first representative of a group distinguished from the preceding one by the more rounded head, shorter muzzle, and larger eyes, as well by the longer and more slender form of the foot.

Allen's galago is found at Fernando Po and the Gabun, and is characterised by the tail being thick and bushy, and also by the extreme length and slenderness of its fingers and toes. The prevailing colour of the fur is blackish-brown, with the forehead, rump, and the root of the tail grey, a tinge of red is on the limbs, the tail is black, and a streak on the nose and all the under-parts are whitish.

If we examine the skull of this species it will be noticed that the last molar tooth on each side of the upper jaw is nearly equal in size to the tooth in advance of it. This will be found an important point of distinction between Allen's galago and all the remaining species, in which the last upper molar is much smaller than the tooth in front of it.

THE SENEGAL GALAGO (*Galago senegalensis*).

The longest-known of all the galagos is the Senegal galago. It was originally described so far back as the year 1796, from specimens brought from Senegambia, which may be regarded as its headquarters. Subsequent discoveries have, however, shown that a galago exists on the east side of Africa to the south of the Sudan, which, although described as a distinct species under the name of the Sennaar galago (*G. sennariensis*), is so closely allied to the Senegal galago that it may probably be regarded as a mere local variety or race. Indeed, it is probable that when we are fully acquainted with the zoology of the vast stretch of country lying to the south of the Sahara desert, it will be found that this galago extends right across Africa.

In addition to the distinctive character of the upper molar teeth already mentioned, the Senegal species has certain marked external features by which it differs from Allen's galago. Thus, in the tail the hairs near the root are pressed down, only those nearer the end spreading out on all sides, so that the whole tail assumes a somewhat club-like form. Then, again, the fingers and toes are considerably thicker and shorter than in Allen's galago. In colour the typical Senegal galago is grey, with the under-parts and a streak on the nose white, and the tail, hands, and feet blackish-brown. The Sennaar race appears to have a rather bluer tinge to the fur, with a darker face, and black rings round the eyes; while the tail is described as being relatively longer. It is of comparatively small size, and appears to be common in the forests of Senegal, and in those on the Blue Nile in Kordofan, and the White Nile in Sennaar. Its chief food consists of various kinds of insects; but it is stated that it will also eat the gum of various kinds of acacia, which we have already noticed as forming part of the diet of the baboons of the Sudan. Its habits are said to be similar to those of the other species.

In South Africa the Senegal galago is represented by a species so nearly allied to it that some writers have thought that the two forms are only varieties. This southern form is the Maholi galago (*G. maholi*), which is a distinctly inland species found as far south as Natal, and also met with in Nyasaland and the adjacent districts. A galago from the neighbourhood of Titi some distance up the Zambesi, has been identified with the Sennaar variety of the Senegal galago, but it would appear more probable that it is one of these. The prevailing colour is brownish, or yellowish-grey, becoming darker on the back, and still more so on the tail; while a broad streak on the nose, the cheeks, and the throat are white, and the inner surfaces of the limbs and the under-parts are whitish with a faint tinge of yellow.

THE SENEGAL GALAGO (½ nat. size).

In the male specimen in the British Museum brought home by the late Sir Andrew Smith—the original describer of this animal—the fur surrounding the eyes is of the same colour as that on the other parts of the head. In other examples in the national collection there are, however, dark rings round the eyes. This variability shows that we must not regard the presence or absence of such rings as indicating a specific distinction between the Senegal and Sennaar galagos.

DEMIDOFF'S GALAGO (*Galago demidoffi*).

The smallest and the last of these lemurs that we shall mention is Demidoff's galago, from the West Coast of Africa. This animal differs from the two species just considered by its more slender and cylindrical tail and smaller ears. The length of the head and body is 5 inches, and that of the tail 7½. The general colour is brown, darker on the sides of the face; the white streak on the nose being narrow; and the chin, throat, and under parts of a reddish-grey colour. The so-called *G. murinus*, from Old Calabar, is probably identical with this species.

THE SLOW LEMURS, OR LORIS.

Genera *Nycticebus* and *Loris*.

With the slow lemurs of the warmer parts of Asia we come to the last group of the lemur family; this group likewise including the pottos of Africa, to be described next. The members of this group may be recognised either by the total absence of the tail, or by its length not exceeding one-third that of the head and body. The only lemur with which these animals could possibly be confounded would, therefore, be the indri of Madagascar; but, irrespective of its larger size, that animal is at once distinguished by the web uniting the bases of the toes, and the full development of the index finger of the hand. Moreover, the slow lemurs and the pottos may be further distinguished, not only from the indri, but likewise from all other lemurs, by the index finger of the hand being invariably very small, and even rudimentary and without any trace of a nail. Then, again, all these lemurs are peculiar in having the thumb of the hand and the great toe of the foot very widely separated from the other digits; this divergence being carried to such an extent in the case of the great toe, which is actually directed backwards instead of forwards.

Apart, therefore, from their distribution, there is no difficulty in distinguishing a slow lemur or a potto from all other lemurs. All the members of the present group have, however, the same number of teeth as the true lemurs, but they differ from the galagos and mouse-lemurs in that the bones of the upper part of the ankle are of ordinary proportions, so that the foot is not abnormally lengthened.

The slow lemurs are purely nocturnal, and are well known for the extreme slowness and deliberation of their movements; the latter characteristic having given their distinctive name to the Asiatic representatives of the group. It was probably their deliberate motions, nocturnal habits, and large glaring eyes, that suggested to the Swedish naturalist Linnæus the name of lemur for the group generally.

The slow lemurs are distinguished from the pottos by having a well-developed but small index finger on the hand, which has the usual three joints, and is provided with a distinct nail. They have no external tail, and are, as we have already mentioned, strictly confined to the tropical and subtropical regions of Asia. There are three species, all of which are very closely allied, although the majority of naturalists have considered it advisable to divide them into two genera, one of which contains two, and the other one species.

The Common Loris (*Nycticebus tardigradus*).

The common loris, or slow lemur, may be taken as the typical representative of the genus *Nycticebus*. The distinctive features of this animal, as the representative of a genus, are that the eyes are not of very enormous size, and are separated from one another by a considerable space; while the general build of the animal—more especially as regards its limbs—is comparatively stout.

The name loris, by which all the slow lemurs are commonly designated, is derived from the Dutch word *Loeris*, meaning a clown, and appears to have been applied to

THE COMMON LORIS ($\frac{2}{5}$ nat. size).

these animals by the Dutch colonists of the East Indian Islands. To the natives of India the slow loris is known either by the name Sharmindi billi, "bashful cat," or Lajjar banar, "bashful monkey." It is an animal about the size of a cat; different individuals or races varying considerably in size, so that while some specimens do not measure more than 13 inches in total length, others may reach as much as 15 inches, or even more. Its proportions are thick and clumsy; the head being broad and flat, with a slightly projecting and pointed muzzle. The large eyes are perfectly circular, and their pupils can be completely closed by the gradual contraction of the iris, which opens from above and below, so that when the pupil is half concealed it takes the form of a transverse slit. The ears are short, rounded, and partly buried in the fur; and are, thus, very different from those of the galagos. The hind-limbs are only slightly longer than the others. With the exception of the muzzle and the hands and feet, the whole of the body is covered with a thick coat of very close and somewhat long woolly fur.

There is a considerable amount of variation in the colour of different local races of this species, although in all cases there is a dark stripe running down the middle of the back, sometimes extending on to the head. In the more common and larger variety, the colour of the fur is ashy-grey above, tending to become silvery along the sides of the back, the under-parts being lighter, and the rump often having a tinge of red. The stripe on the back is chestnut-coloured, and stops short at the hinder part of the crown of the head. The eyes are, however, surrounded by dark rims; between which is the white streak extending upwards from the nose. The ears, together with a small surrounding area, are brown.

In another, and generally smaller variety, the hue of the upper-parts has a distinct tinge of red mingling with the grey; while the stripe on the back is wider, and often of a full brown colour; but, instead of stopping short at the back of the crown of the head, this band widens out into a large brown patch on the crown, which embraces the ears. The eyes, however, although surrounded by brown rings, are not connected with the patch on the head by a dark-coloured area. There is yet a third variety of this creature, found in Tenasserim, in which the general colour is pale rufescent, while the dark stripe on the back, instead of expanding on the crown of the head, merely splits into a fork, of which each prong joins the dark ring round the eyes.

The slow loris is found over a large area in the countries lying to the eastward of the Bay of Bengal. It occurs on the north-east frontier of India in the provinces of Sylhet and Assam, whence it extends southwards into Burma, Tenasserim, and the Malay Peninsula; while it is also found in Siam and Cochin China, and the islands of Sumatra, Java, and Borneo.

Habits. Its food consists of leaves and young shoots of trees, as well as fruits, various kinds of insects, birds, and their eggs. It has been observed to stand nearly erect upon its feet, and from this advantageous position pounce upon an insect. It is generally silent, although sometimes uttering a low crackling sound; but when enraged, and especially if about to bite, it gives a kind of fierce growl. Mr. Blanford, quoting from notes by Colonel Tickell, observes that this animal is tolerably common in the Tenasserim provinces and Arakan; but, being strictly nocturnal in its habits, is seldom seen. It inhabits the densest forests, and never by choice leaves the trees. Its movements are slow, but it climbs readily, and grasps with great tenacity. If placed on the ground, it can proceed, if frightened, in a wavering kind of trot, the limbs placed at right angles. It sleeps rolled up in a ball, its head and hands buried between its thighs, and wakes up at the dusk of evening to commence its nocturnal rambles. The female bears but one young at a time. Many accounts have been published of the habits of the slow loris in confinement. One of the best of the earlier of these is from the pen of Sir William Jones, who had one of these animals as a pet in Calcutta. All observers are agreed that, while these creatures are apt to be fierce when first captured, they soon become docile. They are very susceptible to cold, and when so affected are apt to be fractious and petulant.

There is an account of a tame loris in Loudon's *Magazine of Natural History.* After mentioning that the animal was especially fond of plantains, the writer observes that it was also partial to small birds, which, " when put into his cage, he kills speedily ; and, plucking the feathers off with the skill of a poulterer, soon lodges the carcase in his stomach. He eats the bones as well as the flesh ; and though birds, and mice perhaps, are his favourite food, he eats other meat very readily, especially when

THE SLENDER LORIS, IN WAKING AND SLEEPING POSTURE.

quite fresh ; if boiled, or otherwise cooked, he will not taste it. He prefers veal to all other kinds of butcher's meat ; eggs, also, he is fond of, and sugar is especially grateful to his palate ; he likewise eats gum-arabic. As flesh is not always to be had quite fresh (the only state in which it is acceptable to him), he has for some time past been fed upon bread sopped in water, and sprinkled with sugar ; this he eats readily, and seems to relish much. . . . When food is presented to him, if hungry, he seizes it with both hands, and, letting go with his right, holds it with his left all the time he is eating. Frequently, when feeding, he grasps the bars in the upper part of his cage with his hind paws, and hangs inverted, appearing very much intent upon the food he holds in his left hand. He is exceedingly fond of oranges ; but, when they are at all hard, he seems very much puzzled how to extract the juice. I have, upon such an occasion, seen him lie all his length upon his back, in the bottom of the cage, and, firmly grasping the piece of orange in both hands, squeeze the juice into his mouth. He generally sits upon his hind part (the hair of which is much worn by long sitting), close to the bars of his cage, grasping them firmly with his hind paws; he then rolls himself up like a ball, with his head in his breast, his thighs closely placed over his belly, and his arms over his head, generally grasping the bars of the cage with his hands also. In this position, and also without moving, he remains the whole day. Upon coming into the Channel, the cold weather affected him very much; he was seized with cramp, and I at that time placed him in a small box, which was filled with very soft down. This he felt so agreeable that, when cold, he never left it during the whole day, unless disturbed, and slept in it rolled up in the shape of a ball. He is extraordinarily slow in his motions, and his trivial name, *tardigradus*, well marks his habit in that particular . . . When he climbs he first lays hold of the branch with one of his hands, and then with the other. When he has obtained a firm hold with both hands, he moves one of his hind paws, and, after firmly grasping the branch with it, he moves the other. He never quits his hold with his hind paws until he has obtained a secure grasp with his hands. When he walks, he moves his limbs in the same methodical manner as when he climbs.

"His temper, in cold weather especially, is very quick; but, in general, he is rather timid, and never offers any injury unless incautiously touched, teased, or provoked; he then makes a shrill, plaintive cry, evidently expressive of much annoyance, and bites very sharply." He was obtained from the island of Penang, lying off the Malay Peninsula, and belonged to that variety in which the brown stripe of the back expands into a large triangular patch on the crown of the head.

The Javan loris (*N. javanicus*), said to be confined to the island from which it derives its name, is distinguished by having four brown bands running down the head and face from the crown, one band going to each eye, and one to each ear; the interspaces being pale, and the space between the eyes white. As Mr. Blanford remarks, this coloration is only one step in advance on that obtaining in the third variety of the slow loris mentioned on p. 229, and it is therefore extremely doubtful whether the Javan loris really has any right to rank as a separate species.

The Slender Loris (*Loris gracilis*).

The slender loris, of which we give an illustration on p. 230, representing it asleep, and another on p. 232, is the sole species of the genus to which it belongs. It is distinguished from the slow loris by its lighter build of body and longer and more slender limbs, as well as by the greater size of the eyes, which are separated merely by a narrow space. The ears are also somewhat larger than in the slow loris.

The slender loris is a much smaller animal than the preceding species, the length of the head and body being about 8 inches. In colour it is a dark earthy grey, with a more or less marked ruddy tinge on the back and outer sides of the limbs, and showing a faint silvery wash; the under-parts being much paler. Between the eyes there is the usual narrow white stripe, which spreads out on the forehead; and the cheeks and region round the eyes are darker than the rest of the body. Some young specimens are decidedly reddish.

This animal is confined to the forests of Southern India and Ceylon, and appears only to be found in those which are situated at but a comparatively slight elevation above the sea-level. Mr. Blanford states that its habits are very similar to those of its cousin the slow loris, although its movements are not quite so deliberate. It partakes of the same kind of food as the latter; and sleeps rolled up like a ball, with its head between its thighs, and its hand grasping the bough on which it is seated, as shown on our illustration on p. 230.

The present writer once had occasion to purchase a pair of these animals in the bazaar at Madras, and was surprised to find the number of specimens which

THE SLENDER LORIS.

were exposed there for sale. On the voyage up to Calcutta these pretty little creatures lived mainly on a diet of plantains and rice, supplemented with an occasional cockroach; but as they passed the whole day in slumber, they could scarcely be reckoned as very lively pets.

Sir J. Emerson Tennent, who tells us that this animal has acquired the name of the "Ceylon sloth" in Ceylon, observes that "the singularly large and intense eyes of the loris have attracted the attention of the Singhalese, who capture the creature for the purpose of extracting them as charms and love-potions, and this they are said to effect by holding the little animal to the fire till the eyeballs burst. Its Tamil name is Thavangu, or 'thin bodied'; and hence a deformed child or emaciated person has acquired in the Tamil districts the same epithet. The light-coloured variety of the loris in Ceylon has a spot on the forehead, somewhat resembling the *namam*, or mark worn by the worshippers of Vishnu; and from this peculiarity it is distinguished as the Nama-thavangu."

The Pottos, or African Slow Lemurs.

Genus *Perodicticus*.

In West Africa the place of the slow lemurs of Asia is taken by two species of lemur, which may be collectively known as pottos, although in its proper application the native name Potto appears to be restricted to the first of the two kinds. The pottos are distinguished by the index finger of the hand being quite rudimentary, consisting only of a stump without distinct joints, and unprovided with a nail. The typical potto is further distinguished by possessing a short tail, but since this appendage is rudimentary in the second species it does not afford any characters by which the African slow lemurs can be distinguished from their Asiatic relatives. The habits of the pottos are very similar to those of the loris, but their movements are still more deliberate and sluggish.

THE POTTO ASLEEP ($\frac{1}{2}$ nat. size).

Bosman's Potto (*Perodicticus potto*).

The true, or Bosman's potto, represented in our first illustration in its sleeping posture, and in our second awake, takes its name from having been discovered by the Dutch navigator, Van Bosman, who met with it on the coast of Guinea, and described it as long ago as the year 1705, under its native name of Potto.

It is an animal of somewhat robust build, chiefly characterised by having a tail of about one-third the length of the head and body; the whole body being covered with a thick coat of soft and moderately long hair. The small and rounded ears stand up well above the fur of the head; the large eyes are separated from one another by a considerable interval; and the muzzle is rather broad and not very long. The arms and legs are of nearly equal length. With the exception of the nearly naked nose and chin, which are flesh-coloured, the general colour of the animal is a kind of chestnut tint, with a black or greyish tinge; the throat and under-parts being yellowish-brown. The peculiar half-red, half-grey tint of the fur on the back is produced by the individual hairs being slate-coloured at their roots, reddish in the middle, and paler at the tips.

In addition to the loss of the index finger of the hand, the potto presents a curious peculiarity connected with the joints of the backbone in the neck. The spines, which project from the upper surfaces of their joints, are so elongated that they actually project beyond the general level of the skin of the back of the neck, where they form a series of little humps. We are at present unacquainted with the object of this peculiar structural arrangement.

Like the loris, the potto is nocturnal in its habits, sleeping during the whole of the day, as shown in our first illustration, rolled up in a ball, with the head between the fore-legs, and folded into the chest, and supporting itself, in captivity by grasping the bars of its cage with both hands and feet.

The potto is found over a considerable extent of the West Coast of Africa, having been recorded from Guinea, Sierra Leone, and the Gabun. Unfortunately, however, we have but few details as to its habits in a wild state, this being prob-

BOSMAN'S POTTO.   (From *Proc. Zool. Soc.*—After Sclater.)

ably largely due to the creature having been seldom seen by Europeans. Several specimens of the potto have been exhibited in the Gardens of the London Zoological Society; the animal is, however, extremely susceptible to cold, and requires the greatest care.

The Awantibo (*Perodicticus calabarensis*).

Far more rare than the potto is the lemur represented in the illustration on the next page, which is known only from the regions around the Old Calabar River, flowing into the Bight of Biafra, east of the Niger. The awantibo is distinguished from the potto, not only by its smaller size and more slender build, but also by the tail being reduced to a mere rudiment, and by a still further reduction of the index finger, which is represented merely by a little tubercle on the edge of the hand.

Moreover, the other fingers of the hand, as well as the toes of the foot, with the exception of the first or great toe, have their first joints connected together by folds of skin. The entire hands and feet are relatively smaller than in Bosman's potto. The colour of the awantibo is yellowish-brown above, but paler on the under-parts, becoming whitish in places; and the whole length of the body is just over 10 inches.

This animal has only been known to Europeans since the year 1859. Very

THE AWANTIBO (⅓ nat. size).

few specimens have been received in this country—none of them in a living condition; and we have practically no information regarding its habits. It has been observed that in this animal and the potto the hands and feet are divided into two distinct moieties by the separation of the thumb and great toe from the other digits; this being most marked in the hand by the loss of the index finger. The hands and feet may accordingly be compared to the feet of a parrot; and it is suggested by the writer, who makes this comparison, that in both cases the structure is one specially adapted for long-continued grasping without change of position.

Fossil Lemurs.

We have already incidentally referred to the occurrence of several fossil lemurs in the lower Tertiary strata of Europe ; but it remains to be mentioned that other species have been found in the corresponding rocks of North America. This is a very curious and highly important circumstance, since it suggests that while the New World monkeys and marmosets, which have very lemur-like molar teeth, may have taken their origin directly from the extinct lemurs of that hemisphere, the Old World monkeys may have had an independent origin from the ancient lemurs of Europe.

Curiously enough, although the remains of lemurs have been known for very many years from the lower Tertiary rocks, both of Hampshire and France, it is only quite recently that they have been recognised as such, having been long regarded as belonging to small hoofed mammals. One of these groups of lemurs, represented by several species of different, though relatively small, dimensions, occurring both in England and France, has been described under the name of *Microchoerus;* the term meaning " small pig," and having been applied from the supposed affinity of the creature to the hoofed mammals. These animals were undoubtedly lemurs nearly allied to living forms, their skulls being very like those of the galagos, although their upper premolar teeth more nearly resembled those of the mouse-lemurs. Like all other fossil lemurs, they are, however, distinguished from living forms by the circumstance that the place and form of the lower tusk is not taken by the first of the lower premolar teeth (see p. 203). This is a very important circumstance, since it shows that these ancient lemurs were what zoologists call less specialised than their living relations, and also removes any difficulty as to the descent of monkeys (in which the lower tusk always remains) from lemurs.

Another and larger European Tertiary lemur, known as the *Adapis,* carries the series one step still further back, since it has four premolar teeth on either side of each jaw ; whereas, as we have seen, no living lemur has more than three of these teeth. Here, then, so far as it goes, we have decisive evidence of the approximation of the extinct lemurs to the inferior orders of Mammals, among which four premolar teeth are frequently present ; and we may thus hope in time to discover further evidence of intermediate forms.

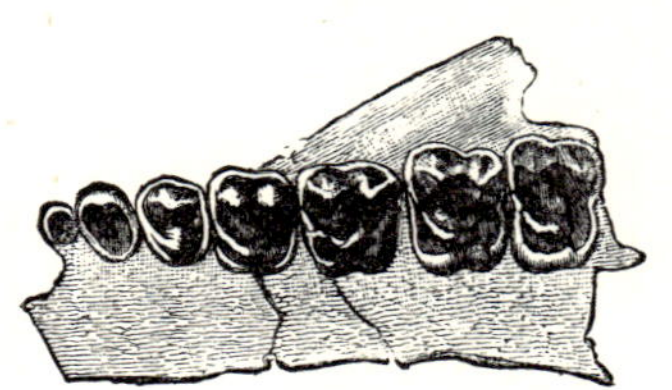

THE LEFT UPPER CHEEK-TEETH OF AN EXTINCT EUROPEAN LEMUROID (*Adapis*).

Some of the extinct North American lemurs, with four premolars, do indeed exhibit certain transitional characters ; but it would be beyond the province of the present work to enter upon their discussion.

We have already called attention at some length to the importance of these extinct European lemurs as helping to explain the peculiar distribution of their modern relatives ; and we may take leave of the subject by mentioning that their occurrence in France and England during the early part of the Tertiary period indicates the prevalence in these countries of a tropical or subtropical climate.

THE TARSIER (½ nat. size).

CHAPTER VIII.

APES, MONKEYS, AND LEMURS,—*concluded.*

THE TARSIER AND THE AYE-AYE.

THESE two strange creatures, although sufficiently nearly related to the lemurs to be included in the same great group, yet differ so markedly, not only from the lemurs, but likewise from each other, as to make it necessary to refer them to two distinct families—*Tarsiidæ* and *Chiromyidæ*. This gives us, for the first time, instances of families represented not only by a single genus, but by a single species.

The Tarsier (*Tarsius spectrum*).

Takes the first of its Latin names from the elongation of the bones of the upper part of the ankle (*tarsus*), after the manner we have noticed as occurring in the mouse-lemurs and galagos, and its second from its spectre-like and ghostly appearance. It is a native of various islands in the Malayan region, being found, among others, in Celebes, Sumatra, Borneo, the Philippines, and some others. It has never, we believe, been exhibited alive in this country, and since accounts at first hand from those who have seen animals in their native countries are always valuable, we commence our notice of this animal by quoting from Dr. Guillemard, who received a living specimen while at Celebes, and, in his *Cruise of the Marchesa*, writes as follows:—"The most interesting addition to our menagerie was a tiny lemuroid animal (*T. spectrum*), brought to us by a native, by whom it was said to have been caught upon the mainland. These little creatures, which are of arboreal and nocturnal habits, are about the size of a small rat, and are covered with remarkably thick fur, which is very soft. The tail is long, and covered with hair at the root and tip, while the middle portion of it is nearly bare. The eyes are enormous, and indeed seem, together with the equally large ears, to constitute the greater part of the face, for the jaw and nose are very small, and the latter is set on, like that of a pug dog, almost at a right angle. The hind-limb at once attracts attention from the great length of the tarsal [ankle] bones, and the hand is equally noticeable for its length, the curious claws with which it is provided, and the extraordinary disc-shaped palps on the palmar surface of the fingers, which probably enables the animal to retain its hold in almost any position. This weird-looking creature we were unable to keep long in captivity, for we could not get it to eat the cockroaches which were almost the only food with which we could supply it. It remained still by day in its darkened cage, but at night, especially if disturbed, it would spring vertically upwards in an odd mechanical manner, not unlike the hopping of a flea. On the third day it found a grave in a pickle-bottle."

If we add that the general colour of the fur is usually some shade of brownish-fawn, with the face and forehead reddish, and a dark ring round the enormous eyes, the above account gives a very good idea of the general appearance of the tarsier,[1] the length of whose body is about 6 inches. This account does not, however, show us any reasons why this animal should be separated from the typical lemurs as the representative of a separate family; and we must therefore proceed to the consideration of this point.

Now, the elongation of the bones of the upper half of the ankle evidently allies the tarsier to the galagos and mouse-lemurs; and if the other characters of the animal approximated to them there would be no reason why it should not be included in the family. It happens, however, that there are very important differences connected with the teeth, and it is on these zoologists largely rely in assigning the tarsier to a distinct family. In describing the teeth of the lemurs it has been shown that the middle pair of incisors in the upper jaw are separated from one another by an intervening space, and it may be added here that they are of small size. If, however, we examine the skull of a tarsier, we shall find that these

---

[1] In Dr. Guillemard's figure, reproduced on p. 244, the ears are longer than in our heading.

central upper incisors are, as in ourselves, of large size, and placed quite close to one another. Then, again, we shall find that the upper tusk is much smaller than in the typical lemurs. Moreover, if we examine the lower jaw, we shall see that the tusk is formed by the canine tooth, instead of being the most anterior of the premolars; the latter tooth being smaller than either of the other two premolars, instead of taking the form and function of a tusk, as in the true lemurs. In having but a single pair of lower incisors, which an examination of its skull would show to be the case, the tarsier agrees with the indri lemur; but in the presence of three premolars on either side of each jaw it resembles the true lemurs. Its whole series of teeth are thirty-four in number—four more than in the indri, and two less than in the true lemurs, and may be expressed by the formula $i\frac{2}{1}$, $c\frac{1}{1}$, $p\frac{3}{3}$, $m\frac{3}{3}$.

It is, therefore, clear that the tarsier differs very markedly from ordinary lemurs; and, if our observations made under the head of fossil lemurs have been understood, it will be apparent that in this respect the tarsier is what zoologists term a more generalised form than the true lemurs, and that it closely resembles the extinct types. Indeed the series of teeth in the extinct microchoere are expressed by the same formula as the one denoting those of the tarsier. We may, therefore, venture to conclude that this animal shows in its teeth signs of affinity with the extinct European lemurs, which have been lost in the true lemurs and their allies. In regard to the elongation of the bones of the upper half of the ankle, the tarsier is, however, evidently a specialised, or highly modified creature; and it is probable that the same structural peculiarity did not exist in the Eocene lemurs.

Another peculiarity of the tarsier is that the two bones of the lower leg,—the tibia and fibula,—instead of being quite separate from one another, as in all other lemurs, are united in their lower half. Then again, in place of only the toe next the great toe being furnished with a sharp compressed claw, and all the other toes having flat nails, the middle toe is also provided with a similar compressed and pointed claw.

We might refer to certain features connected with the structure of the skull of the tarsier, and also mention some peculiarities in the anatomy of its soft parts; but sufficient has been said to show what a very remarkable creature it is when properly studied, and to indicate why it is referred to as a distinct family. It is, indeed, generalised, or little modified in regard to its teeth, but highly specialised, or much modified in respect of the bony skeleton of its legs and feet.

Dr. Guillemard calls special attention to the peculiar leaps made by his captive tarsier; and this habit of leaping is highly characteristic of the species,—as we have seen it to be of the galagos and mouse-lemurs, in which the ankle-bones are modified in the same manner, although to a less degree. The tarsier is described as progressing in the woods by a series of leaps from bough to bough, or along a single bough; and it doubtless makes use of similar leaps to pounce upon its living prey. Its food consists chiefly of insects and small reptiles, and it does not appear that it ever touches fruits. Tarsiers are rare in their native lands, and instead of going in small parties are found singly or in pairs. They are looked upon with great dread and horror by the native inhabitants of the Malayan Islands. According to the late Mr. Cumming, who once had a female and young tarsier alive, the animal is known to the natives of the above-mentioned islands by the name of the Malmag. The same writer also informs us that only one young is produced at a birth; and that when the natives capture one of a pair, they are sure of securing its fellow. When feeding, the tarsier sits up on its hind-quarters and holds its food in its hands, somewhat after the fashion of a squirrel.

THE AYE-AYE (*Chiromys madagascariensis*).

The last of the lemur-like animals, and, at the same time, of the whole order of Primates, is the aye-aye of Madagascar, which has teeth so utterly different from all other members of the order that it was long considered to belong to the Rodent order (rats, rabbits, etc.).

The most peculiar feature about the teeth of the fully adult aye-aye is that the front, or incisor teeth, are reduced to a single pair in each jaw, which are curved, and have their extremities brought to a sharp chisel-like edge, admirably adapted for gnawing and rasping hard substances. The structure of these teeth is in fact precisely the same as in the front teeth of rats and beavers; their sharp cutting-edge being produced by the circumstance that while the body of the tooth is formed of the comparatively soft ivory, the front surface is faced with a layer of hard flinty enamel. And it will be obvious that the result of wear in a tooth of this type will be to produce a chisel-like edge. It will further be apparent that such a tooth, if continually employed in rasping away hard substances, would be very quickly worn away altogether, if it were of the same length as ordinary teeth, and not provided with some kind of renewal. This difficulty is obviated by the front teeth of the aye-aye remaining open at their lower ends, and undergoing a continual process of growth; so that as their summits are worn away they are pushed further up from below. In all these points their teeth are precisely similar to those of the Rodent Mammals. A further resemblance to Rodents is shown by the absence of tusks in the aye-aye; and also by the cheek-teeth being separated by a long gap from the incisors, as well as by being reduced in number, and having their crowns with nearly flat surfaces, instead of being surmounted with the sharp cusps found in those of the true lemur. Indeed, the total number of teeth in the adult aye-aye is only eighteen; these being expressed by the formula $i\frac{1}{1}, c\frac{0}{0}, p\frac{1}{0}, m\frac{3}{3}$, or exactly the same as in many Rodents.

If, then, the teeth of the adult aye-aye are so exactly like those of a Rodent, the reader may well ask why it is not placed among the rats and beavers, instead of among the lemurs. To this it may be replied that in the young aye-aye the milk- or baby-teeth are very much more like those of the true lemurs; while the anatomy of the skeleton and the soft parts is essentially that of a lemur, and not that of a Rodent. The resemblance of the skull and teeth of the aye-aye to those of a Rodent, is, indeed, an excellent instance of what zoologists term an *adaptive* or *parallel resemblance*. When two animals belonging to totally different groups have more or less nearly similar habits, it frequently results that they will closely resemble one another in at least some part of their structure; such particular structure being the one best adapted for a particular mode of life. In all such cases a superficial examination of the animals in question will frequently lead to their being referred to one and the same group; while further minute investigations will reveal the fact that their deep-seated internal structure—which alone reveals their true affinities—is very different. Such was the case with the aye-aye, which was at first referred to the Rodents; its affinities to the lemurs not having been discovered till a fuller examination.

The aye-aye agrees with the true lemurs in having the great toe of the foot furnished with a flattened nail, and capable of being opposed to the other toes; this feature being alone sufficient to prove that the creature has nothing to do with the Rodents. With the exception of this great toe, however, all the toes and fingers, which are very long and narrow, are furnished with narrow and sharply-pointed claws. Although both the hands and the feet are large in proportion to

THE AYE-AYE ($\frac{1}{9}$ nat. size).

the size of the animal, yet the great peculiarity is concentrated in the hands, in which the fingers are much longer than are the toes of the feet. One finger—namely, that corresponding to our middle finger—is more remarkable than the others, being of great length and extreme slenderness. It is probable that this ghostly middle finger is employed in extracting from their burrows the larvæ which, as we shall shortly learn, appear to form a portion of the creature's natural diet.

In size the aye-aye may be compared to a cat; its total length being about 3 feet, of which the larger moiety is formed by the bushy tail. The comparison with a cat may be further extended to the short and rounded head and cat-like face of the animal. The rounded ears are, however, relatively larger than those of a cat, and have the peculiarity of being nearly naked. The fur is long, and composed of a mixture of longer stiffish hairs, with an under-coat of more bushy and shorter ones. The prevailing colour is dark brown, tending to black; the throat being yellowish-grey, and the under-parts showing a rufous tinge. Some of the longer hairs on the back are whitish, thus producing a somewhat mottled appearance in the fur.

The aye-aye was discovered by the French traveller Sonnerat—who likewise first obtained the indri—as far back as the year 1780; and it was described in the first year of the present century by Baron Cuvier, who regarded it as a kind of squirrel. Nothing more was heard of the creature from Sonnerat's time till 1860, when specimens were sent to this country, and described by Sir Richard Owen. The following account of the habits of the aye-aye in its native land was published in 1882 by Mr. L. Baron, a missionary in Madagascar. "The aye-aye," writes Mr. Baron, "lives in the dense parts of the great forest that runs along the eastern border of the central plateau of the island, but only in that part of it which separates the Sihanaka province from that of the Betsimisaraka, and which is about twenty-five miles from the east coast, in latitude 17° 22″ S., or thereabouts. Possibly there are other parts of the country where the aye-aye is found; but so far as my knowledge extends (and I have made inquiries in different parts of the island), this is the only region where the creature finds its home . . . From what I have gathered from the natives, it seems to be pretty common, its nocturnal habits, and the superstitious awe with which it is regarded (and of which I shall speak presently) accounting for its apparent rarity.

"The native name of the animal is Haihay (Hihi); but this is not derived from the exclamations of surprise which the natives exhibited at the sight of an unknown animal, but is simply onomatopoëtic, the creature's call being *haihay, haihay.* The animal, as is well known, is nocturnal in its habits, prowling about in pairs—male and female. It has but one young one at birth. It builds a nest about 2 feet in diameter, of twigs and dried leaves, in the dense foliage of the upper branches of trees. In this it spends the day in sleep. The nest is entered by a hole at the side. The teeth are used in scratching away the bark of trees in search of insects, and the long claw in digging out the prey when found. A white insect called *Andraitra* (possibly the larva of some beetle), seems to form its chief food. I was told that it frequently taps the bark with its fore-feet, and then listens for the movement of its prey beneath, thus saving itself useless labour. It does not flee at the sight of man, showing that for generations it has not been molested by him; which is indeed true, as the following will show. The natives have a superstitious fear of the creature, believing that it possesses some supernatural power by which it can destroy those who seek to capture it or to do it harm. The consequence of this is that it is with the greatest difficulty one can obtain a specimen. With most of the people no amount of money would be a sufficient inducement to go in pursuit of the creature, 'because,' say they, 'we value our own lives more than money.' It is only a few of the more daring spirits among them, who knowing the *odiny*, that is the secret by which they can disarm it of its dreaded power, have the courage to attempt its capture. Occasionally it is brought to Tamatave for sale, where it realises a good sum. Now and then it is accidentally caught in the traps which the natives set for lemurs; but the owner of the trap, unless one of those versed in the aye-aye mysteries, who know the charm by which to counteract its evil power, smears fat over it, thus securing its forgiveness and goodwill, and sets it free."

Another account was published in the following year by the Rev. G. A. Shaw, also a resident in Madagascar, and since it differs somewhat from the preceding, which it supplements in some other respects, it may be likewise quoted. Mr. Shaw starts by stating, in opposition to Mr. Baron, that the name of the creature is derived from *hay ! hay !* the Malagasy exclamation of surprise; the animal being known to the natives as the Haikay (pronounced Hayekaye). Be its origin what it may, there is thus full testimony that the name by which we know the creature is substantially the same as that by which it is known in its native land.

"Being a nocturnal animal," Mr. Shaw continues, "it is very difficult to get any reliable information concerning its habits in the wild state, and native reports are altogether contradictory with respect to these matters. Even with reference to its natural food no satisfactory explanation can be obtained from the people. Many assert positively that it lives on honey; but one I had in captivity would not eat honey in any form, either strained or in the comb, or mixed with various things I thought he might have a fancy for. Others say it lives on fruits and leaves; others that birds and eggs are its natural food. I fancy from what I saw of my captive that both these conjectures are nearer the truth; for after a few days, during which it would eat nothing, and it was thought that the proper food had not been offered (but it was in reality pining or sulking), it took several fruits which I was able to procure for it. It liked bananas; but it made sorry efforts at eating them, its teeth being so placed that its mouth was clogged with them. The small fruits of various native shrubs it also devoured, as also rice boiled in milk and sweetened with sugar; but meat, larvæ, moths, beetles, and eggs it would not touch. But I noticed that when I came near its cage with a light, it almost invariably started and went for a little distance in chase of the shadows of the pieces of bananas attached to the wire-work in front of its cage; and I think that if I could have procured some small birds it would have, if not devoured them, at any rate killed them for their blood, as some lemurs are known to do. It drank water occasionally, but in such a way as to make it highly probable that it does not drink from streams or pools in the ordinary way. It did not hold its food in its hands as the lemurs which I have had in captivity have done, but merely used its hands to steady it on the bottom of the cage. But whenever it had eaten, although it did not always clean its hands, it invariably drew each of its long claws through its mouth, as though, in the natural state, these had taken a chief part in procuring its food.

"In some accounts, given by different writers, the haikay is said to be easily tamed, and to be inoffensive. . . . In each of these qualities, I have found, both from native accounts, and from the specimen I have kept, that exactly the reverse is the case. It is very savage, and, when attacking, strikes with its hands with anything but a slow movement. As might be imagined in a nocturnal animal, its movements in the daytime are slow and uncertain; and it may be said to be inoffensive then. When it bit at the wire-netting in the front of its cage, I noticed that each of the pair of incisors in either jaw could separate sufficiently to admit the thick wire even down to the gum, the tips of the teeth then standing a considerable distance apart, leading to the supposition that, by some arrangement of the sockets of the teeth, they could be moved so far without breaking. The haikay brings forth one at a birth, in which the long claw is fully developed."

It has been observed that captive aye-ayes are very partial to the juice of the sugar-cane, which they obtain by ripping up the canes with their front teeth; and since sugar-cane grows wild in Madagascar, we may infer that its juice forms a part of the food of these animals in their wild state. It is, therefore, probable that the diet of the aye-aye is a mixed one, consisting partly of grubs, partly of the juices of plants, partly of fruit; but whether birds or their eggs also form a part of the bill of fare must be left for future observers to determine. The favourite haunts of these animals appear to be the bamboo-brakes, which form such a large portion of the forests in some regions of the island.

THE TARSIER ACCORDING TO GUILLEMARD. (From *The Cruise of the Marchesa.*)

The Hammer-Headed Bat.
The Naked Bat.
P. J. Smit.

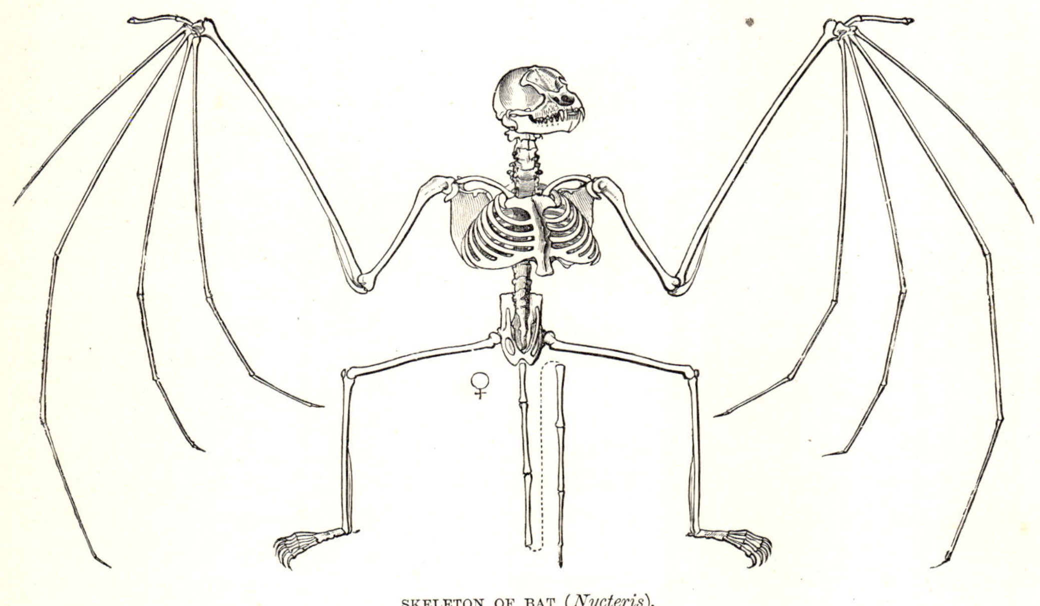

SKELETON OF BAT (*Nycteris*).

CHAPTER IX.

BATS,—Order CHIROPTERA.

IN some cases there is more or less difficulty, especially when we have to take extinct types into consideration, in finding well-marked characteristics by which the various orders of Mammals can be distinguished from each other. With bats, however, there is no such difficulty, since they are sharply distinguished from all other Mammals by possessing the power of true flight, for the purpose of which their fore-limbs are specially modified. We say true flight advisedly, for the reason that there is a kind of spurious flight possessed by certain other Mammals, such as flying squirrels and flying phalangers, which is quite different from the flight of bats, and does not entail any special modification of the structure of the fore-limbs. True flight, like that of birds and bats, is effected by means of alternate upward and downward strokes of the wings, and can be carried on as long as the muscular power of the flyer permits. Spurious flight, like that of the flying squirrels, is, on the other hand, nothing more than a prolongation of an upward or downward leap, by the aid of parachute-like expansions of the skin of the sides of the body, and cannot be extended in an upward direction beyond the limits of the impetus of the original leap.

This power of true flight is, then, the essential characteristic of all bats; and it is a very remarkable fact that among all the host of extinct animals with which we are now acquainted, none have been discovered in any way connecting bats with other Mammals. Indeed, remains of bats very closely resembling existing kinds are met with in the upper part of the Eocene period, which show that the order is a very ancient one, and that we should have to go back still earlier before creatures intermediate between bats and other Mammals were met with. In spite of this, naturalists have, however, no hesitation in believing that bats have taken origin from Mammals of ordinary terrestrial habits. It is found, indeed, that in their essential structure bats are so closely allied to the Insectivores (of which we treat next), such as shrews, moles, etc., that there can be little doubt of their derivation from the ancestral forms of that order; and it is probable that the power of true flight was developed gradually from spurious flight, like that of flying squirrels. Moreover, it will be shown later on that there is a very curious kind of Insectivore, endued with the power of spurious flight, which may give us some inkling of the manner in which bats have been derived from the earlier members of that order of Mammals. Bats are accordingly regarded by zoologists as neither more nor less than Insectivores, specially modified and adapted for an aërial life. Moreover, as there appear to be indications that the Insectivores were connected with some of the extinct lemurs, it is now considered best to place them and the bats immediately after the Primates. This must not, however, be taken as any indication that these groups really occupy a high position in the zoological scale; the fact really being that their organisation is of a low type, and far inferior to that of the Carnivores which are placed later on.

Characteristics. The most obvious and important characteristic of bats being their faculty of flight, and the apparatus for this being mainly furnished by the fore-limb, the order to which they belong has been appropriately named Chiroptera, or hand-winged. In the great majority of Mammals the hind-limbs are as large as, or larger than, the front pair, but in bats the latter (as is well shown in the figure of the skeleton at the head of this chapter) vastly exceed the former in length. In a bat's wing the humerus of the upper arm is only moderately elongated, but the single complete bone in the fore-arm, corresponding to the human radius, has a far greater length, and this extraordinary elongation is carried to a still greater extent in the bones of the hand, all of which, with the exception of those of the thumb, form long slender rods. The thumb is free, and terminates in a hooked claw, which can be used for the purposes of climbing or suspension; but the fingers, of which the third is the longest, are connected together by the delicate membrane constituting the soft part of the wing. This wing-membrane is continued along the arm and the sides of the body, and thence to the hind-legs. There is, moreover, a similar membrane connecting the two hind-limbs with the generally long tail; this membrane being usually supported by a peculiar spur of bone projecting from the foot. The toes are, however, quite free. In consequence of the connection of the hind-limb with the wing-membrane, the knee-joint is directed backwards instead of forwards in the usual manner; and this peculiar arrangement renders a bat's movement on the ground an awkward kind of shuffle.

In order to afford space for the attachment of the powerful muscles necessary to move the wings, the chest of bats, like that of birds, is remarkably large. But as these animals are poor walkers, the haunch-bones are relatively small and weak.

Teeth. The great majority of bats feed solely on insects, and have their cheek-teeth furnished with a number of sharp cusps, admirably adapted for holding and piercing the tough integuments of beetles and many other insects. A few bats, however, are blood-suckers, and these have the front teeth specially modified for piercing the skin of the animals they select as their victims. Others, and among them the largest representatives of the order, are fruit-eaters; and these accordingly have a quite different kind of cheek-teeth, in which the crowns are nearly smooth, and without cusps.

The number of the different teeth in different bats is variable, and is of great importance in distinguishing the different genera; but as some of these teeth may be exceedingly minute, their enumeration requires great care. No bat, it may be observed, has more than two pairs of incisor teeth in the upper jaw; neither are there ever more than three premolars on each side of the upper and lower jaws, so that the number of teeth behind the tusks, or canines, never exceeds six.

So thoroughly are bats adapted for a life in the air, that most of them but seldom resort to the ground, and even when they do so they generally endeavour to leave it as soon as possible by ascending a tree, rock, or wall, whence they either again take flight, or settle themselves into their favourite position of repose, suspended head downwards by the feet. Not only do most bats feed and drink while on the wing, but the females even carry their young tightly clinging to their bodies.

Sense of touch. In their active life bats being mostly crepuscular or nocturnal, while their eyes are relatively small, it is obvious that they must be provided with some special means of avoiding contact with objects during flight. This appears to be effected by the extreme development of a sense more or less akin to our sense of touch, by which the neighbourhood of objects is perceived without actual contact; and it was demonstrated as long ago as 1793, by the cruel experiment of depriving bats of sight and then allowing them to fly in a room across which silken threads were stretched in such a manner as to leave just sufficient space for them to pass between with outstretched wings. The unfortunate bats not only succeeded in passing between these threads without contact, and likewise avoided the walls and ceiling of the room, but, when the threads were placed still nearer together, they contracted their wings in order to be able to pass without contact. In the same manner they flew between branches and twigs of trees placed in their course, and suspended themselves when tired of flight on the walls of the room, just as easily as when they enjoyed the use of their eyes. In the great majority of bats it appears that this sense of touch is situated in the wing-membranes, and in the delicate and frequently enormously elongated ears, which are often provided with a kind of secondary inner ear, known as the tragus. There are, moreover, certain bats provided with an additional organ of perception, which takes the form of expansions of skin from the nose and adjacent parts of the face, forming what is generally known as the "nose-leaf." These folds of skin may be either comparatively small and simple, or so large as to form a kind of mask, communicating a most extraordinary physiognomy to the bats in which they occur. The various membranes forming these nose-leaves are always fringed with long and fine hairs, which evidently correspond to the "whiskers" of the cat; and we may accordingly regard these nose-leaves merely as an excessive development of the cat's whiskers, accompanied by leaf - like growths from the skin of the nose. It has been observed by Dr. Dobson—our great authority on bats—that those species which are without nose-leaves are in the habit of flying at dawn or twilight, while the leaf-nosed kinds are more strictly nocturnal, and are thus much less frequently shot when on the wing. The fruit-eating bats, whose habits are very different from the other members of the order, never have these nose-leaves, and their ears are small and unprovided with a tragus; there being no necessity for the extreme delicacy of tactile perception required in the other groups.

Cry. When on the wing, the ordinary insectivorous bats utter a short, sharp squeak of such an extremely high pitch that to many persons it is quite inaudible, although to others, whose ears are attuned to the reception of such high-pitched tones, these cries are of piercing intensity.

Migrations. The insect-eating species of bats inhabiting the temperate regions, being dependent for their nourishment upon a full supply of insects, must in winter either migrate to warmer regions, or hibernate. In our own country all the species hibernate, and do not appear to migrate at all; and it is probable that this hibernating habit also holds good for the whole of the European bats. It seems, however, that at least one North American species—the *Vespertilio borealis*—migrates to a certain extent during the summer, not visiting the more northerly portions of its habitat till August, when the long intense twilights, which would be unsuitable to its habits, have ceased. In Canada, moreover, Dr. Hart Merriam is of opinion that at least two species of bats regularly perform extensive migrations in order to avoid the intense cold of the northern winter. This eloquent writer observes that "all North American bats, except when their habits have been modified by proximity to man, may be classed as *cave-dwelling* or *tree-dwelling*, according to the places in which they spend the day. As a rule, the cave-dwelling species live in large colonies, while the tree-dwelling live singly or in small companies. Now, it is well known that the temperature in caves, even in high latitudes, is little affected by the external atmosphere, but remains nearly uniform throughout the year; while in holes in trees the temperature is about the same as that of the surrounding air. Hence, animals inhabiting caves can pass the winter much farther north than species living in hollow trees. The hoary bat (*Atalapha cinerea*) is a tree-dwelling species, and its home is in the Canadian fauna, from the Adirondack Mountains northward. Therefore, on purely theoretical grounds, it should be expected to migrate." Now, specimens of this bat have been not unfrequently observed in the autumn and winter from localities so far to the southward of its usual habitat, that there would seem to be no longer any reasonable doubt as to its being truly migratory. It has, indeed, been found so far away from its ordinary summer haunts as the Bermudas, where Mr. J. M. Jones states that it is observed occasionally at dusk during the autumn months hawking about according to its nature in search of insects; but as it is never seen except at that particular season, it is clear that it is not a resident, but merely blown across the ocean by those violent north-west gales which also usually bring numbers of birds from the American continent. The hoary bat is, however, not the only species in which there is evidence of periodical migrations. Thus Dr. Merriam tells us that the silver-haired bat (*Vesperugo noctivagans*), which ranges as far north as Hudson's Bay, is known to visit every spring and autumn a solitary lighthouse situated on a solitary rock off the coast of Maine, fifteen miles from the nearest island and thirty miles from the mainland. This rock being uninhabited permanently by bats, the occurrence of these stray individuals at the spring and fall seems to afford perfectly conclusive evidence of the migratory habits of the particular species to which they belong.

Distribution. In regard to their geographical distribution, it may be observed that bats are found over almost the whole world; one species at least even extending as far northwards as the Arctic circle. They are far more abundant within the tropics and the warmer parts of the temperate zones than elsewhere; and it is to those regions alone that the larger species are restricted. Indeed, the bats, according to Mr. Wallace, may be regarded as some of the most characteristic of the Mammals of the tropical zone, occupying in this respect a position second only to that held by the apes, monkeys, and lemurs, and becoming suddenly much less plentiful, both as regards the number of individuals and of species, when we pass into the temperate zone, and still more reduced in both respects when we reach the colder parts of those regions.

In some instances particular family groups of bats are confined more or less exclusively to particular regions of the earth's surface; although others enjoy an almost world-wide distribution. For instance, while the fruit-bats are entirely confined to the warmer regions of the Old World, and the vampires and their allies to America, some of the more common types of ordinary European bats, like *Vesperugo* and *Vespertilio*, are almost cosmopolitan. It will be found that these cosmopolitan forms belong to the more generalised types, while those restricted to particular districts are usually the more specialised form. It is somewhat curious that, according to Dr. Dobson, bats are quite unknown in Iceland, St. Helena, Kerguelen, and the Galapagos Islands.

Numbers. The number of species of bats known to science is now enormous. In a list published in 1878, Dr. Dobson recognised no less than four hundred distinct species, arranged in eighty genera, and six families. Since that date the number has, however, been so largely increased, that we shall probably be not far wrong in setting it down as but little, if at all, short of four hundred and fifty. With such a portentous list to deal with, it will be obvious that, in a work like the present, all that can be attempted is to indicate some of the more generally interesting and leading types, leaving the others for technical treatises. The old English name Flittermouse, by which these animals were known to our ancestors, and by which they are still designated in certain parts of the country, conveys a very accurate notion of their zoological position, if we use the term mouse in the popular signification, in which it embraces animals like the shrews, as well as the true mice.

The Fruit-Bats.

Family *PTEROPODIDÆ.*

The largest of all bats are the so-called flying foxes, or fruit-bats, of the warmer regions of the Old World, which differ from the other members of the order in their purely frugivorous habits, and in certain details of structure partly caused by adaptation to their special mode of life. It is highly probable, as Professor T. Bell observes, that some of these huge fruit-bats " with their predatory habits, their multitudinous numbers, their obscure and mysterious retreats, and the strange combination of beast and bird which they were believed to possess, gave to Virgil the idea, which he has so poetically worked out, of the harpies which fell upon the hastily-spread tables of his hero and his companions, and polluted, whilst they devoured, the feast from which they had driven the affrighted guests."

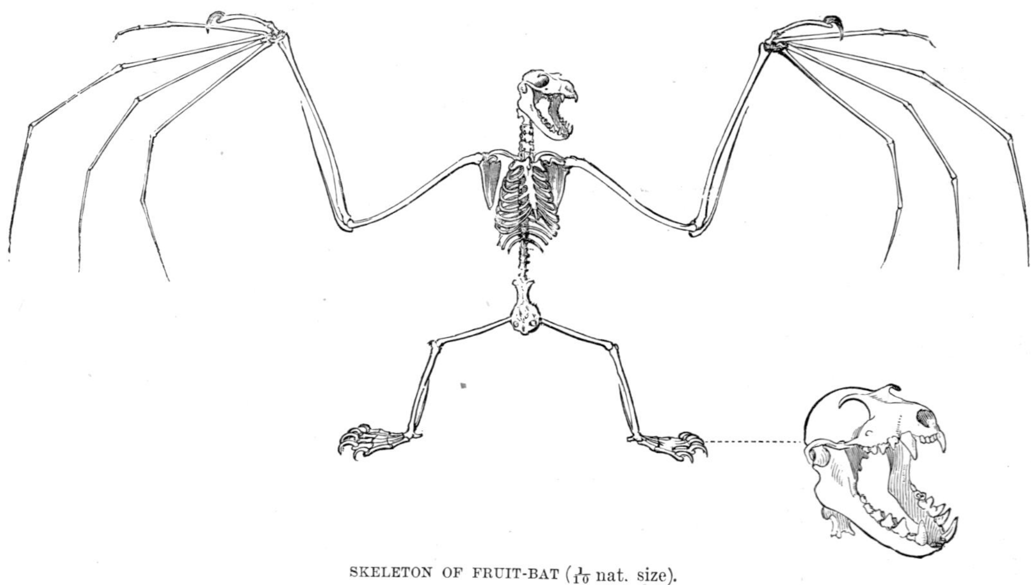

SKELETON OF FRUIT-BAT ($\frac{1}{10}$ nat. size).

Since the fruit-bats differ so essentially from all the other members of the order, both in habits and structure, they are not only referred by naturalists to a separate family,—the *Pteropodidæ,*—but are likewise distinguished as a special suborder, appropriately termed the *Megachiroptera,* or large bats.

As a group, the fruit-bats are characterised by their generally large size, and by the peculiar nature of their teeth, as well as by certain features connected with the wings, ears, and tail. As regards the teeth, they are characterised by the molars having nearly, or quite smooth crowns, elongated from back to front, and divided by a deep longitudinal groove; such a type of tooth being obviously as admirably adapted for mashing up pulpy fruits, as the cusped teeth of ordinary bats would be unsuited. The wings of fruit-bats may be at once distinguished from those of all other kinds by having three (instead of one or rarely two) joints in the second or index finger, as shown in our figure of the skeleton; but the metacarpal bones, or those between the wrist and the fingers, must not be confounded with the proper bones of the latter. Moreover, the terminal joint of the second finger is generally provided with a claw; whereas in other bats the thumb alone is thus furnished. Then, again, a fruit-bat may always be distinguished by its ears, of which the sides of the projecting portion, or *conch*, are united at the base so as to form a complete ring; the ears, as we have already incidentally mentioned, being invariably of small size, and unprovided with an inner tragus. The last distinctive feature of the group that it will be necessary to mention here is that the tail, if present at all, is always short, and is situated beneath the membrane between the hind legs, with which membrane it may have no connection. There are certain other characteristics of the group which require a considerable amount of anatomical knowledge for their due appreciation, and which we accordingly pass over.

Many considerations lead to the conclusion that the fruit-bats are a specialised group, which have been derived by adaptation from ordinary insectivorous bats; and this view has been remarkably confirmed by the comparatively recent discovery of a peculiar species, which, while agreeing with the rest in the general structure of its molar teeth, differs in that these teeth retain cusps representing those of the insect-eating group.

The Common Fruit-Bats, or Fox-Bats.

Genus *Pteropus*.

The best known of the group are the so-called fox-bats, or flying-foxes, taking their name from their long fox-like faces, of which a group is represented in the coloured plate, and a single example in the woodcut on the next page. These bats, constituting the genus *Pteropus* of naturalists, are characterised by their large size, the presence of thirty-four teeth (among which there are two pairs of incisors and three premolars in each jaw), the total absence of a tail, the long and fox-like muzzle, and the thick coat of woolly fur with which the neck is covered.

Fox-bats are found in India, Ceylon, Burma, the Malay Archipelago, the Seychelles, Madagascar, the Comoro Islands, the south of Japan, and most of the islands of the Pacific (the Sandwich and some other groups excepted), as well as in Papua and Australia. Curiously enough, they are quite unknown in Africa, although common in the Comoro Islands, two hundred miles distant. Probably the best known of all the species is the Indian fox-bat (*Pteropus medius*), characterised by its naked and sharply-pointed ears. All who have resided in India are familiar with the long strings of fox-bats which may be seen, as the shades of

HEAD OF WALLACE'S FOX-BAT.
(From Gray, *Proc. Zool. Soc.*)

evening approach, wending their way from their sleeping-places to the scene of their nocturnal depredations. Writing of these bats, the late Dr. Jerdon says that "during the day they roost on trees, generally in large colonies, many hundreds often occupying a single tree, to which they invariably resort if not driven away. Towards sunset they begin to get restless, move about along the branches, and by ones and twos fly off for their nightly rounds. If water is at hand, a tank, or a river, or the sea, they fly cautiously down and touch the water, but I could not ascertain if they took a sip, or merely dipped part of their bodies in. They

THE KALONG, OR MALAY FOX-BAT ($\frac{1}{3}$ nat. size.)

fly vast distances occasionally to such trees as happen to be in fruit." As the first streaks of dawn begin to appear in the east the bats set out on their homeward journey from the field of their depredations, and the scene which ensues on their arrival at their roosting-place is graphically described by Colonel Tickell:— "From the arrival of the first comer, until the sun is high above the horizon, a scene of incessant wrangling and contention is enacted among them, as each endeavours to secure a higher and better place, or to eject a neighbour from too close vicinage. In these struggles the bats hook themselves along the branches, scrambling about hand-over-hand with some speed, biting each other severely, striking out with the long claw of the thumb, shrieking and cackling without intermission. Each new animal is compelled to fly several times round the tree, being threatened from all points, and when he eventually hooks on he has to go through a series of combats, and be probably ejected two or three times before he makes good his tenure."

Full accounts of this bat will also be found in Sir J. Emerson Tennent's *Natural History of Ceylon*, although it is probable that this writer was mistaken in saying that its diet included insects. He observes that a favourite resort of these bats was some tall india-rubber trees near Kandy, in Ceylon, where they used to assemble in such prodigious numbers that large boughs would not unfrequently give way beneath the accumulated weight of the flock. It is also stated that the branches on which they are accustomed to roost become almost denuded of leaves, most of these being stripped off by the bats as they contend with one another for the favourite roosting-places. When suspended in the usual position, these bats move easily from place to place, and from branch to branch, by using each foot in turn, and by climbing, when occasion requires, by the aid of the claws. When feeding, Colonel Tickell states that the fox-bats hang by one foot only, and take the fruit they are about to eat in the other, seizing it by driving in their claws like a fork, and not by a grasping action.

Fox-bats invariably fly singly in long files, and never in close flocks; their flight being a slow, flapping, measured movement. In Calcutta the long strings of these bats may be seen every evening stretching across the sky from west to east, although the number of individuals varies considerably at different seasons of the year. Writing there on 23rd August 1869, Dr. John Anderson observes that " this species has been flying for the last few days from the north to the south of the city, in immense numbers, immediately after sunset. The sky from east to west has been covered with them as far as the eye could reach, and all were flying with an evident purpose, and making for some common feeding-ground. Over a transverse area of two hundred and fifty yards as many as seventy bats passed overhead in one minute, and as they were spread over an area of great breadth, and could be detected in the sky on both sides as far as the eye could reach, their numbers were very great, but yet they continued to pass overhead for about half an hour. This is not the first time I have observed this habit in this species; indeed, it was much more markedly seen in August 1864, while I was residing in the Botanical Gardens, Calcutta. The sky, immediately after sunset, was covered with these bats, travelling in a steady manner from west to east, and spread over a vast expanse, all evidently making for one common goal, and travelling, as it were, like birds of passage with a steady purpose. I observed them, not only on one, but both sides of the river. But in the Botanical Gardens I noticed that, whilst the great mass of bats passed on, a few were attracted by trees then in fruit, and seemed to go no further. This continued for a number of successive nights, but I did not observe the bats returning." What occasioned these enormous assemblages has not yet been explained.

This species of fruit-bat has an expanse of wing of about 4 feet from tip to tip; and it is found throughout the whole of India, Ceylon, and Burma. In the Andaman and Nicobar Islands in the Bay of Bengal, it is, however, replaced by a species (*P. nicobaricus*) of nearly the same dimensions, but readily distinguished by its rounded ears.

The largest of all fox-bats, and consequently of all bats, is, however, the kalong or Malay fox-bat (*P. edulis*), represented in the figure on p. 254, which measures upwards of 5 feet from tip to tip of the wings, and derives its name from its flesh being eaten by the Malays, as, indeed, is that of its Indian cousin by some of the natives of that country. Writing of the Malay species, Mr. Wallace states that they are considered a great delicacy by the natives, and are much sought after. "At about the beginning of the year they come [to Batchian] in large flocks to eat fruit, and congregate during the day on some islands in the bay, hanging by thousands on the trees, especially on the dead ones. They can then be easily caught or knocked down with sticks, and are brought home in basketfuls. They require to be carefully prepared, as the skin and fur have a rank and powerful foxy odour; but they are generally cooked with abundance of spices and condiments, and are really very good eating,—something like hare."

Of the Australian fruit-bat (*P. poliocephalus*) the late Professor Moseley describes a roosting place which he visited in New South Wales in the following words:—"In a dense piece of bush, consisting principally of young trees, the trees were hung all over with these bats, looking like great black fruits. As we approached, the bats showed signs of uneasiness, and after the first shot were rather difficult to approach, moving from before us, and pitching in a fresh tree some distance ahead. The bats uttered a curious cackling sound when disturbed. They were in enormous numbers, and although thousands had been shot not long before by a large party got together for the purpose, their numbers were not perceptibly reduced. They do great harm to the fruit orchards about Parramatta, and the fruit-growers there organise parties to shoot them."

The same observer also records that certain species of fruit-bats, which he met with in the Friendly Islands and in New South Wales, are in the habit of devouring flowers as well as fruits. The particular species observed in the Friendly Islands was doubtless the Polynesian fruit-bat (*P. kerandrenii*), which is found in most of the islands in that region. "These bats," writes Professor Moseley, "appear on the wing in the early afternoon in full sunlight, and at the time of our visit were feeding on the bright red flowers of one of the indigenous trees. Flowers form an important proportion of the food of fruit-bats. In New South Wales, in Botany Bay in May, numbers of fruit-bats were to be seen feeding on the flowers of the gum trees. The bats most probably often act as fertilisers by carrying pollen from tree to tree adherent to their fur. As dark comes on the fruit-bats become more plentiful. It is probably only those specially driven by hunger that come out before dark." These observations show that two of these bats are, at certain seasons, in the habit of supplementing the ordinary fruit-diet by one of flowers; but it does not appear that a similar habit has been recorded in the case of the Indian or Malayan species. It has, however, been observed that the Indian fruit-bat will greedily drink palm-juice from the pots hung on the trees for the purpose of collecting it; and individuals have been found lying at the foot of the trees in a helplessly intoxicated condition.

FRUIT-BATS.

The Tailed Fox-Bats.

Genus *Xantharpyia.*

Closely allied to the common fox-bats are the tailed fox-bats, which are represented by a comparatively small number of species, ranging from India,

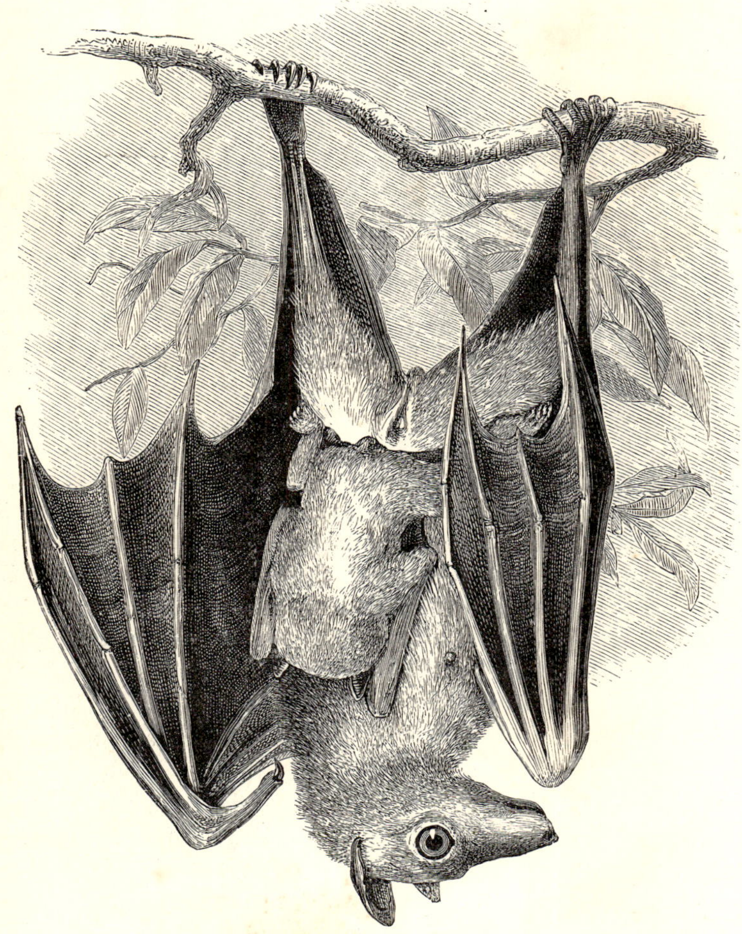

COLLARED FOX-BAT AND YOUNG. (From the *Proc. Zool. Soc.*—After Sclater.)

Burma, and the Malayan Islands to the Persian Gulf, Palestine, Africa, and Madagascar. They are distinguished from all the members of the genus *Pteropus* by the presence of a short tail, which is connected with the membrane between the legs, and likewise by their inferior size and less brilliant coloration, as well as by the fur on the back of the neck being no longer than that on the body. The collared tailed fox-bat (*X. collaris*) is represented in the accompanying illustration.

Many of these fox-bats, instead of living in trees, inhabit caves or deserted buildings; one species being found in numbers in the chambers of the great pyramid in Egypt, as well as in old buildings in Palestine; while a second was observed by Mr. Blanford inhabiting caves excavated in rock-salt in Kishm Island, in the Persian Gulf. Dr. Dobson is of opinion that different individuals of a single species of these bats may inhabit either caves or trees; and he further believes that those dwelling in caves may be distinguished from those habitually frequenting trees by their shorter fur. Like most other members of the family, these bats will travel long distances in their daily journeys for food; and it was at one time supposed that in Nipal they flew between thirty and forty miles out and home. This enormous distance has, however, been shown to be incorrect; the length of the daily journey really being about sixteen miles each way.

The Epauletted Fruit-Bats.

Genus *Epomophorus*.

A striking contrast to the neat and sharp-muzzled heads of the fox-bats is presented by a small group of African species known as the epauletted fruit-bats, so named from the tufts of hair surmounting the shoulders of the males. These bats have fewer teeth than the fox-bats, the total number being only twenty-six or twenty-eight. They are readily distinguished by their remarkably large and long heads, with a bluntly conical or truncated muzzle, the very large, flabby, and expansible lips bordering the capacious mouth, and also by the presence of a tuft of white hair on the margins of the ears. Some of these bats are tailless, while others have a short tail unconnected with the membrane between the legs. In all the species but one, the males, which are larger than the females, are furnished with peculiar pouches of skin on the sides of the neck, from the interior of which project tufts of long yellowish hair, surmounting the shoulders, so as to resemble epaulettes, and thus giving origin to the popular and scientific names of the group.

These bats are confined to that portion of Africa lying to the south of the Sahara Desert, which constitutes the greater portion of the Ethiopian region of zoologists, and are unknown in Madagascar. They are most abundant in the forest regions of the western side of the continent, especially the Gabun district. It is here that we meet with that most remarkable species discovered by Du Chaillu, known as the hammer-headed bat (*Epomophorus monstrosus*), which differs from the rest in the absence of shoulder-tufts in the males. The head in that sex has an enormous muzzle, furnished with a kind of shield-like expansion in front, communicating a most repulsive and hideous expression to the whole face, which reminds one of a very ugly caricature of the head of a mule. Sir John Kirk tells us that the epauletted fruit-bats subsist largely on figs, and Dr. Dobson remarks that their voluminous and capacious lips are admirably adapted to retain and swallow without loss the juicy contents of these and other soft fruits during the process of mastication.

The Short-Nosed Fruit-Bats.

Genus *Cynopterus*.

The short-nosed fruit-bats comprise several species almost exclusively confined to the Oriental region (that is to say, ranging from India to the Malayan Islands), and readily distinguished from the fox-bats by their short and rounded muzzles, marked by a shallow vertical groove, and their small size. The teeth are, moreover, somewhat less numerous than in the latter, being usually thirty-two, but occasionally, owing to the absence of one pair of lower incisors, only thirty. They have generally a short tail, with the same relations to the membrane between the legs as in the tailed fox-bats.

The common short-nosed fruit-bat (*Cynopterus marginatus*), ranging from India to the Philippine Islands, is one of the best-known forms, and is remarkable for its extreme voracity. It is very common throughout India, where it generally inhabits trees,—especially the palmyra palm,—but is occasionally found in caverns and crevices of rocks. This bat is very destructive to fruit, being especially fond of plantains and mangoes. As an instance of its voracity, it may be mentioned that an individual, of which the weight when killed some hours after the feast was only one ounce, consumed two and a half ounces of plantains within a period of three hours. It has been observed that the flight of this species is much lighter than that of the fox-bats, although the general habits of the two groups are very similar.

The Tube-Nosed Fruit-Bats.

Genus *Harpyia*.

Two curious bats, differing from one another considerably in size, and found from Celebes to New Guinea, North Australia, and New Ireland, are distinguished from the short-nosed fruit-bats by their still shorter and more rounded muzzles, but more especially by the production of the nostrils into a pair of long diverging tubes, reaching rather beyond the extremity of the muzzle. Such a structure, except to a less degree in one group of insect-eating bats, is quite unparalleled elsewhere in the whole class of Mammals, and gives to the creatures such an extraordinary appearance that it is difficult to believe at first sight that it is natural. So far as we are aware, no suggestion has been yet made as to the

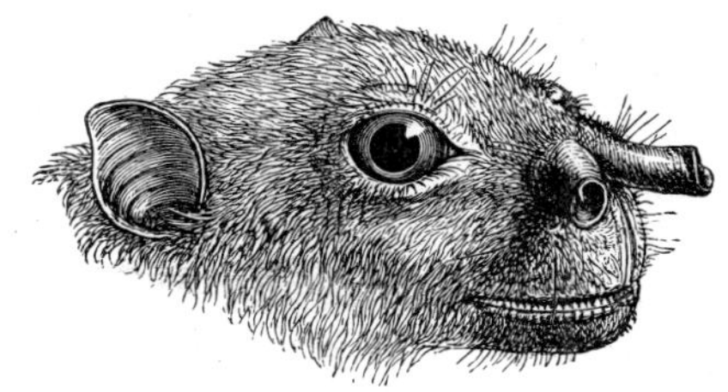

HEAD OF TUBE-NOSED FRUIT-BAT.
(From Dobson, *Proc. Zool. Soc* 1877.)

probable reason for this tubular prolongation of the nostrils, although it is, doubtless, of some special advantage to these bats, of whose habits we have, indeed, practically no information. The tube-nosed fruit-bats are further distinguished by the small number of their teeth, of which the total is only twenty-four.

The Cusped-Toothed Fruit-Bat.

Genus *Pteralopex*.

In our brief survey of the fruit-bats we must not omit mention of a rather large species recently discovered in the Solomon Islands, which is remarkable for the peculiar structure of its teeth. This bat, which is of a uniform dark-brown colour, has the general external characters of the fox-bats, with which it also agrees in the number of its teeth, but the muzzle is much shorter and thicker. The peculiarity of the teeth is that the molars have a series of cusps, almost obliterating the longitudinal grooving characteristic of those of all the fruit-bats. The presence of these cusps clearly shows that the cusped-toothed fruit-bat is the descendant of a connecting form between the insect-eating bats and the fox-bats; and it is upon the evidence of this species that naturalists now regard all the fruit-bats as derived from bats with fully cusped teeth like those of the insectivorous species. The Solomon Islands form a group lying to the east of New Guinea, and extending in a south-easterly direction from New Ireland; and it is just such remote spots as these which appear to be the most favourable for the survival of ancient connecting types of animals like the species under consideration.

The Long-Tongued Fruit-Bats.

Genus *Carponycteris*, etc.

All the fruit-bats hitherto noticed are characterised by the tongue being of moderate dimensions, and the well-developed molar teeth. We come now, however, to a small group comprising seven genera (each represented by only a single species), all of which are distinguished by their long and slender tongues, terminating in recurved papillæ, and likewise by their exceedingly narrow molar teeth, which scarcely project above the level of the gums. All of these bats have long and sharply-pointed faces. With the exception of one West African species, the long-tongued fruit-bats are confined to the Indian, Malayan, and Australian regions, extending from India itself to New Guinea and the Solomon Islands, and they are found on the continent of Australia. They are of relatively small size as compared with the fox-bats. The use of the long tongues of these bats is unknown, but since they can be protruded some distance in advance of the muzzle, it may be that they are employed to lick out the contents of soft fruits while still hanging on the trees; this being confirmed by the small size of the molar teeth, which can be of but little service for mastication.

The small long-tongued fruit-bat (*Carponycteris minima*) is the smallest of all the fruit-bats, being considerably inferior in size to the European noctule described in the next chapter. It has a very extensive geographical distribution, ranging from Northern India and Burma to Australia and New Ireland. It is common in the warm valleys of Sikhim; and, according to Mr. Blanford, generally roosts in trees, although occasionally found in old buildings. It lives on fruit of all kinds, of which it consumes, in proportion to its size, a large quantity. The cavern long-tongued fruit-bat (*Eonycteris spelæa*) is a rather larger species, distinguished by the absence of a claw on the index finger. It inhabits caves in Burma, Java, and Cambodia. The only other species we shall mention is Woodford's long-tongued fruit-bat (*Nesonycteris woodfordi*), from the Solomon Islands, which is remarkable for its brilliant coloration, the body and hairy portions of the limbs being of a bright orange, while the wing-membranes are dark brown. Nothing seems to be known of the habits of this bat.

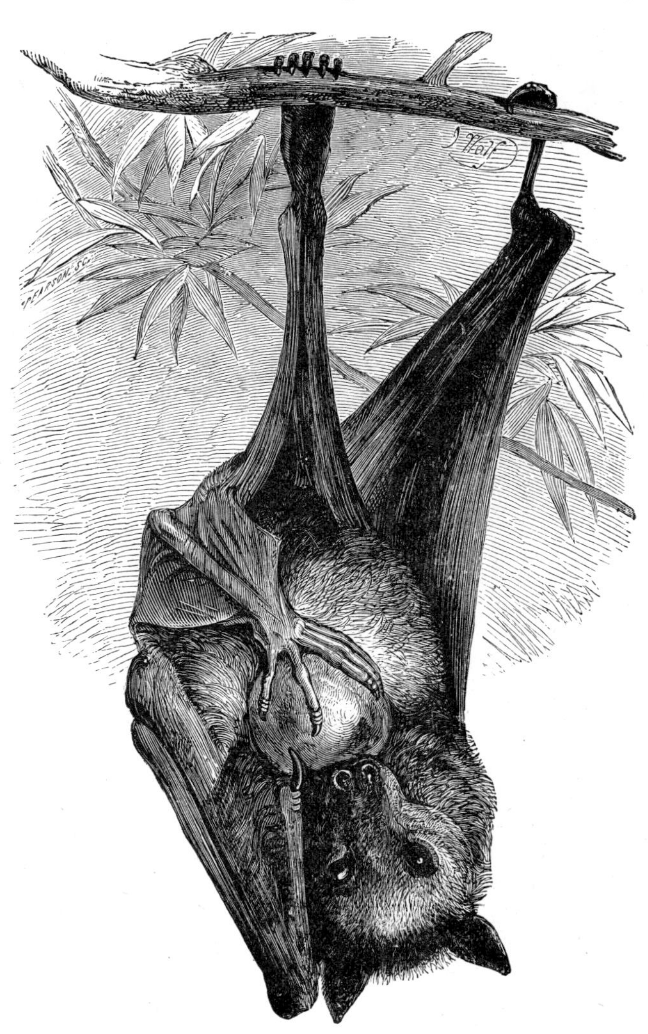

RED NECKED FRUIT-BAT.

CHAPTER X.

Bats,—*continued.*

The Insect-Eating Bats (*Microchiroptera*).

HAVING treated in the preceding chapter of the bats which feed entirely upon fruit or flowers, we now come to the consideration of the much larger group of those which subsist upon insects, among which we must include a few which have acquired frugivorous habits, and likewise those which subsist by sucking the blood of Mammals larger than themselves.   As being generally of much smaller size than those of the frugivorous group (Megachiroptera), the members of the insectivorous group of bats are collectively known to zoologists as the Microchiroptera; and it remains to indicate the leading characteristics (apart from those of an anatomical nature) by which this group may be distinguished from the one treated in the preceding chapter.

Apart from their generally inferior bodily size, the insectivorous bats are broadly distinguished from the fruit-bats by the presence of a number of sharp cusps on the crowns of their molar teeth; these cusps in the upper molars taking the form of the letter W.   There is, moreover, no trace of the longitudinal groove found in the molars of the fruit-bats; the upper molars having their longer diameter placed transversely, instead of longitudinally.   Another distinctive feature is to be found in the index finger of the fore-limb, which has never more than two joints, and usually contains but one; moreover, this finger never terminates in a claw, as it so frequently does among the fruit-bats.   Then, again, the head of an insect-eating bat may be at once recognised by the two margins of the conch of the ear arising from the head from separate points, instead of forming a complete ring at the base, as in the fruit-bats.   Moreover, the tail, which is very generally present and of considerable length, is either contained in the membrane joining the hind-limbs, or is visible upon the upper surface of the same.   The insect-eating bats are further divisible into two minor sections, distinguished from one another by several easily recognised features.   In the first section one of the chief characteristics is that the tail is included within the membrane between the hind legs.   Another is that the inner pair of incisor teeth in the upper jaw are never very large, and are always separated from one another in the middle line by a considerable space.   Yet another characteristic of these bats, with the exception of three species (belonging to as many genera), is that the third, or middle, finger has only two bony joints; to which it may be added that when the animals are at rest it will be found that the first joint of the same finger is invariably extended in the same line as its supporting metacarpal bone.

The Horseshoe and Leaf-Nosed Bats.

Family *RHINOLOPHIDÆ*.

The bat represented in the accompanying illustration is one of the two British representatives of a well-marked and rather numerous family distributed over the greater part of the Old World. This family is technically known as the *Rhinolophidæ*, and includes the horseshoe-bats (*Rhinolophus*) and the leaf-nosed bats (*Hipposiderus*), together with some less important genera. All of them are

THE GREATER HORSESHOE-BAT ($\frac{4}{5}$ nat. size).

characterised by having a well-developed nose-leaf completely surrounding the nostrils, which are situated in a depression of the snout. And they are also distinguished by their large ears, which have no trace of an inner ear, or tragus, and are in most cases completely separate from one another at their origin at the head.

The horseshoe-bats (*Rhinolophus*), of which our figure is an example, always have 32 teeth, of which the incisors number $\frac{1}{2}$, and the cheek-teeth $\frac{5}{6}$ on either side; and they are further distinguished by the shape of the nose-leaf, which consists of two portions, the one immediately over the nose being horseshoe-shaped, and the posterior one pointed. Moreover, the ears have a large process of membrane in front, termed the *antitragus*.

The greater horseshoe-bat has a very wide distribution, being found over a large portion of Europe, the greater part of Africa, and Asia northwards of the Himalaya Mountains, and as far eastwards as Japan. In England, although nowhere common, it is met with in the southern counties, and is occasionally found in the Midlands, but is quite unknown further north, and has never been observed in Ireland. Like the other species, it generally prefers to rest during the day in caves and old buildings, and does not issue forth till late in the evening, when it continues its flight till dark. As we have already mentioned, there seems little doubt that the nose-leaf of these bats is specially intended to aid them in avoiding obstacles during flight, as most or all of the species fly later than the bats which are unprovided with these appendages. Mr. J. E. Harting states that this species (*Rhinolophus ferrum-equinum*) when on the wing appears as large as the noctule, from which it may be distinguished by the greater proportionate width of the wing-membrane. In the caves of the department of the Eure, in the north of France, great numbers of these bats collect for their winter sleep; upwards of one hundred and eighty having been observed in one colony, and eighty in another. It is further noteworthy that these colonies always consist exclusively of either males or females.

The second British representative is the lesser horseshoe-bat (*R. hipposiderus*), which ranges over a large part of Europe, extending as far north as the Baltic. It has been recorded from Ireland, and is also found at Gilgit, on the north-west portion of India, though in Africa it does not extend south of the Sahara. Mr. Blanford states that during the day it hides in caves, ruined buildings, outhouses, etc., often in large numbers. It usually appears about dusk, and, according to Scully, by whom it was observed in Gilgit, has a powerful and long-sustained flight; but Blasius, who made his observations on European examples, says its flight is rather irregular and fluttering. It is generally found rather higher in the air than *R. ferrum-equinum*, and is more frequently found away from dense tree-growth.

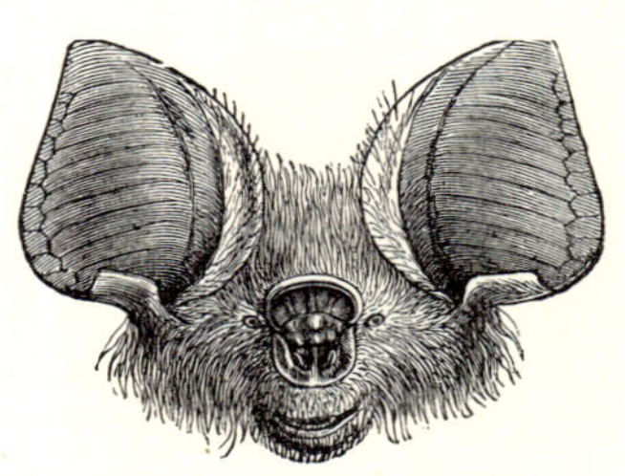

HEAD OF LEAF-NOSED BAT (*Hipposiderus calcaratus*). (From Dobson, *Proc. Zool. Soc.*, 1877.)

The largest of all the species is the great eastern horseshoe-bat (*R. luctus*), which is found in elevated districts from India to Borneo and the Philippine Islands. It has a very large and peculiar nose-leaf, the anterior part of which spreads over the lips; and the colour of the fur and wings is generally jet black. According to Captain Hutton, these bats generally go in pairs, instead of in flocks, although several pairs may not unfrequently be found in large caves. The same observer states that this species commences its flight early in the evening, and flies at a height of about twenty or thirty feet above the ground, its movements being somewhat heavy and slow. There are many other species of horseshoe-bats, among which there is one (*R. megaphyllus*) peculiar to North-East Australia, a second (*R. capensis*) confined to South Africa, extending as far north as Zanzibar, and a third (*R. æthiops*) from West Africa. In the colder regions all the species of *Rhinolophus* hibernate; but the late Dr. Leith Adams mentions that in Malta the little horseshoe-bat, which on the continent retires for the whole winter, may be observed at any season, although of course most plentiful in summer, even in mid-winter occasionally venturing forth at twilight when the warm southern winds are blowing. The horseshoe-bats, with their near allies the leaf-nosed bats, may be regarded as the most highly organised of the entire insectivorous group, as is especially indicated by the great development of their nasal appendages, and also by their compact and delicately-formed bones.

The leaf-nosed bats (*Hipposiderus*) may be distinguished from the preceding group by the form of the nose-leaf, in which the upper and hinder portion does not terminate in a point, and there is also no median process hiding the nostrils. Moreover, the large leaf-like antitragus found in front of the ears of the horseshoe-bats is reduced to a very small remnant; and the teeth, owing to a reduction in the number of the premolars, are fewer than in the horseshoe-bats, the total being either thirty or twenty-eight. Leaf-nosed bats are quite unknown in Europe, but are widely spread over the warmer regions of Africa, Asia, and Australia. Some of these bats exceed in size the largest of the horseshoe group; the largest of all being Commerson's bat (*H. commersoni*), from Africa and Madagascar, next to which is the great Himalayan leaf-nosed bat (*H. armiger*), extending from the Eastern Himalaya to China. Males of this species are just over 4 inches in length, exclusive of the tail. The following account of its habits is taken from Dr. J. Scully, who writes: "This bat usually harbours during the day in caves, or commonly in lofts, outhouses, and sheds that are little used; in the latter localities it suspends itself, by the claws of the feet, from the rafters. When attaching itself in this way to the edge of a beam or rafter, the animal sways, pendulum-like, a few times until the impetus given during flight is exhausted; and it then hangs motionless with its wings folded close to the body. If slightly alarmed by the opening of a door, or any unusual noise in the room it occupies, the head is thrust out and turned carefully in various directions, as if for the purpose of finding out the cause of disturbance. On such occasions I have purposely dropped a heavy book on the floor so as to alarm the bat thoroughly. The animal would at once fly off, and either take several turns round the room or else leave it; but it invariably returned quickly and attached itself to the spot it had previously occupied. It comes out for the capture of its prey about sunset, and its hunting-grounds are gardens, orchards, cleared spaces in woods, or avenues of trees; somewhere near trees always. It is sometimes found flying on a level with the tops of the trees, but more commonly nearer the ground; a very characteristic movement it has is a slow but steady sweep round a leafy tree, or clump of trees, in search of insects which frequent the lower branches. While it was intently occupied in this circular flight I have been nearly touched on the face by this bat, as I walked across the grounds attached to my house in Nipal. And in passing so close to one it could be distinctly heard crunching the hard-bodied insects it had caught between its strong teeth. Sometimes these bats come out of their day retreat before the insects they are in search of are to be found in plenty. On the 25th August, about 6 P.M., I noticed an example flying close to a tree. It circled twice round the tree while I was watching it, keeping about three feet above the ground. Apparently finding that none of the insects it wanted were about, it suspended itself to a small horizontal branch of the tree, just three and a half feet above the ground, and so remained for some time. It was probably waiting for a more propitious hour.

Whether this was really the explanation of the pause in its flight or not, it seems certain that this bat does not ordinarily remain very long on the wing. I have often observed that in the early part of the night it alternated its pursuit of insects with short periods of repose in an outhouse. On one occasion, I observed a bat of this species return three times during the evening (from about 8 to 10 P.M.) to a room I happened to be occupying; and, curiously enough, it always attached itself to precisely the same part of the ceiling. That part of the room, however, was the point furthest away from me, and my presence may have influenced the bat in its selection of the spot."

In addition to the true leaf-nosed bats, of which there are fully twenty species, there are several more or less closely allied kinds which are referred by zoologists to distinct genera. The only one of these we shall notice here is the flower-nosed bat (*Anthops ornatus*), discovered a few years ago in the Solomon Islands, and remarkable for the extraordinary development of its nose-leaf This appendage assumes the form of a large rosette, covering the whole front of the face, reaching from eye to eye, and extending downwards nearly to the upper lip. Above the eyes the upper border of this rosette terminates in three stalked balls, while the remainder consists of overlapping furbelow-like expansions of skin; the obliquely-placed nostrils appearing somewhat below its centre. It is difficult to believe that such an extraordinary structure is solely connected with the sense of touch, and we should rather assume that in this case the great development of the rosette is to a considerable extent an ornamental feature. Mr. O. Thomas remarks that the discovery

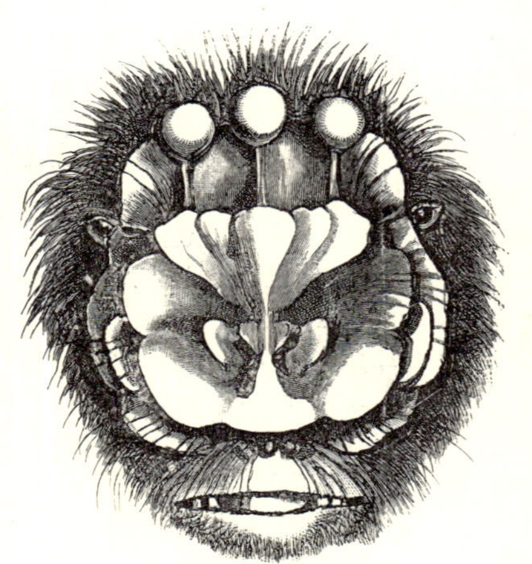

FACE OF THE FLOWER-NOSED BAT (4 times nat. size).—After Thomas, *Proc. Zool. Soc.*, 1888.

of such a form in the Solomon group is a most interesting and unexpected fact, since oceanic islands are generally characterised by the large proportion and great specialty of their frugivorous as compared with their insectivorous bats, a rule otherwise well exemplified in this archipelago.

The False Vampire Bats and their Allies.

Family *NYCTERIDÆ*.

Certain bats agreeing with the preceding group in the possession of a nose-leaf, and found in the tropical and subtropical parts of Africa, India, and the Malayan region, are (from the blood-sucking propensities of at least one of the species) commonly known as vampires; but since that term is exceedingly likely to lead to confusion with the true American vampires, they are better designated false vampires. The five species of these bats, together with seven of another genus, collectively constitute a distinct family.

All the members of this family, which is known as the *Nycteridæ*, are distinguished from the horseshoe-bats and their allies by the presence of a large tragus in the long ears, and also by the smaller development or practical absence of the nose-leaf. The false vampires (*Megaderma*) are easily recognised by their enormous ears being united together for a longer or shorter distance by their inner margins, and also by the divided tragus and tall nose-leaf. Their tail is so small as to be practically invisible; and they have no upper incisor teeth; the total number of their teeth being 28 or 26, of which the incisors number $\frac{0}{2}$, the canines $\frac{1}{1}$, and the cheek-teeth either $\frac{5}{3}$ or $\frac{4}{5}$ on each side. One of the best known species of the group is the Indian false vampire (*M. lyra*), which is found throughout India, from Kashmir to Ceylon, and, although at present unrecorded from Burma, reappears in China. Decisive evidence of its blood-sucking propensities was obtained by Blyth, who on one occasion saw one of these bats fly into his house with a smaller bat in its mouth, which it dropped when pursued. The captured bat was weak from loss of blood, and when put next morning into a cage with its captor was at once attacked by the latter, being seized behind the ear and speedily devoured. Canaries in Rangoon have also been killed by bats, probably belonging to this species —an inference which, if correct, proves the occurrence of this bat in Burma. Blyth was also informed by a correspondent that his house was frequented by numbers of these bats, and that in the mornings the floor of the verandah was strewn with the débris of slaughtered frogs, large grasshoppers, and crickets; while on one occasion the remains of a small fish were discovered. Frogs appeared, however, to be the favourite food of these bats, which could sometimes be heard crunching the bones and skulls of their victims. In correspondence with their different habits, the jaws and

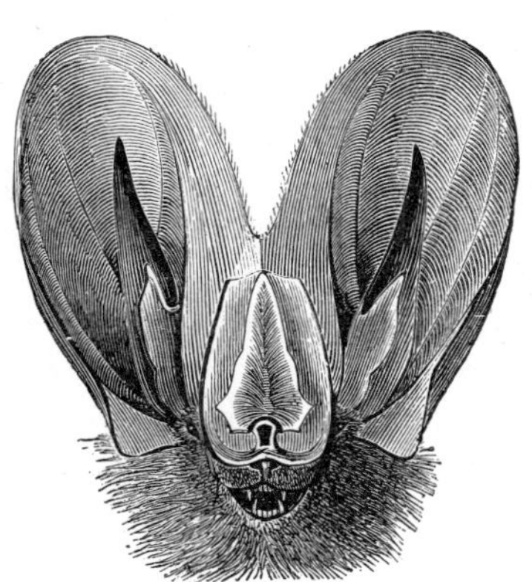

HEAD OF INDIAN FALSE VAMPIRE BAT.

lips of this species, as well as of the other false vampires, differ considerably from those of ordinary insect-eating bats; and we may hence assume that all the species partake more or less extensively of an abnormal diet. The large Indian false vampire, which, like the other species, has no tail visible externally, measures from 3 to $3\frac{1}{2}$ inches in length, while its extended wings have a span of from 14 to 19 inches.

A second species, the Malay false vampire, extends from the Malayan region and Tenasserim to China, while two others are found in Africa. One of the latter (*M. frons*) is characterised by the great height of the nose-leaf, and also by the length of the tragus of the ear. It is an inhabitant of the west coast. These African species have one more upper premolar tooth than the oriental forms.

There does not appear to be any popular name for the bats forming the second genus—*Nycteris*—of this family. They are readily distinguished from the false vampires by the practical absence of a distinct nose-leaf, which is represented only by a slit running down the middle of the face from the nostrils to the line of the ears, on the sides of which are small expansions of skin. Then, again, the ears, although furnished with an undivided tragus, are merely joined by a very narrow band at their bases, which in some species is so slightly developed as to be almost invisible. Moreover, these bats have well-developed tails, and also upper incisor teeth, the total number being 32, of which $\frac{2}{3}$ on each side are incisors, $\frac{1}{1}$ canines, and $\frac{4}{5}$ cheek-teeth. So different, indeed, are the bats of the genus *Nycteris* from the false vampires, that the reader might well wonder why the two are associated in a single family. There are, however, important resemblances in the form and structure of the head and skull, among which—as characters visible externally—may be mentioned the pointed and cylindrical muzzle, and the projection of the lower jaw beyond the upper; these being sufficient to establish the near relationship of the two groups.

With the exception of one species (*N. javanica*) from Java and the Malay Peninsula, the bats of this genus are confined to Africa, where they are mostly restricted to the regions south of the Sahara, although one of them ranges into Egypt.

The Typical Bats.

Family *VESPERTILIONIDÆ.*

With the exception of the horseshoe-bats already described, the whole of the bats found in the British Islands, and, indeed, in Europe generally, may be included in a single family, which may conveniently be designated popularly as the typical bats, and is scientifically known as the *Vespertilionidæ.* All these bats agree with the two preceding families in the relation of the tail to the membrane between the legs; but they are distinguished by the absence of a distinct nose-leaf, the nostrils merely forming circular or crescent-shaped apertures at the end of the muzzle without any complications from foldings of the skin. Their tails are long, and produced to the edge of the membrane between the legs; and their ears are always furnished with a distinct tragus. Apart from certain details in the structure of their skulls which need not be mentioned here, it may be observed that the incisor teeth of the upper jaw are always of small size, those of opposite sides being separated from one another by a considerable interval, while their number varies from one to two pairs. The lower incisor teeth, on the other hand, are, with one exception, three pairs. Moreover, there are generally either six or five cheek-teeth on each side of both upper and lower jaws, the reduction in number in the latter instance being due to the disappearance of one of the premolars.

In addition to being the common bats of Europe, the typical bats have an almost world-wide distribution, and include more than one hundred and fifty distinct species. The absence of the nose-leaf, together with other features in their organisation, indicates that they are less specialised types than the two preceding families, to which, however, they are in other respects intimately related. Accordingly, Dr. Dobson considers that in the typical bats we have the descendants of the ancestral forms which gave rise both to the *Nycteridæ* and the horseshoe and leaf-nosed bats; and we may thus regard all these three families as forming a single distinct branch of the insectivorous bats; the main stem of this branch being formed by the *Vespertilionidæ,* and the other two families forming side branches. The number of these bats being so great, all that can be done here will be to select a few of the better-known examples of some of the more important genera.

The Long-Eared Bat (*Plecotus auritus*).

The well-known long-eared bat, of which we give an illustration in the accompanying figure, is a common, though not very abundant British species, easily recognised by the great length of its delicate ears. It is one of two representatives of the genus *Plecotus*, forming the type of a special group characterised by the

THE LONG-EARED BAT (nat. size).

presence of grooves, or incipient nose-leaves, on the upper part of the muzzle behind the nostrils; and also by the ears being generally very large, and united by their inner margins.

The long-eared bat has 36 teeth, of which $\frac{2}{3}$ on each side are incisors, and $\frac{5}{6}$ cheek-teeth; the premolars being, what is very rare in the family, $\frac{2}{3}$ in number. The ears are much more than twice the length of the head, and are united for a considerable distance; their tragus being also large. The general colour, like that of all British bats, is sombre, being brownish-grey above and paler on the under-parts. This bat has a very wide geographical distribution, being found over the greater part of Europe, in Northern Africa, and probably also in most of the temperate regions of Asia; so that its known range extends from Ireland in the west to the Darjiling Himalaya in the east.

In the great development of its ears, as well as in the presence of groovings on the nose (which in other forms of the group develop into incipient nose-leaves), the long-eared bat and its allies occupy the highest, or most specialised position among the typical bats. This large size of the ears is in all probability connected with the nocturnal habits of this species; and it would appear that these organs to a large extent serve the same purposes as the large nose-leaves of the horseshoe-bats. That the long-eared bat is mainly nocturnal in its habits is clearly stated in the second edition of Bell's *British Quadrupeds*, where it is mentioned that although this species may often be seen hawking after flies with the short-eared pipistrelle in the evening, yet that it is late in coming forth from its diurnal resting-place, and that its flight is continued throughout the night. The presence of this bat may be recognised by its cry, which, when once known, can always be distinguished from that of all other species; and the author of the work just cited tells us how this cry may be heard at all hours of even the darkest night, whether the listener be in the open fields, in the neighbourhood of woods, or near towns. The cry itself is described as being acute and shrill, although not loud; but practice only can enable observers to distinguish it from that of other bats.

In order to protect them from injury during the time that their owner is at rest, the long and delicate ears of this bat are at such times generally carefully folded away beneath the wings; and since the upright tragus is then left standing alone, the creature looks as if it had only short and slender ears. The ears both of this bat and of its North American ally are relatively longer than in any other animal; and it is, indeed, probably solely due to the adventitious width communicated to the body by the wings that the ears do not appear monstrous and out of all proportion. The long-eared bat is a comparatively small animal, the length of the head and body being just short of 2 inches; while the ear measures about $1\frac{1}{2}$ inches, and the spread of the expanded wings reaches 10 inches.

The favourite hiding-places of these bats in inhabited districts are church towers, or within the roofs of open buildings or outhouses; and in such places they may be found in the daytime during the summer months hanging in large clusters, and in the winter carefully ensconced in such crannies and nooks as afford the best protection. In a rock-cut tomb in the Libyan desert visited many years ago by the late Professor Leith Adams, the long-eared bats, which were at that time regarded as distinct from the present species, were met with in swarms; "so plentiful were they," writes Professor Adams, "that during my descent into the crypt I was covered with them, while hundreds fluttered about like bees around a hive." In North America and Vancouver Island, the long-eared bat is represented by an allied species, the American long-eared bat (*P. macrotis*), readily distinguished by some peculiar gland-like swellings in the region of the nose. Its habits appear to be very similar to those of the European species.

The Barbastelle (*Synotus barbastellus*).

The barbastelle appears to be one of the rarest of all the British bats, and, like the long-eared bat, is one of two species severally representing a distinct genus. This bat, which belongs to the same group of genera as the species last mentioned, is readily distinguished from the latter externally by the comparatively small size of its ears; while, if its skull be examined, it will be found to have only thirty-four, in place of thirty-six, teeth; this reduction being due to the disappearance of one pair of premolars from the lower jaw. A further point of

THE BARBASTELLE (nat. size).

difference is to be found in the circumstance that, whereas in the long-eared bat the outer margin of the ear terminates suddenly near the corner of the mouth, in the barbastelle it is produced forwards, so as to extend above the mouth to the front of the eye.

The barbastelle is found over middle and southern Europe, extending as far north as England and Sweden, and it has also been obtained from North Africa and Arabia, while it may extend, as Dr. Dobson suggests, into the temperate regions of Asia lying to the north of the Himalaya.

When examined closely, the appearance of the head of the barbastelle is so peculiar as to render its recognition always an easy matter. Thus, the muzzle is abruptly truncated and marked by a groove leading up each side to the nostrils; the latter being situated in a depression void of hair on the upper surface of the muzzle. The black hair on the somewhat swollen cheeks also adds to the peculiarity of the physiognomy; while the ears are relatively broad, and nearly equal in length to the head. The long fur is darker than that of any other European bat, and on the upper-parts is brownish-black, with the points of the hairs lighter; while on the under-parts the light tips of the hairs are longer. The length of the head and body is 2 inches, and that of the ears half an inch. One white example of this bat has been recorded, and also another in which, while the head and neck were of the normal tint, the body was white.

Contrary to the habits of the long-eared bat, the barbastelle is a solitary species, both when in repose and during active life. " If," observe the authors of the second edition of Bell's *British Quadrupeds,* "in a twilight stroll about midsummer, a person finds himself in close proximity with a bat of somewhat thick and clumsy form, but of rather small size, whose flight is so desultory that it appears to be flapping lazily about hither and thither, seemingly without purpose, and intruding so closely that the flutter of its wings may be heard, and even the cool air thrown by their movement felt upon the cheek, it may with almost certainty be regarded as the barbastelle. Although there is no English bat which resembles the barbastelle in its mode of flight, yet in choice of situation there are several. Where the whiskered bat and pipistrelle are seen, the barbastelle may be seen also; but, having been once observed, it will probably be useless to make search again at the same place. Equally uncertain is its diurnal retreat; most likely not the same place for long together, as we have found it in places where it could not have rested the day previously. A crevice in a wall or tree, the spaces between the rafters and tiles of a cowshed, the timber over a sawpit, the thatch of a shed in a brickyard, or behind a cottage window-shutter, are suitable places of repose for the barbastelle, in all of which situations we have met with it, and always alone." The barbastelle appears earlier in the evening than the long-eared bat, and probably retires as the night advances.

As we have already mentioned, the genus *Synotus* resembles *Plecotus* in being represented only by two species. Whereas, however, the second species of long-eared bat is North American, the second kind of barbastelle is a Himalayan species. The Himalayan barbastelle (*S. darjilingensis*) is distinguished from its European congener by its larger ears, which lack the projecting lobe found on the outer margin of those of the latter. This bat appears to be common in the Himalaya, and has been captured in localities so far apart from one another as Gilgit and Darjiling. It is generally found at altitudes varying from about five thousand to eight thousand feet above the sea. In habits the Himalayan barbastelle appears to be very similar to its European relative; showing itself, however, rather late in the evening, and hibernating in the narrowest crevices and chinks of rocks into which it can contrive to crawl. There are four other bats allied to the long-eared bat and barbastelle, which are referred to three distinct genera. One of these is Hemprich's eared-bat (*Otonycteris hemprichi*) from North Africa and the North-West Himalaya, which is characterised by having only thirty teeth, owing to the reduction in the number of the upper incisors and premolars to a single pair each.

Its ears are considerably longer than the head. The second genus, *Nyctophilus*, comprises one species from Australia and a second from New Guinea, which, while possessing the same number of teeth as Hemprich's bat, are distinguished by the possession of a rudimentary nose-leaf. Finally, we have the Californian cave-bat (*Antrozous pallidus*), in which there are only twenty-eight teeth, owing to the reduction of the number of the lower incisors to two pairs (a feature unique among the typical bats), the genus being also distinguished from all the members of the family hitherto mentioned by the ears being disconnected with one another.

The Pipistrelle, Noctule, and Serotine.

Genus *Vesperugo.*

The pipistrelle, noctule, and serotine, of which the first and second are figured among our illustrations, are the three best-known British representatives of the large and widely-distributed genus *Vesperugo;* the pipistrelle (*V. pipistrellus*) being the common English bat. With these bats we enter upon the consideration of a group of genera, distinguished from that containing the long-eared bat and its allies by several more or less important features. Among these may be mentioned the simple nature of the nostrils, which are without any trace of groovings or foldings of the skin, while the ears are usually of comparatively small size, and are always quite separate from one another.

The bats included in the same genus (*Vesperugo*) as the pipistrelle are very numerous, and vary to a certain extent in personal appearance, and also in the number of their teeth, which is either thirty, thirty-four, or thirty-six. Dr. Dobson says that they may be easily recognised by their relatively stout bodies, their broad and flattened heads and blunt muzzles, as well as by their broad, short, and triangular ears, in which the tragus is usually rather thick and inclined somewhat inwardly. Moreover, their legs are unusually short, and the membrane connecting the legs with the tail almost always has a small supplemental portion situated on the outer side of the spur rising from the heel.

Certain species of the genus approximate, however, in some of their characters to bats of other groups; one coming so close in general appearance to the long-eared bats that, without careful examination, it might readily be mistaken for a member of that group. "This genus of bats," observes Dr. Dobson, "probably contains the greatest number of individuals among the Chiroptera. The common bats of all countries, especially of those lying within the tropical and subtropical regions of the northern hemisphere, generally belong to it. . . . The colour of the fur is generally dark-brown or black, the extremities of the hairs being of a paler colour on the upper surface, and ashy or whitish beneath." One species of this genus (*V. borealis*) has the most northern range of all bats, having been observed flying within the limits of the Arctic circle.

The pipistrelle, which we take as the first example of the genus, belongs to the typical section of *Vesperugo,* in which the incisors number $\frac{2}{3}$ and the premolar teeth are $\frac{2}{2}$ on either side of the jaws. It is a small species, measuring 1·65 inches in length of head of body, and with a span of wing of about $8\frac{1}{2}$ inches. The fur is rather long and silky, of a yellowish-red colour near the roots of the ears, but elsewhere reddish-brown above, and dusky beneath. This bat, the smallest of the British species, is distributed all over Europe, the temperate parts of Asia, and North Africa. It does not enter India, but is found in the valley of Kashmir, and also at our frontier station at Gilgit.

This being the commonest of the British bats, and also one which frequents the neighbourhood of human habitations, we are naturally more fully acquainted with its habits than with those of many other species; and the following account is mainly derived from the excellent description given in Bell's *British Quadrupeds*.

THE PIPISTRELLE (nat. size).

The pipistrelle appears earlier and retires later than any other English bat, making its first appearance as early as the middle of March, and not finally hibernating till winter has actually set in. Its flight is extremely swift and rapid, and accompanied by the sudden turns and descents which have probably been observed by all. The favourite resorts of this species in inhabited regions appear to be old buildings and roofs, but it seems to avoid the roofs of stacks and ricks, which might have been thought to have afforded safe cover. Probably, however, this avoidance may be due to the rats and mice which are so frequently found in such situations. Trees appear to be but seldom selected, either as a temporary hiding-place, or for the hibernation. In uninhabited districts crannies and clefts in rocks serve as shelter. The favourite food of the pipistrelle is said to be gnats; and the abundance of these insects on some of the warmer days of winter is probably the reason why one or more of the bats may be occasionally seen flying about at that season. In captivity this bat will readily eat meat; and it is said that it will at times visit larders for the sake of food of that nature.

In India the place of this bat is taken by a closely allied species, the Indian pipistrelle (*V. abramus*), which also ranges as far east as Northern Australia, and, in summer at least, as far west as Central Europe. It may be at once distinguished from the common species by the outer margin of the ear being straight, instead of concave, below the tip. As the pipistrelle is the commonest bat in England, so its Oriental representative is probably the most abundant species in India, where it ranges from the Himalaya to Ceylon. Its habits are described as being similar to those of the ordinary species, the same partiality for human dwellings being exhibited, and the flight being characterised by similar sharp doublings and turns.

Noctule. Among the representatives of *Vesperugo*, our remarks will, in the main, be restricted to those found in the British Isles; and we accordingly pass to the consideration of a species much larger than the preceding, and known as the great bat, or noctule (*V. noctule*). This species, of which we give a figure on the next page, belongs to the same section of the genus as the pipistrelle, and is perhaps the best known of the larger British bats. Apart from its larger size, it is distinguished from the pipistrelle by its broad and rounded ears, which are set very far apart on the head. The colour of the upper-parts is yellowish-brown, only very slightly paler below; but some examples have been described with a reddish tinge. The length of the head and body is 3 inches, and the spread of the wings from 13 inches to more than 14. This bat has a wider distribution than the pipistrelle, being found not only all over Europe and the temperate regions of Asia, but likewise ranging into Africa north of the Sahara, and also occurring in Java and Sumatra, and entering the confines of our Indian dominions in Nipal and Sikhim, and not improbably Kandahar.

The noctule differs from the pipistrelle in being a tree-haunting bat, and likewise a gregarious species. In winter, however, its retreat may be either in hollow trees, or under roofs and eaves of houses, in which situations numbers may frequently be found together. It appears early in the evening, and its flight is particularly strong and rapid, and takes place high in the air. Its favourite food consists of cockchafers and fernchafers, in pursuit of which it may be seen on summer evenings hawking round large trees, especially oaks. An unpleasant odour is characteristic of this bat.

"The noctule," writes Bell, "is essentially adapted for the capture and mastication of coleopterous insects. The broad muzzle and strong jaws are found quite equal to the reduction of the stubborn elytra of beetles as large as the cockchafer (of which, according to Kuhl, he will consume as many as thirteen, one after the other), and the wings are in no way deficient in power when in pursuit of these insects. During the fine midsummer evenings, when the cockchafers have become abundant, and you hear them humming on every side, the noctule is in his glory. Then he flies high and straight, and you hear his shrill but clear voice as he passes overhead, interrupting himself to dart at some prey, and then passing on. But an observer will not watch his movements long on such an occasion without noticing a manœuvre which at first looks like the falling of a tumbler-pigeon, but on closer observation proves to be simply a closing of the wings, and a consequent drop of about a foot. Sometimes this is repeated every few yards as long as he is in sight. It is occasioned by some large and intractable insect having been captured, and the anterior joint of the wing, with its well-armed thumb, is required to assist in retaining it until masticated. Sometimes, however, food is not so easily obtained. With a cold east wind, or, indeed, a strong wind from any quarter, a change of hunting-ground is required; and the noctule may often be seen taking a humble and silent flight in some sheltered and warm corner,

THE NOCTULE (nat. size).

fluttering about with half-closed wings, and appearing to be very little at home, or indeed like himself, for we recall an instance where several were shot under the belief that they were of some unknown species."

In Sikhim and Nipal the habits of the noctule appear to be much the same as in Europe, but it does not hibernate. In Nipal it appears to be of rare occurrence, as Dr. Scully states that he only procured one specimen, which was caught in the following manner, during the month of July: "About eight o'clock in the evening," writes Dr. Scully, "I heard the very shrill scream of some small animal in my bedroom, and, on going into the room, I found this bat attached to the mosquito net covering my bed. In its flight, it had apparently alighted on the net, and there got its claws so firmly entangled that it could not escape."

In White's *Natural History of Selborne*, it is stated that the noctule is not to be seen on the wing before the end of April, nor later than July. Other observers have, however, seen this bat in Hampshire and Sussex in August and September, while one instance is on record of its appearance in Cambridgeshire as late as the first week in November.

Hairy-armed Bat. Closely allied to the noctule is the British species known as the hairy-armed bat (*V. leisleri*). Its popular name is derived from the presence of a broad band of fine short hairs on the under side of the wing-membrane running from the fore-arm to the wrist. Since, however, this feature is also found in the noctule, it is obviously not distinctive of the species to which it gives the name, and we must therefore seek for another characteristic by which to distinguish the two species. Such a characteristic is found in the incisor teeth. In the hairy-armed bat the outer pair of these teeth in the upper jaw are equal in cross-section at the base to the inner pair, but the height of their crowns is much less; whereas in the noctule the former is much wider at the base than the latter, while it also has the crown hollowed out to receive the summit of the lower tusk, or canine. Then, again, the lower incisor teeth in the hairy-armed bat form a regular semi-circle, with scarcely any overlapping of one over another; whereas in the noctule they have broad crowns, are set obliquely in the jaw, and largely overlap one another. Such characters may seem trivial and unimportant, but they are amply sufficient to prove the specific distinctness of the hairy-armed bat, which is, more-over, a considerably smaller animal than the noctule, the combined length of the head and body being rather less than $2\frac{1}{2}$ inches. Needless to say, however, these two bats are often confounded together, although careful attention to the points mentioned will always serve to distinguish them. Moreover, careful observers will readily discriminate between these bats, even when on the wing, from their difference of habit and mode of flight. " Whilst the noctule," observe the authors of Bell's *British Quadrupeds*, "may throughout the whole of the summer be seen taking its regular evening flight, night after night, near the same spot, the Leisler's bats, on the contrary, will be seen once, perhaps for a few minutes only, and then lost sight of. It appears to affect no particular altitude in its flight, any more than it preserves a regular or prescribed beat. When the weather is fine, you may see this bat passing on in a kind of zig-zag manner, apparently uncertain where to go; generally, although not always, at a considerable elevation, and in a few minutes it is gone." Like the noctule, the hairy-armed bat has a wide geographical distribu-tion, ranging through Europe and the temperate regions of Asia, and having been recorded from one locality in the Himalaya.

Serotine. The serotine (*V. serotinus*) is another large British bat belonging to a group distinguished from that containing the preceding species by the premolars in the upper jaw being reduced to one on each side. This bat has ears of moderate size, with broadly-rounded tips, and the tragus broadest just above the base, and thence gradually diminishing in width to the rounded tip. The general colour of the fur is chestnut-brown above, and yellowish-grey on the under-parts; the hair being long and silky, and the wing-membranes dark brown, or nearly black. There is, however, some degree of individual variation in colour, specimens being occasionally found with a greyish tinge to the fur.

The serotine is of particular interest as having the widest distribution of any known bat, and being the only representative of the order Chiroptera which is common to the eastern and western hemispheres. Seeing that bats are, from their power of flight, able to traverse with ease long distances over sea, it seems at first sight very remarkable that the serotine is the only species which has succeeded in crossing from the Old World to the New. It is, however, probable that most of these animals are unable to withstand the cold of the regions about Behring Strait, where the passage between the two hemispheres is the shortest, and have hence failed to spread themselves in the same manner as purely terrestrial Mammals like the reindeer, elk, and glutton.

The range of the serotine extends from England to Siberia, and from Northern Germany to Northern Africa, whence it is continued through Arabia and Asia Minor to the valleys of the Himalaya. In Africa it is found as far south as the Gabun district on the west coast, and it probably extends to the Camerun Mountains. In America, where it was at one time regarded as distinct from the European species, it appears to be widely spread from Lake Winnipeg in the north to the Isthmus of Darien, and is met with throughout all the West Indies. The serotine from the Gabun constitutes a distinct variety, distinguished by the fur of the under-parts being of a pale yellowish-white, and thus forming a marked contrast with the dark brown fur of the back.

The serotine, which is a comparatively rare and local species in England, is said to have very similar habits to the noctule, so far as regards the length of its period of hibernation, and its consequent late appearance in the spring are concerned. It is nearly always found alone, and has a characteristically slow fluttering flight; while, as its name implies, it does not venture forth till late in the evening, and, in suitable weather, continues on the wing till dawn. The southern counties appear to be the only part of England in which this bat is found; but in France, and other continental countries, it is widely distributed, and far from uncommon. Observers in the country last named state that it may generally be found flying around the tallest trees in forests; and that it frequents the timber yards in Paris, among the woodstacks of which it conceals itself during the day. In North America, where it is known as the dusky, or Carolina, bat, the habits of the serotine appear to be very nearly the same as in Europe. Thus, in writing of these bats, Dr. A. K. Fisher observes that "they are the last to make their appearance in the evening. In fact, when it gets so dark that objects are blended in one uncertain mass, and the bat-hunter finds that he is unable to shoot with any precision, the Carolina bats make their appearance as mere dark shadows, flitting here and there while busily engaged in catching insects. We have to make a snap-shot as they dodge in and out from the dark tree-tops; and we are left in doubt as to the result until in the gloom we may perchance see our little black-and-tan, seemingly as interested in the result as we are, pointing to the dead animal. This species is particularly fond of fields well surrounded by trees."

Parti-coloured Bat. The last of the bats of the genus *Vesperugo*, reckoned as British, is the parti-coloured bat (*V. discolor*), which, while belonging to the same group as the serotine, differs in that the widest part of the short tragus is above, instead of below the middle. Apart from this, the parti-coloured bat is, however, readily distinguished by the comparative richness of its coloration, which has a somewhat marbled appearance, owing to the light tips of the hairs. Above, the colour of the fur is reddish-brown, with the tips of the hairs white; while all the under-parts are of a dirty white tint. Up to the year 1874 only one individual—captured at Plymouth—of this bat had been obtained in Britain, and we are not aware that any instance of occurrence has been recorded since. It has accordingly been suggested that the Plymouth example may have been imported in the rigging of some ship. On the Continent the parti-coloured bat is widely spread, but it is chiefly found in mountain districts; its range extending from Italy and France to Southern Sweden and the Ural Mountains. In Asia it has been observed in Western Siberia and Eastern Turkestan.

Silver-haired Bat. The last member of the genus to which we allude is a North American species, known as the silver-haired bat (*V. noctivagans*), which is the sole representative of a group characterised by having three premolar teeth on each side of the lower jaw, and also by the hairiness of the membrane between the legs. In the upper jaw there are two premolars on each side. The fur above is dark brown, becoming silvery-white at the tips in the region of the back; and there is a very characteristic white spot at the base of the brown ears.

The silver-haired bat has the most northern range of any American species, extending to Hudson's Bay, and southwards to California. In the Adirondack Mountains, near New York, Dr. Hart Merriam states that it is by far the commonest of all the bats. "Like many bats," writes Dr. Merriam, "it has a decided liking for waterways, coursing up and down streams and rivers, and circling around lakes and ponds. In some places its habit of keeping directly over the water is very marked. At Lyon's Falls it is exceedingly abundant, particularly just below the falls. I have stood, gun in hand, on a point on the east bank of the river, and have seen hundreds passing and repassing, flying over the water, while during the entire evening not more than two or three strayed so far that if shot they would fall on land. Several that were wounded and fell into the water, at a distance of twelve or fifteen feet from the bank, swam ashore. They swam powerfully and swiftly, for the current is here quite strong, and would otherwise have carried them some distance down stream. Next to water-courses, the borders of hard-wood groves are the favourite haunts of the silver-haired bats. By standing close under the edge of the trees one sees many that at a little distance would pass unobserved. While searching for their insect-prey they may be seen to dart in and out among the branches, and to penetrate, in various directions, the thick mass of foliage over-head. They often pass within a few inches of one's face, and yet it is rare that a sound is heard from their delicate wings. In the early dark the silver-haired bat emerges from its hiding-place; after a few turns about the immediate neighbour-hood, it generally takes a pretty direct course for water. I have seen it start from the summit of a high, densely wooded hill, circle around for a few minutes, and then, keeping far above the tree-tops, sail leisurely towards a distant river till lost from sight in the valley below. And, standing on the banks of the large stream that winds along the foot of the hill, I have seen the bats flying over at a height several hundred feet, all moving in the same direction—toward a more distant river. Whether it remains abroad all night, or limits itself to comparatively brief excursions in evening and early morning, can only be conjectured. I am inclined to favour the latter view, for the reason that the greater number always disappear before the darkness becomes sufficiently intense to hide them from sight."

We may conclude this somewhat long account of the genus *Vesperugo* (which is, however, short in comparison with the extent of the genus) by mentioning that there are three species which differ from all the rest in having only a single pair of incisors in the upper jaw. These species are *V. schliefenii*, of Africa; *V. dormeri*. of Southern India; and *V. parvulus*, of Central America.

The Hoary Bat and Red Bat.

Genus *Atalapha*.

Omitting all mention of two genera of bats (*Chalinolobus* and *Nycticejus*) unknown in Europe, our next representatives of the family *Vespertilionidœ* will be two species of a genus known as *Atalapha*, which is confined to the New World. All these bats have only a single pair of upper incisor teeth; the number of incisors in both jaws being $\frac{1}{3}$, and the cheek-teeth either $\frac{5}{5}$ or $\frac{4}{5}$, so that the total

HEAD OF HOARY BAT.—After Dobson.

number of teeth is 32 or 30. They are also characterised by the membrane between the legs being more or less hairy; and by the expansion and inward curvature of the extremity of the tragus of the ear.

The largest of the more typical species of this genus is the well-known hoary bat (*A. cinerea*), ranging from Nova Scotia to Chili, and characterised by its ashy-grey colour. Dr. Hart Merriam, writing of the habits of this fine bat in the Adirondack Mountains near New York, observes that it " can be recognised, even in the dusk of evening, by its great size, its long and pointed wings, and the swiftness and irregularity of its flight. It does not start out so early as our other bats, and is consequently much more difficult to shoot. The borders of woods, water-courses, and roadways through the forest, are among its favourite resorts; and its nightly range is vastly greater than that of any of its associates. While the other species are extremely local, moving to and fro over a very restricted area, this traverses a comparatively large extent of territory in its evening excursions, which fact is probably attributable to its superior powers of flight." Of the migratory habits of this bat, which is rare in the Adirondack region, we have already written.

Far commoner in the Adirondacks is the red or New York bat (*A. noveboracensis*), which is of smaller size, and conspicuous for its bright golden fur, tipped more or less markedly with silver. This species, which is second only in beauty to the hoary bat, is widely distributed in North America, and represented by several varieties in South America. According to the writer last quoted, it generally makes its appearance earlier than the other species, and may even be occasionally seen abroad on cloudy afternoons long before the shades of evening have begun to fall.   Dr. Coues states that "in most portions of the United States the red bat is one of the most abundant, characteristic, and familiar species, being rivalled in these respects by the little brown bat (*Vespertilio subulatus*) alone.   It would be safe to say that in any given instance of a bat entering our rooms of an evening, the chances are a hundred to one of its being one of these two species. The perfect noiselessness and swiftness of its flight, the extraordinary agility with which it evades obstacles—even the most dexterous strokes designed for its capture—and the unwonted shape, associated in popular superstition with the demons of the shades, conspire to produce repulsive feelings that need little fancy to render weird and uncanny."

As is the case with many of its North American allies, this bat generally hibernates in large colonies, which select for their retirement a cave or hollow tree. The following account of a visit to a cave, in the year 1816, probably refers to this species, and gives a good idea of the vast numbers of individuals composing one of these colonies.   The describer, Professor J. Green, as quoted in 1842 by Dr. J. D. Godman, writes that " I this day (November 1st) visited an extensive cavern about twelve miles south of Albany, New York.   I did not measure its extent into the mountain, but it was at least 300 or 400 feet.   There was nothing remarkable in this cave except the vast multitudes of bats which had selected this unfrequented place to pass the winter.   They did not appear to be much disturbed by the light of the torches carried by our party, but upon being touched with sticks, they instantly recovered animation and activity, and flew into the dark passages of the cavern.   As the cave was, for the most part, not more than six or seven feet in height, they could very easily be removed from the places to which they were suspended, and some of the party who were behind me disturbed some hundreds of them at once, when they swept by me in swarms to more remote, darker, and safer places of retreat.   In flying through the caves they made little or no noise; sometimes upon being disturbed in one place they flew but a few yards and then instantly settled in another.   These bats, in hibernating, suspend themselves by the hinder claws from the roof or upper part of the cave; in no instance did I observe one along the sides.   They were not promiscuously scattered, but were collected into groups or clusters of some hundreds, all in close contact.   On holding a candle within a few inches of one of these groups, they were not in the least troubled by it; their eyes continued closed, and I could perceive no signs of respiration."

As an instance of the weight of the young which female bats have sometimes to carry with them, we may refer to an account by Mr. W. H. Hudson, who states that in La Plata he once captured a female bat, which, although mentioned by another name, appears to have belonged to a variety of this species.   This bat had attached to her breast two young, which were so large that it seemed incredible how she could fly when thus burdened, much less with sufficient speed to catch her insect food.   Mr. Hudson states that these young ones were fastened on each side of the body of the parent; and when forcibly separated from their hold were incapable of flight, and fluttered feebly to the ground.   The weight of the young in this instance was not, indeed, so relatively great as in the case of the opossum, where seven or eight young may sometimes be seen clinging to the tail and back of the female; but then it must be remembered that the opossum has only to climb, when it can use both its claws, teeth, and prehensile tail to aid its movements. The bat, on the other hand, had to seek its living in the empty air, pursuing its prey with the swiftness of a swallow, "and it seemed wonderful to me," writes Mr. Hudson, "that she should have been able to carry about that great burden with her on one pair of wings, and withal to be active enough to supply herself and her young with food. In the end I released her, and saw her fly away among the trees, after which I put back the two young bats in the place I had taken them from, among the thick-clustering foliage of a small acacia tree. When set free they began to work their way upwards through the leaves and slender twigs in the most adroit manner, catching a twig with their teeth, then embracing a whole cluster of leaves with their wings, just as a person would take up a quantity of loose clothes and hold them tightly by pressing them against the chest. The body would then emerge above the clasped leaves, and a higher twig would be caught by the teeth, and so on successively, until they had got as high as they wished, when they proceeded to hook themselves to a twig and assume the inverted position side by side; after which, one drew in its head and went to sleep, while the other began licking the end of its wing, where my finger and thumb had pressed the delicate membrane. Later in the day I attempted to feed them with some small insects, but they rejected my friendly attentions in the most unmistakable manner, snapping viciously at me every time I approached them. In the evening I stationed myself close to the tree, and presently had the satisfaction of seeing the mother return, flying straight to the spot where I had taken her, and in a few minutes she was away again and over the trees with her twins."

As the narrator well remarks, this incident is noteworthy not only as a touching instance of parental affection, but likewise for the circumstance that the young bats, which up to the time of their capture had existed in a kind of parasitical condition, when thrown upon the world were quite capable of taking care of themselves. In other Mammals born in a helpless state, the power of accommodating themselves to new conditions, and the instinct of self-preservation, are acquired gradually, whereas in these young bats they were assumed in a moment.

The Tube-Nosed Bats.

Genus *Harpyiocephalus.*

The production of the nostrils into a pair of tubes has already been noticed as distinctive of a genus of fruit-bats (p. 259), and it is, to say the least, remarkable to find the same feature reappearing in a less marked degree in a group of insectivorous bats belonging to the *Vespertilionidæ*. These tube-nosed bats, constituting the genus *Harpyiocephalus*, are restricted to Tibet, India, Ceylon, and the Malay Archipelago, and Japan, where they always inhabit hilly districts. They are sufficiently distinguished at a glance from all the other insect-eating bats by their divergent tube-like nostrils, of which the apertures are circular. It may, however, be added that their teeth are 34 in number, of which there are on each side $\frac{2}{3}$ incisors, a single canine, and $\frac{5}{5}$ cheek-teeth. Moreover, the upper surface of the membrane between the hind legs is characterised by its thick covering of hair.

The greater number of the eight species of these bats occur in Tibet and the Himalaya, some of them also extending into the highlands of India and Ceylon; there is also one from Java and some of the other Malayan Islands, and another from Japan. The white-bellied tube-nosed bat (*H. leucogaster*) of the Himalaya is remarkable for its brilliant coloration, the fur being golden-orange on the head, the base of the hairs greyish, and on the back pale rufous-brown with grey at the base. The fur on the membrane is bright ferruginous, the upper surface of the inter-femoral membrane and toes being well covered. Beneath, the fur is white throughout on the chin and throat, the rest of the lower parts having bicoloured fur—grey at the base with white tips.

HEAD OF TUBE-NOSED BAT.—After Dobson.

Writing of its habits in the North-West Himalaya, Captain Hutton says that it occurs at an elevation of about 5500 feet, but does not appear to be common in the hills, the Dehra-Doon being probably its true locality there. An example which flew into a room at Jeripani (below Masuri), at night, kept low down in its flight, instead of soaring towards the ceiling, passing under the tables and chairs, as if afraid to emerge into the broad glare of the lamps. This is likewise the mode of flight when searching for insects in the open fields, where it skims closely and somewhat leisurely over the surface of the crops and grass.

DAUBENTON'S BAT, NATTERER'S BAT, ETC.

Genus *Vespertilio.*

Daubenton's bat (*Vespertilio daubentoni*), represented in the illustration on p. 284, is a well-known although local British species, which we select as our first example of the genus *Vespertilio*, second only in point of the number of its species to *Vesperugo*, and the type of the family *Vespertilionidæ*. The bats of this genus have 38 teeth, of which there are $\frac{2}{3}$ incisors and $\frac{6}{6}$ cheek-teeth on each side of the jaws. As Dr. Dobson observes, they are easily recognised by the circumstance that the upper incisor teeth are so implanted in the jaw as to diverge from one another; and also by the large number of the cheek-teeth, which exceeds that obtaining in any insectivorous bats yet noticed, and is only equalled in four other genera, of which three are mentioned later on. Moreover, the second cheek-tooth in the upper jaw, belonging to the premolar series, is invariably characterised by its minute size. Then, again, the ear has a characteristic elongated oval form, and its tragus is very narrow.

The genus appears to be of unusually wide geographical distribution, and is found throughout the temperate and tropical regions of both hemispheres. "Most of the species," writes Dr. Dobson, "appear to be dwellers in woods, some either habitually or occasionally live in caves or under the roofs of houses. The position of attachment of the wings to the hinder extremities, and the size of the

foot, appear to be connected with the nature of their dwelling-places, the inhabitants of caves having larger feet more or less free from the membranes, while those
living in woods have much smaller feet inclosed in the wing-membrane to the base
of the toes." The bats of this genus being of a more delicate organisation than
the species of *Vesperugo* are less capable of withstanding the effects of cold, and
have therefore a less northerly range than the latter. And in the countries
where the bats of these two genera hibernate, those belonging to the present
genus are later in awakening from their winter slumber than are the species of
Vesperugo.

Daubenton's bat belongs to a group of the genus characterised by the large size

DAUBENTON'S BAT (nat. size).

of the feet, and also by the wing-membrane rising, as a rule, from the shin-bone or
the ankle, as well as by the middle of the free margin of the membrane between
the legs forming a very acute angle. Moreover, the tail has one or two joints
projecting beyond the edge of the membrane last mentioned, and the spur arising
from the ankle to support the same is of very great length. The wing-membrane
extends below the ankle to the metatarsus; and the ears are characterised by
their oval form, and are rather shorter than the head. The length of the head and
body is 2 inches, and the span of the wings 9 inches. The fur is brownish-black
at the base, and usually reddish-brown on the upper-parts and ashy-grey below;
although there is considerable individual variation in this respect.

This bat is chiefly characterised, so far as habits are concerned, by its partiality for the neighbourhood of water, and from this peculiarity it is frequently overlooked, even in districts where it is abundant. So close, indeed, does it fly to the surface over which it skims, writes Professor Bell, that it is "difficult to distinguish between the creature itself and its reflection. The flight, quivering and slow, is performed by very slight but rapid strokes of the wings. It may, indeed, be said to vibrate rather than fly over the surface of the water. It could not well fly in any other manner so near the surface without often striking it, and this it seldom, or perhaps never, does, although it often pauses to dip its nose into the water, whether to drink or to pick up some food we have been unable to ascertain. The Daubenton's bat is, we suspect, rather an abundant species in the middle parts of England; at least it is plentiful in some parts of Warwickshire. We have sometimes seen these bats so thick on the Avon, near to Stratford, that at certain spots there could not have been fewer than one to every square yard, and this abundance has extended over a very considerable space. It resorts indiscriminately to buildings or trees during the day, though we think the preference is given to the former." The last observation is in harmony with the opinion of Dr. Dobson already quoted, in which it is stated that the species with large feet choose buildings for resting-places in preference to trees.

This bat is found in England, Scotland, and Ireland, and appears to extend over the great part of Europe, having been recorded from Finland to Sicily. It also extends into Asia, where it probably ranges over most of the temperate regions to the northward of the Himalaya, while on the eastward of the Bay of Bengal it extends southwards into the Tenasserim provinces. It is sometimes termed the water-bat.

The rough-legged bat (*V. dasycneme*) is another species belonging to the same group of the genus, which has been recorded from the southern counties of England. In it the wing-membrane extends only to the ankle; and the species is readily distinguished from the rest by the form of the tragus of the ear, which approaches that of the serotine, and also by the thinness of the hair on the face. It is widely distributed on the Continent, but has only of late years been recognised as British.

The reddish-grey, or Natterer's bat (*V. nattereri*), is also a British species of very local occurrence, and belongs to the second or typical group of the genus *Vespertilio*. This group is characterised by the smaller size of the foot, by the wing-membrane generally extending down the leg as far as the base of the toes, and also by the obtuse angle in the middle of the free hinder margin of the membrane between the legs. Moreover, the tail is either wholly contained within the margin of that membrane, or has only its extreme tip projecting beyond; while the spur arising from the ankle to support this membrane is shorter, reaching only to half, instead of three-quarters of the distance between the ankle and tail. The colour of its fur is lighter than that of any other British species. This bat is characterised by the relatively small size of its head; and its fur is of a reddish-grey colour above, and whitish beneath. Owing to the smallness of the head, the total length of the head and body is somewhat less than in Daubenton's bat, but the span of the expanded wings is 2 inches more, and thus reaches 11 inches.

In habits it is a sociable species, being found in large numbers in its favourite places of repose, which are generally buildings, especially church-towers. Thus, in the year 1848, an enormous colony was discovered in the roof and tower of the church of the village of Arrow, near Alcester. Its range extends from Ireland to the Ural Mountains, and from the south of Sweden to the Alps.

Another closely-allied British species is Bechstein's bat (*V. bechsteini*), which is limited to Europe, and is of rather larger size than the last; the length of the head and body being 2 inches instead of 1·65 inch. It is distinguished by the hinder margin of the membrane between the legs being naked instead of fringed, and also by the shorter tail, of which the length is less than half that of the head and body. The colour is reddish-grey above, and greyish-white below. It is very rare in England, but has been taken in the New Forest.

We must not leave this group of the genus *Vespertilio* without referring to an African species remarkable for its gorgeous coloration. This is Welwitsch's bat (*V. welwitschi*), from Angola, on the West Coast. In this bat (which is closely allied to the last species), while the head and body are reddish above and straw-coloured beneath, the naked wing-membranes are variegated with orange and black, the dark portions being of a triangular shape, and occupying the spaces between the second and third, and third and fourth fingers, and also the space included between the fourth finger, and a line drawn between the wrist and the ankle; the remaining portions being orange. Then, again, the membrane between the legs is margined behind by a black band, and dotted over with small black spots; similar dots also occurring upon the orange-coloured portions of the wings between the arms and legs. Hodgson's bat (*V. formosus*) of India and China, which is more nearly related to the under-mentioned whiskered bat, has an almost identical coloration, the only difference being that the membrane between the legs is wholly orange, and the black spots are wanting from the wings.

While on the subject of brilliantly-coloured bats, we may mention two other species belonging to different genera. One of these is the Indian painted bat (*Cerivoula picta*), belonging to a genus (*Cerivoula*) closely allied to *Vespertilio*, but distinguished by having the upper incisor teeth parallel instead of divergent. In this bat the fur on the upper-parts is of a deep orange or ferruginous red, and that beneath paler. The wing-membranes are black, with orange spots and lines of orange along the fingers and on the margins, while the membrane between the legs is wholly orange. So brilliant indeed is the species, that it is said to have the appearance of a gorgeous butterfly rather than a bat.

Our second example of contrasting coloration is the white-winged bat (*Nycticejus albofuscus*), the River Gambia, on the West Coast of Africa. The genus *Nycticejus*, which has been incidentally mentioned on p. 280, is closely related to *Vesperugo*. In colour the body of the white-winged bat is dark amber-brown both above and below; and the naked skin of all the portions exposed when the creature is at rest is likewise of a nearly similar hue. On the other hand, those portions of the wing-membranes lying external to a line drawn from the elbow to the knee are pure white on both sides, thus contrasting very markedly with the dark tint of the body and limbs. All the other known members of the genus have the body and wings more or less uniformly coloured; but, as observed by Mr. O. Thomas, the describer of this singular species, many of the smaller bats of the Gambia, belonging to several distinct genera, have dark bodies with white wings. That there is some good reason for this peculiar style of coloration among the Gambian bats is evident, although no explanation has hitherto been offered. With regard to the coloration of Hodgson's bat, it has been shown by the late Mr. Swinhoe that in the Island of Formosa this species is in the habit of hanging suspended on the fruit of the longan tree (*Nephelium*). "Now this tree," writes Mr. Swinhoe, "is an evergreen, and all the year through some portion of its foliage is undergoing decay, the particular leaves being, in such a stage, partially orange and black. This bat can, therefore, at all seasons suspend itself from its branches, and elude its enemies by its resemblance to the leaf of the tree. It was in August when a specimen was brought to me. It had at that season found the fruit ripe and reddish-yellow, and had tried to escape observation in the semblance of its own tints to those of the fruit." A similar explanation will doubtless hold good with regard to the Indian painted bat, which feeds on plantains, which, when ripe, are of a bright yellow or orange colour, speckled with black, and thus almost exactly similar to the bat.

With the whiskered bat (*V. mystacinus*) we resume, and at the same time conclude, our survey of the British representatives of the genus. This bat, while agreeing in the relative size of the feet, and other leading characters, with Natterer's, belongs to a subgroup distinguished by the tragus being straight and more or less blunted at the tip, instead of being acutely pointed and inclining outwards. This bat is of small size, the length of the head and body being only $1\frac{1}{2}$ inches, and the spread of the outstretched wings $8\frac{1}{2}$ inches. The fur on the upper part of the body is dark chestnut, tending to black, and dusky beneath. It takes its name from the fringe of long fine hair on the upper lip. It is a solitary species, although on some occasions a considerable number may be seen together on account of the abundance of food in particular localities. In its mode of flight and general habits it is very similar to the pipistrelle; hiding during the day in situations as various as are those favoured by different individuals of that species. Its range includes the greater part of Europe, while in Asia it has been found in Syria, the Himalaya, and North China. It may be mentioned that no less than twelve species of the genus *Vespertilio* are peculiar to the New World, and that the whole of them are characterised by the small size of their feet.

Schreibers' Bat. This bat (*Miniopterus schreibersi*), which ranges from Germany to Japan and Australia, and is the sole representative of its genus, differs from all the preceding forms by the great elevation of the crown of the head above the face. The same feature is found in the South American and West Indian tall-crowned bats (*Natalus*), of which a head is shown in the figure. Both these bats are distinguished by the presence of a gap in the middle line between the first pair of incisor teeth, and by a second gap between the second incisor and the tusk. The American tall-crowned bats, while agreeing with *Vespertilio* in the number of their teeth, are further distinguished by the small size of the tragus of the ear. On the other hand, Schreibers' bat has but thirty-six teeth, owing to the absence of the first pair of premolars.

Sucker-Footed Bats.   Our notice of the Typical Bats may conclude with genera, each represented only by a single species, which are peculiar in having sucking organs on the thumbs or hind feet. One of these species is the tricolor bat (*Thyroptera tricolor*) of Brazil, and the other the golden bat (*Myxopoda aurita*) of Madagascar. Both have thirty-eight teeth, as in the genus *Vespertilio*. In the former the suckers on the extreme toes are in the form of round discs on the lower surfaces of the thumbs and the soles of the feet; while in the latter the sucker on the thumb is horseshoe-like, and those on the feet are smaller. Both these bats are further remarkable for possessing three joints in the third or middle finger of the wing, in which respect they resemble the second family of the Free-Tailed Bats.

HEAD OF TALL-CROWNED BAT (3 times nat. size). (From Dobson, *Proc. Zool. Soc.*, 1880.)

By the aid of their suctorial discs these bats are enabled to climb smooth polished surfaces, after the manner of cuttle-fishes; but a good and satisfactory account of their habits is still a desideratum. The occurrence of the two forms of sucker-footed bats in such widely remote regions as Madagascar and Brazil is one out of many instances indicating an intimate connection between the faunas of South Africa and South America.

The Free-Tailed Insectivorous Bats.   The bats remaining for notice are arranged in two families, and differ so markedly from those described that they may be regarded as forming a separate branch derived from the same stock as that from which the Typical Bats have originated. From the circumstance that in many of these bats a greater or smaller portion of the tail is completely detached from the membrane between the hind legs, the whole group may be conveniently referred to as the Free-Tailed Bats; and to them we devote a special chapter.

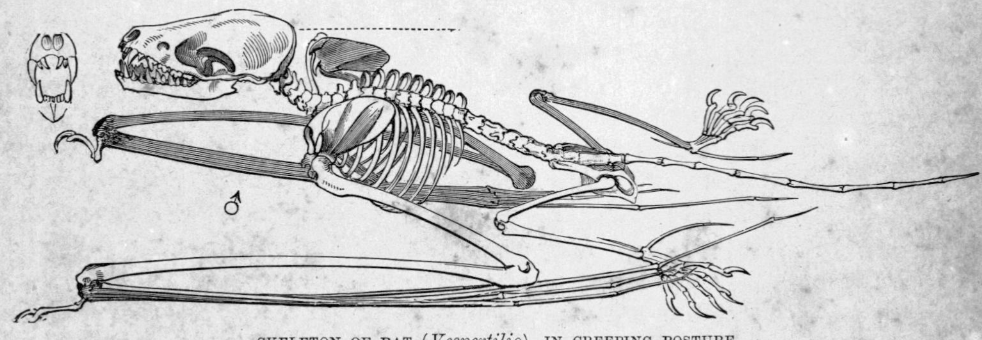

SKELETON OF BAT (*Vespertilio*), IN CREEPING POSTURE.

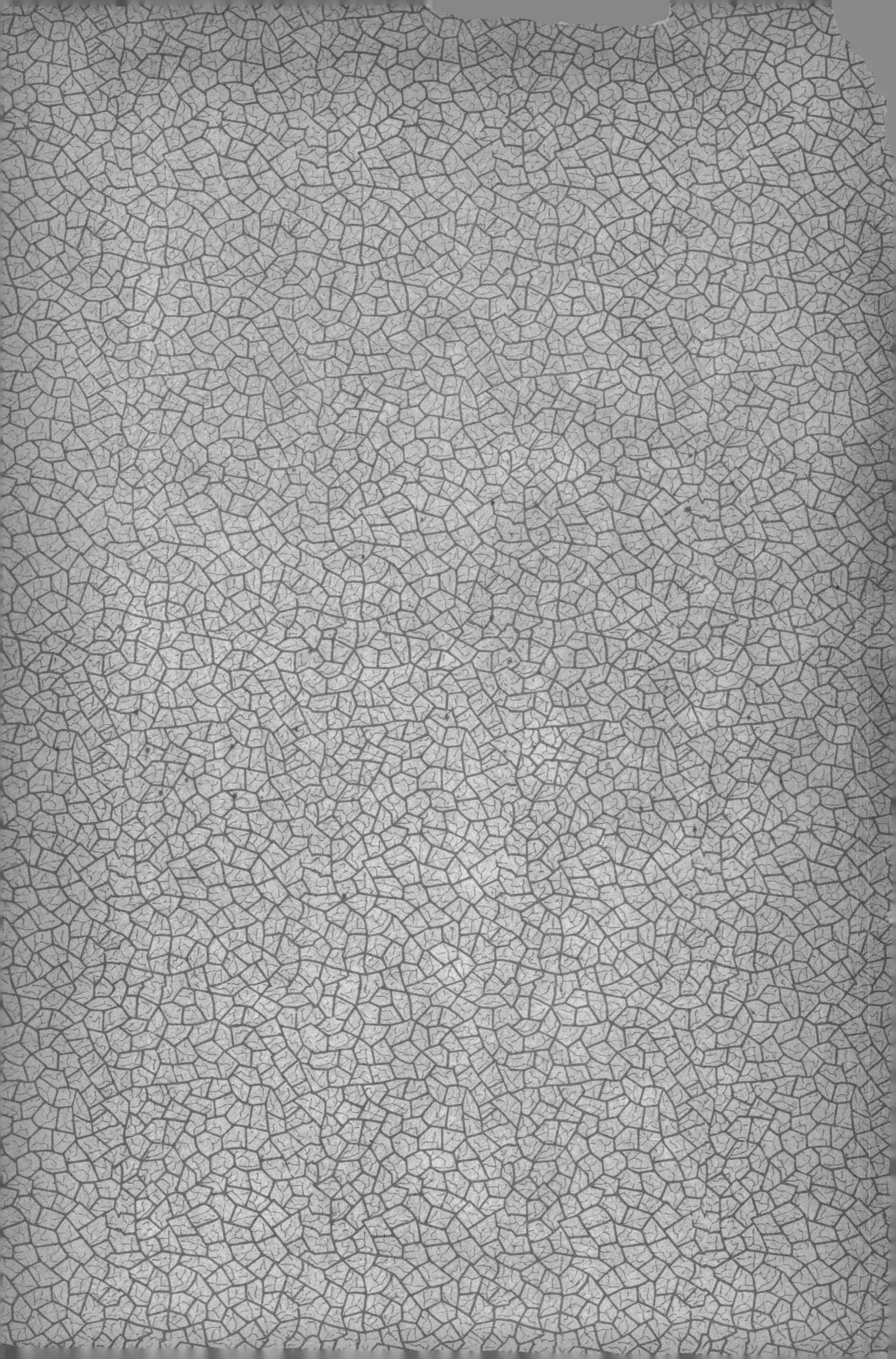